The Economic And Social Problem

Flürscheim, Michael, 1844-1912

The Economic

.... and ....

Social Problem

By MICHAEL FLURSCHEIM,

Author of " Rent, Interest and Wages "; "The Real
History of Money Island and Clue to the
Economic Labyrinth," etc.

Published by

JEFFERSON PUBLISHING COMPANY,

BASIL BARNHILL, Manager,

XENIA, CLAY COUNTY, ILLINOIS.

THE ECONOMIC
AND
SOCIAL PROBLEM

BY

MICHAEL FLURSCHEIM,

AUTHOR OF "RENT, INTEREST AND WAGES," "THE REAL
HISTORY OF MONEY ISLAND AND CLUE TO THE
ECONOMIC LABYRINTH," ETC

PUBLISHED BY
JEFFERSON PUBLISHING COMPANY,
BASIL BARNHILL, MANAGER,
XENIA, CLAY COUNTY, ILLINOIS, U. S. A.

Michael Fluerscheim

CONTENTS

THE ECONOMIC AND SOCIAL PROBLEM.

CHAPTER I.

A PROBLEM AND ITS SOLUTION

The great social problem is First the question why a growing number of workers have to go without necessaries and luxuries though only too anxious to produce them for each other, and Second what are the obstacles interposed against the exertion of their productive power?

> "I gave a beggar from my little store
> Of well earned gold He spent the shining ore
> And came again and yet again still cold
> And hungry as before
> I gave a thought, and through that thought of mine
> He found himself a man supreme divine
> Bold clothed, and crowned with blessings manifold,
> And now he begs no more"
>
> —*Ella Wheeler Wilcox*

A caravan trudges wearily through the hot sand of the desert. At last an oasis is reached, and all rush toward the life-giving fluid. But only a meagre quantity is found, hardly sufficient for all, and already the more vigorous travellers are making use of their strength to monopolize this supply Weak and tired pilgrims whose strength had barely sufficed to permit their reaching the oasis, despair of being able to force their way to the spring

Fortunately the leader approaches, and his exhortations are heard He asks the strong ones to moderate their greed, and to let their poor brethren obtain some of the water. He shows them how wrong it is for them to store away water for future use before others have as much as quenched their thirst.

Who has not heard this gospel, preached in the holy writings of all peoples, resounding from every pulpit of our churches? They are old, very old, these admonitions—as old as humanity. Our parents have heard them before us their parents before them, and their echoes come down to us faintly and more faintly, from the ever-receding generations of the past

But do not let us, in pondering over these glorious teachings of the brotherhood of man, of unselfish love and devotion, of charity and benevolence, of the division of the last loaf and coat, forget to look after our caravan, which, meanwhile, has continued its march.

The desert now lies behind the pilgrims, and a wonderful valley opens before their astonished eyes. As far as they can see, extends quite a forest of fruit trees bending under their precious loads, while blooming meadows crossed by lovely little rivulets invite the wanderer to a delicious rest. Sweet feathered songsters fill the balmy air with their delightful melodies. A real paradise, from which cares and troubles of any kind seem forever banished, opens its inviting arms to our footsore travellers. Nearer and nearer they approach to it, already they see the entrance of the valley, and in a few hours they expect to rest there refreshed and happy.

But, oh how dreadful! A roaring torrent separates them from the valley, its foaming rapids interpose a seemingly impassable barrier between our poor pilgrims and the lovely paradise.

A few intrepid men throw themselves into the seething waters, but most of them perish before the eyes of their companions, who cannot succor them. Only a few hardy swimmers succeed in reaching the opposite shore. The majority cannot swim and must remain on the barren side of the stream.

By irrigating the soil they raise scanty crops, and with the help of the fruits thrown over from the other side they manage to eke out a bare living. Unfortunately, most of the fruit thus thrown fails to reach the bank of the stream, and that which is successfully aimed is nearly always injured in its fall. The majority of the lucky ones, moreover, prefer to take their ease in the paradise they have attained to, little heeding the entreating voice of the leader which is wafted to them over the stream.

Again and again it makes itself heard, that old and well-known command of charity, and more than ever since the world exists, it is obeyed. A few of the successful swimmers, a Leo Tolstoy, for instance, seeing how little can, after all, be accomplished by alms-giving, renounce their enjoyments rather than monopolize them, and, braving all hardships, return to their brethren so that they may partake of poverty with them.

Good, well-meaning men they, and those also who without tiring, throw fruits over, most of which are spoilt or never arrive, and are carried to the ocean by the waves of the stream. Wiser men, however, those few exceptional thinkers who spend day and night of their lives considering whether it might not be possible to construct a bridge by which the whole caravan could be brought over into the happy valley. They are not in the least deterred by the jibes or threats of the others, even of those whom to help they strain every nerve. "A bridge over such a wide and unfathomable stream! What a Utopia! The fools had better make use of their precious time to throw us some more fruits!" Such are the shouts occasionally coming over to them from the other shore.

Humanity has arrived at the border of the desert through which it has been wandering during so many centuries. A hard and continuous fight against terrible odds has marked the different stages of the struggle so far. Where the stronger managed to secure a larger share the weaker ones suffered in consequence, and the exhortations of the moral leaders again and again demanded justice, or at least charity. Where entreaty proved without effect, threats had to help. The most terrible torments of supposititious hells, cruel inventions of human fanaticism, have been shown in prospective to the hard-hearted rich, whose entrance into heaven has been made to appear more difficult than the passage of a camel through a needle's eye.

Meanwhile, gradually, almost imperceptibly, the outlook on the march has changed. Let us listen to some of the observers.

"On the virgin soil of America's prairies 100 men, with the help of powerful machines, produce in a few months the bread required by 10,000 men during a year. The wonders obtained in industry are still more astonishing. With those intelligent beings the modern machines, the achievements of three or four generations of inventors, mostly unknown, 100 men produce the clothing which 10,000 men require during two years. In well-organized coal-mines 100 men extract yearly enough fuel to supply warmth for 10,000 families in a rough climate" (Kropotkine, "The Conquest of Bread")

Let us double, yea, even treble the number of persons required to cater for man's wants, and we arrive at the result that less than one-tenth of the population could supply all with the necessaries of life. This accords with the calculation of others. Dr. Theodor Hertzka, for instance, the well-known Austrian economist, who, in "Die Gesetze der sozialen Entwicklung," figures out what labor will be required to produce the common necessaries of life for the 22,000,000 inhabitants of Austria, with the result that agriculture and all industries, including mining and building, need 615,000 persons, during present working-hours, 300 days a year to provide the whole population with the necessaries of life. But these 615,000 laborers are 12.3 per cent of the population able to work, excluding all women and all persons under 16 years or over 50 years of age. Hence, should the 5,000,000 individuals, instead of 615,000 be engaged in work, they would need to work only 36.9 days every year to produce everything needed for the support of the population of Austria. But should all the 5,000,000 work all the year—say 300 days—each would need to work only about one hour per day. To produce all the luxuries now used, in addition, these 5,000,000 would need to work only another half hour a day.

A book could be filled with statistics proving our immense progress in the arts of production and communication. I give a few items from an address delivered in Boston by Professor Frank Parsons. "Steam and electricity and mechanical contrivances have multiplied the productive power of labor many-fold. A sewing machine will do the work of 12 to 15 women   A M'Kay machine enables one workman to sole 300 to 600 pairs of shoes a day; while he could handle but 5 or 6 pairs a day by former methods. A good locomotive will pull as much as could 800 horses or 8,000 men ; 4 men with the aid of machinery can plant. raise, harvest, mill, and carry to market wheat enough to supply with bread 1,000 people for a year. A girl in a cotton mill can turn out calico enough in a year to clothe 12,000 persons, more or less, depending somewhat on the size of the persons, and the number of changes of cotton they have   The total machine power of the country is equivalent to the labor of half a billion willing slaves, or an average of 20 to every human worker. On the basis of slavery, the Athenians built up a civilization in which every free man might have ample leisure for culture, and civic and social life   On the grander basis of service by the power of Nature, we are building up a civilization in which all shall be truly free, and shall enjoy ample leisure for development and association with far greater means for both than the Athenians ever possessed.   In Athens, during her palmiest days, there were 5 or 6 slaves for every free man, our machinery already equals 20 for every worker, and in another fifty years may equal 40, 50, 60, or more for every man ; or 100, perhaps, for every family And these splendid servitors of steel and brass are exempt from the pangs of hunger and cold, are never oppressed with weariness, lose no liberty in their servitude, and find no misery in subjection "

From *Brotherhood*, of May, 1900: "Mr Ernest H Crosby tells of a factory he inspected where the manufacture of cheap socks was carried on. The manager showed him 400 sock-making machines The machines run 24 hours a day, and only 50 boys are needed for all shifts 5,000 dozen of socks are made daily   Under the old method, this work would have required about 50.000 men or women "

Leone Levy has calculated that to make by hand all the yarn spun in England by the use of the self-acting mule would take 100,000.000 men   It is reckoned that 30 men, with modern machinery, could do all the cotton spinning done in Lancashire a century and a half ago.

William Godwin Moody, of Brooklyn, author of "Land and Labor in the United States" and "Our Labor Difficulties," sworn and examined before the Senate Committee on Education and Labor, in 1885, says: "Now one girl with her loom will weave as much cloth as could 100 women in my mother's time   One man will go into the field to-day and will do the work that required from 50 to 100 men to do when I was a boy." Question   "Do you mean in agricultural pursuits?" Answer   "Yes   A single man with a reaping machine, one of the smallest capacity, with 6 or 7 feet cutting board, will go into the field and will cut and bind from 15 to 20 acres of grain in a day of ten hours   When my father went into the field with a sickle upon his arm, it took four men a full day to cut and bind a single acre, and the Scotch Agricultural Society reported, in an examination upon that matter that it required five men for one day to cut and bind one acre of grain, but now one man will cut and bind from 15 to 20 per day, or, going beyond that, one of the improved machines will cut and thresh and sack the yield of 50 acres in a day.'

"The steam-gang plow, combined with a seeder and a harrow, has reduced the time required for human labor (in plowing, sowing and harrowing) to produce a bushel of wheat, on an average, from 32.8 minutes in 1830 to 2.2 minutes at the present time. It has reduced the time of animal labor per bushel from 57 to 1½ minutes. . . Before Whitney's invention it required the work of one person ten hours to take the seeds from one and a half pounds of cotton   The machine will now do, in the same ten hours, more than four thousand times as much   . A steam shovel will do in eight minutes what one man can do, with difficulty, in ten hours. The dirt may be unloaded from a train of cars in six minutes, that would require, with a shovel, a day's work of ten men. A stone crusher will perform the work of six hundred men "—(The Social Unrest, John Graham Brooks)

We see as far as productive power is concerned, that the paradise of our picture has been reached. Where this power has increased from ten to twenty-fold, on the average, in the course of centuries, there ought to be more than enough product for all; and other exhortations ought to take the place of those which long ages have so accustomed us to, that the following admonition of an American Fabian is quite in its place   "London boasts of her £6,000,000 in missions, etc, besides uncounted sums in private almsgiving while New York records with pride her $5,000,000 spent in municipal charity, her $5,000,000 in organized charity, her $5,000,000 given by societies, $5,000,000 by churches, and $10,000,000 of private personal giving—$30,000,000 in all

' Instead of exulting in the fact that she gives $30,000,000 a year 'to the poor,' New York should rather hide her head in shame that she has so many poor to give to   What sort of an economic system is this which works so badly that $30,000,000 a year will scantily serve to patch it up? Is this peace or is it war which requires a city to expend $30,000,000 a year in the gathering up and caring for part of the crushed, the diseased, the mangled, and the disabled of its citizens?

"A really intelligent community would as soon think of boasting of its epidemics and diseases as of its expenditure for 'the poor' —would as soon vaunt itself on the length of its death list, as upon the magnitude of its charities. Pompous rehearsals of the sums given 'for sweet charity' are to be sighed over rather than rejoiced in "

Few of those who discuss *the social problem* are aware of the fact that the term has entirely changed its meaning. Formerly the wealth of the few was not only in glaring contrast with the poverty of the many, but it supplied one cause of this poverty. One only for, in any case, primitive methods of production transportation and communication, the destructive agencies of nature and of man did not permit wealth-accumulation by the producer When, in addition, a powerful minority robbed the masses of a more or less considerable portion of their share the explanation of the prevailing misery did not offer any difficulty to the student of history.

As though by a sorcerer's magic wand, the Spirit of Invention created a new world The spoilt children of the twentieth century, with its enormous technic progress, can hardly realize that men are still living who travelled on roads inferior to those of ancient Rome, in vehicles not much superior to those used two thousand years ago, men, who saw the spinning-wheel and hand-loom supply most of the people's clothing other commodities being produced by similar primitive methods Productive power has grown at least ten-fold within a single century *

I speak advisedly when I say productive power or productivity, instead of production, for actual production lags more and more behind potential production, productivity. It is this discrepancy which we usually call *overproduction*, though in reality it is *underproduction*, and this underproduction is the riddle of the economic Sphinx the social problem of modern civilization.

We have underproduction in a double sense · a relative underproduction as compared with potential production or productive power, and an absolute underproduction of the necessaries of life mostly needed by the unemployed starving workers, starving, because without purchasing power, without purchasing power, because unemployed, and unemployed in consequence of relative underproduction Tailors go in rags and cannot buy clothing or

---

* The best and shortest summary of this progress has been given by Professor E E Dolbear 'The nineteenth century received from its predecessors the horse, we bequeath the bicycle, the locomotive, and the automobile We received the goose-quill, we bequeath the fountain-pen and typewriter We received the scythe we bequeath the mowing machine We received the sickle, we bequeath the harvester We received the hand printing press, we bequeath the Hoe cylinder press We received the painter's brush, we bequeath lithography, the camera, and color photography We received the hand loom, we bequeath the cotton and woolen factory We received gun-powder, we bequeath nitroglycerine We received twenty-three chemical elements, we bequeath eighty We received the tallow dip, we bequeath the arc light We received the galvanic battery, we bequeath the dynamo We received the flint lock, we bequeath automatic Maxims We received the sailing ship, we bequeath the steamship We received the beacon signal-fire, we bequeath the telephone and wireless telegraphy We received leather fire-buckets, we bequeath the steam fire-engine We received wood and stone for structures, we bequeath twenty-storied steel buildings We received the stairway, we bequeath the elevator We received ordinary light; we bequeath the Rontgen rays We received the weather unannounced, we bequeath the weather bureau We received the unalleviable pain, we bequeath aseptics, chloroform, ether, and cocaine We received the average duration of life of thirty years, we bequeath forty years"

the raw material out of which to make clothing, because the money to buy it with is inaccessible through absence of work, due to an insufficient demand for other people's clothing.

Workers in the building-trades are houseless, because too many houses have been built and few more are needed. Thus deprived of work, they cannot pay rent. And so we could go on through the whole list of necessaries and luxuries. Everywhere we find want, through absence of employment, due to the so-called "overproduction" of really underproduced goods, and overproduction not in one department of production, balanced by a temporary underproduction in another, but a general overproduction. Occasionally we still find fossils who confound the commercial crisis, which embraces all departments of production with those difficulties under which certain expiring methods of production suffer in consequence of new inventions, such as hand-weaving after the introduction of the power-loom, or nailmaking by hand after machine nails came up.

To increase the confusion we hear the very men who raise the cry of overproduction in the face of absolute and relative underproduction, speak of *overpopulation*, as if we could have overpopulation and overproduction at one and the same time, overpopulation being necessarily correlated with underproduction of the necessaries of life. Overpopulation may in reality exist where the system of production is so primitive that the yield of the land is insufficient to produce sustenance for all its inhabitants. Parts of the United States may have been overpopulated before the white man came here, where the Indian hunter did not find game enough in his tribe's territory to supply nutriment for all; although a much larger population afterward found plenty of food in the same region, when the white farmer had begun to plow the soil. Intensive culture under the progress of agronomy can feed increasing populations on areas where a few farmers working on primitive systems almost starved. P. Kropotkin, in "Fields, Factories and Workshops," cites instances of crops of 80 bushels of wheat to the acre. Under special conditions, the yearly food of a man, about 8½ bushels of wheat, has been obtained from less than a twentieth of an acre, which is an equivalent to over 170 bushels to the acre. Thirty tons or 1,120 bushels of potatoes have been dug in Minnesota from one acre in one single year. The Island of Jersey, in the British Channel, is famous for market gardening. Kropotkin gives the wonderful results obtained by a single gardener, with the help of 36 men and boys, on 13 acres, "equivalent to what a farmer would usually obtain from 13 *hundred* acres of land." He shows how even a well populated country, like England, without reducing the area devoted to other industries, could amply feed herself from her own soil, independent of all food importations, except tropical produce.

In this way the population of the earth could be increased tenfold, twenty-fold, a hundred-fold and more, without having to fear starvation. Which shows how little Malthusianism, the fear that population has the tendency to outgrow the means of existence, need trouble us in a time which has no more vexing problem than how to keep back production, because the supply in our markets show an increasing tendency to outrun the effective demand; i. e, the demand backed by purchasing power Notwithstanding this prominent economists (John Stuart Mill, for instance) let the bug bear of overpopulation run through their works, everywhere appearing as the main danger and the inevitable outcome of any improvement.

How enviable were our forebears with their simple problem of poverty through lack of productive power! How different and difficult a problem is this which faces us, want through a teeming productivity; misery appealing to inexhaustible sources of wealth! What disposition can be made of it, until the key to the well-filled storehouse can be found? And the key must be found, or our civilization is doomed.

To help us in our task let us make use of a familiar artifice: let us transport ourselves to Robinson Crusoe's Island and there present the case free from confusing side issues

Robinson Crusoe, on his island, had to work all day to satisfy his needs. When he got Friday to work for him, things began to improve. He got a little leisure once in a while, and could think of producing articles of luxury. More slaves were procured The result was complete exemption from work and a greater amount of luxury for Robinson, while the slaves had to work all day long with their primitive tools to provide this luxury and the necessary means of subsistence for all Often the men suffered want That was the social problem of the past A ship arrived bringing them all the tools and machines which technical science has given to civilized humanity Very soon the slaves learnt how to use them Their productive power increased immensely Where formerly the work of thirty slaves, and that of their families, was necessary to provide the entire colony with clothing, a single producer was sufficient now, and yet everybody was clothed better than before, for the cotton gin the spinning jenny, the improved weaving-machine, and other inventions of the same kind so much facilitated the work for the one worker that he was enabled to achieve more than a hundred could before. Great progress was also made in agriculture, in bread-making, house-building, and, in fact in all industries, which before had been carried on by hand Everywhere hands could be spared, and yet there was a larger production than before, so that all could live in abundance The unemployed workers could now produce articles of luxury, which before could not be obtained Furniture, carpets, table services, and jewelry works of art of all kinds were made—in fact, all such things as the settlers could wish for. In time, machines and tools as well as methods of production, improved more and more, so that workers in all branches could be spared. What did it matter? A great many more articles of luxury were invented and provided. One of the slaves, who was very talented, entertained the company with musical and theatrical performances, another wrote books, others built pleasure carriages and yachts, etc. The general well-being increased continually with the increasing facility of satisfying every wish, and the labor time was reduced all around.

All this was very good until one day Robinson got up in bad humor, and gave the order to stop the general good living of the slaves, which did not please him. 'He alone had a right to enjoy all those luxuries which everybody had been partaking of, and the slaves ought to be satisfied if they got enough to eat and to drink, and had protection against wet and cold. All indulgence beyond this point only made them lazy and vicious.' From that day the slaves were forced to live accordingly.

A week after this, when Robinson took a walk, he saw a great number of slaves standing about, doing nothing. He angrily called his head man, and gave him strict orders that only those who worked were to eat, and have clothes and lodgings. He was perfectly astonished when, some time after this the head man came to tell him that a number of the men were dying of want.

"Are you mad?" Robinson asked him, "has not the island got more of all the good things which man needs than we could wish for, and can we not produce as much more as we like? Are there not victuals enough? Are we short of clothing or of houses?"

"On the contrary," the head man humbly replied, "we are forced to build new store-houses, because the old ones are filled to the top with food and clothing, and a great many of the dwelling-houses are empty."

"Well?" asked Robinson, whose astonishment increased.

"Yes, sir, that is all right, but you ordered that only those who work are to be fed, clothed and housed."

"Certainly, and that was only right. Why don't the lazy fellows work?"

"Because there is no work for them."

"No work?" said Robinson, more and more astounded, and feeling his head to be sure that he was not dreaming. "No work? Are you crazy, my man?"

"No, sir," replied the head man, who felt offended. "I have got all my senses about me, and should be very grateful to my master if he would show me what work I am to give the men. In the brewery, to begin with, three men were employed who had plenty of work in providing the beer for our people. Since your lordship has forbidden this luxury, so that only the beer for your table has to be brewed, I had to take away two of the brewers, and the third is only busy one-tenth of his time, so that he is also doing the work of others, who consequently are out of work now. It is the same with the people who made the carpets and all the other articles of luxury   Your lordship is abundantly provided for, but the others are not to have any, so I have to take the workmen from their work of production."

Robinson learnt a great lesson that day, which our economists and statesmen, as it seems, have yet to be taught; a lesson which, in fact, we ought to ponder over, if we don't want it driven home to our minds some day in a fashion we shall hardly relish; the lesson that *we cannot produce if we do not consume*

In order to simplify matters I made the workers of the island Robinson's slaves.   To make him the owner of the land, whose "free" inhabitants were his tenants or wage-workers, would merely complicate the relation, without changing anything in the final result. They are just as dependent on Robinson if they cannot get away or if emigration only means the exchange of one Robinson for another   They are what Robert Hunter calls "wage-slaves whose owners have been freed from caring for them when sick or unemployed."

Robinson would only employ them or let them have land when he needed their products or their labor.   Under the original primitive condition he needed all of these products which they could spare after providing for their own sustenance   Then there was plenty of work for all   There was no question of overproduction and want of employment in those days; it was "the good old time," when all went well as long as nature behaved, men kept the peace, and master or landlord was not too harsh and exacting.

The trouble began only when modern improvements became accessible, when each worker could easily produce ten times as much as before, and when Robinson would not allow their consumption to keep up with their increased productive power, while his own consumption could not be forced up sufficiently to take care of the balance   Then the workers starved because their work was too productive, in which case it proved immaterial whether this starvation was due to non-employment or inability to obtain land, and whether overproduction or overpopulation was looked upon as the cause

They were in the position of men athirst, yet at the same time drowning in rising waters; rising, because the poor fellows were not allowed to use the water for their own needs.   They had been much better off before the flood rose, at the time when pumping procured just enough water for daily use; because then the owner of the precious liquid had to let them have enough to keep them alive, for dead men could not pump any water for him.

This misery-producing effect of abundance under monopoly, the key to the modern social problem, is so little understood, that before we proceed let us consider another object lesson

Let us suppose a group of one hundred free workmen and one employer.   The one hundred workers are producing all necessaries and luxuries, each one having his speciality; the employer gets one-tenth of all they produce Each worker will thus have only nine-tenths of what he produces, the employer will get the production of ten workers The question whether the work of supervision and organization, and perhaps of invention, accomplished by him is worth as much as he gets for it, and whether through the employer's work every worker, in spite of his giving up one-tenth gets more wealth than he would without the employer's management, is one of no importance in regard to the question before us All we want to know at present is whether the employer's confiscation of one-tenth of all the wealth produced will in any way interfere with free exchange It evidently will not, whether he consumes his share of wealth or puts it aside for future consumption.

The workers, instead of exchanging the product of a full day's work, only exchange that of nine-tenths, the employer takes the balance, and everybody has full work all the time.

Let us suppose, now, that the productiveness of labor by means of inventions increases ten-fold, a too moderate estimate, if we compare to-day's results with those of the Middle Ages. Let us further suppose that wages—that is, that part of the product left to the worker—have quadrupled in that time, which is far from being true. In what ratio will the share of the employer have risen, if he gets the balance? P is the product, of which formerly W (the workers) enjoyed nine-tenths, and E (the employer) one-tenth W had together 90 P; E 10 P Now W enjoy 4×90 P $= 360$ P, and the total of production being 1,000 P, E will get the balance, or 640 P.

Let us suppose that his needs have increased ten-fold, yet his income has increased sixty-four-fold.

We might consider it unjust that one man should get so much, and others so little We might reply to statisticians like Giffen, who exultingly point to the increase of the workers' incomes as a proof of their increased prosperity, that their relative income, instead of having quadrupled, has decreased 60 per cent, if we take into account the increase of productive power But all this would have nothing to do with the circulation of goods. Every worker would be able freely to exchange his products with every other worker, and there would be no want of work for any. Whether E takes his lion's share in articles of consumption, or whether he prefers taking it in new tools and machines, by which he further increases the productiveness of labor, is immaterial The latter forms of investment might be of greater advantage to the workers, because it is not impossible that a small part of the increase of wealth due to new machines would fall to their share. But even supposing that it only increases the income of E, it could not do them any harm, so long as E continues to invest his surplus in the old way But let us suppose now, that E is the owner of all the available land, and by that agency, of all the forces of Nature, all its accumulated treasures, without which work is impossible—and

we have to make such a supposition as otherwise there would be
no earthly reason why the workers should not have left their employer as soon as his share exceeded the value of his services   They
would very soon have made for themselves as good machines as
they had made for him. Let us further suppose that E made up
his mind that he had machines enough, and did not want any
increase of luxuries for the time being. A new feature of the
problem would in this case present itself which had not been observed before   There would no longer be work enough for all
the workers   They would like to continue as before, working full
time and exchanging with each other the products of their work,
giving the lion's share to E, but E will not let them have the use
of natural opportunities any longer than he needs their services,
which they furnish in payment   One-half of the tribute they are
in the habit of paying is all he needs, and the natural consequence
is that half of the work will be all he requires, and all he allows to
be done on his land   He now uses the rest of the land as a deer
park.   There being no other way of going to work than by using
E's land, our workers will have to work half time, though they
would be happy if they were allowed to make use of their leisure
to produce for themselves the goods they are so much in need of
Naturally E only pays them half wages for half work   Very
soon fifty of the workers will come to E and propose to him to
work cheaper than the others, to give him a larger part of their
products if he will allow them to work full time. E accepts,
and from now on there is no more work for fifty of the workers,
for the remaining fifty do all the work, and leave a larger share
to E than the hundred left him before   Let us suppose that E
increases his consumption fast enough to use up the new savings
he makes in this way, as otherwise there would not be full work
even for the fifty cheaper workers; but things do not rest here
The fifty unemployed ones, pushed by hunger, finally underbid
their former co-workers, and get the work themselves, or rather
forty of them get it, for they work so hard, long, and cheap now
that E gets as many goods out of them as before out of the fifty,
and since he does not need any more goods for the present, there
is only work left for forty   These forty, reduced to starvation
wages by their underbidding their former friends, call in the help
of their wives and children. By these means they begin to get
along a little better, until the thereby increased production becomes
too much for E. who consequently dismisses ten of the party
The unoccupied reserve of workers amounts now to the number
of seventy and their families   Want drives them to underbid the
thirty, who with their families are working overtime to make a
decent living   Finally a man working with his whole family gets
no more for fifteen hour's work than he formerly got alone in
eight hours   'There is no help for it," say the lawgivers they
appeal to, "work is slack   Emigrate (to other countries, where

the same state of things exists) or else go to the poor-house! We cannot fight against the laws of supply and demand."

The workers, not knowing how to strike at the root of the evil, ask for a maximum working day of eight hours, for a prohibition of the employment of married women and of children, while others even want the State to fix a minimum of wages. When the law-givers of all parties hear this a terrible noise is raised against these "socialist and anarchist agitators," who want to sap the foundations of our prosperity, the liberty of each man to work as long as he pleases, and to sell his work and that of his wife and children to whomsoever and as cheaply as he likes. They ask the workers how they can afford to lose the wages of overtime and the earnings of their wives and children, when, even as it is, they hardly know how to make both ends meet

In this way things get worse every day If a certain part of the unemployed did not set up as superfluous middlemen, thus artificially adding to the cost of goods by waste in the work of distribution, and thus forcing E to spend a little more, and to occupy more workers; if others, by becoming criminals and paupers, did not make more work, especially by compelling E to employ some of the men as policemen and soldiers, thus reducing the army of the unemployed; if the employers in different countries did not from time to time quarrel amongst themselves, and lead the unemployed workers mutually to kill each other, thus reducing their numbers and destroying the overproduced wealth; if these and similar means of decreasing *overpopulation* and *overproduction* were not adopted, there would have been a terrible catastrophe long ago

We have seen now that the cause of the evil is that E monopolizes part of the workers' product and does not take this share as fast as they are ready to deliver it, preventing them at the same time from working further until he feels ready to accept the part due to him. We have further seen that the power of thus impeding production is given to him by the ownership of natural opportunities, in a word, of *Land*

But the monopolization of the land by a minority is not the only cause of our abnormal circumstances The division of labor necessitates an exchange of products Where the stage of primitive barter is passed, the exchange of products demands a medium of exchange, and if this medium does not adapt itself elastically to the demands of the market, a new calamity arises which remains to be illustrated in an other phase of our island's history To avoid confusion, private land ownership and its effects are entirely eliminated in this illustration.

Things were getting rather turbulent on Robinson's Island. It was not for the first time. There had been a revolution before, when the people would no longer put up with Robinson's land monopoly. He had owned the whole island, and only those who obtained land from his lordship could live on the island, and could only live on what Robinson was gracious enough to leave them of the fruits of their labor, which was not much   But some agitators had managed to get a foothold in the island, and their teachings opened the people's eyes   They began to see that they had as much right to the land as Robinson; and that Robinson was only one weak man, whereas the islanders numbered thousands of strong men, that they only had to *will*, and Robinson would have to obey So they willed common land-ownership, and the land was owned in common   It was taken without compensation, but the people were generous enough to pay Robinson for improvements, although they themselves had made the improvements in part payment of their rents   They consented to give him bonds to the full amount of these improvements, on which they agreed to pay a moderate interest up to the time when they could redeem them This would not have taken very long, because the inventive spirit of the islanders had immensely multiplied their productive power, and they were enabled to put aside in a few years wealth enough to pay the whole of their debt to Robinson, capital as well as interest

Robinson foresaw that this new state of affairs would not at all suit him   It would have thrown upon his hands immense stores of commodities which he did not need, and which he could not dispose of unless he took in exchange other commodities equally useless to him at the time. He could only eat five meals a day, any victuals in excess would soon have spoiled   He could not wear more than one suit of clothes or one pair of boots at a time, and if his stock of clothing was too large, the moths would eat it He might leave the commodities in possession of his debtors until he needed them, some time during the balance of his life, or the life of his children; but he wanted interest, and the people were not fools enough to pay it, having no need of the goods   For they had free access to the land, and so their labor easily created all the other means of production necessary to supply plenty of every- thing.

But Robinson was a sly old humbug who knew a thing or two Progressed division of labor long since had called forth a demand for a convenient means of exchange, and finally a scarce metal, called *gold*, was in preference used for that purpose   Long before the revolution which Robinson foresaw, he had induced the islanders to pass a law that debts could not be paid in *any* product of labor but only in that *one* scarce product the yellow metal, called *gold*. While he owned the island he had made the people bring to him almost all such metal found by them, and at the time of the revolution he possessed nearly all the gold on the island When improvement bonds were issued, capital and interest were made payable in gold   To obtain gold, people had to sell their products of labor   Robinson was practically the only gold owner and he was, besides, over-supplied with goods of all kinds This resulted in a mad competition for Robinson's gold, through which prices and wages went down most fearfully The more these went down, the more goods and labor-days were needed to pay Robinson's dues, and as Robinson's wants were limited, the excess of supply over demand increased all the time I do not mean real demand, for the people had an unsatisfied and urgent demand for all the goods in the market; but they had no gold with which to pay for them. Most of the gold they did receive had to be paid again to Robinson for interest. who spent only a part of it The surplus he lent to those islanders who could give him the best security. The interest on these new debts again went to swell Robinson's income, and consequently the unconsumed part of it. This meant that an increasing gold debt had to be paid by the people, who, in order to obtain the gold, tried to sell their products in a market in which the great gold monopolist spent a continually diminishing fraction of his gold income, and in which the people were less and less able to make up for the deficit by their own purchases, because more and more of the gold they obtained for their sales to Robinson had to be paid back to him for interest, and so could not be spent on purchases A terrible struggle ensued. The people did their best to save gold by improving their tools and processes of production, but every such improvement only made matters worse. As it cheapened prices and increased the savings of Robinson, it narrowed the market and rendered the chances of employment more precarious, especially as the taxes were payable in gold, and those who did not pay their taxes were finally driven off their land.

I have intentionally magnified the predicament of the islanders, in order to put into full light the effects of a money liable to monopolization; but I am fully aware that where land is freely accessible, even money-debts of the kind described cannot produce such extreme misery. Unfortunately, the question how much of the evil would remain after land nationalization was accomplished, if unaccompanied by a thorough currency reform. is merely an academic one, for in our real world both Money and Land-monopoly are carrying on their nefarious work jointly, helped by their progeny, Interest.

Their evil work, however, is dependent on the development of production, just as a breach in a dam may remain harmless until the level of the water is raised beyond a certain height, a height which might otherwise be desirable; for if there were no breach it would enable the river to turn water-wheels, float ships, and irrigate fields, instead of destroying lives and wealth. In a like manner, the rising stream of production would prove a blessing were it not for the breach in the dam: the monopolies which make it leave its natural bed, i. e., a consumption, which keeps pace with production This breach causes the destructive inundation of overproduction, or rather underconsumption, and consequent under-production   Every new machine, every improved process of pro-duction and distribution raises the level of the stream and though beneficial in itself, under the influence of monopoly it becomes a destructive agency

In this light we have also to look at the Trusts   Judged by them-selves, they are meritorious organizations   They diminish wasteful competition and they save labor, exactly as the railroads and the steamboats do.   Under Land and Money-monopoly, however they are made to become as great a curse as the other labor-saving inventions, as the power-loom and the linotype   So the fight against the trusts closely resembles that against machinery once waged by labor.   Both fights are equally vain, the wheel of progress can never be turned back by the means which ignorance employs

The road over which reform moves lies neither in the destruction of machines, factories, or trusts, nor in their nationalization, it lies in their democratization, their gradual appropriation by the workers of all classes, voluntarily co-operating; and the purpose of this book is to show how this can be accomplished by certain fundamental proceedings.

The most important one, the Restoration of the Land to the people as a whole, is discussed in Chapter II, which aims to show how easily this great reform can be effected on the basis of justice to all classes, without having recourse to the confiscatory methods of the so-called Single Taxers   Chapter III takes up the Money Question, showing how a fundamental currency reform could be gradually introduced without interfering with existing obligations and contracts.   Chapter IV deals with the Circulation Problem, including international balances and tariffs   The nature of Capi-talism and the part played by Interest in the great problem form the subject of Chapter V while Chapter VI, entitled "Democracy," takes up the political weapons required by the people in the fight for freedom and the accomplishment of social reform   The work which can be done, parallel with the political one, by private initiative and by co-operation will be discussed in Chapter VII Chapter VIII discusses 'Trusts and Socialism," while the con-cluding chapter takes a parting look at the battle field

While the most pressing questions are being treated, a new science of political economy arises before us : a real science, in which results correspond to promises because it is built on the eternal foun-dations of justice and truth   At the same time proof is furnished that a peaceable evolution is attainable on such foundations and that otherwise a violent revolution is unavoidable   I hope I have suc-ceeded in giving the light touch demanded by the average reader, without, on the one hand sinning by superficiality, or, on the other, falling into that ponderosity which, unfortunately, disfigures most works on economics

CHAPTER II.

LAND.

"Place one hundred men on an island from which there is no escape, and whether you make one of these men the absolute owner of the other ninety-nine, or the absolute owner of the soil of the island, will make no difference either to him or to them   Our boasted freedom necessarily involves slavery, so long as we recognize private property in land   Until that is abolished. Declarations of Independence and Acts of Emancipation are in vain   So long as one man can claim the exclusive ownership of the land from which other men must live slavery will exist, and, as material progress goes on, must grow and deepen!" (*Henry George in "Progress and Poverty"*)

Land differs from other human possessions in five particulars:

1   It is a product of nature, the stock of which is limited
2   It is indestructible
3   It cannot be carried away

These are three important qualities which make land the safest investment in the world, for there is no limit to man's products, they are perishable and most of them can be carried away by thieves

4   Land can produce wealth without human labor   I well know that this is against the theories of orthodox political economy, against one of its useless and positively harmful distinctions according to which wealth is a product of human labor and which refuses to accord to nature's work, unaided by that of man, its wealth-producing power   It is this kind of sophistry which has given to political economy the title of the dismal science   Why should a tree, never touched by human hands and sold on the stump, have less title to the term wealth than the board sawn from it?   Or do we call this tree a product of labor because man has created a market for it?   Then land, too, would be a product of human labor, because merely the presence of man has given it a market value   Though nature can produce wealth without the help of man, man cannot produce wealth without the help of nature, and in most cases nature does the lion's share.   Is it not pitiable to call the steer of the pampas the product of human labor, merely because one man has branded him to prevent his appropriation by other men?   I shall return to this point further on

5   Land is indispensable to human existence   Not only by co-producing all our food and raw-materials, but as an abode.

These five qualities of land here enumerated render it essential to deal with it differently from any other of man's possessions   Its limited quantity gives to its possession the character of a monopoly, its indispensability makes the monopoly a dangerous one

This character of land makes its appropriation by individuals intolerable Man has a sacred right to life and liberty, and, as neither of those rights can be enjoyed without access to land, land monopoly is a denial of man's sacred rights

But can we speak of land monopoly where there is no entail, where free trade in land exists, which is said to have the tendency of bringing it into the hands of those who put it to the best use, at the same time producing the most extended division of land?

History teaches the very contrary, to wit, that free-trade in land inevitably leads back to concentration, as brooks and rivulets finally help to form the ocean

The best proof of this fact is supplied by the history of France, since that memorable night of August 4, 1789, which overthrew feudalism and introduced a century of free-trade in land

Toubeau, a French author best known for his advocacy of intensive agriculture in 'La Repartition Métrique des Impôts," drew attention to some surprising statistical data regarding the division of the French soil, in a paper which first appeared in the *Philosophie Positiviste* of July and August, 1882 Its title is "Le Prolétariat Agricole en France depuis 1789, d'après les Documents Officiels' Who would have believed, without these official figures, that only one-tenth of the French soil is owned by peasant proprietors, by men who cultivate their land by their own work? No doubt most of the members of the 1889 International Congress of Land Reformers— of which Toubeau was elected secretary—learned this fact for the first time from his lips

In round figures, the official "Statistique Internationale de l'Agriculture de 1873'—from which Toubeau took his data—gives 49 million hectares (1 hectare = 2½ English acres) as the inhabitable surface of France after deducting the area taken up by rivers and lakes   The area covered by forest heath, swamp grazing land, and wilderness amounts to about one-third of the whole = 16 million hectares Houses and gardens take another million Another third = 16 million hectares is leasehold property cultivated by tenants Of the remaining third, 12 millions are taken up by large properties They represent 60,000 farms of 200 hectares on the average   This part of the soil is cultivated by laborers   For the peasant proprietor 4 million hectares are left, to which we may add a certain amount of the grazing land of the gardens and the house area, say 1 million hectares   We thus arrive at the stupendous fact that in the paradise of the peasant proprietor only one-tenth of the soil belongs to men who work it with their own hands   The number of these properties is 2 millions, with an average surface of 2½ hectares. This number seems to be in contradiction with the statistical tables, which give us 14 million properties Now, one-half of these 14 million properties pay less than 5 francs land-tax and on 3 or 4 million of these the tax cannot be collected at all, either because the owners are insolvent or because the properties are so small that the expenses of collection would be greater than the amount of the tax. In fact, the government statistician realizes that a great number of these so-called proprietors are such only by name. He says "Half of the land-owners possess only a small house with a very modest garden, sometimes an insignificant portion of an old common, or an undivided portion of a yard, open space, passage, or building-lot. In this way, in a great number of cases, in reality they have only the name of proprietors." Four million more pay only a land-tax of from 5 to 20 francs and therefore their holdings are so insignificant that their owners cannot make a living off their land. Toubeau then deducts the larger owners, the towns-people, etc., and thus arrives at his figure of 2 million families who subsist on their own land by their own labor.

The number of 3¼ million holdings given in the official statistics shows that if Toubeau erred, he did so on the right side; because, of these 3¼ millions, quite a number often belong to one proprietor, and 1¼ million of them are worked by tenants, while the balance of less than 2 million includes the large properties worked by laborers. Anyhow, the number of peasant proprietors does not affect the quantity of land owned by them, which—as Toubeau shows—is not over one-tenth of the French soil, and here we have to consider that a man cannot be called a proprietor in the full sense of the word if a great part of his property is mortgaged, and thus practically belongs to the mortgagee. Under the French system of an equal division of inheritances the partition of the small properties is continually progressing. If no immediate partition of the land takes place one of the children takes over the land, while the others take a mortgage for their share, which then is mostly sold to outsiders. This only means deferring the partition in many cases where land has finally to be sold to satisfy the mortgagee. While the small properties get thus subdivided through inheritance, the same cause has a tendency toward increasing the large properties. Rich people are in the habit of leaving wills, and for one case where such a will divides a large real estate, because there are not enough other assets to satisfy all the heirs, there may be ten cases where small properties which come into the market are bought by some rich man to enlarge his neighboring domain.

Toubeau's opinion that actually the peasants owned more land before the French Revolution than they do in our time is justified by a passage in Taine's 'Les Origines de la France Contemporaine L'ancien Régime," p. 453. "Vers 1760 un quart du sol, dit-on avait déjà passé aux mains des travailleurs agricoles." ('Towards 1760, it is said, that one quarter of the soil had already passed into the hands of the agricultural workers.")

On the preceding page Taine describes how many domains passed into the hands of merchants, lawyers, rich townspeople, a process also going on in our time wherever land can be freely bought in the market. We have seen the obvious reason. Land is indestructible, whereas the products of labor are more or less short-lived. Neither can land be carried away by thieves, like most of the things produced by man. While almost all products of human labor decrease in value through the lapse of time, unless new labor is added, the value of land, as a rule, increases. Fallow land becomes richer in chemical components. Trees yielding fuel and timber grow spontaneously on it. Anyhow, its price rises under normal conditions through the greater demand that follows technical progress and with the growth of population and wealth; rents become enhanced.

The very reverse takes place with most products of human labor. Independent of the destructive effects of time on them the price at which their equivalent can be produced falls continually, owing to our progress in the arts. As is to be expected under such conditions the rich and knowing investors give the preference to land, and this raises still more its selling price. In this way, the rate of interest at which rent is capitalized into the selling price of land falls so low, while the selling price becomes so high, that the worker who needs land prefers to rent it or is forced to do so, as he has not got the means wherewith to buy. The little capital he possesses is wanted in his business, and anyhow, it cannot be invested at the low rate of interest with which the rich landowner is contented.* Or, if he buys, and borrows part of the purchase money on a mortgage, usually the rate of interest of this mortgage is so much higher than the net rate yielded by the land, that a two-third mortgage generally swallows the whole of the rental value. This explains how even in a country like France, where a little over a hundred years ago the Revolution threw a great part of the feudal property into the market, the number of tenants and laborers who work on other people's land by far exceeds that of the men who work their own freeholds. It is even more astonishing that the same fact obtains in the United States of America, a country most of whose land—within the memory of the living generation—was practically thrown open, free of cost to the hardy pioneers. Let us take our figures from the census of 1900.

If we go as far down as 100-acre farms, we may suppose we have reached the utmost limit where an American farmer can work the land with his own hands and those of his family. In this case only one-sixth of the cultivated area comes into consideration. Of this we have to deduct that portion which is worked by tenants, to obtain the area worked by peasant-proprietors. As the farms worked by tenants figure up to about 40 per cent of the whole area only ten per cent, or one-tenth of the whole area remains for the peasant-proprietor.

In case 100 acres should be considered too low a limit for this

* De Lavergne, the enemy of peasant proprietorship, speaks of "That turning aside of capital from the cultivation of the land to its purchase, which is one of the chief vices of our French rural economy."

class of farms, we must not forget that, on the other hand, the mort-gages have been left out of calculation. As the mortgagee prac-tically owns the land, whose rent he collects in the shape of interest, to the proportion of the mortgage, this takes off a larger percentage of land from the freely-owned area than the inclusion of certain farms above 100 acres could add to it, especially as the mortgages stand at a very high rate of interest.

The tendency towards concentration of landed property in this country is also evidenced by the fact that from 1870 to 1900 the smaller farms under 100 acres only increased from 2,075,338 to 3,297,404 = 60 per cent., while those above 100 acres increased from 584,647 to 2,424,354 = 413 per cent. Those above 500 acres increased from 19,593 to 149,686 = 763 per cent., or almost eight-fold, about 13 times more than the farms below 100 acres.

Let us now take the case of a still newer country, usually presented as a model by the followers of Henry George. In New Zealand the number of occupied acres in 1904-5 was 36,511,154, of which 27,013,683 were in holdings of over 1,000 acres, 29,142,776 in holdings of over 640 acres, and only 991,542 in holdings up to 100 acres, inclusive. The holdings over 1,000 acres numbered 4,211, those over 640 acres 6,820, of a total of 68,680 holdings, which means that one-sixteenth of the holdings (belonging to one-seven-tieth of the people) embrace three-quarters of the occupied land. Of these 893 holdings, or one seventy-seventh of all the holdings, belonging to three per cent. of the population, embrace as much as 56 per cent. of the total occupied land. But if we want to get at the number of peasant properties we have to consider that of the 36,511,154 acres only 16,392,221 are held as freeholds, 3,574,038 are leased from private individuals or public bodies, 1,667,676 are leased from natives and 14,877,219 are held from the Crown under different tenures. The mortgage debt amounts to 37 per cent. of the value of the land assessed, without improvements, or 23 per cent. of the value including improvements. The interest rate varies from 5 to 8 per cent.

If we counted as peasant proprietors all land owners up to 100 acres we could hardly estimate the area thus owned, after the per-centage of indebtedness is deducted, as figuring up to more than one per cent. of the occupied area, and if we go as high as a thou-sand acres, because of the prevalence of grazing—and it is almost impossible in this case to manage the farm with the owner's and his family's unaided labor—we do not arrive at a higher percentage than in France, one-tenth of the occupied land.

That the same state of things prevails also in Australia is indicated by the following utterances of an old friend A. J. Ogilvie, of Richmond, Tasmania, meant as an attack on the superstition that the desire to own a piece of land is deeply engrained in human nature.

"'But,' we are told, 'you forget the land hunger. Man naturally craves for the absolute ownership of the soil he tills, and without it loses half the stimulus to exertion   He wants to sit under his own vine and fig-tree

"Here are three statements rolled into one   Take the last first 'He wants to sit under his own vine and fig-tree'

"True, and the result of your system of absolute ownership is that ninety-nine men out of one hundred can get no vine or fig-tree to sit under, and the hundredth finds that the vine and fig-tree under which he sits are not his but his landlord's, who charges him heavily for the privilege, and this even though he has planted the tree himself, and watered it with the sweat of his toil

"Year by year all over the civilized world, the ownership of the land is passing out of the hands of the occupier   One man rears the fruit, another stretches out his hand and takes it   The very institution which you defend as securing to the producer the full value of his produce is the institution that compels him to part with it

' How comes this?

"Because the unearned increment, though certain, is deferred, and falls therefore, to him who can afford to wait, and who accordingly waits

'Sooner or later the day comes when a mortgage has to be redeemed, or death brings the property into the market, and then the man of large and independent means, who does not mind getting a low rate of interest for a while in consideration of large profits thereafter, easily outbids the working owner, who has to earn his living, and must have quick returns

"Thus it is that not only is the rich non-occupying owner fast superseding the poorer working owner, but the large non-occupying owners are also eating up the small ones, and the tendency of the times is for the whole land of the country to pass gradually into the hands of a few enormously rich people

"We have not got into this second stage yet out here, but we are well on into the first   And so inevitably and steadily land is coming to belong, not to him who has the best right to it, not to him who wants it most, not to him who will put it to the most productive use, or even to any use at all, but to him who can afford to give most for it, for the mere purpose of squeezing other people

"You offer the name, but you cannot confer the reality   We withhold the name, but guarantee the reality

"For what is the land hunger?

"It is the natural craving for a permanent home, and for the fruits of our labor   and we guarantee both these, you do not

"The natural desire of a man is for a dwelling which he can regard as his home, for so long as he chooses to dwell in it, for a piece of land which he can cultivate and build upon and improve as his interest or fancy may dictate, without the fear of a notice to quit, and the certainty that when he quits of his own accord he can realize the full value of his improvements at the time of his retiring

'If you say further that all these things shall be his own, you are conferring no further privilege You are only summing up the privileges already enumerated in a compact, sweet-sounding phrase

' That he shall possess his home so long as he chooses to dwell in it, his land so long as he chooses to fill it; this is the land hunger But to want to own the land without using it, to leave and yet retain the ownership for the mere purpose of preventing other people from using it, except on payment, this is not the land hunger at all

"Directly a man has lost the desire to dwell in his home and till his land, and wants to go elsewhere and live on the rent, he has lost the land hunger, and retains only the ordinary desire to make money.

"Therefore, when under these circumstances we require him to give up the land, securing to him the value of his improvements, we violate no craving of his nature; we only take from him what he has ceased to value, the land, and allow him the one thing he continues to value—his money—to invest elsewhere

"Further, it is the nature and not the extent of the occupancy that satisfies the land hunger A home and land enough to afford employment are all that is wanted for the purpose

"The Irishman's poor cabin is as much his home to him as the duke's palace to him and an acre or two satisfies the craving to be working for oneself, as thoroughly as 1,000 acres would Therefore so long as we leave a man land enough to provide him full employment, much more when we leave him enough to employ many hired servants, we may take, at a valuation, the broad acres on which he merely runs his flocks, without jarring any legitimate feeling."

Even in England, where the feudal system has long held sway, where the entail is still the rule, even in England the saleable freehold exists and tells its usual sad history

Macaulay, in Chapter III of his "History of England," where he treats of the yeomanry, says "If we may trust the best statistical writers of that age (1685), not less than a hundred and sixty thousand proprietors, who with their families, must have made up more than a seventh of the whole population, derived their subsistence from little freehold estates The average income of these small landholders—an income made up of rent, profits, and wages—was estimated at between 60 and 70 pounds a year It was computed that the number of persons who tilled their own land was greater than the number of those who farmed the land of others I have taken Davenant's statement, which is a little lower than King's"

What a change for the worse these figures present! Considering the difference in the value of money, we must take at least £150 as the equivalent of the £60 to £70 of two centuries ago   Now, we certainly cannot go below holdings of 5 acres when we want to find men who can make an income of £150 a year from the land, and the total number of holdings above 5 acres, and not exceeding 50 acres, in 1889, was for all England and Wales 203,861.   The "Financial Reform Almanac," from which I take these figures does not give the number of these holdings which are freeholds, but to anyone knowing England, it is evident that only a very small proportion of this land is owned by the parties who cultivate it.   On the other hand, Macaulay may have included holdings above 50 acres   Erring largely on the right side by compensating the two causes of error, we arrive at the conclusion that, in spite of an eight-fold increase of population, the number of people who make a living on their own land by their labor has not increased, while it ought to be eight times greater.   Where, two centuries ago, "the number of persons who tilled their own land was greater than the number of those who farmed the land of others," it is notorious that tenant farming is the rule in the England of 1908, and a man's tilling his own land has become such a rare thing that it plays a very insignificant part in the English corn yield

The great scientist Alfred Russel Wallace finds in England the same causes at work which I indicated in the case of France, in "Studies Scientific and Social".

'It is a favorite dogma of some reformers that all the evils of the present day would be got rid of by what they term 'free trade in land'   They seem to think that if all obstacles to the sale and purchase of land were abolished, if entails of all kinds were forbidden and the conveyance of land made as cheap and expeditious as it might easily be, the obstacle that now exists to the growth of a body of peasant proprietors would be got rid of   This notion appears to me to be one of the greatest of all delusions.   The real obstacle to peasant proprietorship or small yeoman farmers in this country is the land hunger of the rich, who are constantly seeking to extend their possessions, partly because land is considered the securest of all investments and which, though paying a small average interest affords many chances of great profits, but mainly on account of the political power, the exercise of authority, and widespread social influence it carries with it   The number of individuals of great wealth in this country is enormous, and owing to the diminution of the more reckless forms of extravagance, many of them live far below their incomes, and employ the surplus in extending their estates   The probabilities are that men of this stamp are increasing, and will increase and the system of free trade in land would serve chiefly to afford them the means of an unlimited gratification of their great passion"

The following verses from "Land and Labor" the excellent organ of the English Land Nationalization Society illustrate in a

happy vein the chances the average English peasant has, under the
present free trade in land system, of securing enough land to make
a bare living on

THREE ACRES AND A COW.

"I hear thee speak of a bit o' land,
  And a cow for every laboring hand,
  Tell me, dear mother, where is that shore,
  Where I shall find it and work no more?
  Is it at home this promised ground,
  Where the acres three and a cow are found?
  Is it where pheasants and partridges breed?
  Or in fields where the farmer is sowing his seed?
  Is it on the moors so wild and grand
  I shall find this bit of arable land?"
    "Not there! not there, my Giles!"

"Eye hath not seen that fair land, my child,
  Ear hath but heard an echo wild—
  The nightmare of an excited brain,
  That dreamers have like Chamberlain
  Far away, beyond the ken
  Of sober, practical business men,
  Far away beyond the sight
  Of men whose heads are screwed on right;
  Where castles in the air do stand,
  Behold the cow and the bit o' land!
    'Tis there! 'tis there, my Giles!"

Many more proofs might be given that the formation of large
estates is the inevitable result of free trade in land, experienced
everywhere since the times of old Rome, when Plinius found in
large landed properties the cause of Italy's ruin.

The contention is made that free trade in land not only brings
the land into the hands of those who use it to best advantage, but
that this is to the benefit of the community at large. Facts show
that neither premise nor conclusion is correct, and that Ricardo was
right when he claimed that "the interest of the landlord is always
opposed to that of every other class in the community." The interest of the landlord is to collect for himself the highest rent or
net produce attainable In figuring this rent or net produce the
expense for labor stands among general expenses, which are deducted from the gross product to obtain the net product But for
the laborer his wages are his own net product, and thus finally all
gross products resolve themselves into net products of other people Every cent paid out for machinery, manure, seed, fences,
cattle, etc, is finally spent for labor of some sort, and is the net

product of somebody else   In this way all gross products an.
practically all net products, from the point of view of the communit
The well-being of the people consequently depends on the quant:
of gross products

Take, for instance, the case of a large proprietor owning 10,000
acres   If he lets the land to a hundred small farmers, or employs a
hundred laborers, the gross product of the land may be $100,000.
while his net income from the rent obtained, or from the crop sold
after deduction of wages and other expenses, may not amount to
over $10,000   If he lets the land to a grazier or raises cattle on
his own account, the gross product may not exceed $20,000 and
still leave him a larger net amount in the end than he obtained in the
other case. His preference will naturally be for the highest rent
and so only a few cow-boys find employment, where a hundred
families might have earned their bread   Which is of greater benefit
to the community as a whole?   The State, the representative of all
citizens, would probably refuse the higher rent and lease the land
to the hundred farmers   Leaving all higher considerations aside
and looking at it only from the financial side, this policy might
even in the end yield a larger income to the public exchequer
through the taxes paid by the farmers and their purveyors, the
urban producers, who make their clothing, the wire of their fences.
their furniture and household goods, their machines and their tools
Supply and demand are beneficial regulators in the case of commodities that can be produced in any quantity, but not in the case
of a limited commodity like land   Free trade in land could never
have found such a number of defenders if it had not been looked
upon as the best antidote to feudal monopoly; whereas in reality
it merely substituted the plutocrat for the aristocrat, a worse for a
better master   The capitalist landlord has not been connected by
a family tradition of centuries with the land and its occupiers, to
him his land is nothing but the equivalent of other investments
which he gave up for it   Its rent replaces the interest which those
investments yielded, and he expects his rent to fall in somewhat
after the quasi-automatic process in which his coupons were cut
and cashed before he exchanged the bonds to which they were attached, for the land he bought with their proceeds   As he never
cared who finally had to pay the interest represented by these coupons so the tenant of his land to him is merely a rent-paying machine, to be exchanged for another, so soon as it does not regularly
perform its functions

This is still more conspicuous where the capitalistic ownership
is indirectly exercised through the mortgage and, especially, where
the mortgagee is not a person but a corporation, often one who
represents thousands of poor people, as in the case of savings banks
and insurance companies   To these institutions it is a case of mere
figures. It is no longer a question of one man's relation to his
fellow-man who works for him, but that of the impersonal capital

to its interest   The right of capital to earn interest seems such a self-evident one, that anybody who refuses to pay his interest dues is considered as defrauding capital of its rights   Neither can the savings bank be blamed for not granting facilities, as it is merely the agent of others who have brought their savings   The real landlord is yonder poor widow, who has invested her few dollars in the bank, or perhaps the farmer's own laborers, who have not the least idea where their interest comes from, and dream not that they are the oppressors of their poor master, who bitterly refers them to his own misery when he refuses to raise their wages   A remarkable illustration, this of the so-called *"class war"* !

But what other system is better adapted to bring the land to the most rational use, if free trade in land, instead of accomplishing this purpose, has the pernicious effect of concentrating possessions in the hands of the few to the detriment of the many?   The reverse of free trade entail?   Perhaps, if rationally organized i e. so as not to keep the land in the possession of the exploiter, but to insure permanent possession to the workers   If feudalism was the father of aristocratic entail, the Germanic Mark and the Russian Mir might give us a precedent for democratic entail'   Of course, periodical re-allotments, only possible under a primitive system of cultivation, would not be practicable under scientific farming.   Nor are they essential to Mark or Mir, of which they rather are the greatest obstacle   An allotment which in place of his well cultivated land, assigned to an industrious farmer the neglected field of a thriftless neighbor, obviously discouraged the better man and had a tendency to bring him down to the other's level

A slight change in the American Homestead Laws would have provided an improved "Mark" with all the advantages of the old plan without its inconveniencies   Let us suppose that this country had added the following simple clause to her Homestead Law "This land is to remain freehold property of the settler during his life and that of his descendants, provided that he or they occupy the said land themselves   The title does not include the right of sale or lease   Whenever personal occupation of land by the settler or his descendants ceases, the land reverts to the previous owner the United States, with full right of free disposal, free of any charge but the price originally charged to the settler, plus the payment for the improvements made by the dispossessed party at their assessed value."   An inventor who enriches the world with a product of his brain has its ownership guaranteed for only 17 years; why should the first occupier of a piece of land, which is not his product, have a right of eternal possession, the right to use and abuse it, also to cede this right to others?

Though it might have had a deterrent effect on mere speculators holding land for a rise, and meanwhile, like dogs in the manger, keeping bonafide occupiers at a distance, such a law would not have held off a single real settler   On the contrary, the increase of free land at their disposal, besides the effect on general social conditions, concentration of wealth in particular, would have brought over the best class of immigrants from the whole world   Even if the whole of our present population were farmers, there would still be available 100 acres for each family on the average, if we take only the occupied area into account   Of course, the State would not reallot homesteads that come back into her possession without a just compensation for the increase of value in price or rent

A Homestead Law with such a condition, insuring to the community the reversion at cost price whenever the party to whom the homestead has been given ceases to occupy it either in person or through his or her descendants, would have produced wonderful results , but, unfortunately, a law of this kind has never existed The American abortion bearing the name of "Homestead" has been a most serviceable instrument of landlordism and capitalism   Only Germany in her new Chinese colony has shown a practical approach to something in the nature of a real Homestead Law   The State buys the land from the former occupiers at a certain price based on the land tax paid by them, or rather the land rent, as the soil of China nominally belongs to the Emperor   The land is then sold to the settlers at the market price resulting from supply and demand   The right of pre-emption is reserved to the State, in case the buyers want to sell at any future time.   If the government makes no use of this right, it demands a tax of 2 per cent on the selling price and, furthermore, one-third of the unearned increment, of the profit made on the original price—of course, taking first account of the improvements made by the owner   This third has to be paid anyhow, once within 25 years, whether the land changes hands or not   In addition to this, a yearly tax is demanded amounting to 6 per cent of the selling value of the land   This tax cuts off the soil under the feet of land-hoarding speculators, who, besides the interest on their outlay, lose every year as much as 6 per cent of the selling value of the land they leave unused , and, in the best of cases, they have to give up one-third of their final profits   It is understood that the 6 per cent. cannot be deducted from the profits from which the State gets her third.   As the tax is one of the conditions of the purchase, all the advantages of a land-value tax are reaped by the State without the stigma of confiscation

A valuable proof in the progress made in land reform occurs in Germany since the society now called the League of German Land Reformers was founded, through my instrumentality, in 1888, a time at which the mere idea of land nationalization was generally ridiculed in the Fatherland   Such proof is furnished by one part of the address with which the government's representative, Contre-Admiral Tirpitz introduced the new law in the Reichstag   He put stress on the fact that the financial point of view had stood in the second line only in the motives which caused the government to bring forth this law , motives which any one would have looked for in the pages of "Progress and Poverty" rather than in the speech of a representative of Germany's emperor Better than this, a representative of the Bund der Landwirthe, the league of the agrarians, Germany's big land owners, not only approved of the law, but would have liked to see the third of the State's share in the profits raised to one-half The manner in which this progressive law may affect the development of the German colony will be shown in time.

However, the best system of securing enough land for the occupier and the rental income for the community is Common Land-ownership

Of all which has ever been written on this subject nothing can approach the wonderful work of Henry George, the pioneer of the modern land reform movement "Progress and Poverty" has opened a new world to untold thousands who had previously refrained from social reform work, because socialism did not seem attainable or even desirable and no other solutions were in sight The mere looking out for such meant a dive into the dismal abyss which the science of economics presented to the ordinary mortal, until Henry George's poetic prose, his wonderful imagery, a limpid style such as had not been known since Macaulay fascinated his hosts of readers, rendered economic subjects more attractive than the ordinary novel Here lies the imperishable merit of the book, not in its scientific theories, which unfortunately contain many sad errors

The book is too well known to require any recapitulation. To those of my readers who have not read it, I merely offer the advice to study it They may not agree with everything in it, in fact if they have any notion of economic realities they will shake their heads over several strange theories such as the relations George finds between wages and interest, his absolute negation of the wage-fund theory through his ignorance of the currency problem, and his ideas as to the cause underlying commercial depressions But they will acquire the absolute conviction that justice and expediency demand that the ownership of the soil must belong to the people as a whole, and that no thorough-going reform in the social domain is at all possible without the restoration of the land to the community With unmitigated delight we follow the author's sledge-hammer strokes against the greatest crime man ever committed on this planet —the crime of selling and pawning God's own, this earth the great heritage of humanity One after another of those sophistic defences with which the usurpers and their gang of venal or ignorant lackeys have tried to prop up the foul wrong crumbles before those mighty strokes. Nothing will hold together *Not the right of discovery or first occupation,* claimed by the human mite left stranded for a few seconds by the ocean of time on some little nook of this globe which, according to this mitish knowledge, was never before alighted upon by any fellow-mite of his, whereupon the little mite prefers

a title to that nook for all times to come, including the right of use
and abuse, of letting to fellow-mites against heavy tribute, or withholding the use, though fellow-mites should die miserably in consequence   Not the *right of conquest* based on superior power, driv-
ing other mites from the locations previously occupied by them—
a dangerous title anyway, for it legitimizes Democracy's claim to
the right of expropriation without compensation, whenever it has
the power to enforce the claim   Not the *right of purchase* from
other mites, whose title, after we have proceeded backward through
the centuries, finally finds itself based upon some pretence of first
occupation or conquest   Not *any right whatever given by king or
parliament,* by His Majesty, the chief mite, or the mite-hive's
representatives   Not even the assent of all the mite-hives which
ever crawled over this little dustball of the universe during a few
pulse-beats of eternity, on their journey from the unknown to the
unknowable, even if this assent be engrossed ever so visibly on the
hides of defunct sheep, goats, or asses. Can a thief give a valid
title to his booty?

George shows that the right given by improvements can only
extend to the improvements, not to the land on which they are
made   What produces most of the land's value are not the improvements made by the landowner, but those made by other
outside of his land   If an untouched piece of original forest land
existed near New York City it might be even more valuable than
the improved farm land near it, through the value of the timber,
but the main value of both improved and unimproved land would
be created by the neighborhood of millions of men and women
who need this land as a place of work and residence   What gives
to land most of its value is not the labor of the owner, but that of
all humanity since untold ages

A Stephenson broods over the problem of transportation by steam-
driven wagons on iron-shod roads, others invent new plows, sowing, and reaping, and threshing machinery—and land far off in
Dacota's prairies, as worthless before as the water of the ocean,
acquires an immense value   Not through the work of the cul-
tivator, which covers it with the waving corn, for he is getting his
wages from the proceeds of this corn after the rent of the land has
been paid   This rent is due, not to the corn which can be grown
on the land, for that could have been done since immemorial times,
but to the railways and steamers which permit the sale of this corn in
the London market, cheaper than the neighboring Essex farmer
can supply it, which puts the farmer into communication with the
rest of the world, from whence all he needs is brought to his door
at reasonable rates   It is further due to the inventors of that
machinery which enables one man to do the work of a hundred

An inventor finds a system of freezing establishments and cool-
storage ships, through which Australian carcases of sheep and cattle
can be cut up by the Smithfield butcher and served to the Londoner

as fresh as the meat of animals slaughtered yesterday—and millions of Australian acres double and treble their value in consequence Talk of this value being due to the improvements of the landlords! Why should they be entitled to land values produced by this and similar work done all over the world, including the work of the meanest hand in an English factory, which enables him to buy this Australian meat or this Dacota wheat, and thus pay some of the rent of the distant land? Germany's warriors are victorious on the fields of Koniggratz and Sedan, and the farmer at the gates of Berlin sells his land for building purposes at a price exceeding its cost more than a hundredfold. Was it his merit? The State erects irrigation works on the Grand river of Colorado, and land—bought a few years before as a homestead, almost for nothing—soon sells for $600 an acre, because water becomes attainable at a moderate charge which changes the desert land into fertile soil, producing innumerable crops without manuring Is it the merit of the chance land owner that the State or private parties carry out irrigation works? Only the community can be the rightful heir of the fruits of this work of present and past generations, which made the world of to-day, can rightfully claim the additional value, the unearned increment, as it is called, thus created Rather a misnomer, for, as Miss Helen Taylor said "Those who earn it don't get it, and those who get it don't earn it"

With kindling eyes you read on and on, more and more eager to follow the great leader to the ramparts where the advocates of wrong vainly try to defend their parchment fortresses Alert you listen for that word of command by which the glorious captain will direct the attack.

At last you come to the study of Chapter II, of Book VIII Can you believe your eyes? Are you reading aright? Is it possible that the very man who has just proved with a logic as transparent as crystal that private property in land is doomed and must be exterminated, if humanity is to live, that this very man now advises you to leave this property in the possession of its present owners, on the grounds of expediency and to content yourself with taxing it? Again and again you read the page, but there it is, it cannot be wiped out. Was the great prophet after all only a poor, erring human being?

It is almost unbelievable that a man like Henry George should have thus left the straight plain road he had opened, and should instead have chosen a crooked by-path full of thorny weeds, and ending in a quagmire For such a course he must have had most powerful motives, certainly worth examination

When, however, we investigate his reasons our astonishment increases, for all he has to say in explanation of such a sudden departure from the principle which the whole book has been advocating, is contained in the following few lines

"To do that (confiscating all the land and letting it out to the

highest bidders) would involve a needless shock to present customs
and habits of thought—which is to be avoided   To do that would
involve a needless extension of government machinery—which is to
be avoided   It is an axiom of statesmanship, which the successful
founders of tyranny have always understood and acted upon—that
great changes can best be brought about under old forms. We,
who would free men, should heed the same truth   It is the natural
method   When Nature would make a higher type, she takes a
lower one and develops it   This is also the law of social growth
Let us work by it   With the current, we may glide fast and far
Against it, it is hard pulling and slow progress '

That is all

George, as we see, sets out from the axiom that land nationalizers
want to confiscate the land, though most land nationalizers, like
myself, will fail to remember ever having met one single partisan
of our special method of land restoration who even dreamt of
proposing such a measure. It is, however, quite consistent with
George's convictions to leave out of consideration any other method
of accomplishing land restoration

The idea of compensation is so absolutely antagonistic to his
thoughts and principles that he cannot even conceive how those·
land nationalizers who propose compensation—and, as I have just
said, they all do—can be honest. In his opinion, we do not really
want to obtain the land for the people at all, we only want 'to
draw a red herring across the track" of land restorers as one of
George's disciples once stigmatized my work for land nationalization
in New Zealand   George's words are "For to say that men must
be compensated if they are prevented from doing a thing, is to say
that they have a right to do that thing   And this those who in-
telligently advocate compensation, know   *Their purpose in advocating compensation is to prevent abolition*" ("A Perplexed Philosopher," p 276)   Now, it is certainly not a feeling of unkindness
towards co-workers on another plan which begot such thoughts,
for he was the kindest of men and the most loyal of friends   No
it was his firm and unshakeable conviction of the absolute injustice
of compensating anybody for ceasing to perpetrate a wrong   Private land ownership, in his eyes, is a theft, and if anybody were
to be compensated, let it be not the robbers, but their victims the
landless people whose heirloom has been taken away from them
since times immemorial   Emerson gave expression to the same idea
regarding compensation to slave-owners   "Pay ransom to the
owner, and fill the cup to the brim   Who is the owner? The slave
is the owner pay him!" "Let bygones be bygones," I have heard
George say repeatedly in public, "only don't sin any more!"
"Let the people forgive the past, the immense amounts wrested
from them by the landlords and only demand to be at last reinstated
in their rights "

According to him, it makes no difference how the land-owners got into possession, whether they inherited, stole, or bought their land in good faith The law demands restitution without compensation from anybody who bought stolen property, why should there be any difference whether the stolen object is a watch, or a piece of God's earth?

He usually compared private land ownership with slave property Both confer the right of claiming the work of fellow-men without any compensation In fact, we might say that the slave-owner gives some kind of compensation to the slave whose services he makes use of, for he feeds and clothes him, provides him with shelter, medical advice, and assistance, whereas the landlord demands his rent, little caring how the tenant makes a living The tenant often has to work harder than a slave to pay his landlord, and has to "find" himself.

"Compensation for the selling value of a slave, which disappears on the refusal of the community longer to force him to work for the master, means the giving to the master of what the power to take the property of the slave may be worth What slave-owners lose is the power of taking the property of the slaves and their descendants, and what they get is an agreement that the government will take for their benefit and turn over to them an equivalent part of the property of all The robbery is continued under another form What it loses in intension it gains in extension If some before enslaved are partially freed, others before free are partially enslaved" ("A Perplexed Philosopher," p 263) We shall see further on that this is an error that compensation can be given without the imposition of any new tax

Other arguments are given and more might be added

A strong one has already been alluded to on a previous page The original title—in Europe anyhow—is based on conquest in the last resort, on the right of the strongest Since the landless people now are stronger than the land-owners, the latter could have no valid objection to confiscation were the people sufficiently united for land restoration to overcome by force any possible resistance, for the new title would have the same foundation as the one it superseded History has seen such cases On that memorable night of August 4, 1789, of which Carlyle says "Dignitaries, temporal and spiritual, Peers, Archbishops Parliament-President, each outdoing the other in patriotic devotedness, come successively to throw their own untenable possessions on the altar of the Fatherland With louder and louder vivats—for indeed it is after dinner, too—they abolish Tithes, Seignoral dues, Gabelle, excessive Preservation of Game nay, Privilege Immunity, Feudalism root and branch "

It was a voluntary surrender only in appearance, in reality, the old spent force which once had conquered the privileges yielded to the new force, which did not content itself with what was surrendered, but confiscated a good part of the remaining monopoly, the property of the land

When a people emerges from despotic government, and takes its destinies into its own hands, assuredly it may also overthrow the institutions of the old régime, revolution has its own laws, those of the strong

So has reaction, the revolution backward   The following passage taken from Macaulay's "History of England," Chapter II, shows to members of the English Liberty and Property Defence League— a league of drones formed for the defence of the liberty of exacting tributes from the land-using workers, and of the property wrested from the people, the land—that their own party supplied a very valuable precedent how to treat vested rights, even where founded on cash payment   Their own actions in the past have deprived them of their strongest defence against plans of confiscation

Single-taxers (the infelicitous title assumed by those followers of Henry George in the United States and in England's colonies, who have adopted his land-restoration method) may point out to the Liberty and Property Defence League of how little value their own party accounted the right based on honest purchase, how it was they who first in England made use of Henry George's argument in regard to land that the owner of stolen property has the right to take possession of it without any compensation, wherever he finds it, never mind what consideration has been given by the actual possessor

"Property all over the kingdom was again changing hands   The national sales (under Cromwell) not having been confirmed by Act of Parliament, were regarded by the tribunals as nullities   The bishops, the deans, the chapters, the Royalist nobility and gentry re-entered their confiscated estates, and ejected even purchasers who had given fair prices"

It is hard to see, however in what way confiscation could be justified on such grounds in the United States, where most of the land was parted with by the people's elected representatives, who acted in perfect agreement with their mandators   Though Henry George was not the first who wrote against the prevailing system of private landownership, yet before his great book appeared not one man in a thousand was conscious of the fact that trade in land differed fundamentally from the trade in any other marketable object   Though the abuses due to the system were painfully felt, the system itself was attacked only by a few socialists whose opposition to private land ownership formed only a part of their antagonism to any kind of private property used for revenue purposes   The people, as a whole, were just as ardent defenders of the freehold as they were of other private property   Would it be just under such conditions to turn round on and punish with confiscation men who acted on views which we ourselves entertained but yesterday ? We should act like that good Christian who wanted to justify his attack upon one of "the Lord's people" by accusing them of crucifying Christ. When his victim defended himself by stating the fact that the circumstance had taken place a couple of thousand years ago, he replied . "No matter, I had never heard of it until yesterday !"

It is hardly fair to style landowners "robbers" under such circumstances, and certainly nobody has a right to indulge in such aspersions and to ask for confiscation, who himself held the ladder by which the burglars entered the house

A state which proceeded on these lines would furnish a very bad precedent   To-day it confiscates the land which it sold for hard cash, because private landownership is robbery, to-morrow it declares that the public debt has long since been more than repaid by the interest the creditors have received in the course of years, and interest is robbery   Consequently the debt is repudiated without any other compensation to bondholders than to call them robbers, never mind whether they are the original lenders or those who bought their papers only yesterday, trusting in the State's good faith   The day after, socialists obtain the majority and declare every employer a robber, they confiscate the factories built by the workers, and, of course as they make it out, belonging to them by right

We can leave the question aside whether the confiscation of the land is a crime or a justified action, for Talleyrand's famous word applies here   "C'est plus qu'un crime c'est une faute."   (It is more than a crime, it is a blunder)   Even the proverbial Yankee who sent his son into the world with the advice, "Make money, honestly if you can but make money anyhow !" preferred the honest way, if it was as practicable   If I shall therefore succeed in proving that compensation is the practicable method and further that it is the cheapest, I should think that we may as well take that way which most people in our generation believe to be also the honest way, never mind what George and his disciples may think of it

It is not with books like "A Perplexed Philosopher" that such men as Herbert Spencer are gained over to our side   The great sociologist certainly acted wrongly when he gave up the idea of land restoration because he could see no practical way of accomplishing it without wronging the present owners   Such a withdrawal was not moral in a man who had recognized that "with this perplexity and our extrication from it abstract morality has no concern   Men having got themselves into the dilemma by disobedience to the law, must get out of it as well as they can, and with as little injury to the landed class as they may "

Henry George would have been better entitled to cast stones at Herbert Spencer if "Progress and Poverty' had proposed a practical reconcilement of the interests of the people with those of the landowners

On page 282 he reproaches Herbert Spencer for not even so much as alluding to his proposal of taking land values, not land, for ignoring it "because there is on that line no place for proposing or even suggesting compensation. Compensation to the ultimate payers of a tax is something unheard of and absurd."

Even here George is wrong, as I pointed out to him before he wrote this passage. When in 1865, in Prussia, the land tax was imposed on the properties of certain nobles, who, as former independent sovereigns, i e., direct dependents of the German Empire, had been exempt from this tax, they were compensated to the full capitalized amount of the tax (at 4½ per cent or 22 years purchase), because a tax on land confiscates a proportionate part of the land's value which is nothing but the capitalized rent, and any deduction from this rent correspondingly reduces value, or selling-price. Whether we take away a man's land, or the rights which this land gives him, and which alone constitute its value amounts to the same thing. If we give him no compensation, we are guilty of confiscation

I should have had a better right to accuse the illustrious Spencer that he maintained errors long after he had a chance of correcting them. After his letter in the *Times* (November 1889), giving as his principal reason against carrying through land nationalization that the interest which would have to be paid to raise the funds required to compensate landowners would exceed the rent obtained by the State, I showed him how, through the rise of rent on the one side and the falling of the interest-rate on the other, there would be a growing surplus sufficient to pay off the whole debt within a measurable time. Granting, as implied in the answer I received, that pressure of work and the state of his health prevented the philosopher from giving a complete reply, still he cannot be excused for failing to investigate the facts placed before him. If found true as they were bound to be, they withdrew the foundation on which his opposition to land nationalization had been based, a reform without which—according to him—the law of equal freedom is infringed

As confiscation is not on our programme, let us see whether as George says, land nationalization 'would involve a needless shock to present customs and habits of thought."

Certainly not in England, where by far the greatest part of the land does not belong to the people who use it, and is not used by those who own it, where it does not change to any great extent existing habits and customs, whether the tenants, the land users who were the highest bidders, have to pay their rents to the agent of the Duke of Westminster, Buccleuch etc, or to the official of the government. Even in the United States almost 40 per cent of the land is worked by tenants and some of the rest is mortgaged so heavily that the nominal owner is practically the tenant of the mortgagee. Similar conditions exist pretty well in the whole of the

civilized world   If we take all this into consideration, we come to
the conclusion that, after all, the substitution of the State for the
private landlord would not involve so very great a "shock to existing customs and habits of thought "

But to impose a tax that shall gradually grow until it swallows
the whole rental value of the land, thus gradually to confiscate the
basis of this property guaranteed by the State like any other property, to put on the shoulders of one class of citizens the whole of
,the State's charges, this, according to Henry George, could be done
without any "needless shock to present customs and habits of
thought "

He goes on: "To do that (nationalize the land) would involve
a needless extension of government machinery, which is to be
avoided "

When George wrote this he was almost totally unacquainted with
the political condition of European countries, he reasoned from the
impressions received in his native country, the United States   Even
thus he left out of consideration the working of cause and effect
Instead of arguing The powerful monopolies which have arisen
out of private landownership have corrupted our government
machinery to such an extent that we cannot possibly entrust it
with the administration of the land of the nation, he ought to have
reasoned · The destruction of those influences which have made the
government of the United States almost the most corrupt on earth,
among which our system of landownership takes the first place.
can alone restore purity of administration to such a degree that we
may safely confide the land of the people to their government   If
he had gone to Germany he would have found the Prussian State
domains among the best administered farm land in the country.
The States' forests are models of a perfect management. The
national mines and railroads are well managed   The effects of
land nationalisation on employment would render government employees more independent and less liable to obey unjust dictates
from above, so that even the political dangers which might be feared
from a further extension of government influence would be less
than under our type of administration.   A landowning democracy
where every citizen has a· stake in the country is certainly less cor-
ruptible than a landless rabble

And, must we ask, has corruption no influence on tax collection ?
When we behold American officials, charged with the assessment
of personal property, so blind that they cannot see the contents of
large palaces full of the most valuable furniture and objects of art,
but consider them as not in existence, and as if the millionaire who
exhibits them daily to his guests possessed bare walls and the
simplest pine furniture, when we see the Mayor of Cleveland, Tom
L Johnson, prove to the railway pass-owning tax assessors that
their assessments of railway property are made at only one-tenth
of the actual value, can we expect such officials to obtain much

better eyesight under the single-tax? It is true, land values are more visible than the contents of a palace, though not more visible than the real estate of a railroad, but a much thicker gold varnish is at hand to render opaque the assessing official's spectacles. It is already thick enough in the case of our present land assessors

'It is an axiom of statesmanship, which the successful founders of dynasties have understood and acted upon—that great changes can best be brought about under old forms We, who would free men, should heed the same truth'

Perhaps, but not when some day the old form threatens to bring back the old contents Who guarantees us against a repetition of historical facts, such as those connected with the English land tax? Every land reformer is familiar with the manner in which England's landlords used their legislative power to reduce this tax, a remnant of their military dues in times of feudalism, to about one twenty-fifth of its original signification, by leaving the valuation on which it was imposed unchanged since the time of William III, whereas the value of the land increased twenty-five-fold since If this tax had been collected from the actual value of the land as it ought to have been, its proceeds would have redeemed England's public debt

Or take German experience, showing how even those nobles who were compensated for subjecting themselves to the land tax helped in the agitation, anyhow passively, to have this tax practically repealed by demanding that its proceeds should be used to relieve the rates, which were mostly on the shoulders of the landowners The German "Lex Huene" and the so-called "Landlord relief bill" of the recent English Tory government are twins, but the German case is even more iniquitous Only a generation had passed since the equivalent of the tax had been handed over to these noble landlords in interest-paying State bonds, yet who could have anticipated that so soon a time would arrive when these very men, while complacently continuing to cash the interest coupons of these bonds, would try to get rid of the tax they had undertaken to pay with the proceeds of these same coupons?

And a time would come also when a new Pharaoh knows not Joseph, when Henry George's arguments would be forgotten, and when the landholders would unite in a fight against his victorious single-tax, with the success which united and strong minorities often gain against divided and indifferent majorities Shall we, with open eyes, expose our children to this danger? No, the hydra, Land Monopoly, can never be effectually destroyed until we cut off and burn out all its heads, the land titles as well as the rental income Otherwise we shall see the experience of old Hercules repeated while one head is cut off, another is rapidly regrowing

Though the danger is not so great as under Single-taxism it is not totally absent even under land nationalization

This is proved by such an outrage as the "Rebate of Rent Bill," brought in at the end of the 1900 session of the New Zealand legislature Here we had a government deliberately attempting to make a present to State tenants of 10 per cent of their rents, which means courting the favor of these tenants by offering them the nation's property Where the whole of the land belongs to the nation, there will be naturally more State tenants than at present, and consequently the number of electors influenced by such gifts must be proportionally much greater Who guarantees us that the Seddon of another generation might not offer to relieve the tenants of half the rent they agreed to pay, or even the whole?

The case proves the old truism that economic and political reform must go together The most advanced political freedom has no guarantee of permanence where the economic and social position of the people is on a low level, of which Rome's history supplies the best illustration On the other side, it is equally true that not only are political arms required to fight the battle of economic reform, but that political reform affords the sole means of preserving the results of victory The land and its fruits can only be secured to the nation by preventing the servants of the nation from becoming its masters, by giving the citizen the power of effectually carrying out his will through the referendum Where the constitution cannot be changed without a vote of the majority of all who are entitled to vote, and where the new laws are made part of the constitution, attempts of the nature just described are effectually barred

If Henry George wanted to conserve old forms he ought just to have fought the freehold, which is a new form and a mere transitory stage between two kinds of tenancy, the ruling system the world over, though the forms of the tenancy contract gradually changed If we look at the mortgage as a kind of tenancy contract, and if we exclude those remaining freeholds which are worked by paid laborers a very insignificant fraction remains where the freehold is worked by the owners We have found that this holds good even in France, the reputed home of the peasant proprietor, and in new countries like this and Australasia

But even supposing the freehold to be the old form, would it be real statesmanship to bring about the great change by the method which George proposes? The very reverse is true, in fact, his system is the only one which has absolutely not the least chance of being carried through If confiscation should ever solve the land problem, if the people should ever reach the state of mind without which such a measure cannot possibly be carried—looking at might as right—they would not stop at mere taxation, they would take the land and all there is on it Not Single-taxism but Communism would be the result of such a mental state, and a much more logical result, too

If George wanted to follow "the law of social growth," "the natural method," which to "make a higher type takes a lower and develops it," he had no other way but to develop the prevailing lower type—private tenancy—and to develop it into the higher type of public tenancy, and this means land nationalization, not Single-taxism.

"With the current we may glide fast and far, against it, it is hard pulling and slow progress."

Of all the vain delusions under which Single-taxers suffer, the worst is the professed belief that most landowners will voluntarily consent to the imposition of the Single-tax. The landowners would not dream of such a thing, even if it could be proved to them that they would gain more through the relief from all other taxes than they would have to pay if taxed as high as 100 cents in the dollar on unimproved rental values. One of my best friends in New Zealand, a farmer owning about 500 acres which is by no means a large farm in that country, a convinced socialist, would not listen to Single-taxism, because he could not see why landowners alone should have to bear all taxes while the majority of the people were relieved altogether. That is human nature and we have to reckon with it. Besides, no juggling with figures could make him see how this relief from taxation of all non-landowners would not increase his own charges. Leaving out of consideration the fact that all small landholders in town and country entertain the hope of some day extending their holdings, and thus entering that class which, according to the Single-taxers, will have to bear the brunt of the battle, it is rather disgusting thus to play the "beggar your neighbour" game.

"Vote for this law! It will not hurt you, it will only weigh upon the richer men!" is certainly not a battle-cry apt to inspire a nation. This appeal to the lower instincts invariably and justly proves to be a bad policy. If, in this instance, it were effective, the Single-tax would give no final satisfaction, far beyond the intention of its apostles, the ultimate goal would be sought.

Another serious objection to the Single-tax campaign is that, by substituting a tax and practically a tariff problem for the great land reform, it shifts the entire battle-ground, to the great disadvantage of the reform. Many people who are enthusiastic for land restoration do not believe in free trade: the inevitable outcome of Single-taxism, which preaches the substitution of the land tax for all other taxes and duties. It has been the cause of creating antagonism to land law reform (or land reform, the usual name) from motives absolutely strange to the same. A man may honestly believe that protective duties benefit his country, and still he may be an ardent land reformer. The intermixture of tariff legislation and land reform has thus done a great deal of harm, especially in the United States and the British Empire. In these countries many enlightened men are thorough protectionists, who, in that respect, have to stand up against men with whom they are united in the fight for a much more important issue.

But all this is nothing compared with the most serious obstacle in the path of the Single-taxer the mortgage To tax away the rental value of the land destroys the best part of the mortgagee's security, and mortgagees are shrewd enough to be perfectly conscious of this fact They would be absolutely unmindful of their interests if they did not carefully watch the chances of success which Single-taxism might have Long before its principles could ever be embodied in a law, mortgages would be called in all over the country * It can easily be imagined that in these circumstances new mortgages could not be contracted, and nothing would remain to the unfortunate landowners but to submit to a public sale The prices which the land would fetch in such a market would not pay off the mortgage, and the mortgagee would not only enter into possession of the land with all its improvements, but probably also of his debtor's other property as well, while the poor mortgageor would be completely ruined. Do Single-taxers really believe that our farmers will join their ranks, with such prospects before them, no matter what the future effect of the measure may be? I, for my part, have never yet met with such self-sacrificing farmers, and I have known a good many Individualists, as they mostly are, you could much sooner obtain their adhesion to communism pure and simple, which, at least, would give them an equal share in the total wealth

Difficulties like these were too glaring to quite escape the notice of George's followers As is usually the case, where the straight path has been forsaken, concession has had to follow concession, each step taking them farther away from the original goal Land restoration They came to the conclusion that it would not do to cut the dog's tail all at once, but that a gradual increase of the tax until the hundred cents in the rental dollar or five cents of the capital value dollar have been reached would be the only method likely to be carried They—the radical anti-compensationists—do not see that this system would leave much more of the unearned increment in the hands of the present landowners than a rational system of land nationalization It is easy to prove this

More than a quarter of a century has passed since "Progress and Poverty" was first published in this country a quarter of a century which has seen a very lively agitation for the Single-tax. Yet there are few States in the Union where we have progressed so far that the land is assessed and taxed independently of improvements, the first step towards the Single-tax Practically not even this slight advance in the direction of the Single-tax, after which the tail-cutting business, the real campaign, is to begin, has been reached so far Now let us suppose that the next ten years may witness the first instalment of a tax on land values, independent of improve-

---

* Taxing also the mortgages would only precipitate the process of having the mortgagees look out for other investments or of raising the interest rate paid by the mortgagor, high enough to compensate the mortgagee for the tax, as is now done wherever this most foolish of all taxes exists

ments, beyond present taxes, to the amount of as much as one-tenth of the rental income, and that we shall find such self-sacrificing land owners or such a radical landless majority that the tax is raised every ten years one-tenth more, a supposition so absolutely optimistic that no sane statesman would build upon it In this highly improbable case it would take a century before the community could enter into the enjoyment of the full rental This practically unattainable result would be equivalent to the enjoyment of the full rental by the present land owners for another 50 years. Now, if we are able to show that under a system of full compensation the land could be fully paid for without imposing any new tax, within not more than 25 years, can we not claim that the arch-enemies of compensation give practically a much higher compensation than those who advocate honest purchase of the land? This proves what Mr Joseph Hyder, the able general secretary of the English Land Nationalization Society, said in "Land and Labor" of February 8. 1899. "The real controversy is not between compromise and no compromise, but between two or more different compromises; not between compensation and no compensation, but between two or more different methods of compensation For to say that landlords shall keep all the rent, less whatever tax can be levied upon it, is in reality to offer compensation in the hope that it may afterwards be cut down by taxation."

We should be much farther advanced if it were not for the stubborn extremism of Single-taxers, who insist on their special "ism," oppose all other methods proposed, and thus prove themselves the worst enemies of land restoration The final answer I usually get from their leaders, when I have driven them into a corner, where they can no more gainsay my arguments, is "Let this proposal (of compensation) come from the landowners, not from us!" As if landowners all over the world were not perfectly satisfied with their monopoly! As if they could be expected to initiate land reform of any kind! Many of them will oppose both land nationalization and the Single-tax, but whereas we perhaps can get them to meet us halfway on a plan of compensation, they would fight tooth and nail any attempt at confiscation America had a civil war of four years' duration on less incitement. The proverb says. "Build a golden bridge for your enemy," and it is for us to propose fair means and ways to attain our end, we must not wait for the other side to take the initiative If they do take it, it will be on the lines of British landlords when they passed the Ashbourne and other recent Irish land acts which strengthened landlordism by widening its base, just as the New Zealand "Land for Settlement Acts" have done in the past

However, even the Ashbourne Acts—although they merely created

---

* The existing land taxes left out of consideration in this calculation are amply balanced by that part of the tax which is shifted, of which more, later on

new landowners—have rendered our cause a great service by showing how easily compensation can be carried through without costing the people a single penny The land was paid for by means of the difference between the cheaper interest rate at which the State could obtain the purchase money, and the higher rate at which the rent was capitalized in the land price In this way, though a reduction of rents to the amount of 25% was allowed, the land is paid for within 46 years But instead of belonging to the State at that period, through whose good credit the operation had become possible, it was made in favor of certain privileged individuals, besides the former landlords The tenants, who accidentally were in possession at the time of the law, became landlords without paying a single penny, by simply continuing to pay their old rent, reduced by one-quarter for the next 46 years, unless they preferred to purchase right out at the official valuation The *Times* of January 28, 1890, gives the inevitable results One tenant bought the farm he cultivated at £550, and soon sold it, subject to the repayment of this sum, for £970 Another farm bought for £538 was sold, subject to the purchase money, for £1,280 One which had fetched £755 was sold by the fortunate tenant who obtained possession of it through the new law, subject to the purchase money, for £1 725 £3,975 profit were made in these three cases, more than three-fold the purchase money was obtained Those who bought on such onerous terms pay, in the shape of interest, a more burdensome rent than their forerunners, when their state of distress resulted in the legislation which, from the oppressed, made them the oppressors It matters little whether the title under which the power of oppression is exercised is that of the landlord or that of the mortgagee, whether the tribute is called rent or interest, whether the oppressor is the nobleman, whose ancestors had conquered the land, or the former tenant, who has been fortunate enough to enter into possession when the new law passed, and who retires from active work supported in a town by the new tenant's or mortgaged owner's labor.

The difference between the rate of interest at which the price which is to be paid for the land is capitalized from the rent, and the rate which the State would have to pay for the purchase money, would be at least as great in this country as in Ireland. The one rate will not be less than 5%, the other not over 3%, and instead of a reduction of 25% on present rates, a progressive country like this, with a rapidly growing population, could count on a rapid rise.*

* This has been contested. It has been said that under free conditions rent will fall because speculative withholding and rackrent are absent: wages of labor thus obtaining the increment caused by progress I think this leaves out of sight the fact that nature produces wealth without human labor though certain theorists deny it, saying that without the presence of man there is no market and consequently no wealth in the economic sense Neither should we have professors of political economy without the existence of man, a redeeming feature of the calamity

On the Matapom river in Virginia, where seagoing ships can load timber by merely throwing a plank to the shore from the ship, I have seen

While the rental income of the State would thus increase from year to year, the interest rate, paid for the bonds issued for the purchase of the land, would decrease through the laws of supply and demand.* The demand for safe investments is growing

land, in the sixties, where they counted that from one-half to one cord of wood grows yearly on each acre without any labor, and a cord brought $2 in the standing tree   Of course this wealth production by nature would not have existed without the presence of people who wanted wood and of others ready to cut and ship it, but this does not in the least alter the fact that nature produced wood on this land worth a certain price before any worker touched it, that nature added something to the productivity of labor which this labor could not produce to earn anywhere else.

Is the value of the herd of cattle, living and procreating on the open prairie, entirely created by the labor of the cowboy who branded them?

I pick out these special cases as examples, because here the part done by nature, without the assistance of labor, is so clear and unmistakable that no amount of sophistry can eliminate it, but the same fact exists more or less wherever labor uses land inside of the margin of cultivation; i e, inside the line beyond which more land is found free than there are workers ready to use it   Such a margin exists in few civilized countries   Even in the wilds of the Scotch Highlands not a foot of land can be had free, nor could it be had free even under land nationalization, for rich men would always be ready to pay a certain rent for such land for its use as a deer park

These deer parks indicate another land use forgotten by our theorizers— the use for health, comfort and pleasure, the value of which grows with the wealth of the people   The inhabitant of our slums, where a thousand and more people are crowded on a single acre, is just as fond of a cottage surrounded by a garden as his betters   Where now a thousand people live on one acre, these will, in better times want a hundred acres and more—though the single acre may fall in price, the total of the city's surface will yield a much higher rent, because large areas of agricultural land will be covered with houses and gardens   And where further out the rent now only corresponds to the yield of wheat or corn, it then conforms to the higher income of the market gardener, whose produce is eagerly bought by a teeming wealthy population, and to the craving for their own pleasure-parks by the well-to-do, far more numerous than in our times of artificially restrained productive power

Thus it can safely be asserted that with the increase of population and productive power the value of land and consequently of rent will increase all around, with which position Henry George is in full agreement

* The bonds could either be given in payment to the landowners, or they could be sold in the market, in which most of the former landowners to whom the money is paid would be looking out for these new solid investments and thus return the money to the State   Under our wonderful system, which permits bankers to buy interest bearing United States government bonds with money obtained almost free of interest on the deposit of these bonds, the nationalization of our land, our railroads, telegraph, etc, on this plan, instead of creating a money stringency, would cause the bond sales to make money more abundant

all the time through the savings of untold thousands of persons who, taught by experience, shun investments in business and prefer land values and government bonds. The supply of the latter does not grow fast enough to keep pace with the unconsumed portion of the incomes that look for new investments, a portion rapidly growing, through the effects of compound interest. However, on the other hand, land values now offer an elastic field for investment, ever widening with the demand—not through any extension of the never-widening area, but through an increase of price in consequence of demand. As rent cannot increase equally fast, being limited by the paying capacity of the tenants and the yield of the land, such values cannot rise proportionately to the demand unless the rate of interest at which rent is capitalized is forced down.

A few figures will illustrate this. Suppose that the demand for L (land) and P (the price paid for it) has quadrupled, while R (rent) has only doubled, I (interest rate) would be reduced to one-half; for P is the product of R multiplied by 100 divided by I. Therefore, whenever P rises to 4P, while R rises only to 2R, I must fall to one-half, or the total of 4P could not have been reached. If P rises from $100 to $400, though R only increased from $5 to $10, this implies a fall of I from 5% to 2½%, for at 5% an R of $10 corresponds only to a P of $200, while at 2½% an R of $10 capitalizes to a P of $400. Or, as it is often expressed in England, the price of the land has increased to 40 years' purchase from 20.*

Just as slave values disappeared on the day of Lincoln's proclamation, so land values cease to exist when land nationalization is accomplished. It must not be forgotten that I use the word value only in its economic sense of market price. The real value of the negro, as well as of the land, their use-value, not only remains after their liberation from private ownership, but rises; for free men are finally worth more to the community than slaves, and free land will be made to produce more wealth than that which is monopolized by individuals.

For the former land values, which—in the capital market—elastically extend with the demand for them, government bonds are now substituted, deprived even of the limited power of price extension they now possess in consequence of their temporarily excluded

---

* Of course this is only a rough outline, not quite corresponding to the actual facts, which are influenced by various data. For instance we may find a local rise in the price of land based on the expectation of a future rent increase reducing the rate of interest, on which the capitalization is based, below the regular rate. The demand of land-hungry peasant proprietors, or neighboring owners of large properties, desirous of enlarging their possessions, may work in the same direction. The difficulty of selling land or of collecting rents rapidly may, on the other hand, raise the rate of interest at which the rent is capitalized above the interest rate of bonds, which will take place the more certainly the more the rate of the latter falls below a certain limit. For instance, it is not likely that at a bond interest rate of ½% rent will multiply with 200 (200 years' purchase) to obtain the land price. Perhaps only a hundred years' purchase would be obtainable.

convertibility, which makes the fall of the general interest rate rai e
correspondingly the bonds' price, their exchange rate. A fall of
interest from 5% to 2½% would result in a rise of 5% bonds, inconvertible for a long period, from 100, the supposed price of issue
to 200, or, to be exact, to some price between 100 and 200, according
to the date at which the bonds can be reimbursed at par The loss
of capital must be just made up by the gain in interest This is the
reason why certain bonds are quoted at a premium on the stock
exchange.* As a matter of course, in our case, the State would not
forego the right of reimbursement or conversion for a period, as it
did in the case of certain bonds in the interest of financiers under
Cleveland It would reserve the right to convert the bonds to a
lower interest rate or to pay back their amount at any moment.
This right of conversion or reimbursement at any time would keep
the price of the bonds at or below the par level, consequently the
interest rate, which the State would have to pay for her bonds, would
permanently fall †

Each reduction of the interest rate and consequently of the
interest dues on the bonds, besides the interest saved on the reimbursed bonds—compound interest, for once, working on the side of
the people—would increase the profit margin made by the State between the rising rental income and the decreasing interest disburse-
ments The amortization of the public debt would thus proceed by
leaps and bounds, and this would further restrict the field of interest-
bearing safest investments for private capital The effect would be
the increase of the demand for the said investments and of the pressure on the interest rate How beneficially this would affect production and trade is left for discussion in the chapter on Interest; here
we refer to it only because of its rent raising consequences to add

---

* 4% U S bonds 130 in May. 1906

† The falling of the interest rate which I expect from land nationalization independent of currency reform, is not without historic precedents of
similar conditions I quote from Adam Smith's "Wealth of Nations," Book
I, Chapter IX 'The province of Holland on the other hand in proportion
to the extent of its territory and the number of its people, is a richer country than England The Government there borrow at 2%, and private people
of good credit at 3 The wages of labor are said to be higher in Holland
than in England, and the Dutch, it is well known, trade on lower profits
than any people in Europe "

See also in Kahn's "Geschichte des Zinsfusses in Deutschland," where
we learn that the interest rate of mortgages in Hamburg was 2⅛% previous
to 1842

At the time of which Smith speaks comparatively few bonds of any
government existed—only 2500 million dollars according to Fenn—and land
was mostly tied up so that little opportunity of this sort was open for the
investment market In Hamburg, at the period mentioned the savings of
its rich citizens seeking good investments near home, were very large, while
the demand for money on mortgage was comparatively small

Incidentally we might note that the low interest at which money could
be obtained by business men in Holland had an effect on wages not at all
in accordance with Henry George's strange theory that interest and wages
rise and fall together

another element to strengthen my assumption that the period required for the amortization of the debt, incurred through the purchase of the national land, would not exceed 25 years, and that not a single tax would have to be imposed for the purpose. The income made out of the margin between the rent paid by the land users and the interest of the bond issued for the purchase of the land from its present owners, would suffice for the purpose If such a plan had been carried out when "Progress and Poverty" first appeared, all the land could belong to the people by this time, free of debt, though full compensation was given. I need not say that the rent paid by the land users to the State is not a tax, but merely the equivalent for the special benefit obtained through the use of land.

Of course, the term of the debt's final amortization might be extended indefinitely, if found convenient The probability is that it ' would be extended, because the State might have good use for part of the rental income for the benefit of the new landlords, the citizens, of which I shall have something to say further on There need not be any hurry, for the interest rate would fall through the mere excesss of the savers' demand over the supply of safest investments, an excess caused by the substitution of the unelastic, or eventually narrowing field of investment in government bonds to the elastically widening land value field The rate thus would fall, even if not a single bond were reimbursed

This part of my work is necessarily limited to a demonstration of the practicability of land purchase by the State without imposing any new taxes upon the people No need to treat questions of detail such as the expediency of purchase and administration by the States, the counties, or the municipalities of the individual States of the Union or of purchasing gradually, or at once. Many who would have been afraid of a financial operation on such an immense scale ten years ago have of late become so habituated to business running into the billions, that a few zeros more or less have lost much of their former bogey power However there are methods of a gradual nationalization which may prove less objectionable to many For instance, the right of preemption given to the State at present values for all times, whenever a sale takes place, would cut off the future unearned increment from investors by enabling the community to purchase whenever there is a profit in the operation A number of Prussia's cities begin already to go part of this way in taxing away a portion of the profits made on land sales It is an idea proposed as far back as 1870 by Professor Adolf Wagner and since then taken up by the league of German land reformers Anyhow whatever method may be found preferable let us aim at full public ownership by all means! Let us never be satisfied with a tax no matter how high, even if it were only that a tax keeps up private ownership and does not touch the right of the landowner to use and abuse his power as he sees fit

Provided he pays his tax, nobody would under the Single-tax prevent another Duke of Sutherland from clearing thousands of

hard-working people from his land, from their fatherland, from making another of those bloody entries in Clio's book by which his
family scutcheon has forever been tarnished   All that would be
asked of him is to pay a tax equivalent to the highest rent which the
poor, despairing crofters—driven unmercifully from the homes and
the soil which they and their forefathers had tilled in the sweat of
their brows—might have been willing to pay. What of that? His
income from other sources, from bonds and stocks of all kinds, from
houses and factories, allow him this sport   He wants a deer-park,
and he can afford to pay for it as well as the American Winans who
bought Scotch land from sea to sea for this purpose

Nor could the Single tax have prevented facts like those reported in the following newspaper extracts

A Millionaire's Freak —Mull, an island on the coast of Scotland, is the property of Earl Beauchamp   It has an area of 237,000
acres, and a population of 4,691 living in 1,030 houses   Among its
products are oats, barley, flour and potatoes, and the inhabitants
have also had a fair export trade in sheep and cattle   A millionaire
has recently secured the sole ownership of the island, and wishes to
turn it into a deer-park for the amusement of himself and friends
He has, therefore, given the whole population notice to quit, and has
decreed the pulling down of all the houses —*Barrier Truth*

Deer-Forests in the Highlands —The acreage of deer-forests in
Scotland is increasing   Fifteen years ago they extended in the
Highland counties to 1,711,892 acres, last year (1898) they were
2,287,297 acres   These figures are exclusive of certain forests, such
as Glencannich and North Affaric, with regard to which no return
has been obtained   I observe, says a London correspondent, from
the Parliamentary Report, that in several cases the sheep-farms of
1883 have become the deer-forests of 1898 —*The Highlander*

Suppose that under the Single Tax the Rothschilds and a few
hundred other millionaires in England and America should share
this whim of turning Great Britain into a deer-park, and British landlords should sell at reasonable figures because of the new tax, which
destroys the selling value of their land   Under existing laws, what
could prevent these men from having their will?   Certainly not the
land-value tax, even if it were as high as it would be were the present
values taken as a basis of calculation i.e., 200 million pounds a year
The income of Rockefeller and Carnegie alone is at present valued
at 12 to 15 million pounds each   that of the Rothschild families is
higher and without going any farther we have already obtained
one-quarter of the yearly tax required   But how long would it be required?   How long would there be a rental value of 200 million
pounds in a depopulated England, in that magnificent new deer-
park?   That value would follow British enterprise wherever the
evicted people went   The United States, Australia, New Zealand
Canada, South Africa, would see their land values rise as the British
land values fell, and finally, the 200 million might be reduced to

something like 5 shillings an acre, to 20 million pounds, or less even, a mere trifle for such magnates * That such an event is practically impossible is begging the question, because it is only saying in other words that the Single-tax is impossible.

In fact I can see no reason why this system should at all do away with some of the worst abuses of landlordism, abuses of daily occurrence. Even in Germany, where property is much more equally divided than in England, there are instances of large landowners who buy up all the surrounding land until whole villages disappear, sometimes to let the land become overgrown with forest. The same takes place in Austria Henry George's plan would not in the least increase the financial sacrifice of such purchasers. They would have to buy and sacrifice only the improvements, as they do anyhow; the unimproved value of the land would disappear in consequence of the tax, and this tax would not be higher than the present interest on their purchase money.

Nor could a mere land-value tax do away with cases like the following which are quite of common occurrence in England and Scotland Here are a thousand acres, used as grazing land for sheep, and yielding the landlord a net rental of £1,000 in sheep and wool, after labor to the amount of, say, as much as £200 has been paid If the land were let out in allotments, it would yield a rental of £2 an acre, and it would keep at least 100 families against 2 in the other case The gross product would be at least four times, the net income of the landlord twice as large: but the landlord prefers the lesser income, because the division into small holdings would interfere with his sport In the Paris Congress of land-reformers, my departed friend William Saunders, in narrating his Wiltshire experiences, told of a landlord who preferred to accept 15 shillings an acre from a farmer rather than £3 paid for allotments—a rent at which the laborers his tenants, yet made a living, while the farmer, who paid only a fourth, failed

Sport may not have been the only cause for this anomaly The landlord was perhaps afraid that allotments would render the laborers too independent, so that neighboring farmers would have to pay higher wages, and thus be unable to afford as much rent

What difference would a tax make in such cases? The landlord would simply pay the tax, even though it should reach the height of the rent offered by the crofters, and would still retain the farmer (and his sheep) who takes part in the hunt, instead of interfering The State could not prevent this comparatively unproductive use of the land—unproductive in a double sense in wealth and in men Under the Single-tax all it has a right to claim is its tax.

* Since I wrote this, I have learned that Dr William Clarke published an article in the *Contemporary Review* of December, 1900, in which he predicts that England will gradually be turned into the pleasure domain of the world's aristocracy and plutocracy The population which did not emigrate would serve as their flunkeys and shopkeepers,

Nor would a mere land tax prevent those abuses of the land-lord's power so often experienced in England, attacks on the liberty of conscience, the prohibition of building dissenters' places of worship, or attempts against the tenants' political independence, coercion of voters through the Damocles sword of notice to quit always gleaming over their heads

Nor would it render possible the construction or reconstruction of towns on improved plans which might be adopted by a land-owning community, for under the Single-tax the community's power does not exceed its taxing privilege Once the tax is paid it has nothing farther to say beyond the issue of comparatively trivial building regulations

Henry George was principally misled in his assumption that the self-interest of the individual must bring about the best use of the land. The tax would, according to him, be at a level with the highest rent which the average land user would be ready to bid for the land, and no man could pay this rent without putting the land to the best use The question still remains whether what may appear the best use to the owner or his tenant is always the best use in the interest of the community

We have already seen that the interest of the community is very often opposed to that of the individual, real or supposed The individual has the passion of hunting and shooting, and his interest, as he understands it, drives him to deplete a large area of land of its inhabitants so that his game may not be disturbed Or he may destroy thousands of homes because sheep-runs are more productive —not of human happiness—but of rent On the other side, the community prefer sheep to deer, and citizens to sheep The State, if it realizes its own welfare, cannot allow a condition wherein—as was said in England centuries ago—sheep will swallow men, and it certainly cannot allow deer to develop a still greater appetite for human flesh than that possessed by sheep. The State's principal object must be to see the greatest number of happy persons grow up under her protection, and only her citizens will protect her against outside attack. Neither sheep nor deer will take up arms in her defence in the hour of need *

Therefore she cannot afford to allow the letting of the national

---

* In Peru and in Egypt part of the soil was distributed to the soldiers Diodorus says "This was done to give a solid basis to their patriotism It is absurd to confide the public safety to those who have nothing in the country worth the trouble of fighting for ' (Ch Letourneau 'Property Its Origin and Development " p 145)

The famous passage from Pliny's writings where he describes the fate of Rome's soldiers who did not own a square foot of land as worse than that of the wild beasts which have their lair applies to Great Britain's soldiers who fight for a country in whose soil most of them have no part whatever, while their foes in Africa were endowed with the strength of Antæus through being in continual touch with their own soil And how much land is owned by our own regulars?

land become a mere financial manipulation, à question of the largest rental income in each special case

"Cash payment is not the sole nexus of man with man, how far from it,' says Carlyle. The landowning State would soon find that out, and would lease the land on principles not quite following the mere "supply and demand" theory Cases might arise where a high-born or low-born capitalist offered a million pounds a year for a certain county of Scotland, whereas fifty thousand poor crofters could afford only £10 each, and yet the crofters would be allowed to continue raising oats and hearty men and women on the land, whereas the capitalist would have to look elsewhere for partridge coverts For, fortunately, no agent of Lord Gobbleland or of John Brown—retired partner of Smith, Brown & Baker—would have the letting, as they would even under the Single-tax, but poor Hodges, who wants a little croft on which to grow potatoes for his children, and Jones, the artisan, and Mill, the factory hand, who want a home market for their goods, not barred off by protective Chinese walls, and who know that fifty thousand crofters use more shirts, coats, boots, and hats, and other manufactures or produce, than a dozen Gobblelands. these are the men whose agents will have the letting of that land Even if these agents will collect £500,000 less a year, and even if the tax-paying power of the 50,000 tenants and their purveyors should not make up the deficit in the common purse, they will not mind so very much, as long as their—the people's—eating, their shirt and coat-wearing power continues to grow, which, strange to say, has more weight with these deluded beings than all the calculations of learned professors, who want to convince them that they are acting against all the tenets of a sound economic doctrine, according to which the land ought to go to the highest bidder That is not the State's business to procure employment to such men as they That such unscientific proceedings would merely result in a further over-population. That if there is no demand in the market for their work or produce, they must get out of the country as fast as they can, or put on khaki to shoot Chinese and other people who presume that they can do as they like in their own country, instead of recognizing that their paramount God-taught duty is to buy the over-produced goods of Old England The idea of wasting £500,000 rental income of the State to provide a market for 5 million pounds' worth of home produce, and thus sustaining not only the 50,000 crofters and their families, but also many thousands more. who exchange manufactures for their food and raw materials! To provide, instead of this only a living for Gobbleland's 50 game-keepers may be a poor policy, but by letting the nation's land according to the gospel of Supply and Demand we have at least the consolation of working within the lines of orthodox political economy It is true, Supply and Demand will not defend England should the foreigner succeed in invading the country Nor would it feed the nation if some day foreign fleets cut off the corn fleets of distant regions, or where those corn-growing regions have joined the ranks of England's enemies Lord Gobbleland's partridges certainly would not go very far towards supplying the necessary food, the oats grown by the 50,000 crofters might do more good Their arms, and those of the artisans and mill-hands they provide with a living, will form a better army than the 50 gamekeepers—officered by Gobbleland, if he is not in India tiger-shooting or taking his ease in Paris But what does all that signify when Gobbleland's £500,000 additional land tax is taken into consideration?

Otherwise the system of administration of the public land need not give us much concern. We have enough precedents to prove that the officials of public bodies are as capable of undertaking this work as the agents of our landlords The Prussian administration of the royal domains may be considered the model of a perfect management, and the Birmingham administration of the land belonging to the city is accounted as, at least, equal to any management of private landlords Neither will the question how the management and revenue is to be divided between the central and local governments offer insuperable difficulties

The length of leases or, rather, the periods of revaluations of rents, present a more disputable field In any case, I do not think that these periods ought to extend as far as many leases of city property given by English landlords, i.e., 99 years The only advantage which the private landowner may find in such long terms does not exist for public bodies The former has the tendency to prefer benefits obtainable during his own life to the superior opportunities of his successors A tenant who obtains a 99 years' lease will certainly pay a somewhat higher rent than he would for a shorter lease The additional amount thus realized by the lessee may be a mere trifle when compared with the loss in the next generations, with their largely increased rental values; but the proverbial bird in the hand will not fail to claim its superiority over the bush species. Public bodies, however, are longer lived than individuals, and though, unfortunately often addicted to a very short-sighted policy, are not quite so inclined to sacrifice the future for the present The long-lived lessor will find it good business to take advantage of the short-lived lessee's natural inclination to value the shilling which he himself enjoys higher than the pound which he might save for his unborn descendant, and to prefer shorter leases at lower rents to longer leases at, presently higher—but in future relatively much lower rents The privilege reserved by English landlords of confiscating improvements after the longer lease has run out does not add much to the inducement of the long lease, and prevents improvement on the property towards the expiration of the lease

With regard to urban lands I should prefer the system adopted by the City of Wellington New Zealand, in its leases of the reclaimed land (land formerly covered by the bay and now nearly the most valuable business location) The land is leased for a term of 21 years at a stipulated rent. The tenant has to pay rates, taxes and assessment At least six months before the expiration of the lease the tenant can demand a valuation of the rent for another term of 14 years, and so forth Three valuers are appointed, one by the tenant, one by the corporation, and the third by the two valuers thus appointed. In ascertaining such new rental, the valuers shall not take into consideration the value of any buildings or improvements then existing upon the premises, but they shall value "the full and improved ground-rental of the premises" that ought to be payable during the new term The corporation prescribes the kind of building which the tenant has to erect on the land The tenant has a right to have his lease renewed by the corporation at the new valuation If he does not demand a valuation, it means that he has no wish to renew the lease; and the corporation enters into possession of the land and improvements without paying for the latter The tenant's only chance to get compensation for them is to find a party who takes the lease off his hands and pays him for the improvements

Of course, it may happen that these improvements, though they have been very costly, are worthless under the circumstances. Let us suppose, for instance, that when the tenant took the lease, the quarter of the city that he erected buildings in was looked upon as a fine location for residences, but, through the growth of the town, had become a business locality—as has occurred in certain portions of most American cities—and in consequence of this change, the ground-rent for the land has been considerably raised In this case he could only recoup by increasing the rent of the residence built on the land, which is impossible, because the locality is much less desirable for such a purpose than it was before, whereas its inner arrangements render the house absolutely unfit for business purposes As the higher rent can thus be recouped only by pulling down the house and building business premises on the ground, no tenant could be found who would pay more for the house than what can be obtained from parties contracting for its removal Or business premises might have been erected which were perfectly suitable 21 years before, and paid well at the lower rent, whereas now, when the rent is raised, only a building of much larger dimensions could be made to pay If the land were freehold, the owner would not hesitate to pull down the old building and erect a new one, provided the increased rent not only pays the interest of the new building, but, if capitalized, also soon refunds the cost of the old one, or in other words, provided the unearned increment obtained from his land amply compensates him. But under the changed conditions this increment goes to the community, and tenants, in tendering, have to take into account any possible loss on their improvements They will not rent unless they feel sure that the rent they pay will allow them to lose on the improvements when the lease runs out

The condition that the tenant has to pay rates, taxes, and assessments of any kind under the Wellington system renders a special betterment clause unnecessary, which, otherwise ought to be inserted in every lease of public land and, meanwhile, ought to form part of our land tax laws

Any increase in the rental value directly traceable to public improvements made in the neighborhood of any property ought certainly accrue to those who pay for such improvements. Even under the Wellington Corporation leases, where the city benefits by such improvements after 21 years, there is no reason why the lessee should obtain the full benefit of any betterment through public improvements made while his lease runs.

A new municipal tram line passes the land he holds, a public railway station is erected, a park is opened in its immediate neighborhood, or the street is widened. All this is done at the expense of the public It would certainly not be fair to make a present to the lessee (under present conditions to the landowner) of the increase in rental value thus created, which was not expected at the time the lease (purchase) was made, to let him reap where others sowed. The betterment clause would force him to contribute to the improvement in proportion to the profit he derives from it, giving him the benefit of the doubt as to the exactness of the assessment

A very valuable lesson in land administration has been supplied by the little State of Hamburg, in Germany. When the new free port was constructed in 1884, a contract was made between the Senate of Hamburg and the Norddeutsche Bank, by which 30,000 square metres of the 40,000 square metres (11 acres) belonging to the State in that section were—not sold or given away, as our short-sighted government sold or gave away land traversed by our railroads—but leased to the bank, on terms which left in the possession of the community the increase of value certain to follow the improvement created. It was done without any oppressive condition against the bank, and the company founded by it—both which did a profitable business The State became, so to say, a partner of the company, putting in its land against the company's capital The buildings were valued at 300 marks per square meter, while the State put in its land at 500 marks, and shared in the profits at the rate of 5 to 3; every surplus beyond 3½% being counted as profit In this way the State has received a yearly rental of 525,000 marks since 1889 for its 8 acres But that is not all, for, beyond its share, the State obtains another 10% of the net profits made by the company, after the 3½% and a moderate reserve are deducted, and this 10%, with the accumulating interest, is employed to purchase for the State shares of the company A yearly lottery determines the numbers which have to be given up for this purpose at par In the year 1900, the State had thus obtained shares to the amount of

223,000 marks Finally, since 1899, the State has the right of purchasing the remaining shares at a price not under 110% and not above 150% It is calculated that without paying out a single penny the State will own the whole property within 50 years. The *Deutsche Volksstimme*, from whose 2nd August number of 1900 I extract the above information, says that this system, which thus rescued the land from private speculation and made it subserve the public interest, has in no way hurt the development of the Hamburg free port, nor have buildings of inferior value been constructed on the leased ground. On the contrary, the buildings, constructed on plans approved by the State, are of a superior quality, and the company has not found the least difficulty in obtaining mortgages. Eight million marks have been borrowed in this way on a building value of about double the amount The dividend has been 5% of the capital invested, which in Germany is considered quite satisfactory.

Enough has been said to prove that practical business men can devise as good systems of land-use for the community as the landlords have been able to find in the past; better ones, in fact, because the landlords only consider their personal advantage, which, as we have seen, is not identical with that of the community. The community will let the land on a different plan, certain to bring not only greater financial results, but also more beneficial to the citizens as a whole.

I have now shown that as a method of land restoration, land nationalization is preferable for various reasons to the Single-tax First, because it does not sacrifice principle to expediency It stands for a straight and full restoration of the land to the people, while the Single-tax leaves it in the possession of the present landowners, which can never yield the full benefits expected from land restoration, as it preserves many of the old abuses and does not even prevent the return of those which it reformed.

I have also shown that the inferiority of the Single-tax system to land nationalization is due not only to principle, but expediency While land nationalization can be carried by methods commending themselves to the justice and fair-play of the average citizen, the Single-tax appeals to the instinct of spoliation and thus can never hope to convert a majority of the nation I have further shown that the dishonest method is practically also the costliest and slowest

The result of the false policy adopted by Henry George and his followers has been that, during a quarter of a century's agitation practically no progress has been made towards land-restoration on Single-tax lines in this country. I believe that the great man has almost as much retarded land restoration, by the advocacy of a false method, as he has furthered it by his general work The very word "taxation" stinks in the nostrils of the overtaxed American, while the idea of nationalization becomes more popular from day to day The service done by our railroads, express and telegraph companies has been found bad and expensive; their political influence pernicious and, in spite of the efforts made by the interested parties, who even founded a special bureau for the purpose of spreading lies through the press as to the failure of nationalization and communalization wherever tried, the conviction gains ground that no matter how objectionable nationalization might be, it could certainly not produce worse results than the present system The real facts can not well be quite suppressed. Foremost among them that Prussia now clears 135 million dollars a year from her nationalized railroads, by which her debt could soon be paid off without levying any special tax, in spite of better service, lower passenger rates and one-tenth of accidents per passenger mile. State railroads are found in over fifty other countries, and I think this country stands alone as one in which not only the railroads, but even the telegraph and parcel service are private monopolies Finally the question is bound to force itself on the public why what is so successfully done elsewhere cannot as well be carried out here.

Consul-General Richard Guenther, writing from Frankfort (Consular Report, Friday, May 10, 1907), says that the Prussian State railroads, after payment of the interest of the debt, showed in 1906 an excess of earnings over expenditures of $135,650,000 (565,-200,000 marks). From 1882 to 1904 the excess in earnings has amounted to $1,205,000,000 These sums represent from 6 to 7 per cent of the capital originally invested in the roads; and from 14 to 16 per cent of the capital debt as yet not repaid out of the earnings.

If the followers of Henry George had done their duty, if his unfortunate errors had not switched them into the Single-tax siding, the popularity of land nationalization might be further advanced than railroad nationalization. It is high time that an American land reform league should take the lead in this great fight, instead of leaving the honor to socialists. The latters' error of pressing for the nationalization of much else that had perhaps better be left in private hands, at least for a time, will be less and less in the way of their victory if they remain the only champions of free land, if the pretenders of the championship continue to fight for a lie that calls highly taxed land, free land Those are the most dangerous reactionaries who keep progress back by pretending to fight its battle

There is still time to make the change, which, after all, is only one of methods, not of principle.

History has often supplied the proof that great men's followers are far less accessible to compromise than their leaders Henry George supplied me with a proof of this in 1889 at Paris, where, supported by him and William Saunders, of London, I had called a Congress of the different schools of land reformers When the tenor of a joint resolution was debated, he tried to have it run on Single-tax lines but, finding no support outside of his direct followers, he finally joined us in the acceptance of the resolution, which then was unanimously passed by the Congress The final line of this resolution reads "This meeting declares that individual property in the soil must disappear and become replaced by appropriation for the benefit of all " As a contrast to this conciliating attitude of the master, let me exhibit that of one of his disciples, Mr J. Dana Miller, who in June, 1907, refused for his "Single Tax Review" a free contribution, in which I put up for discussion the question of a change of methods, for which I think the time has come.

The nationalization of public utilities, of railroads, telegraphs, telephones and parcel-service, would further land nationalization as much as the latter would support the agitation for the nationalization of public utilities. The close relation between them will presently be illustrated. I do not wish to see my opposition to the Single-tax misconstrued. I am fully aware that there is much to be said in favor of a tax on land values. I attack the plan only because it comes before us with the pretension of supplying the best method of land restoration For such a purpose it is not only the worst proposal that could have been made at all events in this country, but it marches under false colors by overstepping the dividing line between taxing and confiscation, or robbery. An uncertain dividing line, anyhow, for any robbery may be called a tax; any tax may be raised to the point of confiscation

The very history of taxation proves this. Taxation originated in robbery, and robbery finally became reduced to taxation, either through the resistance of the robbed, or because it did not pay to kill the goose that laid the golden eggs. The robber knights at first robbed the passing merchant of all his goods and often of his life The armed people of the cities or the Imperial forces destroyed a number of their castles The fact now impressed itself upon the remaining robbers that dead merchants do not bring merchandise and that the danger of loss stopped commerce, so that to take all, finally meant to get nothing Thenceforth only a certain portion of the goods were stolen. In the course of time the stealing business became a vested right, and, when the State took over the knight's vested rights, the knight's toll became the State's tax, the progenitor of customs duties

The origin of income and inheritance taxes is not a whit more reputable The robbery of the whole income and heritage finally stopped the creation of incomes and heritages and had to be limited, after which it took the name of income and inheritance taxation

Thus a certain amount of confiscation, of robbery, adheres to any system of taxation, and to find out the exact dividing line between robbery pure and simple, and the exaction of a fair contribution towards common needs, constitutes a special department of political economy, called the Science of Taxation.

Therefore, one may look at Single-taxism without compensation as a robbery of present bona fide landowners, and still advocate a reasonable land tax, or rather a land value tax, by which is meant a tax on the value of land apart from improvements Such a tax unites the two criterions of a just tax benefit received with ability to pay Even in conservative Germany a heavy municipal tax begins to be levied upon building lot profits, as it is recognized that generally such profits are created entirely by the community and not by the work of the landowner Strong evidences of this well known fact have been lately brought into special notice by the large increase of values due to elevated and subway railroad constructions in some of the great centres New York, London, and Berlin, especially In some cases the price of suburban property has increased more than four fold in the course of a few months. In London, for instance, there is a suburban building zone from five to ten miles from the centre, where blocks of houses are standing on land of £600 lease value. After the construction of the Tube, some of this land has been let at ground rents ranging from £2,500 to £3,000 A striking instance of how such improvements, instead of benefiting the tenant, benefit only the landlord, was given after Waterloo-bridge, in London, was thrown open to the public, free of toll. The saving to the workers living near the bridge on the right shore who had to come over the bridge every day, which amounted to six pence a week, was at once added to their rent Increase of wages has the same effect During the late tory ministry in England it was officially stated how little the government employees at Woolwich profited by a rise of wages because rents rose with them It has been correctly pointed out by Henry George that if a benefactor willed a yearly pension to every inhabitant of a certain town, the only effect which such a benevolence produces would be a corresponding rise in rents and land values To enjoy this pension, people would have to move into the town, and as this is impossible without living on the land, the landowners would demand in higher rents or land prices the full equivalent of the benefit thus connected with a residence on their land

That a land value tax is an equivalent for benefit received from the community and thus also corresponds to the taxpayer's ability to pay, is not its only recommendation With one of the arguments in its favor the one generally adduced by Single-taxers, viz that it cannot be shifted, I do not quite agree Though it is true that as a rule the landlord takes all he can extort from the tenant, this power of extortion depends in the last resort on the rent-paying power of the latter Now, as any tax relief obtained by the tenant raises his rent-paying power, the landlord may certainly recoup, by a higher rent, any tax shifted on his shoulders from those of the tenant If a tenant pays $300 rent and $50 taxes and you make the landlord pay the $50 taxes, will not the rent at once rise to $350?

This is entirely in agreement with Henry George's own teaching, according to which all progress in the last resort increases the landlord's rental income Now, the Single-tax would certainly mark a great progress over our existing system of taxation, and thus would increase purchasing and rent-paying power all round, which according to George's own theory, raises rent proportionately If this is not shifting, what is?

And if all taxes were abolished for the Single-tax on land values, would it not enable the tax saving tenants to pay higher rents? Rents would rise in exact proportion with the economized taxes, if it were not for the land kept out of use by speculation which is offered cheaper in consequence of the higher tax. However, we must not count too much on this element of the calculation, because once the landowners got over the loss caused by the imposition of the Single-tax, they would find as ample compensation for holding land out of use, in the increase of rents, and consequently of land values, as they do now. Of course, the new increase of rents might be taxed away, too, the proceeds being used for public improvements, but these, too, have a rent-raising effect, and thus Rent would continually race ahead of the Single-tax

There is one way only which precludes shifting of land taxes, and that way is closed to Single-taxers. Instead of using the proceeds of the tax for the relief and benefit of the tenants, they ought to be applied towards the purchase of privately owned land—whose price the tax would cheapen in this case—for the community, in other words, to further land nationalization. No shifting then, because there is no relief of the tenant's taxes, the rackrenting finds its only antidote the community's competition in the land-leasing business

This rackrenting, this charging all the traffic can bear, i.e, all the tenant can afford, is also the answer to the attacks against building laws, which force the landowner to restrict the height of houses, or to leave open certain parts of the space. Such laws do not raise rents, as is pretended, for rents are always at their highest, but they lower the value of the land Nothing has, on the other hand, so ʾraised the value of land in the business part of American cities as the invention of sky-scrapers, which permit the use of more of the air space which belongs to the landowner. Office rents have not fallen in consequence of this putting half a dozen houses, one upon the other but the ground, ʾwhich thus is better exploited, has correspondingly increased in value, so that the most expensive sky-scrapers are not as costly as the land on which they are erected Or rather, the land which was formerly worth only a little more than the low house on it, is now more valuable than the high building it supports If ever we should succeed in building a hundred-story edifice, rents will not fall, but the land on which such houses stand, or are to be erected will correspondingly rise in price The first separate assessment made in 1904 of land and improvement-values in New York City, has developed the astonishing and unexpected fact that in those quarters, in which the most expensive and luxurious buildings are to be found, the value of the bare land is greater than that of all the improvements. The total valuation of real estate in greater New York was $4.798.344.789. of which the land was assessed at $3,679.686 935 and the improvements at $1,100,657,854, so that the percentage of land valuation to valuation of real estate was 77% to 23%. If we take the borough of Manhattan alone where practically all the costly structures are situated, their value only amounted to $600,000,000, while the land was assessed at $3,000,000,000, five times as much   Ten of the most recently constructed sky-scrapers aggregate a cost of $9,543,000. while the land on which they stand was assessed at $16,072,000, 70% more than the buildings Sixteen of the leading hotels, including the Waldorf-Astoria, were assessed at $6 445,000; the land on which they stand, at $20,805,000   Ten of the larger and more costly mansions on Fifth avenue are assessed at $5,065,000, the land at $13,355,000.

Taxes on land where they do not relieve the tenants, or laws restricting its use, not only do not raise rents, but they have the very opposite effect, they lower rents, paradoxical as it may sound They do this by forcing the speculative owners of unoccupied land to hasten its sale, all such restrictions and taxes reducing the expected profit, and making it more expensive to wait for the final recuperation.

The present system has the effect of favoring the speculator who holds land out of use, in the face of an urgent demand, until he can secure his usurious price, while it punishes the improver by taxing his improvements   Here is a man who erects a fine house, an ornament to the place, and at once he is fined for his bad action by a heavy tax on this house. Next to him is a plot full of weeds, or of the garbage from the neighborhood, owned by a speculator who finds his land increasing in value in consequence of the new building. This man is encouraged in his dog-in-the-manger game by the low tax on his unimproved land In some countries this tax is not even levied on the selling value of the land, but on the income derived from it, which in such a case is practically nil: agricultural rent on city property It seems unbelievable that the League of German Land Reformers has had to fight for laws that change assessments levied according to rent actually derived, into assessments on selling value At last town after town adopts the new system, and the householders who, through ignorance oppose the reform, find themselves benefited by it, as it hits only the speculative holder of unimproved land

Another advantage of the land tax is that it cannot be dodged, as the taxable object is evident before everybody's eyes. The tax could also be made an excellent accessory to land nationalization if a plan, often proposed, were adopted in connection with it, i e, allowing the landowner to be his own assessor, with the understanding that the community is to have the privilege to purchase from him at any time at the assessed price. The taxpayer thus finds himself between the Scylla of paying too much in taxation and the Charybdis of receiving too low a price for his land.

I have adduced enough to prove that if the American followers of Henry George were content to style themselves tax reformers, they would be accepted as valuable helpers in fiscal reform, though in this case they could hardly pretend to the position of workers for a thorough social reformation. But they call themselves Single-taxers, they want to make the land-value tax, the sole tax, and a tax productive enough to permit the abolition of all other taxes; which practically means a confiscation of the rental value of the land, the basis of its selling value. They thus leave the domain of tax reform to enter that of robbery, pure and simple, and in this way they have become the worst enemies land restoration ever had. Their very name is obnoxious to the two opposite wings of the community, the fair men who want to combine reform with justice, and the revolutionists who aim at the subversion of all property rights. To one they are mere robbers; to the other timid weaklings who do not dare to face the full consequences of their teachings.

In another way their agitation has injured land restoration, i.e., by misleading land nationalizers. One wrong is generally the father of another. The Single-taxers' wrong, of preaching the confiscation of private rent to relieve the landless from all taxation, has begotten the unjust proposal of land nationalizers to use the public rental, after it has been restored to the people and thus belongs to all equally, for the relief out of the public purse of those who justly pay more than the average share of taxation. Whereas in the one case the rich are to be robbed to relieve the poor; in the other the poor are to be robbed to relieve the rich. Land nationalizers forget that the idea to use the rental income for public expenses, though logically in the Single-tax plan, of which it forms the very essence, in reality is absolutely out of place in their own scheme of restoring the land to the people. Taking the rental from private landowners in the form of a tax means if the point of confiscation is left out of sight, that each landowner is taxed according to the benefit he receives from the community through the use of the land he owns. However, the case changes where the land has been honestly bought back by the people, and where the land-users rent this land from the community. Their rent is a fair equivalent for the benefit they receive from the land, but it is no more a tax. It is a rental income belonging by right in equal parts to the landowners, the people of the country. Public expenses ought to be paid by means of taxation as before, and on the most approved principle; i.e., each citizen ought to pay taxes in proportion to the benefit he receives from the State. To confiscate the common rental income for public expenses under the new conditions would work a similar injustice on most of the new landowners as the Single-tax would on many of the present ones. It would mean that each citizen is to pay as a tax his equal share in the national rental, though his dues are unequal on the benefit-received principle, for the rich receive greater benefits from the public than do the poor. The whole apparatus of public defense, of police and of justice, protects property; while the funds spent for public education in its higher branches benefit the wealthy far more than the poor. Is it just to force the poor to pay as much as the rich for the soldiers and policemen to protect their property? Yet this is exactly what would be done if the share of the poor in the national rental were used for public expenses, instead of being paid over to them or used otherwise according to their wishes. To assume that these wishes run in the direction of relieving the rich of their just proportion of taxation is certainly an idea which might never have occurred to land nationalizers, if Henry George's confiscation plan had not been first in the field, in which the heavier load it lays on the wealthy to some extent is equalized by the greater benefit they obtain out of the tax fund, which in so far lessens the wrong inflicted. Land nationalizers do away with this wrong altogether; but, forgetting the exceptional conditions under which the proposal to use the common rental income for common needs had arisen, they adopted this part of George's plans, though they rejected those features of his teachings which alone could justify it. I repeat, while George's plans involved robbery of the rich, the use of the common rental, bought with common funds, for public expenses, means simply robbery of the poor. This is not only an injustice, but also a bad policy, for it means leaving unused the best weapon in the arsenal of land nationalization.

The share of each family in the United States in the common rental may be estimated at about $200 a year. The prospect of obtaining by legal methods such a contribution to the budget of the workers, or a correspondingly high insurance in the case of invalidity and old age (at least $600 a year) would call forth quite another enthusiasm for land restoration than the mere hope of a relief from taxation figuring up to a much smaller sum for the man of the people.

There would not be found insuperable difficulties in the way of raising a public revenue by a just and sufficient taxation without any taxation of the land. The income tax, if imposed where the income is made, not where it is spent, not only works on the ability-to-pay principle, but also on that of benefit-received, for, without the help of the community no income can be obtained. Alcohol and tobacco, if the monopoly of their sale is given to the State, could be made to produce a very large fiscal revenue. This also would be a tax on the ability-to-pay principle, because nobody is forced to use these noxious commodities, and though the tax-payer certainly does not enjoy an equivalent in any benefit received—rather the reverse—he would at least indemnify his fellow-citizens for the damage done them by his use of the two poisons—by the one through the employment it provides for our police, criminal courts, prisons and asylums, by the other through the contamina tion of the air and the injection of poisonous gases into the lungs of his fellow-citizens

We shall see in Chapter VIII how an extension of the State's monopoly of distribution from one or a few to all products would by itself yield such enormous savings that a fraction of them would, if put aside for public expenses, suffice to amply provide for them. Savings due to the work of society are certainly not wrongfully used for the benefit of all.

Inheritance taxes on fortunes above a certain amount, supplemented by the substitution of the State for indirect heirs, where no will is made in their favor, might supply another bountiful source of revenue.

Before closing this chapter, I have to say something more on a subject already touched upon, nearly related to the land question and now in the centre of public discussion. Public ownership and management of public utilities It is one of those important questions which are yet open in this country, despite the unanimous favorable verdict passed upon it elsewhere I refer to the reports of Professor Frank Parsons in his "Railways, the Trusts, and the People" The facts given are of the highest importance; the arguments lucid and convincing I have to limit myself to a few points.

Concerning the fear of political influence and graft, Parsons finds it easy to prove from the examples of Germany, Holland, Belgium and Scandinavia, as well as Australia and New Zealand, that independent railroad boards and civil service regulations have proved an effective protection against this danger. Anyhow, in this country an objector to railway nationalization on such grounds would present the case of the passenger on a storm-tossed boat who jumps into the sea for fear of drowning. The worst that public ownership and management could do would be nothing compared to what private ownership and mismanagement has been doing, and is doing, in this country.

Professor Parsons correctly says on page 516: "In answer to the objection that government ownership would put the railroads in politics, we may ask· 'Where are they now?' It is doubtful whether they could be in politics in any worse form than they are to-day, and it may be further remarked that it is not' necessary that the railroads should be in politics at all in the objectionable sense, under a common-sense system of public ownership with a non-partisan commission, railway courts, and solid civil service organization, such as is provided for in the Pettigrew Bill" To this, a quotation from Professor Richard T Ely is added· "Our American railroads are incomparably more 'in politics' than the German railroads. Not only this; those German railroads which have been bought by the State, I believe, are less 'in politics' than they were when they were private property Our terrible corruption in cities dates from the rise of private corporations in control of natural monopolies, and when we abolish them we do away with the chief cause of corruption "

The defenders of the existing private monopolies must find it
rather a hard task to frighten the people with possible abuses of
political power under National ownership, when even the worst
abuses of this power could not begin to approach those continually
perpetrated by the existing monopolies, which own legislatures,
courts and press Next to the political bugbear, the inferiority of
public management to private management is usually put into the
foreground of the discussion. This reasoning is due to a kind of
atavism, an inherited notion under whose influence we overlook the
fact that "private management" in our father's time was entirely
different from that of our existing corporations The master and
owner of the little workshop, with his few journeymen, who practically was only the foremost worker of the shop or the owner of
the little factory, in continual personal contact with his employees
and hands, represented private management in its good sense That
of our corporations has mostly preserved only the bad side of private
management its personal greed, while it lacks the good sides of
public ownership and operation devotion to the public good.
What guarantee have we that a stock company is sure to bring
better managers to the top than the public administration? Is the
control of the largest number of shares, through ownership and
proxies at a stockholders' meeting, a better test of efficiency than
that of the largest number of votes at a national. state or city election? Is the method of procuring the votes so vastly superior in
one case than in the other? And the result? I entirely agree with
Professor Richard T. Ely, where he says "Management of the public finances so corrupt as that which has characterized the private
railways of the United States, would have produced a revolution
long ago   For every failure of municipal ownership and
management which it would be possible to adduce, twenty failures
of private ownership and operation could be named."

The most corrupt political bosses this country ever produced
from Tweed to Cox, from Sweeney to Quay—and in this specialty
America beats the world—are poor bunglers in grafting compared
with some of our great railroad chiefs. It is questionable whether
the "earnings" of all the bosses in the Union during a whole generation reach those of the great Harriman alone The methods of
the graft may differ, the result remains the same

But why do we assume that public management in this country
would be sure to be inferior to private management? The following facts stated by Professor Parsons seem to prove the reverse
"As high as 20 per cent of the railroads of the United States have
been operated at the same time by government agents called re-
ceivers, and the success and honesty with which these public managers, responsible to the Federal courts, performed the duties of
their calling under infinite difficulties, bringing the roads back to
prosperity after they had been wrecked by private enterprise, shows
the possibilities of public management of railroads under reasonable

safeguards. The very same men that now manage our railways would gladly manage them with equal ability, far more justice and public benefit, and infinitely more happiness, if they were the honored and respected servants of the Republic, than as they are now, the suspected, accused, and condemned leaders or agents of the forces of predatory wealth that are preying on the public, defying the law, and corrupting the government, and are denounced by many of our best people as enemies of the Republic and guilty of treason under the Constitution "

To get at the core of the partiality for private management, we find it due to its effectiveness during a period now more and more receding that of competition   We are too apt to forget that this competition gradually becomes a thing of the past in the distribution (exchange) and transportation of products   Concentration brings such immense advantages into this domain that it saves far more than the most effective management, due to the competitive struggle, could ever yield   Take the case of a hundred competing post-offices splendidly managed by a hundred commercial geniuses and imagine the cost of a letter when compared with that obtained under our centralized system   The waste through competition in this case would far outweigh the savings attained through a better organization   The organizers of our corporations know this, and their best efforts are successfully directed towards a centralization of their enterprises, in spite of the ridiculous Sherman law.   It is estimated that seven men now control the railroads of this country, and when centralization has so far progressed that all the roads are managed from one central point, the service can be made still more effective, waste can be still further eliminated   We are coming to this, and if we come to it, the saving will not be due to the genius of the manager, but to the fact of the central management.   But even if this were otherwise, and if private management provided better men than universal suffrage, would the public benefit by the greater success of the monopolists' chief?   Does it now benefit by it?   The crisis which is already thundering at our doors, while this is written, is certainly not an affirmative answer   And if we go so far as to admit the temporary advantages of allowing the superman's domination, the effects on the race are certainly pernicious. The worst effect, however, is found in the mortality of the superman, who very often is superseded by idiot heirs, whose power is established without the brains to make it beneficial to anybody.

I here refer to what the opening pages of the chapter on Democracy contribute to this subject of dominion by the enlightened minority over the ignorant masses

The ignorant masses !   To whom is their ignorance due and why should not better men rise from their ranks than the best now at the head of our affairs?   The community will find such men at its service after the present avenues are forever closed, where ambition finds its best paying remuneration, from the paltry standpoint

of the dollar   The very class of men we find now at the head of
our big corporations will then try to force their way to the direction
of the public administration, as Professor Parsons indicates   But
the people begin to find out that it is not merely a question of dollars; that considerations of a far higher nature are coming into the
foreground   It is a question whether the corporations are to own
the nation; or the nation the corporations.

Smithianism has been too long dominant in political economy;
its sway over universities, press and rostrum has been too general
to yield at once even to the most stubborn facts, or the revolt would
have come long ago.   Land nationalization would, however, bring
such powerful forces to the side of public ownership against the
private corporations, that the victory would soon be won.   Between
land and public utilities the most intimate connection exists.   A
railway or tram-line stands in the same relation to the adjoining
land as a lift in a sky-scraper stands to the rooms of the building.
Without this improvement the rooms would only have a fraction
of their present rental value; and without the railway or tram-line
the lands it connects with the centers would be far lower in price
The lift is the vertical railroad, the railroad the horizontal lift   To
give the right of running and owning the lift to an outside party
would be just as sensible on the part of the house-owner, as it is on
that of the people as owners of the land to let private parties own
and run their horizontal lifts, their railroads and trams   The lift-
owner would have it in his power to determine the rent of the rooms
according to the rate of his fares demanded from the occupants and
their visitors; a power virtually exercised by the owners of our
means of transportation.   The house-owners run their lifts free of
charge, and can well afford to do so, because they obtain correspondingly higher rents   So the community as land-owner could
afford to give general free transportation and still do a good business, in consequence of the higher rents which the land thus served
would fetch.

Landownership and transportation, like Leda's twins, thrive
best when unseparated   Independent transportation enterprises
often starve, though land values along their lines rise materially
through their activity, and land values are kept low where the transportation monopolies take all the traffic will bear.   Together they
are a strong thriving unit   The same principle holds good for the
supply of gas, water, electricity, telegraphs and telephones

The question of compensating present owners of public utilities
is as easily solved as that of compensating landowners.   In both
cases growth of population increases the incomes out of which the
purchaser gradually cannot only pay the interest on the capital, but
obtains a growing fund for redemption of the debt, a fund largely
increased through the falling of the interest rate   To be absolutely
just in the valuation of such properties we must try to get over the
perfectly natural attack of hydrophobia (fear of water) which we

are experiencing when we meet with their inflated values As a rule
the market price expresses the capitalized value of the income derived from the properties or expected in a near future It is identi-
cally the same case as that of land values. To offer our corporations
mere payment of cost of construction and of running material would
be like offering to the landowner the value of his improvements only.
To offer first cost, including the cost of the right of way, would be like
offering the landowner first cost of his land plus improvements
Justice in both cases demands that we pay present market values,
which include a lot of water, said water being the capitalized value
of incomes obtainable from the property over and above the interest
on the original outlay It makes not the least difference in which
way the price of the water is expressed, whether in a low nominal
capital, accompanied by a high stock exchange quotation, or a high
nominal capital and a lower quotation. I give an illustration (See
Pohlmann in "Deutsche Volksstimme.") The French "Compagnie
des Mines de Houille de Courrières" (Courrière Coal Mining Co,
in which over a thousand human lives were lately lost) was
founded in 1852 with a capital of 600,000 francs, divided into 2,000
shares of 300 francs each Dividends began in 1857 and gradually
rose from 150 francs per share to 2,300 francs in 1891, which means
that the invested capital brought from 50% to near 800%. This
enormous profit began to be compared by agitators with the low
wages earned by the miners, which proved unpleasant, and so the
owners managed to disguise it by inundation. In 1896 they raised
their nominal capital to six millions, issuing 60,000 shares of 100
francs each, so that each shareholder obtained 30 new shares for
one of the old ones Things looked better now, for, though the
dividends still rose—in 1900 to 125 francs for each new share, or
3,750 francs for each of the original shares of 300 francs—it only
spelt 125%, not 1,250%, the real percentage, which would have too
much horrified the public when the terrible catastrophe brought
about by the economies of the management destroyed so many
human lives To the market price of the mine the watering did not
make the slightest difference, for it matters not whether this price
is computed in 60,000 shares at 2 800 francs a piece, the quotation
of 1901, or in 2 000 shares (the original number) of 84,000 francs
a piece In both cases the market value of the mine was 168
million francs, and to expropriate it for less would have been a
proportionate confiscation This example shows that the often expressed opinion that watering of stock raises the people's tribute
payments is erroneous because based on a confounding of cause
and effect The tribute is always as high as the market will bear.
The amount of the nominal capital only influences the interest rate,
i e , appearances, not the interest sum the reality
    To recognize the injustice of all proposals which tend to expro-
priate such properties below their market value does not imply
that the State is to buy at extravagant market prices, when it is

in her power to press down these values to reasonable figures without any interference with so-called vested rights To find out how this is done we may look for valuable lessons to those clever men who organized our trusts They did not invent boycot and blackmail, but they make profitable use of it When they want to buy out a competitor they fix their own price, which he generally is forced to accept, though no law compels him to do so They arrange conditions in a manner that no choice is left him He finds it impossible to obtain railroad cars when he wants them His raw materials rise in price, while the finished product falls The threats of the trust force his best customers to refuse touching his goods His bank refuses further credit Everything suddenly turns against him, and ruin stares him in the face so that finally he is only too glad when an offer of purchase is made to him The people when they want to buy out present proprietors can profit by their example without resorting to any injustice They can make use of the law that their demand is the creator of value in the economic sense, by regulating this demand according to their interests Wherever they find that extravagant prices are demanded for a property they can simply agree to reduce their demand for the product and to retire the laborers What would those Courcelles mines be worth to-morrow if the people refused to buy another pound of their coal, and the workers left the mines, without others taking their places? Practically nothing at all Under such conditions any price offered by the nation would be gladly accepted This price ought to be the capitalized profit which would remain after a reasonable reduction of the coal price and a just increase of wages under fair working conditions Such a price would certainly not be based on 1,000% dividends The same principle would hold good in the case of railroads wherever no exclusive monopoly has been granted or as soon as the monopoly has expired New roads would be built by the people and nobody could blame them if they gave their exclusive custom to their own roads Anyhow, the State can hold out longer than private companies in bringing down rates and can thus force on sales just as the trusts have done with their competitors, with the difference that the State would only use her power to obtain reasonable terms, not to ruin competitors It is the policy which Bismarck applied, or threatened to apply, in Prussia at the time when she gradually bought up the private roads The same policy would be used in the case of mines, oil wells, trams, gas and water works etc , wherever feasible, and in regard to land in general The people need very little land for their maintenance if they make use of intensive culture The desert land still owned by the community, if brought under a perfect system of irrigation as indicated in "Arid America"—the excellent work of William E. Smythe —would by itself suffice to provide a large population with all the foodstuffs they require and abstention from the cultivation of pri-

vately owned land would soon force down its price to a reasonable
level

New centres built on agricultural land, on the Garden City plan
(see Chapter VII) would depopulate the old cities and reduce their
land prices All this would not be confiscation, but merely a reasonable pressure on the real estate market, through the influence
of supply and demand

Let the people once unite on first principles and the rest will
be easy No need of injustice to demolish injustice! Monopoly's
value is based on the people's readiness to be fleeced Let us cease
being ready victims and vested rights will lose the most valuable
part of their vestments or such vestments are purchasable for a
trifle in the old clo' market of the world's vanishing ghettos

The gamblers are beaten at their own game and, as it is not
good form to appear a bad loser, they will take their defeat much
more calmly than might be inferred from the noise they are now
making, while the stroke is merely impending

CHAPTER III.

MONEY

The physical and commercial qualities of the precious metals have since
immemorial times made them the preferred money-substances, but their great
scarcity i e, the insignificant proportion which the amount produced of this
merchandise bears to that of all other merchandise (about 1 400), and the
consequences of this disproportion makes the comparatively few capitalists
the fanatical defenders and the producing and indebted masses more and
more the inveterate enemies of metal money From this it is easy to
prognosticate that its final doom is sealed under the reign of universal suffrage

THE flood of money debates which submerged this country in the
nineties has so wearied the people that it requires a considerable degree of optimism to expect a patient hearing on this subject However, no full view of the great problem is obtainable without going into the Money Question, and all I can do to mitigate its
tedium is to treat the subject with the utmost brevity compatible
with clearness.

Money is called the life blood of the economic body, and just
as blood was circulating for millions of years before Harvey ex-
pounded its laws, so money has been and is used by millions who
have not the least conception of its real nature Many of those
who know most about it have a personal interest in concealing
their knowledge So early as 1577 we find the keen and piercing
intellect of Bodin remarking thus "For men have so well obscured
the facts about money that the great part of the people do not see

them at all. The moneyers do as the doctors do, who talk Latin before women, and use Greek characters, Arab words, and Latin abbreviations, fearing that if the people understood their recipes they would not have much opinion of them"

I do not wish to fatigue the reader with the many conflicting definitions given of Money by economists, but shall follow the course adopted through the whole of this book, of taking the word as nearly as possible in the meaning given to it by the custom of everyday life. In this sense I shall confine the term to anything which is legal tender for debts, i e, which has to be accepted as the final settlement of a debt by the creditor to whom it is tendered * In Great Britain sovereigns and half-sovereigns are legal tender for all debts, smaller coins are only legal tender for debts up to 40 shillings, and Bank of England notes for all debts above £5, except the debts of the bank. British coins and Bank of England notes, therefore, are Money in Great Britain. If I give the English system as an example, instead of the American one, it is merely because I do not want to call up at this stage the subject of bimetallism

Other means of payment or exchange, such as those bank notes which are not legal-tender, checks, bills of exchange, promissory notes, etc., are not money, but money representatives, money promises. They are included with money under the general name of currency, but whereas money is only that which has been made legal tender for debts, currency is anything which passes as a means of exchange and payment. Money is always currency, currency is not always money   There are three kinds of money

1. Any kind of merchandise may be made money by law or general agreement   We might call this money *merchandise money,* or *commodity money*   A number of different kinds of merchandise have been chosen as commodity money at different times and in different countries   Cattle have been formerly mostly used, of which "pecuniary" (from "pecus" = cattle) still reminds us   Different metals paid out by weight come next in order   Certain shells, salt, fish-hooks, etc, have been or still are money in certain countries   Whether a special form is given to the money commodity, whether it is marked by some kind of stamp, or whether the special form and the stamp exist concurrently, makes no difference so long as the value of the money, as such, does not differ from that of the raw material it contains, as is the case with the newly-minted English and American gold coins, for instance   It is self-evident that the parity between the value of the coin as money and the coin as bullion, as merchandise exists only so long as no abrasion has taken place, and can only be maintained while free coinage exists, for without free coinage, which enables any possessor of bullion to

* We shall yet see that "legal demand" would be a far better term than "legal tender" There is no great need of forcing creditors to accept money tendered them   Most of our calamities arise from the legal right of demanding something which is less and less obtainable

have it changed into coins of equal value, free of cost, coinage becomes a monopoly, and coins obtain a monopoly value liable to differ from their bullion value. Without free coinage coins enter the confines of money, class 2.

2 The stamp is applied to a commodity which would fetch an appreciable price even if the stamp had not been added; but the stamp increases this value, more or less. Silver, copper and nickel coins at present belong to this class, and also gold coins which, through seigniorage or wear and tear have a higher value as money than they possess as bullion. Class 2 offers a transition to class 3.

3 The commodity value has entirely disappeared, the value imparted by the stamp alone remains. We have reached *Token Money* or *Money of account.* In our time it is exclusively known in the form of paper money—not to be confounded with bank notes payable or supposed to be payable in legal coin. The best known prototype of this class is the French Assignats of the eighteenth century, but money of this kind was already used in remote antiquity, in China, Rome and Carthage, in the shape of small pieces of leather supplied with certain signs, iron, whose commodity value was destroyed, in Sparta, etc.

The wooden tallies issued by the English Treasury up to the reign of William III belong to the same class. They were accepted in payment of taxes by the Treasury, but not paid in gold or silver.

What has more than any other cause contributed to complicate the money problem is the difficulty of drawing a sharp line between this third class of money and a special kind of currency, called bank or treasury notes. Where these are merely money promises, they are not money; but where they have been made legal tender they are legitimate money, even though, as in the case of the Bank of England notes, the bank has to pay coin for them on demand. With most kinds of legal-tender bank or treasury notes this obligation does not exist, for though at some time or other coin was obtainable for them, the practice has become obsolete, and to all ends and purposes they are just as much mere tokens, or paper money, as the French Assignats were. To this class belong the notes or Argentina * Brazil, Greece, Portugal Spain, Turkey,

---

*The Argentine Republic offers an interesting example of the hybrid nature of certain kinds of paper money. In 1869 the province of Buenos Ayres issued real paper money on which was printed· "La Provincia de Buenos Ayres reconoce este billete por 1 peso moneda corriente." (The province of Buenos Ayres recognizes this note for 1 peso, current money.) The present paper money of the Argentine Republic has the inscription· "La nacion pagara al portador a la vista por medio del Banco de la nacion Argentina 1 peso." (The nation will pay to bearer at sight through the bank of the Argentine nation, 1 peso.) Which means that for the paper another paper of the same kind is handed over on demand. This paper is legal tender money, and is issued even for small change down to 5 centavos. As a peso in paper is worth about 45 cents, the 5 centavos paper is worth about 2 cents. These notes are not only a hybrid between paper money and money representatives, but also one between treasury and bank-notes.

etc. Austria-Hungary and Russia resumed specie payments after a very long period of non-convertibility, but I do not think the payments have been permanently resumed in Russia. In spite of the text of the notes promising coin, her people there had so entirely ceased to associate paper roubles with coin that the peasants in many cases refused the new coins at first, because in their eyes—exclusively familiar with the paper—they were not roubles.*

Though the hybrids just enumerated are responsible for most of the confusion reigning in the field of currency reform, the elasticity of the boundary line between class 1 and class 2 is equally productive of mischief. Thus the main bone of contention between monometallists and bimetallists is the question whether or not the value of gold or silver as merchandise can be kept at par with their money value where both are made legal tender for all debts, after a permanent relation between the amounts of metal respectively used in the gold and silver coins has been established; or, in other words, whether both together can be kept within our first money class. It is evident that, whenever the merchandise value falls below the money value, the coin has, for the time, passed from class 1 into class 2. A possible temporary excess of the merchandise value over the money value can be left out of account, because dealers in the precious metals will at once take care to eliminate such coins from the money domain altogether, by selling them as bullion for melting purposes. Coins selling at a premium in legal tender are practically no longer money, but a merchandise.

Without wishing to prejuge at this stage which class of money proves the best in practice, we can at least conclude that each presents a degree of evolution from the preceding class, an evolution corresponding to a more advanced state of civilization, just as the use of class 1 itself was a decided progress from primitive barter. It is barter still, but improved barter, or, as it has also been called, a double barter. The tailor who wanted to exchange a coat for a table had not only to find a person who wanted a coat, but one who at the same time had a table to dispose of. If by custom certain commodities are accepted in exchange by everybody, whether specifically required or not, because, through this general acceptance, other things which are required can be procured for this special commodity, the work of our tailor is much simplified. He has only to find someone who wants a coat and is willing to give the generally accepted commodity for it. He is sure then to obtain a table in case one is in the market, even if the owner of the table does not want a coat, because the latter will certainly accept the special commodity, for which he in his turn can obtain anything he may need

* This recalls a remark made by Thompson in his "Political Economy,' of the Scotch bank-notes down to 1845. "The people will take guineas instead, if they must but they pass them off as soon as possible as a pretentious, unthrifty, eminently un-Scottish kind of money, much inferior to a native bank-note coined in any corner of Scotland."

The next step will perhaps be that the community makes its taxes and fines payable in this special generally accepted commodity, and finally, not only the prices of all goods and services are computed in the quantities of the special commodity for which they are obtainable,* but debts are made payable in our commodity, which becomes legal tender, and consequently money. When it is supplied in exchange for anything else, or when it is handed over for a debt, we call the transaction a payment. bartering becomes buying and selling.

It is generally considered that the adoption of certain metals as the money commodity, because of their comparative indestructibility, their homogeneousness, their divisibility and their general use in the arts, marked a further progress We shall yet have to consider whether another of their qualities—their scarcity—usually given as their principal claim to the money honor is not more in the nature of a disqualification than of an advantage, through the dangers it involves.

A further good quality of metals, usually stated, is their impressibility (I should prefer to use the word "coinability") Metals offer the great advantage of delegating the trouble of weighing and assaying each piece to special parties, instead of forcing this work on every receiver of money. It is a perfection, however, which in its consequences supplies the most powerful weapon for the gradual but certain dethronement of the precious metals from their money kingship The stamp itself obtains a value more and more independent of the raw material to which the stamp is applied, until, after class 2 is passed, the value of the raw material entirely disappears, and class 3, token money, is reached—a very ancient class, for the money of some high civilizations of the past belonged to it, and it is capable of a perfection to which the other classes cannot aspire.

The money of the first class is the remnant of a stage of development not far distant from the savage condition Credit, the child of confidence and trust, is not born. The money accepted has as much value if sold as an ordinary merchandise as the commodity which is supplied for it The money of the third class, however, has no other value but that imparted by the stamp, for the material on which the stamp has been affixed is practically worthless Parting with valuable goods for a mere token of no independent market value presupposes a certain amount of trust in others, the trust that they will pay equal honor to the stamp

Robert Ellis Thompson says, in his "Political Economy," p 152 "If barter may be compared to the rude mode of transpor-

---

* Jevons draws special attention to this function as a measure of value by pointing out that 'between one hundred articles there must exist no less than 4,950 possible ratios of exchange all such trouble is avoided if any one commodity be chosen, and its ratio of exchange with each other commodity be quoted"

tation on human backs, and coin to transportation in carriages by horses, paper money is the steam carriage, whose use calls for larger precautions against danger, but whose superior utility far outweighs that consideration", and further on, pp 156, 157 "The third and the most perfect form of money is *money of account.* It possesses in a still higher degree all the advantages that make paper money better than coin." (Under paper money Thompson understands bank-notes, money promises, "money of account" is his expression for token money) "As much as paper money is less material than coin, by so much is money of account less material than paper money" After comparing money of account related to bank notes with a flying machine as related to a steam carriage, he goes on "It is the money of civilization, its use involves a degree of intelligent insight into the true nature of wealth and of exchanges; and a strong confidence in the general honesty and trustworthiness of mankind, that are impossible to the savage or half-civilized man. . . It originated in the communities of Italy; from there it came to Amsterdam, Hamburg and Stockholm." (Thompson here leaves out of sight the token money of ancient times, i e , that of China, Carthage, Rome, Sparta, etc.) He relates that the republics of Venice and Genoa authorized their creditors to establish banks on the basis of the certificates of the city's debt After stating that the bank of Venice dated from 1171, he proceeds

"Then to secure a uniform currency, the Government decreed that all wholesale transactions should be paid in the form of a transfer of bank stock—unless otherwise stipulated—so that whoever had a boxful of coins gathered from the four quarters of the earth through the manifold channels of Venetian trade, took them to the bank to get credit upon its books according to their weight and fineness. The standard by which their value was estimated was called 'money of account,' to distinguish it from the various moneys that were translated into it. The Government treated these masses of coin as payment for the privilege of a credit in the bank's book, and all idea of their repayment was lost sight of."

Benjamin Franklin says "Paper money, well founded, has great advantages over gold and silver, being more light and convenient for handling large sums, and not likely to have its volume reduced by demands for exportation No method has hitherto been formed to establish a medium of trade equal in all its advantages to bills of credit made a general legal tender "

David Ricardo says "The whole charge for paper money may be considered as seigniorage Though it has no intrinsic value, yet by limiting its quantity, its value in exchange is as great as an equal denomination of coin or of bullion in the coin It is not necessary that paper money should be payable in specie to secure its value, it is only necessary that its quantity should be regulated." . . . "A regulated paper currency is so great an improvement in commerce that I should greatly regret if prejudice should induce us to return to a system of less utility The introduction of the precious metals for the purposes of money may with truth be considered as one of the most important steps towards the improvement of commerce and the arts of civilized life But it is no less true that with the advancement of knowledge and finance we discover that it would be another improvement to banish them again from the employment to which during the less enlightened period they have been so advantageously applied "

In "Munera Pulveris," p 21, John Ruskin says· "The use of substances of intrinsic value as the material of a currency is a barbarism, a remnant of the conditions of barter, which alone renders commerce possible among savages."

In a letter to Col Edmund Taylor, December, 1864, Abraham Lincoln said "Chase thought it a hazardous thing, but we finally accomplished it and gave to the people of this Republic the greatest blessing they ever had—their own paper to pay their own debts."

In thus considering the third class the highest evolution of money, I do not wish to prejudice the question whether it is also to be considered the best money under any circumstances, this important question will be treated later on Our first task was to define and classify

We have now to investigate what constitutes the *value of money* If I were a German professor of political economy I should begin with a definition and history of Value, which, by itself, would compass not less than 500 pages, to contribute my share to the Dryasdust library on that famous subject Fortunately my apprenticeship has not been passed in a university, but in practical business in banking, manufacturing and trading Before I ever read a book on political economy I had a twenty-five years' practical survey of the field covered by this science This enables me to get through with our friend "Value" in a few lines and without entering into those tedious elaborations, to which we may well apply Macaulay's estimation of ante-Baconian philosophy· "Words, and more words, and nothing but words, had been all the fruit of all the toil of all the most renowned sages of sixty generations . . . The taint of barrenness had spread from ethical to physical speculations " We may add, "and not only to physical speculations but to speculations of a still more important nature—to those of political economy" If anything were necessary to prove how thoroughly infected all domains of human thought have been with scholasticism, it may be found in the fact that two and a half centuries after the Novum Organum, the science which has the task assigned to it of teaching humanity a fair and just system of production and distribution prefers to waste its precious opportunities in barren speculations about the nature of "Value"

I shall at once simplify my task by leaving "Value in use" entirely aside, for it is self-evident that an object must have value in use before it can have a market value or value in exchange, the only kind of value economic science need concern itself about   Nor need we trouble about certain values in use which have no market value because of their abundance, such as water and air under normal conditions.   Anything has a market value for which something else is currently offered in exchange   We can call this other thing its price.   Price alone determines value in an economic sense, the only kind of value we are concerned with in this treatise   We can safely resign the balance of the whole value-field to those parties who are fond of scholastic playthings, and once for all have done with that bugbear of students in the field of economics.

There is only one way to find the value of money it is to obtain the prices of goods and services   In other words, *the value of money is its purchasing power.*

There is no other gauge; just as money measures the value of merchandise, so merchandise measures the value of money *
This holds good for money of all three classes, with the only difference that, as the value of the money of the first class corresponds to that of the merchandise it is composed of, it is immaterial whether we speak of the value or price of this merchandise or that of the money made out of it

Gold is the money material adopted by the principal commercial nations which are using money of the first class, for even in the four bimetallistic countries France, Italy, Switzerland, and Belgium the silver money no longer belongs to the first class, free coinage has been given up—of which more when we discuss bimetallism   Consequently, we may as well speak of the value of gold in such countries when we speak of the value of their money. It is immaterial whether for instance, in England we speak of the value of the pound sterling, or of the value of the 123 374 grains troy of standard gold composing it, as anyone who carries this quantity of standard gold to the British mint can obtain a sovereign free of cost for it, a right to which we give the name of *Free coinage.*

In the United States whoever brings 25 8 grains of standard gold, nine-tenths fine, to the mint can demand its free coinage into a gold dollar   As gold dollars are no more coined he obtains a five dollar piece for five times 25 8 grains.

This definition of the value of money is certainly simple enough, and seemingly beyond any possible chance of dispute, yet even here, as everywhere in monetary science, confusion has crept

---

* Professor Simon Newcomb says "The fluctuations of money escape our notice Our whole education leads us to look at the dollar as absolutely invariable It is like the earth We do not see it move The sun and stars appear to move round the world and commodities appear to move while gold stands still whereas in both cases the actual fact is the reverse of appearances."

in, and we cannot proceed without devoting some space to two causes of error.

One is due to the jargon of the Stock Exchange When its devotees speak of dear or cheap money, they do not mean the only thing which these words really signify the increased or decreased purchasing power of money, but the rate of interest at which money can be borrowed. We often find money very cheap —in Stock Exchange parlance—in times of commercial depression, because capital is shy, and prefers the 2% to 3% it can obtain on best securities to any high percentage offered in commerce. On the other hand, in times when the discount of the Bank of England is at its lowest, often money cannot be borrowed at all, unless a security is offered that the average business man cannot supply * The rate of interest is low, but the risk premium is exceptionally high This difficulty of finding money, this height of the risk premium, forces the business world to sell goods at any price, and usually such times of exceptionally low rates of interest are accompanied by low prices But low prices of merchandise mean a high price of money, whose purchasing power has risen, has appreciated Thus when the bill-broker says that money is cheap, it is dear. On the other side, when he finds it dear, it is cheap, because when industry and commerce are flourishing, when capital finds remunerative investment in business, it does not compete so sharply for the securer investments bearing a lower rate of interest. In such times the price of consols falls, because many people sell them to take stock in industrial enterprises, and the Bank of England rate rises because the business world eagerly offers bills for discount But when industry and commerce are in a flourishing condition, prices generally have a rising tendency, and, consequently the purchasing power of money becomes reduced So money is cheaper at the very time when the broker tells us that its price has risen

But this is not the only source of error in this field When the fall of prices during the last thirty years is discussed (this was written in 1901 before the trusts forced up prices), you hear that this does not imply the appreciation of gold, of money, but that it means, through our technical progress goods are produced at lower prices The worthy gentlemen who reason in this way do not see that their argument is on a level with that which denies that John is taller than Charles because Charles is shorter than John It is absolutely immaterial whether less gold is given for woolen goods because woolen goods can be produced at one-half the price of x years ago—the same worker being able to spin and weave during the same number of working hours a much greater quantity of wool by means of our improved machines—or

* As Emory Storrs once said, after being frequently told that money was plentiful, yet whenever he tried to borrow was asked for collateral he did not possess, "it isn't money that's scarce, it's collateral"

perhaps because gold has become scarcer in proportion to the demand and costs relatively more to produce All we want to know is whether or not it is true that twice as many woolen goods have to be given for the same quantity of gold If they have, then the purchasing power of gold measured in woolen goods has doubled, and if all other goods have fallen in price at the same rate gold in general has correspondingly appreciated If, on the other side, the new gold mines opened within the same period had produced so much gold that the offer of gold in the market had increased much more rapidly than the supply of all other classes of merchandise for gold, the prices of merchandise might have risen in spite of reduced cost of production, and gold might have depreciated

The relation between the quantity of money offered for goods and the quantity of goods supplied for money—in other words, the law of supply and demand—determines not only the price of goods, but also, at the same time, the price or the value of money We must be very careful, however, not to infer from this definition—usually called the *quantity theory*—that there is anything like a fixed relation between the quantities on both sides of the equation, such as, for instance, John Stuart Mill *seems* to assume, when he says (Book III, Chapter VIII, par 2 of his "Principles of Political Economy") "If the value of money in circulation was doubled, prices would be doubled If it was only increased one-fourth, prices would rise one-fourth" He qualifies his dogma, however, in Chapter XIII of the same book, when he discusses *the effect of credit on prices*. He could not fail to see that elements more powerful than the mere money or goods quantity come into play and make such a raw conception of the quantity theory impossible.

Anyhow, Mill realized that it is not the quantity of the money stock we must consider, but the quantity which circulates in the market Money may be plentiful, but it may be locked up in the safes of misers, and the poor producer who wants to sell his goods to obtain the money he needs may find a good deal of truth in the facetious German saying "Money by itself does not confer happiness, we must possess some of it" Prices may thus be very low, in spite of a large stock of money

Then we have the rapidity of circulation which plays an important part in the problem Francis Bowen illustrates this influence well when he says "The circulation of money and merchandise bears some relation to the momentum spoken of in physical science, which is composed of the velocity multiplied by the mass The movements are equal, though the velocity should be increased ten-fold provided that the mass is but one-tenth as great So also the momentum of wealth is its value multiplied by the rapidity of its circulation"

On the other hand, the quantity of goods offered in the market by itself has no influence on the prices of goods and money, but only the quantity offered for money Where exchange transactions are mostly done by barter, a comparatively small quantity of money may correspond to a much larger turnover of goods than where business is done solely on a cash basis. And barter has played, and still plays, a much more important part in business transactions than many people are aware of. Many of the Australian farmers' business transactions are performed on the basis of mutual exchange. Prices and sums are expressed in money, but no money passes In some parts of the world even barter has not yet been reached. Even in progressive New England the farmer's wife, during the first half of the nineteenth century, still made her own soap, candles, sugar (maple), linen, and part of the woolen apparel of the household. The farmer brewed his own beer, made his own cider, or pressed a sour wine from poor grapes. Rosegger, an Austrian author still living, tells us in one of his most humorous writings, from his own experience, how the peasants in his native village tanned their own leather, which the shoemaker, while he boarded in their houses, made into shoes in exchange for produce, in the same way in which the weaver made cloth from the homespun wool or yarn Often the peasant had his own loom Most of the furniture was home-made, from the table and chair to the mattress made from home-spun and woven flax, and filled with hair cut from the farmer's own horses, or feathers from the geese of the barnyard Similar primitive conditions still obtain in many parts of the world

But barter in our times is a less important substitute for money in business than credit, and especially one form of credit—money representatives. In some countries the check does most work of this class A buys some goods from B, B from C, C from D, and so on until Z buys from A Each gives a check; and if all transactions have been made on the same day, all these checks come into the bank at about the same time, and they are booked for and against the parties. A large turnover may thus take place without a penny of money having passed, even if the parties have different banks For such a case the banks, among themselves, have an institution, called a clearing house, where all bring their checks payable at the other banks, and these are compensated just as the checks of those who bank in the same establishment are compensated in its books. In England, the balances are paid by checks of the Bank of England, and thus billions are turned over without the use of coins to any great extent "In a return," says M'Leod, "laid before Parliament by an eminent city firm, it was shown that out of £2,000,000 payments and receipts by the firm, only £40,986 were paid in gold, silver, and copper, all the rest in different forms of credit and some bankers found that in banking only 0025 per cent. were paid in coin: all the rest in credit"

The bank clearings in the United States for the year ending

September, 1906, were $157,749,000,000, which were settled by paying $5,793,000,000 (3 69%) in cash.

Next to checks bank notes, bills of exchange, promissory notes, and I O U 's are the principal forms which the money representatives usually take. It is impossible to estimate exactly their quantity relation to the money stock At all events I think M Leod's estimate exaggerated when he calculates the credit (resting on 110 millions of actual coin in Great Britain) to amount to 10,890 millions, or about one hundred of credit to one of coin. I came to the conclusion that the relation does not exceed 40 to 1 and if we deduct those debts which are compensated by other debts due to the debtor, the proportion will probably not exceed 30 to 1, nor be less than 20 to 1 According to the director of the United States mint, the debts of the world payable in gold in the year 1893 amounted to $60,000,000,000, while the stock of the world's gold amounted to $3,582,605,000, which is 17 to 1, but I think this is far below the real indebtedness at the present time This lowest figure is, however, quite ominous enough, for it means that if all creditors press for payment in money, only one dollar in seventeen can be forthcoming. If we assume that our largest financial concerns owe on the average about six times more than their money stock amounts to, we are on the safe side. J C Leaver states in "Money," p 20, that the chief London banks, exclusive of the Bank of England, owe to the public £227,000,000, and that the cash in hand and at the Bank of England amounts to £27,000,000 (less than one-eighth).

George Clare, in his "Money Market Primer," which has been included in the list of books recommended by the Council of the Institute of Bankers, says "The sum due on 31st December, 1890, by the banks of the United Kingdom, under the head of Deposit and Current Accounts, was estimated by the "Economist" on the basis of the balance sheets published by the joint stock establishments at, in round numbers, 650 million pounds, while our whole stock of legal tender does not exceed 126 millions .
and of these 126 millions it is quite likely that half to two-thirds are in actual circulation among the people, leaving a balance of, say, 50 or 60 millions available for banking purposes."

Sir Robert Giffen in a lecture delivered in London March 26, 1908, figured the banking liabilities of England at over 900 million sterling· available reserves at not over 50 million

A similar state of things obtains in the English colonies. The different banks of New Zealand, including the savings banks, owed in 1904 for deposits about £27,000,000, to which about £1,500,000 bank note circulation has to be added The gold and silver available for these debts amounted to somewhat less than £4 000 000, about one pound for eight due If we deduct £9,000,000 of fixed deposits, for which a certain time is given within which the banks are supposed to be able to raise the money—a very vain hope when we consider the similar position of the English money market and of other countries, besides the fact that financial crises usually extend over the whole world—£19,500,000 were left, which the creditors could claim from one day to another, and of which only four shillings in the pound (one-fifth) could be paid

On June 30, 1906, 6,053 National Banks of the United States* owed $4,819,974,251 for deposits, against a cash reserve in bank of $651,233,603, or 13.51%, a little over one-eighth Other commercial banks owed for deposits $4,860,399,428, against a cash reserve of $308,808,254, or 6.35% The Savings Banks owed $3,300,000,000 for deposits, against 26 millions in cash, = 4-5% All three together owed in round figures 13 billion dollars, with a cash reserve of only one billion, or 8% = one-thirteenth But this cash reserve includes greenbacks, bank notes, gold and silver certificates Gold coin, bullion and gold certificates amounted to only 487 millions or 3¾% = one twenty-sixth of their gold debts, which almost exceeded threefold the whole gold stock of the world At that date the money in the United States treasury as assets figured up to $325,400,000, that in circulation outside of the treasury and the banks at $1,728,000,000, so that the total, including the money of the banks, amounted to 3 billions gold, silver and paper The gold alone would hardly figure up to more than one-half of this, so that the whole gold of the country would only pay one-ninth of the bank debts, leaving all other debts out of account

Under such conditions, the actual money stock can only have an indirect effect on prices, and consequently on the value of money. Tooke and Newmarch, in "A History of Prices and of the State of the Circulation from 1793-1837," give some interesting facts proving this, showing how the state of credit is of much more importance than the money stock, and how periods of low prices at different occasions coincided with a larger, and of higher prices with a smaller money stock Most instructive is the course of the English crisis of 1847

Prices at the Stock Exchange fell enormously, from one day to another as much as 1¼% discount was paid, which is at the rate of 450% per year. General ruin was in view, when at last the Government promised a suspension of the Bank Act At once the panic disappeared, and large treasures of sovereigns and bank notes came out of their hiding places That there was no exceptional demand for gold was proved by the fact that during the whole time of the crisis there was no diminution in the issue of bank notes, and what is more, as soon as the permission was given to the bank to issue more notes, not quite £400,000 in all were

---

* A special institution of this country, organized on the plan of keeping your pudding and still eating it These banks deposit in the United States treasury, bonds whose interest they pocket, and on the strength of these bonds they obtain money, almost interest free, which they lend out at high interest, thus getting double interest for their capital.

demanded This was specially mentioned in the defence which the
Chancellor of the Exchequer made in the House of Commons
He said that the money in the hands of the public was sufficient,
but that its circulation was lamed by a panic, as all reports received
by him proved   The Government was asked for assistance from
all sides but everyone said   'We don't want any bank notes, we
want confidence   Tell us that you will assist us, and we have
enough   When we know that we can obtain bank notes we do
not need them   It is indifferent how high the interest rate demanded, confidence will at once return "

Here we see clearly that it was assuredly not the gold coins
which the people wanted, and not even the bank notes, but only
the certainty that they could obtain them in case they wanted them
Bank notes, they knew, could not be converted into gold in case
a general attempt had been made; for even in ordinary times, without any repeal of the Bank Act, the issue of 15¾ million pounds
of notes is permitted to the bank (at that time not less than 14
millions) without any gold cover, and the suspension of the Act
might have largely increased the amount for which no coins and
no bullion were in stock   The people made no attempt to demand gold for the notes   The notes were legal tender, they could
be used to pay off liabilities, and that was all they wanted

We have thus arrived at the conclusion that the condition of
credit determines the value of money, a credit the foundation of
which is the certainty people possess, or believe they possess, that
monetary engagements can be regularly kept, that the money promised will be forthcoming when due and demanded   The actual
money stock of the country—as a remarkable historical example
has just shown us, and as the facts of everyday life prove—plays a
much less important part than other causes of which the temporary disposition of the money-creditors is the principal one   When
I use the word 'money-creditors." I do not mean merely the rich,
powerful as their influence necessarily must be

The financial crisis of 1893 in this country, whatever may
have started it, became so acute through the fears of the poor savers, who became afraid for their balances at the savings banks,
and came in crowds to claim their own in cash   Savings banks
cannot keep much ready money in stock, but are forced to invest
the deposits for more or less extended terms, so that they may
obtain the interest which their depositors claim from them. If an
exceptional demand be made, when a tightness in the money market disables them from borrowing at reasonable terms enough to
tide them over the temporary difficulty, they must of necessity
suspend payment The simultaneous demands made by their depositors thus caused a pretty general temporary suspension of
these banks   Other financial institutions, whose creditors pressed
for money in the same way, followed suit and finally the excite-
ment of the small savers became the panic of the nation, Money

was as good as unobtainable, and as much as ½% per day, or 180% per year, was paid by solvent parties supplying the best kind of securities

This crisis of 1893 is especially instructive because there was no exceptional cause for the sudden alarm No war threatened the country or the world; no catastrophe of nature had caused unexpected losses: the crops were good The Chicago Exhibition brought millions into the country and into circulation, politics indicated fair weather It was merely the case of a sleep-walker quietly stepping along the border of a chasm He has not the least fear; he has passed over much more hazardous places before without heeding them But suddenly something or other awakens him, he becomes conscious of his danger; he sees it, and headlong he falls. The chasm between the amount of money due and the actual money stock may have been much wider at other times: but the people did not pay any attention, and went on with their daily routine, when some mere trifle occurred Perhaps it was a report from somewhere that there was danger of suspensions—a danger threatening them all the time and sometimes even with much greater force, but a report now, spreading and swelling through the very effects it brings about When this report makes them start and survey the position, they recognize the patent fact that there is absolutely no money to be got if they really should choose in a body to claim their dues The simplest calculation would have shown this all along; but their thoughts were elsewhere, and thus they had not seen what now suddenly—like an apparition illuminated by the lightning of an ink-black night—gives challenge to their horror-smitten minds

But not all are sleep-walking, awakening only in panic times, and dearly paying for their previous blindness. Our financiers have their eyes open all the while, and though they do not know the hour of the impending catastrophe, they see the chasm and they know their danger This knowledge finds its expression in the high risk-premium demanded, so high that the average debtor cannot pay it The permanent load of usury presses with a much heavier weight on the people than the dangers and losses of the occasional crises. These are the acute outbreaks of a chronic disease which is sapping the life-energy all along, growing in violence from year to year, from crisis to crisis Take away the terrible nightmare generated by the certainty that whenever an exceptional demand for money may occur a crisis must ensue, and our wild struggle for life will have lost its intensity at once But this struggle must be hopeless with a money whose quantity corresponds to that of a certain precious metal, a quantity so ludicrously small when compared with the demand that a credit building about thirty times as high as the diameter of its narrow foundaton had to be erected on it to enable us to carry on at all while all the time invention succeeds invention, technic progress follows technic progress and creates a continually growing demand for more currency. We have seen that the banks of one single country, leaving aside all other debts, owe twenty-six times as much gold as they possess, and about three times as much as the whole gold stock of the world, coined and uncoined, figures up to

The danger inherent in this state of things has been realized not only by financiers but by growing numbers of thinking men of all trades, and it is the soil on which has grown bimetallism.

Bimetallism has been attacked on the ground that it is impossible to make two different commodities—two precious metals—at the same time the standard of value, that if both are coined as legal tender money, one of them has generally to lose its money character, becoming a mere merchandise for the time This seems plausible, for bimetallism presupposes free coinage of both metals at a certain unchangeable ratio Suppose this legal ratio to be sixteen to one, this would mean that anybody bringing to the mint 25 8 grains troy of "standard" gold has a right to claim for it a new gold dollar containing the same quantity of gold, and anybody bringing to the mint sixteen times the 25 8 grains of 'standard" silver can claim one silver dollar, which is to be legal tender for all debt, just like the gold dollar But will the market price of the two metals—which follows supply and demand—permit the maintenance of a fixed ratio? You could certainly not buy in the market the above quantity of silver say, for ninety cents, and thus make ten cents profit on every dollar coined,—no matter how much lower sixteen pounds of silver could be produced than one pound of gold,—as long as the mint gives a silver dollar which is legal tender, for the silver. But the price of money would fall together with, and in the same way in which the price of silver falls; the price of merchandise would rise, and especially one merchandise—gold, provided its cost of production did not cheapen in the same proportion with that of silver It is certain that if it costs more to produce one pound of gold than sixteen pounds of silver, the price of standard gold must rise above one dollar for 25 8 grains, and consequently, not only will no more gold come to the mint which gives only a dollar for this quantity, but the existing gold dollars will be withdrawn from the market and will sell as bullion

Gresham's law will come into operation, according to which the better money is driven out of the market by the inferior one,[*]

---

[*] Better and inferior in the sense of the market price of the material coined As William A Whittick points out in his "Value and an Invariable Unit of Value" (Philadelphia 1896) 'The best money is that money that performs the money function the best and at the least cost The use of a valuable metal as a tool of exchange is just as absurd as would be its use in the manufacture of spades and shovels, and other tools of industry An iron or steel shovel would always drive out a gold shovel just as cheap money drives out dear money For three centuries this paradox has been the apologist of an absurd system of money—a system in conflict with the universal law that the fittest survives The money that runs away from its

and the country will practically have a silver currency This is not a mere theory, but has been the result of bimetallism wherever tried Generally either gold or silver became a merchandise, and was withdrawn from its circulation as money, at least as far as wear and tear had not too much reduced the weight of the coins My own experience during my apprenticeship in a banking house proved to me the fact most unpleasantly in the beginning of the sixties. It was a continual calculation whether gold was at a premium, or silver, and accordingly, gold or silver coins of different kinds were bought to be sold as bullion Many a weary day had I to assort sack pyramids of silver five-franc pieces into four different kinds. Those up to and including Louis XVIII (till 1824) contain a certain amount of gold, and therefore were sold to Allard's refining establishment at Brussels Those of Charles X (1824-30) contain less gold, and were sent separately to the same firm, fetching a little less. The newest pieces after these reigns, those of Louis Philippe, the Republic, and Napoleon III were sorted out to go off as silver bullion to Amsterdam, while those of these last three reigns which were too much worn to pay as bullion were sent to the nearest branch of the Bank of France, and we drew bills of exchange on Paris against them. They alone were left in circulation, or in the vaults of the bank, the others disappeared, as fast as bankers and money-dealers could get hold of them. Gresham's law began to produce its usual effects, the money with the greatest raw material value disappeared from the money into the bullion market

There is nothing in this which reasonable bimetallists will not agree to, as they are fully aware that bimetallism could only succeed if carried internationally if all commercial nations—anyhow, the principal ones among them—open their mints to the free coinage of gold and silver to any amount at the same ratio, both metals being legal tender for all debts This would so increase the demand for silver that its price would never fall below the relative money value assigned to it by the law. The use as money is paramount to any other to such a degree that the market value of the metal is bound to conform to its money value as long as the value of its use in the arts does not prime the money value, which might finally be the case if the money value fell too low. This might happen to silver in case the ratio between the two metals were put farther apart than the late market price of silver put it, if this ratio were beyond 32 to 1 As far as gold is concerned, the limit of the ratio in the opposite direction also depends on the value which gold would maintain for its use in the arts, independent of its money value The ratio is said to have been as low as 1 to 6 in Japan in the sixteenth century, and August Boeckh's "Political Economy

duties—that refuses to circulate—is according to this absurdity, the best money The soldier who runs away from the field of battle is, by this reasoning, the bravest and best soldier " of Athens," I am told, speaks of times when silver had a superior value to gold.

Snobbism is the principal value creator in the case of gold Snobs wear gold watch chains or use gold plates, not because the metal is better than some cheaper materials for the purpose, but because it is costly. If, without in the least changing its qualities, its value fell, we should see some more expensive material take the place of gold. Universal bimetallism, by depriving gold of its exclusive money monopoly and thus depreciating its price, would at the same time also reduce its value in the arts Instead of bring-ing about its withdrawal from the money market, bimetallism would perhaps effect the contrary, it might bring more gold to the mint

One weighty objection has been made to this by the antag-onists of bimetallism *cost of production* Though in the first place supply and demand determine the price of commodities, these gentlemen maintain, correctly enough that this price cannot oscillate far from cost of production in the long run, which renders the arbitrary fixing of a relation between the two metals impossible, as long as we cannot do away with variations in cost The argu-ment seems irrefutable, and so it would be if an important element in the cost of production of both metals had not been left out of consideration the effect of bimetallism on the *margin of produc-tion*. Ricardo in his law of rent, which plays an important factor in this calculation, calls it the margin of cultivation, by which he means the most unfavorable conditions under which production is still carried on, conditions which just yield the lowest wages at which labor would engage in the work, and the lowest profit at which capital will consent to invest. At this margin the price of a commodity is finally determined, when production is forced there by the demand for it. this demand not being satisfiable under better conditions. The price cannot be below cost at this point because it is exactly on the margin where labor and capital will yet join in production If the price were lower than cost at this point, the margin would come inward to a line where better con-ditions obtain, and this would be the new margin of production. Nor can the price be above cost at the margin, for the extra profit thus obtained would induce production under inferior conditions, as long as the usual wages and the usual profit are obtainable. In other words, the margin would be forced outward until again no extra profit is obtainable, the margin would still determine the price A growth of the demand forces the margin still further out, which can only be done if the price increases accordingly In case land (including mines) forms a prominent factor in the production of the commodity—which is not the case in the manufacture of watch-springs, pens and needles, but is the case in the mining of iron ore, for instance,—the extra profit made inside the margin takes the shape of Rent.

Ricardo in fact limited his law to such cases where the extra profit appears as rent, and, though since then extended to all production and consequently to all profits—especially by Professor Boehm-Bawerk and his disciples—we may still call it Ricardo's Rent law. Though usually illustrated by its effects on wheat production, this law is however still more applicable to the precious metals than to wheat for while a larger consumption of wheat is soon met by a correspondingly increased production through a slight pushing back of the margin of cultivation, the scarcity of the precious metals renders this effect on the margin much more powerful It is quite certain that the remonetization of silver would make many mines pay which now lie untouched, just as the demonetization of this metal has stopped the working of many mines which before yielded a dividend The farther the margin is forced back, i e., the less fertile the least paying mine yet worked, the higher is the cost of production, and, according to Ricardo's law, the cost at the margin determines the market price.

In other words, as long as they are money materials, with a fixed price, it is, within certain limits, not the cost of production which dictates the market price of the precious metals, but their market price which determines the cost of production The remonetization of silver would at once open to it the money market, together with gold: and its value, as money, would determine its market price as long as this value is not inferior to that in the arts As the latter was found at a ratio to gold which bimetallists would probably never adopt· the ratio of 32 to 1, whereas the ratio they propose varies between 20 to 1 and 15 to 1, we may leave out of consideration this contingency of the value of silver in the arts ever exceeding its money value under bimetallism Thus the only question will be how far down the limit of the ratio might be narrowed without forcing gold out of the money use. This question cannot be answered, for nobody can foretell what value gold would preserve after it ceases to be used as money.

I think even a reduction of the ratio to that of Japan in the sixteenth century of 6 to 1 need not necessarily drive gold out of the money use, and as long as this does not happen, such a ratio would simply mean that new silver mines will be opened and gold mines will be closed until the least fertile silver mine produces six pounds of silver at the same cost at which the least fertile gold mine produces one pound of gold.

The result is that under any conditions likely to occur the relative cost of production for the two metals will always correspond to the ratio of value which the international monetary convention gives them

To be quite exact, I have, however, to add a few words in regard to another element entering into the cost of mine produce particularly, though not quite absent in other fields of production: gambling.

Del Mar ("History of the Precious Metals") states that the 450 million dollars of gold produced in California, from 1848 to 1856 inclusive, cost in labor alone some 2,250 millions, or five times its mint value, but this is not the cost I mean. His cost price includes the element of speculation, of gambling, which makes lotteries such paying enterprises, because the dazzling effect of great prices entirely blinds the gambler to the well-known fact that, *on the average*, a lottery ticket only brings back a part of the price paid for it. This element of gambling may be responsible for the fact that certain gold and silver mines are worked, though they swallow every penny expended, in the hope of finally striking the long-expected lode; but still there remains a margin beyond which speculation refrains, and this is the margin which is narrowed by the depreciation and forced out by the appreciation of the metal. Speculation may have the effect of forcing the margin beyond its economic limit, but this artificial level must finally follow the same laws as the economic one.

Whether and how far bimetallism would narrow the margin of production in gold mines, thus cheapening the cost of gold by destroying the rent of now rent-yielding mines, depends on the question whether the large increase of legal tender money would have a price-depressing effect on money or not. It may seem preposterous merely to express a doubt as to the absolute certainty of a general depreciation of money under bimetallism; but I have already shown that we must not accept the quantity theory in the literal sense given to it by some tyros. No matter what kind of money the twentieth century may have, business will continue to be done by means of the money representative, the money promise; but this assuredly does not signify that the amount of the stock behind the promises is of no importance whatever. The admission of silver would certainly increase this stock, but whether this increase would be sufficient is more than doubtful as I shall presently show. Taking the price of silver as it stood before its demonetization began, the actual yearly production of both metals for some time to come will hardly much exceed 750 million dollars. From this we should have to deduct a very considerable part, at least one-half, for abrasion, loss, and use in the arts; but I refrain, because we have to add, on the other side, the increase of the silver yield through the opening of new mines, which would be rendered possible by the rise in price following its remonetization. The present world stock of gold is figured at 5,000 million dollars; that of silver is unknown, as we cannot even guess at the amounts hidden and circulating in the East. Let us add another 5,000 million, and thus bring the total of our stock of precious metals to 10,000 millions. The yearly increase would, therefore, be one-thirteenth of the existing stock. To reach the amount of money promises so as to make our money representatives represent a reality instead of a dangerous fiction, our stock of 5,000 million dollars gold, which forms the basis of a credit building of say, thirty times its basis, would have to be increased to 150,000 millions of the new bimetallistic money. Consequently it would take, at the present rate of production, almost two centuries before the 150,000 millions were reached. But this calculation presupposes two conditions. (1) Our gold and silver production must never fall below the present figures, and, what is much more important, (2) Our turnover must not increase.

Now, whoever has realized the enormous increase of trade within the past century, in spite of the fettering effect which our social conditions have exercised, with our currency system as one principal hindrance, will agree with me when I prognosticate such an immense increase for the next couple of centuries that, before the 200 years are passed, money representatives would have got farther ahead of the actual money stock than in our time, though the stock of the money metal had increased thirty fold, so that the basis of this circulation would certainly not be as broad as the one we now possess, one to twenty, or thirty perhaps forty. A child can see that our productivity in thousands of commodities of all kinds must always far outrun our productivity in two special commodities in spite of our artificially interfering with general production by forcing it into dependence of that special production of two precious metals. The relation of all production to the production of gold and silver is now about 400 to 1, but as only one half of the production of the precious metals is used for money purposes, the relation to be considered is 800 to 1.

Independent of this, however the mere cheapening of general merchandise production through further technic progress would, as in the past, cause an appreciation of money, because the progress in the production of the precious metals does not keep step with it.

For the time being, the remonetization of silver would be beneficial for all that. The mere temporary widening of the insecure foundation on which our whole financial circulation rests, would greatly revive confidence, and would largely increase credit, trade and, consequently, production, until soon the money promises would as much outrun the money stock in both metals as they are now exceeding the gold stock. For a time prices might rise, and thus debtors would be eased in a double manner. The depreciation of the money would reduce their debt, and the greater demand for products of labor would give them a chance of satisfying their creditors.

But this help would only be a temporary one, and would be obtained at a ridiculous sacrifice. Millions more of workers would be employed in digging ores from the ground, extracting, transporting, and perhaps also coining the precious metals, as well as in feeding, clothing, housing the metal producers, making the water-pipes, machines and tools or means of transportation, etc.,

they require And what would be the real practical outcome of all
this labor? Simply taking the money material out of one set of
earth-holes to put it into another, where most of it will practically
be as undisturbed as at the time before the miners went down to
get it, that it might be shifted from the vaults of Nature to the
vaults of the banks There the greatest part of the silver and gold
might lie till Doomsday, without serving any other purpose than
to form the basis of the credit paper circulation which will always
be the real tool of exchange and payment

I forgot another result the creation of a large number of new
millionaires and the further enriching of others, the owners of the
gold and especially the owners of the silver mines How far the
latter form the officers of the bimetallistic army of which the debtor
class are the soldiers may be left uninvestigated This is the plight
we have come to at the dawning of the twentieth century by drag-
ging into it that old fetish of a past civilization the commodity
money

Prince Bismarck once told a story in the German Reichstag
of a ferocious watch-dog kept on a chain for a dozen years because
he might otherwise have proved dangerous For twelve long
years the animal ran forward and backward in front of its kennel
as far as the chain would permit until a deep rut had been worn
into the ground in the form of a semi-circle Meanwhile, the dog's
teeth gradually decayed, danger faded away, and liberty was at last
granted to him The chain was taken off and the dog released
The poor creature might have gone where it listed, but habit had
so accustomed it to its old groove at the chain's length that it continued in this groove until it died A stupid dog! Certainly, but
are we less stupid in continuing in the old groove of commodity
money, the old relic of primitive barter, when the greater part of
our business is actually done by means of money promises, widely
outrunning the world's money stock and are thus practically mere
tokens only Like the dog, we do not make use of our liberty to
run free from the old chain from which in reality we have long
since been released—the old chain of distrust and ignorance. Why
continue making believe we trade by means of gold and silver, a
belief sadly destroyed to our great cost whenever we want to put
it to practical test As the currency of our world is in reality
money of our third class—token money to the extent of at least
nineteen-twentieths—why preserve the virtually worthless one-
twentieth which exposes us to such terrible dangers, when practically the question in nineteen cases out of twenty lies not between
gold and paper money, but between *no* gold money and paper
money? Because we must have some *standard and measure of
value*, is the reply we mostly obtain even from comparatively un-
prejudiced men A nice standard of value indeed, which is continually varying! The very quality of the precious metals which
their defenders always fall back upon, makes them a bad standard

of value I mean their *intrinsic value*, as it is falsely called. Falsely, for there is no such thing as an intrinsic value Value—in the sense of market value, here meant—is a relation, the mere result of supply and demand Where was the intrinsic value of the bag of gold found by the dying Arab in the desert? Gladly he would have given it for a drink of water, but the water was not forthcoming, and consequently the gold was valueless No supply of water, no demand for gold in the water market then and there! It is true gold has a market value in most times and places, and water has not, but it is not true that this gives us a right to call value intrinsic in one case, and refuse to call it intrinsic in the other, nor does the value of gold remain more stable than that of most other commodities

The friends of gold money point to the large stock which serves as a huge reservoir to eliminate the effect of a varying supply, but the very effect of this large stock disqualifies gold as a standard of value As value is a relation, the most serviceable standard must be the one which most closely keeps unchanged its relation to the objects it has to measure It is true that an unchangeable yard-stick is a better standard of length than a changeable one, but it is true only under existing conditions. In a world, however, in which everything without exception gradually grows, or in which everything decreases in size in the same proportion, though an unchangeable yard-stick might have the advantage of showing the general rate of growth or of diminution of things, and thus form a scientific instrument of great value for philosophers and historians who are interested in such phenomena, still, such a yard-stick would not be as practical and advantageous for the purposes of everyday life as one which changed in size at the same rate with everything else To the merchant who purchased cloth by the unchangeable yard-stick before the cloth increased in length, and who sells the cloth by measure at the old price, the increase would yield an extraordinary profit, and his customers would be losers at the same rate If, on the other hand, everything in the world—except the yard-stick—became shorter, the merchant would lose, if under a contract to supply goods at the old prices without any regard to the change of length Which is exactly what happened in regard to most goods sold by the gold yard-stick, whose admirers boast that it has remained unchanged while other things have varied The man who, for the last forty years, has been under a contract to supply a regular quantity of wheat yearly— say, as rent for land—has this land much cheaper than his neighbor who pays a money rent, for the same amount of money will now buy more wheat, and the same quantity of wheat will fetch less money in the market than it did forty years ago We have always to keep in mind that the price of goods measures the price of money as much as the price of money measures that of goods More goods have to be sold to pay now a money debt of forty

years' standing than were obtainable for the money when it was
borrowed. And a money of this class is called a perfect standard
of value! Just as a yard-stick, which increases or decreases in
length in the same proportion with all other things in this world,
would be a much better measuring instrument of length than an
unchangeable one, so a money which changes its value in exact
proportion with that of all kinds of merchandise would be a much
better measuring instrument of value, to all intents and purposes,
than one the value of which remained unchanged. As value, in
its economic sense, is a mere relation, the standard which changes
as the things it measures change, and thus keeps up the same
relation to them, is more perfect than the standard which has remained fixed, and has thus varied in the only direction in which its
stability is of practical importance in its relation to the things it
measures.

Thus the defenders of silver are perfectly correct when they
maintain that silver has for the last four decades been a more
perfect standard of value than gold, because its price fell and rose
with that of other merchandise. But we have not the least guarantee
that this relation will keep up for the next four decades. Processes
of manufacture may be found which reduce the average cost of all
kinds of merchandise one-half, while silver may become scarcer and
rise in value instead of falling at the same rate as other commodities.
In this case our children would be in the same predicament with
silver debts incurred in our time as we were in regard to gold debts
made in 1870 and due in 1900. After what I have said about
the relation of the money quantity to the turnover, according to
which it is not likely that even the greatest increase in silver-mining
which we could expect would be likely to keep up with the growth
of our turnover in all merchandise and our money demand, it may
be realized that such a change in the relation of the silver price to
the price of merchandise would almost inevitably occur.

Nor will it help us to look round for other classes of merchandise to serve as the money commodity, for we have no certainty
that their price relation to other commodities will not vary considerably in the course of time. Wheat has been proposed, for instance, but its price variations are even greater than those of the
precious metals.

The clumsiness of wheat as money, independent of the cost of
storage, would not be so great a drawback as we might think at first.
That a bushel of wheat is not as handy a means of exchange as a
dollar is undoubted, but that a paper note promising a bushel of
wheat is as easily pocketed as a paper note promising a dollar is
equally true, and most of our business is done by means of paper
representatives. Even the smallest payments might be thus made.
An Argentine five cents bank-note is worth a trifle more than two
cents, and our postage stamps are also passing as money among the
people. The wheat would remain in the storehouses as most of the

gold and silver is doing, only to be handled over in the exceptional cases in which the holders of the wheat-warrants, the new bank-notes, would want the real money

The want of scarcity, the other indictment made out against wheat-money by its opponents, is an indictment the very preferring of which exhibits the degree to which the financiers have prejudiced public opinion. They stand up for scarcity as if it were a good quality of money, whereas it makes a dangerous weapon in the hands of the money-owners. The scarcer the money material, the stronger the monopoly which the possession of money confers, the tighter the corner into which the money creditors can squeeze the money debtors, the higher the usury they can exact from them. In fact, here we have the unavowed main reason why the financiers have used their powerful influence to force through the demonetization of silver, and thus to increase the scarcity of the money material. That England, the world's creditor, has always been the stronghold of monometallism, is not fortuitous. Through the demonetization of silver the debt due to its capitalists has been increased in purchasing power by untold millions, and the tribute chain they have laid on the balance of the world has been made proportionately heavier.

Cattle and wheat money are certainly clumsy currencies, but they have one immense superiority over gold and silver money everybody can produce wheat or raise cattle by his labor, provided he can gain access to land, the condition without which existence is impossible. Few can gain access to paying silver or gold mines, and to obtain their product somebody has to be found who is ready to sell it for other goods. The more the productive power of labor increased, and consequently the easier it was for the money owner to procure other goods, the more difficult it became for the producer to exchange his product against the scarce gold or silver money. The owner of this money has his choice among the products of the land. All are at his disposal, the producers are at his feet, anxious to sell their goods for the scarce money which they not only need to buy necessaries of life with—barter might do that to a certain extent—but mainly to pay money debts, which are growing all the time, through the usurer's interest charges, in consequence of the very difficulty of obtaining the money.* With a money consisting of ordinary products of labor the usurer's chain could never have been forged, for while on the one hand the debtor could produce the money by means of his labor, not depending on the goodwill of a customer who owns the scarce metal, on the other the treasuring

---

* Tolstoy in "Money" gives an interesting proof of this from the history of the Fiji islands, whose financial ruin was accomplished by a money fine imposed by an American man of war. They might gradually have paid the fine if it had been levied in their produce but gold was not found on the island and to procure it they had to run into debt at a high interest rate and upon other onerous terms which ended their independence.

of the new money through its perishability necessitates so much labor that the money owner perforce becomes more dependent on the worker than the worker on him

We are only too apt to forget that money is not merely a measure of value and means of exchange but is also demanded in payment of debts. Whatever advantages the precious metals may offer in the two first-mentioned qualities are greatly outweighed by the terrible danger their use as money implies in consequence of their having been made exclusive *legal-tender for debts*. We have seen that the amount of debts in gold currency countries exceeds at least twenty-fold the value of the gold they possess, which gold is practically the only legal tender for these debts.

The power of extorting interest for the loan of the scarce money enables the money owners to double their demands within fourteen years at 5%, a percentage rather below the average rate of gross interest (interest proper, plus risk premium), which the debtor pays. Experience has confirmed what arithmeticians could foretell in such a case—that the chain of usury weighing upon the producers gets heavier from year to year, while the victim's power of self-ransom grows weaker and weaker.

Thus the monopolists of the scarce money have it in their power to fix their own prices at which they will accept labor's product, or even to decide whether they will be gracious enough to accept it at all. Most of us are the slaves of the money power, with the titular dignity of free workers. In the case of skilled labor the title may be even more sonorous, though the facts are unaltered. The poor professor at a German university, to whom the State gives the title "Hofrath" to make up for a not forthcoming increase of salary, is just as really a slave of the money power—underpaid and bowed down by the cares of keeping soul and body together, of educating his children and preserving appearances—as a simple laborer.

Need we wonder that, under such conditions, the wealth purchasing power of gold increases?

A nice standard of value, indeed! A standard changed at the will of the creditor class who, independent of the regular and certain increase of their claims, which the widening gulf between the demands of compound-interest and the gold-earning power of labor creates, can at any time force on a financial panic that will put the produce of the workers and the workers themselves at their mercy. It is just as valuable a standard as a yard-stick which a merchant can lengthen at his own will when he goes round to make his purchases of dry goods.

If it were not for the power of that wonder-working giant, Habit, the fact—that with a full knowledge of all these conditions we are still religiously conserving the gold standard—would be inconceivable. Only habit—which veils our eyes so that we see, without heeding, the wonders of Nature all around us, the development of the tiny acorn into the mighty oak, the metamorphosis of the humble caterpillar into the brilliant butterfly, our own birth and being— only habit makes us support the worst monstrosities without think- ing about them. And even where we think, it is generally in the direction of justifying or sanctifying that which is, merely because it is As an amusing proof of this truism, I cannot abstain from quot- ing a few passages out of "Money and Its Laws," by Henry V. Poor.

"They (the precious metals) are the foundation upon which rests the superstructure of civilized society Without them there could have been no exchanges, no wealth, no government no in- stitutions, no history, nothing but the eternal iteration of savage or barbarous existence. . Without them utter chaos would at once take the place of the order which now conducts to prosperous ends the industry of every laborer . As without such stand- ards there could be neither industry, wealth, nor civilization, the in- ference is irresistible that the universal demand for the precious metals at their cost, and the uniformity of their supply, are, equally with moral laws, 'part of God's providence with man.'"

Then, speaking of the possibility of leaving money for the en- dowment of scientific institutions, and pointing out that this could not be effected by "dedicating thereto great store of food or cloth- ing," which are speedily perishable, he says that, "in this way, through silver and gold, man can invest himself, as it were, with the attributes of immortality No commercial people ever have adopted, nor will they ever voluntarily adopt, standards of value other than those providentially appointed"

This man evidently believed in a bimetallistic providence, and if ever he became a monometallist, he would have to change not only his currency theories, but also his theology and religion.

H. D Macleod once made the striking comparison of modern circulation to the movements of a top which spins round on a very fine metallic point As our civilization rests upon such a circulation, it is no wonder it is in continual danger of toppling over, and that it keeps going only by continual whipping! Under such conditions we need no longer be surprised at Mr Poor's giddiness Not every- body can stand the continual turning of a top on which he is forced to dwell.

My quotation from this amusing book reminds me that I have said almost nothing about the function of money as a store of wealth

The fact is, I could not well imagine that anybody in our times should be so hare-brained as to recur to such an obsolete con- ception, unless the reading of "A Thousand and one Nights," with its treasure-troves and its Ali Baba caves, or of Dumas' "Monte Cristo" has turned his head Our modern Monte Cristos, our Rockefellers, Rothschilds, Vanderbilts, Carnegies, etc., own very little gold and silver, the security of their wealth rests on something much more solid—on human stupidity, which makes something exclusive legal tender which does not exist in nineteen cases out of twenty, and so gives to the creditor class the power of claiming enormous tributes for its loan, on still greater human stupidity, which permits the few to own part of God's earth given to all, and to claim tribute from those who want to use it

The wealth of our present world, including the land values, exceeds 500 billion dollars while the total value of its precious metal stock does not reach 10 billions, in fact would not reach 5 billions if these metals were demonetized Of every \$50 of wealth about \$1 now is, of every \$100 of wealth \$1 would then be based on the possession of gold and silver What pitiably insignificant stores of wealth!

An American lady wrote a tale, describing the discovery of immense deposits of gold The State, their owner, distributes the metal among the people at the rate of \$10 of gold per day per inhabitant The result is a general catastrophe, because not one of these "rich" people wants to work any longer, and all would have had to starve if the gold had not finally been confiscated and destroyed.

Let us contrast with this starving Golconda our America as it would be if there were not a particle of gold or silver in the world, either above or below the ground, if this country had only its present thrifty population, its soil, climate, and minerals of different kinds, exclusive of the precious metals Does anyone imagine that production and distribution would stop, that less wealth would be produced? On the contrary, it will be quite clear to all who have learnt to understand the real function which the precious metals and the money made out of them are playing in our economic system that, once freed from their pernicious effect on distribution, and consequently on production of wealth, our country would soon be much richer in everything required by human beings, and that our civilization would rise to higher levels, in spite of our Poor friend and his co-religionaries.

Another standard of value—labor time—has often been proposed, and tried, for instance, in Owen's "Labor Exchanges" (see Chapter VII)—a very poor standard, as the failure of all such experiments proved A good standard only with men like that peasant who had his tooth extracted by a celebrated dentist, and who protested when he was asked to pay two dollars for the operation "Two dollars! Why, man, our barber at home only charges me a quarter, though he pulls me about the room for a couple of hours, and you want two dollars for two seconds!"

Until the period arrives when communist utopias become a reality, until the hour spent by an Andrea del Sarto at his canvas or by a Newton at his desk shall be estimated as valuable and worth the same pay as that spent by a washerwoman at her tub or a crossing-sweeper with his broom, labor time—as a measure of value—must be relegated to the domain of those day-dreams which give a zest to the poet's compositions, but which are better left out of economic dissertations As long as labor is paid according to its current value—found as the result of supply and demand, the higgling of the market, as long as its price does not correspond to mere time units, so long will the labor-time standard remain a mere theory—and a false one at that—without any practical application, in spite of the most learned disquisitions of a Karl Marx and his disciples

The device of counting skilled labor in multiples of ordinary labor does not advance us in the least, so long as we have no gauge for the magnitude of the multiplier

Proudhon expressed it in these words "The value of labor is a figurative expression, an anticipation of effect from cause. . . It is a fiction by the same title as the productivity of capital Labor produces, capital has value, and when, by a sort of ellipsis, we say the value of labor, we make an 'enjambement,' which is not at all contrary to the rules of language, but which theorists ought to guard against mistaking for a reality Labor, like liberty love, ambition, genius is a thing vague and indeterminate in its nature, but qualitatively determined by its object; that is, it becomes a reality through its product. When, therefore, we say This man's labor is worth five francs per day, it is as if we should say The daily product of this man is worth five francs "

It seems unnecessary to insist upon the fact that nothing can be a standard of value without being obtainable in the market. It is a truism, for how can we gauge a standard of value except by the result of supply and demand, higgling in the market and how can this result be obtained unless there is a real supply? To find out the value, the standard of money, it must be offered in the market like any merchandise, and only its regular and permanent supply can enable us to effect a continual verification of its price-relations to other merchandise. If I at all insist on this self-evident truth, it is because I have met with the assertion that gold might be preserved as a standard of value for paper money, even though the paper were not convertible into gold, a single gold piece being sufficient to preserve the standard The persons who maintain such nonsense cannot see that the value of this gold piece is its purchasing power for goods, which can be estimated in no other way but by a market operation, and this single market operation may take our gold piece out of the market for ever Where is now the standard for all other market operations? It is self-evident that these market operations must be continuous, as the purchasing power of gold in general can be found only by its regular supply for other goods offered, in exchange In other words, except under the compulsion of the socialist State neither the value of gold nor that of any other commodity can be found in any other way but by the higgling of the market, which higgling implies the offer of the real article in quantities more or less corresponding to the demand, nothing can be a standard of value without being permanently in the market.

Vagaries of this kind arise mainly from an abuse of imagery, whose office is to illustrate, but not to prove. Measuring lengths and weights is an entirely different process from measuring values, though the poverty of our language forces us to the metaphorical use of the same term. We measure a length and a weight by finding out how many times the length or weight of a measuring tool of a certain length or weight is contained in the length or weight of the object whose length or weight we want to ascertain. We measure the price or value of a certain class of merchandise by finding out how many coins of a certain price or value the market is ready to offer for it, which is attained by a number of business operations in which the objects whose value we want to ascertain are exchanged for the measuring objects. It is a never ceasing, continually varying operation, absolutely depending on the mutual supply and demand of merchandise and money. If all the yard sticks in the market are burned, except one, this one stick can serve as well to ascertain the lengths of the cloth to be sold, and not a single yard of this cloth will be under- or over-measured in consequence. It is totally different, however, if the value measuring tool runs short. In the crisis of 1857 most staples in England fell 27% on the average within two weeks. Was it that cost of production had suddenly fallen? Certainly not, it was simply because the quantity of the legal tender money obtainable for these goods had suddenly decreased. Whenever it is shown that the supply of yardsticks or pound weights influences the length and weight of merchandise in the same way in which the supply and demand of coins influences the price of merchandise, the metaphor will have become a reality instead of a misleading illustration.

Criticizing standards of value can be productive of little good unless something better than the existing ones is proposed, for even an inferior standard is better than none at all. From the negative part of my work I therefore now proceed to the positive. From the pulling down business, I come to the constructive department.

The money of the first class has been found wanting. The money of the second class is only money of the third class burdened with an unnecessarily expensive raw material. Instead of putting the money stamp on cheap paper it is affixed to expensive silver, copper, nickel, or whatever material coins are made of. Much labor is wasted, and for all that, forgery is easier than in the case of paper money, the raw material of which can be prepared in a special way with water marks, and other distinctions, which are imitable by paper makers only, and their trade cannot so easily be followed in secret as that of the coiner.

J. Shield Nicholson, in "A Treatise on Money," says (p. 220) "As to forgery, it is a curious fact that in Scotland spurious sovereigns are more frequently met with than forged £1 notes, and the art of engraving notes has made much progress since England had £1 notes in circulation (1826) "

Del Mar, in his "Science of Money," says "The silk-threaded distinctive fibre-paper, the water-marks, the printing in colors, the highly artistic vignettes, the geometrical lathe work, the numbers, the signatures, and other mechanical safeguards of the modern paper-note render it far more difficult to imitate than coin "

We shall now pass on to class 3 *Token Money* Many economists fail to see that this money is of an absolutely different nature from the money of the first class, from commodity money For instance, Dr C F Taylor, when he says that the present idea of money "is like writing a deed to a house on a plate of gold of equal value with the house It is an enormous waste Money is a title to wealth, and money made of gold and silver is just like the titles to property written on gold and silver " In this he absolutely misconceives the nature of our gold money, for this money is no title to wealth, but a marketable commodity which is bartered for other commodities It is true that certain peculiarities, especially the stamp, and our legal tender laws have made it the most marketable of all commodities, but for all that its value is that of the commodity it is composed of no more nor less Mr Taylor's argument applies to money of the second class, which practically is token money printed on an expensive raw material, a material in some cases almost as valuable as the merchandise bought with the money This certainly is unmitigated folly Either we live under a reign of trust and confidence, of order and good faith—in this case token money, printed on a valueless material and issued under certain precautions, yet to be discussed, is the best money in the world Or we are anarchistic barbarians, distrusting ourselves and our government—in this case no money is good enough which is not a merchandise sufficiently valuable, without its form and stamp, to purchase as much in the market as we gave for it, and only money of the first class will do this Money of the second class ought never to be produced at all, except in small coins found more convenient than paper counters of the same value, so that the greater convenience warrants the extra cost

The objection, often made against token money, belongs to the intrinsic value domain which I have already exhibited at its real worth But even on the principle that value is a relation, it seems impossible to compare a thing which has no market value at all with real wealth, with merchandise of any kind At least, such is the objection made by men like Professor Karl Knies (Heidelberg), who has written valuable books on money and credit According to him, money must be a merchandise, because you can as little measure the value of a commodity by anything else but the value of another commodity as you can measure a length without something that has a length

We might agree with the learned gentleman without, in consequence, being compelled to exclude inconvertible paper money from the money category. What is the autograph of a celebrated man? What is a postage stamp even when cancelled by the post office? Are they commodities or not? Both sell as merchandise in the market and Professor Knies cannot take their merchandise quality from them. He will also have to agree with me that their merchandise or market value in no way depends on the amount of labor they embody *

To a certain extent their value depends on their scarcity, for an autograph which can be had by the million or a common cancelled postage stamp which can be had anywhere for the asking, are practically worthless, even if the former is in the handwriting of the most celebrated man, or if the other has the most beautiful picture impressed on it. But scarcity alone does not give value to an autograph, for the signature of a boor who wrote his name once in his life does not gain any value thereby. The only real element of value in an economic sense in these, as in all cases, is supplied by the market, by supply and demand

It is the price which the market is ready to pay. This makes a picture of Raphael valuable in our markets, while among the negroes of Central Africa it might not fetch as much as its canvas without the painting on it. This gives value to the autograph, to certain cancelled postage stamps, and to the piece of paper money. There is no difference in kind from an economic point of view between the mercantile value of Raphael's Sistine Madonna, an autograph, a cancelled or uncancelled postage stamp, and an inconvertible bank or treasury note. Their mercantile value is what they will fetch in the market. The motives of the buyers have as little to do with the matter as in any other case. A race-horse which has just won the Derby will equally be a merchandise whether bought with the intention of making sausages from it or of winning races through its help. Nor will the merchandise character of a piece of paper be changed in the least whether it is bought because a great artist painted something on its surface because a great man appended his signature to some words written on it or because the Government printed a certain text and applied a certain stamp. Neither does it make any difference whether the picture is bought for its artistic value or for its scarcity, for the purpose of adorning a drawing-room or of completing a collection. The economic classification of a postage stamp or bank-note does not change in the least whether they are bought for a collector's album or if the one is used to prepay a letter and the other to purchase goods. The fact that a certain piece of paper printed with certain signs is accepted

---

* Professor Senior says very correctly 'Any cause of limiting supply is just as effective a cause of value in an article as the necessity for labor for its production. The cost of producing money is only important as affecting the supply. Limit the supply and it does not matter whether there be any cost of production or not.'

MONEY 101

as money at a certain price in the market does not change its commodity character, and in so far, we might as well have refrained
from dividing money into three classes In thus dividing it, we do
not pretend that the money of our third class is not as much a
commodity as our money of the first class, but merely that, whereas
money of the first class maintains its market value after it ceases to
be used as money—a new gold eagle being worth ten dollars, even
if sold as bullion—the money of the third class loses its market
value after losing its money quality Even this is only true within
certain limits, for if gold coins cease to be money after gold has
been demonetized, then value as bullion will no doubt decrease
thereby, and paper money though demonetized, may still conserve
a value for collectors or amateurs of certain classes of wall-paper

In this way, I maintain that token money is money even according to the German professor's limitation But if, according to
a common saying, the best proof of the pudding is in the eating,
the best proof of the money quality of inconvertible paper notes
must be that they actually pass as money in many countries of the
earth Facts, however, have no power over academicians They
often act like the physician who had declared a patient incurable,
and who, when the man had the impudence to recover, in spite of
the doctorial dictum, quietly told him, "Scientifically you are dead,
sir!" Or our learned professor may imitate one of his colleagues,
who, when shown that facts did not agree with his theory, replied,
"So much the worse for the facts!"

It is, however, insufficient to prove that paper money exists
scientifically as well as practically, we have to show that it is a
better money than our metal money, or any money of our first and
second classes. The general opinion is that paper money has been
a failure Gold has fluctuated considerably, but it never has shown
such variations of value as most of the paper moneys we are acquainted with As a warning example, three different historic cases
are usually produced Law s bank paper, the French Assignats, and
the notes of the American confederacy From parity with gold to no
value at all, are fluctuations which no commodity money ever experienced, and it is not to be wondered at that, with all their drawbacks, our gold and silver currencies, are generally considered as
superior to paper currency The ground thus taken seems unassail-
able, for the money of our first two classes can never lose its value
to such an extent as paper money, but for all that, I intend to prove
that paper money can be made a more stable standard of value than
gold, silver, or bimetallic money

Adam Smith, M'Culloch, Ricardo, Tooke, Stuart Mill, Jevons,
and other great authorities have freely acknowledged, and the facts
of every-day life have proved, that paper notes, though inconvertible
into gold, if made legal tender, can be kept at par with gold coins
under certain conditions, i e, they take the place of gold coins withdrawn from circulation. 15¾ million pounds of notes issued by the

Bank of England are not backed by gold, and yet they are at par with gold, as they will always be required for internal circulation That paper money has often been of great benefit—even where it did not keep at par with gold—is also well known.

R. H Patterson says in "The Economy of Capital" (p 447) "How did England manage from 1797 to 1815, when there was hardly a guinea in circulation? That period was the most trying which the British Empire ever came through, a period remarkable for a great expansion of our trade and commerce, nevertheless, though gold almost disappeared from circulation, no difficulty was found in settling the foreign exchanges and the Government was even able besides to obtain large sums of metallic money to pay and feed our armies abroad and to subsidize those of other states."

The difficulty remains of finding the exact margin for the quantity of inconvertible paper money which can be kept floating at par. Must not the paper depreciate, when a certain amount required for internal circulation is overstepped, when, according to Gresham's law—that the bad money drives out the good—the gold coins have disappeared, and gold has to be bought at a premium for outside payments?

The history of *American Greenbacks* has shown this very clearly; for it is an exaggeration or downright falsehood, which has helped more than anything else to discredit paper money, to contend that what brought greenbacks into disrepute, what finally reduced their gold-purchasing power to almost one-third of their nominal value, was the law which made the interest of certain loans and the custom duties payable in gold These people do not reflect for one moment what the loans were contracted for. At that time many goods required by the country, especially for war purposes, could not be produced fast enough within the States, and had to be bought outside where greenbacks were not accepted, but where gold or other salable merchandise of some kind were demanded in exchange. Now for the time the merchandise or gold thus demanded could not be produced in sufficient quantity, and money had to be borrowed abroad to pay for the passive trade balance. The parties who lent this money wanted their capital and interest guaranteed in gold, for nobody could tell whether greenbacks would ever procure them gold at their face value or goods at a corresponding price, when even the very continuance of the Union was in question So the foreign loans had to be made payable in gold, capital and interest, and it became necessary to ensure a sufficient gold revenue to pay for the incurred debts. It is true the Government might have accomplished this otherwise than by making the duties payable in gold These duties might have been made payable in greenbacks, with which the Government would have bought in the market the gold it required But foreign exchanges naturally were against a country which had an unfavorable balance of trade to pay for and no gold in stock for the purpose. Gold had to be borrowed in some way or other at its market price, which grew with the demand for it The Government's financial measures had nothing to do with the premium thus paid for gold, which was produced by the foreign exchanges. The only difference would have been that instead of paying duties in gold which they had to purchase at a premium with greenbacks, the importers would have to pay their duties in greenbacks, but the amount of the duty would have been raised sufficiently to enable the Government to purchase the gold it needed The only difference would have been to force the importers to provide the Government with enough greenbacks to buy gold, instead of having to buy the gold themselves Greenbacks were bound to fall in value in either case, as long as their issue exceeded a certain quantity demanded for internal circulation. Still, their fall would never have been so considerable if the Government had not committed the folly of authorizing the so-called *"National Banks"* to issue a currency of their own, even making them a present of the interest profit thus obtained. This concession added unnecessarily to the inflation

The friends of paper money would do well to profit by an experience daily realized in any department of reform work the experience that exaggeration and radicalism overshoot their mark The greatest enemies of a rational currency are those radical apostles of paper money who want it issued to any amount, secured by real estate This class of currency reformers finds its principal adherents among land-owning farmers, who thus hope to obtain from the State cheap money on mortgages Such a concession would merely add to the unearned increment by forcing up the prices of land, and thus the compensation which the community would have to pay some day when the people take back their own; but leaving this aside, the whole plan shows an entire ignorance of the currency question There can be only one kind of security behind money, and that is its wealth-purchasing power.

If real estate is the wealth on which the money is issued, the money, if issued beyond the needs of circulation, is only good if the real estate can at any time be obtained for it, which is not at all the intention of the men who propose the plan They do not dream of handing over their farms and houses to anyone who presents for redemption the money lent to them on such security They merely want to keep this money for an indefinite time, or at least for an extended period, at a low rate of interest. Their real estate is not in the market for the money they received, in fact, usually it is not in the market at all, most certainly not at those very periods when people want to see something substantial for the paper in their hands—the times of crises and panics, for at such moments their property would certainly not fetch more than was borrowed on it, and probably not even that Thus the security is no security at all in the only sense in which a security is needed, i e, to keep up the full purchasing power of money, the security that its issue does not exceed the quantity of merchandise offered for money in the market

Can we blame gold fanatics if they stick to their gold standard as long as experience justifies them in the belief that gold, with all its fluctuations of value, is after all not subject to such excesses in this direction as most of the paper currencies on record? But they leave out of sight the fact that not a single case is known in modern history where an inconvertible paper money was issued under normal conditions, for the purpose of providing a better money than metal coins Invariably such money was issued in times of wars or revolutions, or at least as the result of acute financial distress Under such conditions it could hardly be expected that the issue would conform to rules adapted to maintain a fixed standard of value for the paper, which in no way proves that such rules might not be devised.   •

On the contrary, a closer investigation will show us the feasibility *A perfect standard of value* for money is reached when the average price of merchandise does not vary, and this can only be obtained where the quantity of the money supply in the market adapts itself to the demands of the market, where more money appears when prices tend to go down, and where the surplus disappears when the tendency is in an upward direction This is impossible in the case of metal money, whose supply depends on the goodwill of those who control the bullion market, but it is within the reach of possibility in the case of paper money, which can be supplied to any amount at the shortest notice, whose issue can thus be adapted to the market's exigencies, more money being issued when prices fall, and money being retired when prices rise Thus, while *our present law fixes the price of gold, the new task is to fix the average price of goods through a regulation of the money circulation* All those commodities which constitute an appreciable portion of the general turnover are tabulated, their prices being multiplied with their turnover The addition of the sums thus obtained gives us the average figure which has to guide us in the issue or withdrawal of paper money.

Before I quote from "Honest Money," by Arthur l. Fonda, of Denver, Colorado, a detailed description of his scheme, I want to say that, though perhaps its best exponent, Fonda is by no means the originator. A number of other proponents are mentioned in "Rational Money," by Professor Frank Parsons (C F Taylor, Philadelphia), and in "The Measurement of General Exchange-Value," by Correa Moylan Walsh (Macmillan, 1901), though both lists are far from complete For instance, the article of Professor Marshall, of Cambridge, is not mentioned, which appeared in the "Contemporary Review," of March, 1887, nor does either of the two authors speak of Silvio Gesell, one of the most energetic propagators of the principle, whose first publication on the matter dates from 1893, the same year in which Fonda came out with the plan; nor of Professor Alfred Russel G. Wallace, who proposed the

scheme in 1898 It is probable that such a simple and valuable
method of obtaining a money with an invariable standard has recommended itself to many others unknown to fame

The "Arena," of September 1897, published a reproduction of
a Treasury Note issued in 1780 in the State of Massachusetts,
promising payment not of a fixed quantity of gold, but of a sum
equivalent to the gold proceeds of given quantities of corn, beef,
wool, and leather This multiple standard was intended as a safe-
guard against fluctuations in the value of the currency, and is
described by the editor as the most nearly honest piece of money
ever issued in a civilized state. This strange money points in the
direction of a proposal made by W Stanley Jevons in 'Money,"
and, it seems, as far back as 1822, by Joseph Lowe, and 1833 by
G Poulet Scrope.

The plan was that of using the multiple price standard, not to
regulate the money, but as a standard of value for money contracts,
by increasing the amount due if the higher sum of the table indicates a depreciation of money, and decreasing the amount if the
reverse takes place Only mere theorizers could ever make such a
proposal; any business man would at once have seen its impracti-
cability Its adoption would keep all financial engagements in a state
of perpetual fluidity. The amount of pensions, salaries, fines, taxes,
duties, debts, in fact of financial engagements of any sort, would
fluctuate continually according to the results of this kind of tabular
standard Just imagine what that means! A man has to pay his
butcher bill of last year, another has signed a promissory note, and
so on through thousands of mutual engagements of daily life.
Before any payment is made the tabular standard must be consulted; a discount has to be taken off or a premium is added, according to this tabular standard; and these complicated calculations
are to be carried on daily, hourly, and mostly by men to whom the
job of multiplying quantities with prices and adding the products,
when they buy a bill of goods, is already sufficiently complicated.
When they have borrowed money, the calculation of the interest
they have to pay is hard enough for them, and now they are also
to add or deduct percentages varying with the money standard.
Most of them will have to rely on the cleverer people who understand "this new fad"; and we know what that often means Adding
another trap for the unwary and ignorant, and heaping additional
work on everybody, would cause this tabular standard to be looked
at as such an unmitigated curse that people would rather put up
with all the dangers of our monetary fluctuations than correct them
in this insane fashion.

The general abhorrence of inconvertible paper money entertained by most English economists of that period, alone can explain
how intelligent men should have passed by the only practical application of the tabular standard to stumble into such impossible
proposals Had they been less prejudiced they would easily have

seen that, instead of using their tabular standard to change the amount of money obligations leaving the money circulation itself untouched, the obligations might have been left untouched by changing the money circulation according to the tabular standard for the purpose of balancing the variations of the latter. By thus steadying the price of merchandise, the value or price of money, its purchasing power, remained invariable, and money obligations could safely be left alone. These enemies of paper money ought to have seen that the danger they were afraid of—Inflation—can be guarded against by means of the very instrument of which they wanted to make such a preposterous use. Just as a fall of prices demands the issue of more money, so prices rising above the normal at once indicate that too much money has been issued. Business men, members of Congress, or chambers of commerce through their experts can thus easily find out at any time whether an under- or overissue has taken place, and whether an increase or a restriction of the money circulation is called for, thus controlling the parties entrusted with the note issues.

Fonda says "Let a commission be appointed by Congress to select a sufficient number of commodities, say one hundred, to be used as a standard of value. This selection should comprise the commodities most largely bought and sold and most independent of each other in their values, preference should be given to those which are products of this country—but foreign products should also be included—and to those which are reliable in quality and of which the prices are regularly quoted—such, for instance, as wheat, corn, oats, rye, barley, cotton, wool, tobacco, rice, gold, silver, lead, copper, tin, iron, steel, cotton and woolen cloths leather, hides, lumber of various kinds, sugar, beef, pork, mutton, etc. The aim should be, while not including all commodities, which would of course be impossible, to include a sufficient number and of such varied kinds as to fairly represent all. Less than a hundred might be sufficient, or it might be better to take more than that number. With the aid of statisticians, the average price of each of the commodities selected, in their principal markets for a few years past, should be ascertained and tabulated. The commodities, of course, should be of specified grade and quality, and in a specified market, but not necessarily the same market for all. The length of time over which the average of prices should extend would be determined as closely as possible by the average length of time that existing indebtedness had run (The reason for this will be explained later.) In addition to the average prices of each commodity, the approximate amount or value annually consumed in this country should be ascertained.

From these data, a table should be prepared showing the amount one dollar would have purchased, on the average, of each of the commodities for the time determined, and from this a final table should be made taking such multiples of the amounts found in the previous table as should represent their proportionate consumption—in other words. their relative importance in trade

For example, suppose the time selected were five years, as representing twice the average time existing debts had run; that during that time one dollar would have bought, on the average, 1 25 bushels of wheat, or 3 bushels of corn, or 100 pounds of pig iron, or ten pounds of cotton, all of specified grade in specified markets; that, further, the importance of each of these commodities in the trade of this country was in the approximate proportions of 5, 3, 2 and 1, respectively. Then the final table would show

$$5 \times 1\ 25 = 6.25 \text{ bushels of wheat} = \$5\ 00$$
$$3 \times 3 = 9 \text{ bushels of corn} = 3\ 00$$
$$2 \times 100 = 200 \text{ lbs. of pig iron} = 2\ 00$$
$$1 \times 10 = 10 \text{ lbs. of cotton} = 1.00$$

Total $11 00

Considering these four commodities only, the dollar, as the unit of value of our system, would be defined by law as one eleventh of the sum of the values of 6 25 bushels of wheat, 9 bushels of corn, 200 pounds of pig iron, and 10 pounds of cotton. This illustrates the method of arriving at, and the definition of the standard Extended to all the commodities selected, the definition would be the same with the substitution of the proper figures This would evidently provide a standard that would closely represent the average purchasing power of one dollar for the time selected. As to the length of time over which this average should extend, if there were no such thing as existing debts, it would clearly be of little importance what the value of the unit selected was, just as it would be of no importance now whether the foot or the pound had been originally fixed at greater or less than their present length and weight, but because of the vast amount of existing indebtedness, the value of the unit that is to be made permanent should be most carefully fixed at the value it had when such indebtedness was created, so as to do as little violence as possible to outstanding obligations The fact that in the past the debtors have been wronged to the advantage of creditors, by an increasing value of money, furnishes no excuse for a reversal of this injustice and a wronging of creditors by permanently fixing the value of the dollar at what it was twenty or thirty years ago The debtors and creditors of to-day are not the same individuals who stood in those relations in the past, and two wrongs do not make a right

The object should be, therefore, to determine as closely as possible how many years, on the average, existing debts have run. and take twice that period for the total length of time over which prices should be determined This would doubtless work a slight injustice to those whose debts are of a longer standing—though a less injustice than they are subject to now—and would be a slight injustice to the creditors of more recent date; but as some time would be occupied in getting the system to work, so that the actual value of the money would correspond with the standard, the injustice would be more or less distributed, and would at most be slight   It would be substituting only a gradual rise in prices for the decline that has been going on, until prices were back to the level of perhaps two or three years before, and then fixing the level at that point.

After the statistical work outlined above has been completed, Congress should repeal the present monetary laws, substituting for the definition of the "dollar" the new definition agreed upon   It should then provide a currency or money to take the place of that now used. This currency should be a paper money similar to our "greenbacks" It should be a legal tender for all debts public and private (except, of course, such as by their terms are payable in gold). In fact, the only difference between such notes and existing "promises to pay" of the government would be that the new notes, as is evident from the new definition of the dollar, would be promises to pay *a definite value*, and not a definite quantity of one commodity of uncertain value.

The notes could be made redeemable *in any commodity at its current market price*, and should contain a pledge, on the faith of the government, that the amount of the currency in circulation would be at all times so controlled by the government that its actual purchasing power would conform to the standard on which it was based

To carry out this pledge, it would be necessary to have a small corps of statisticians who would receive and tabulate the current market prices for each day, and who would calculate therefrom the aggregate prices of the specified quantities of all the commodities constituting the standard—in similar form to the final table before mentioned, and of which an example has been given If this aggregate for any day were more or less than the total of the standard table, it would show that prices in general had risen or fallen, and some money should be withdrawn from circulation, or more issued until the daily total corresponded with the standard total.

Doubtless several plans might be proposed for putting such a money into circulation and controlling its volume The following seems to commend itself by its simplicity and effectiveness of control for at least a part, if not all, of the issues, viz The money to be loaned by the government on approved securities, such as their own bonds, other bonds of states, counties, cities, railroads, etc ; warehouse receipts gold and silver deposits etc. First-class commercial paper, when guaranteed by solvent banks, might also be taken, especially in case of threatened panic In short, such securities as would be considered the safest for banks and trust companies to loan upon, all under such proper restrictions and safeguards as would insure their safety as collateral. The rate of interest charged for such loans to be a *variable one,* decreasing as prices tended to fall, and increasing as they tended to rise, and without other restrictions This would absolutely control the volume of money, within narrow limits, since more would be borrowed at a lower, and less at a higher rate, of interest, yet the control would be elastic. While the loans should be for a short time, they could be renewed at pleasure, and as often as desired, at the current rate of interest, the security remaining good

Such a plan would not interfere with general banking business to any considerable extent In order to prevent monopoly, the loans should be open to all on equal terms, and the list of approved securities acceptable as collateral should be made as wide as possible, consistent with safety. It would probably be found by experience, however, that the principal borrowers direct from the government would be the banks, who would reloan the money (at a sufficiently higher rate to pay them for their trouble) to their customers, on local securities, commercial paper, etc, as they now do The legal tender provision of the notes would be necessary only as specifying the medium in which payment of debts should be made, to prevent misunderstanding, and for the protection of debtor and creditor alike The new dollar being a quantity of value, and not of a specified commodity, a loan might be returned in any commodity of that value but for some such provision The provision could in no case wrong a creditor, for what he would receive in payment for the debt would be a positive guarantee to deliver him the *value* specified in any commodity he chose Making the money redeemable in any of the commodities on which it is based would be only a form, and might be omitted, it is suggested merely as obviating any objections to an irredeemable money Of course, the government would never be called upon to so redeem money, since the holder of it could exchange it for the commodity wanted in the open market to equal advantage No reserve of commodities of any kind need be kept, therefore, for redemption purposes One great difference between this plan and existing systems will, of course, be seen at once the present system promises a definite amount of gold, and must, therefore, keep a gold reserve, but as no one really wants the gold, except in exchange for commodities, this plan proposes to do away with the necessity of a gold reserve by guaranteeing that the money can be directly exchanged for such commodities at the current market price—which is all that can be done with the gold*—and that the average purchasing power of such money shall not vary as gold does" ("Honest Money," pages 158-173)

The nationalization of commerce, proposed in Chapter VIII, would make the new paper actually redeemable in merchandise obtainable from the issuer, like the exchange notes of the co-operative

---

* This ought to read "could be done with gold if, in consequence of its present monopoly position, it had not become an instrument of extortion and blackmail"

societies or the Mutual Banks of Chapter VII The State in such a case would pay for its merchandise purchases with the new money and would accept it in payment

Even without the centralization of commerce the general accessibility of the new money can be secured through People's Banks on the Raiffeisen system, of which the first was founded in 1849, in the Westerwald, Germany—the mother of over a thousand offspring These banks, together with another kind of people's bank on the Schultze-Delitzsch system, and the different kinds of co-operative institutions organized by the people, possessed, in 1892, a capital of 1,250 million dollars Though the Raiffeisen banks lend on personal security, the losses were only about 60 cents per member in that year As they are based on an extensive or unlimited liability, each member watches his fellow-members, which is not difficult as the members usually live close together

In Italy, 28.68% of the members were then engaged in small industries and trades, 8 40% were artisans, 15 40% were school teachers, Government employees, etc , 19 08% small cultivators and 3 18% laborers The balance were agriculturists, manufacturers and traders, or persons without a calling One thousand societies existed with over 150 million lire capital (30 million dollars) They lent out over 500 million lire, and had about 400,000 members. The losses in Milan, a society with $2,500,000 capital and reserve, had not reached ten cases in twelve years

A leading feature of these banks has been the capitalization of profits, a principle especially to be recommended to co-operative societies in general The security offered by these banks can best be concluded from the fact that in 1866 and 1870, the two war years when deposits were withdrawn wholesale from other banks, they were actually pressed upon the Raiffeisen banks, without a time limit, as long as they proved trustworthy and used the money for productive purposes The Rhineland law courts even allowed trust money to be lent them

How much greater will be this security where the money due does not consist in a scarce commodity, but is expanding with the demand! These banks could be the main instrument through which the state issues the new money to the producers and traders, as long as trade is not nationalized Their collective security is good enough to procure them the loans of all the new money which will be wanted as a cover of their check accounts

Then there will be the Postal Savings Banks, which do such splendid service in some other countries and which we are sure to get as soon as the only argument against them in this country is put aside· the personal interest of our private bankers, just as we shall yet obtain a parcel post when the six reasons of Postmaster Wanamaker, why we should not have it have been met, the six express companies The new Postal Savings Bank, with a branch in every post office in the country, would not only accept deposits, but might also grant loans against certain specified securities, which, in case of need, it might obtain from the State's money-issuing department. It could also attend to free transfers of accounts all over the country, as it is doing in Austria-Hungary, where, in 1906, 1500 million dollars were transferred through the Postal Savings Bank, and 3700 million dollars were paid with the checks drawn on this institution Switzerland copied this excellent system in 1906, and Germany intends to do so now.

Professor Erwin Nasse sees a certain difficulty in the work of exactly finding the quantities of the different articles which are to form the basis of the calculations. Others have discussed the question whether wages, tools of production and land values, i e., rent, ought to be included in the lists. In any case, we shall never quite eliminate all sources of inaccuracy, but by the wanderer lost in the wilderness, even the rough indications of the native he meets, as to direction and distance, will be welcomed. He will not refuse to avail himself of them because a map with exact delineations would be preferable Even an approximate price standard is better than none at all, and certainly no system of tables made out on the best available data would hide from us fluctuations like those, for instance, which, in the English crisis of 1857, caused the prices of the principal staples to fall 27% within two weeks, not because their cost of production had decreased so much within that short period, but because money had suddenly become exceptionally scarce. Patterson, in "The Economy of Capital," mentions cotton, going down from 7 to 43½% for the different numbers between August 15 and November 5, 1866, in consequence of the scarcity of money (p 366) It would never do to give up the attainable because perfection seems out of reach However, I do not think the difficulty quite so great as Nasse finds it New Zealand gives fairly exact statistics of the turnover made in the different trades, and there is no reason why other countries should not succeed as well. Of course, we would not take *retail prices*, but the prices obtained by the producer If we gave retail prices, we should only increase the total of each article in about the same proportion without affecting the result. If prices vary in different parts of the country, we should take the middle price *Raw materials* would figure several times in the list wherever they are used as the component of other merchandise, but so would manufactures which enter into the composition of other fabrics, such as leather in shoes and saddlery wares, cotton thread in cotton cloth, etc. This can only affect the quantity relation which each article can claim; but as the same addition to quantity takes place in all branches of manufacture it does not sensibly affect the final result. It makes no difference whether in our lists the price of every article is multiplied with half or double the quantity· the average will not change thereby. Neither can it well be avoided that some manufactures which enter into the composition of others will not appear in the list, because they are produced in the same factory, and thus do not pass through the market, as, for instance, where the yarn is spun and woven in the same works or where the tannery and boot factory are in one hand and the product thus will only figure once where others manufactured by different firms are counted twice. This does not matter much, however, as such causes of error will occur in different branches, and thus will compensate each other in a certain measure. *Land values and rents*, on the other hand, ought not to figure in the list, for their relation to the value of money is not the same as that of the products of labor. Though both rise with the rise of prices and the depreciation of money, it does not follow that the opposite tendency will force them down, for the simple reason that the fall of prices in our times is mostly due to the greater productivity of labor in consequence of technic improvements, and that this fall has by no means kept pace with the increase of this productivity. The balance appears to a small extent in a rise of wages, to a larger extent in the increase of profits, including interest, but chiefly displays itself in the rise of rent. Rent and land values have risen much faster than the value of our metal money, which is easily accounted for by the fact that, though the quantity of our metal money does not increase so rapidly as the productivity of labor, still it increases quicker than the surface of available land. The price of the latter, therefore, is forced up more rapidly. The inclusion of land values and rents in our tabular standard would therefore simply falsify the result. We might see prices of goods fall with rising land values and rents, and if we included the latter in the tabular standard they would produce a corresponding counter effect on the influence of the price fall, and thus at all events prevent a sufficient issue of new money. On the other hand, a new issue of money would cause such an upward tendency of land values that the currency restriction this would entail would overstep the real necessity.

Wages ought not to figure in the tables, because they form a part of cost price. As C. M. Walsh correctly remarks, "what laborers give in return for their hire is not the labor, which nobody wants, but the product of that labor." To count wages, after having counted the product paid for with these wages would have the same effect as the double counting of raw materials. Of course, Fonda's plan of lending out the new money and of regulating its issue through the interest rate, a flood-gate lowered and raised according to the demand, is meant only for that portion of the money circulation which is in excess of a certain minimum below which the demands of the market can never fall. The money required below this line need not be lent out but can be paid out for public improvements, for instance the construction of railways, canals etc.

It is questionable whether the regulation of the money circulation need ever entail a withdrawal of money from circulation. In all probability it will only mean a restriction of the issue. My reason for believing this rests on the steady increase of productive

power, population and trade, liable to assume much greater proportions than those we are used to in our time with its unnatural
fetters on circulation, mostly due to our currency system More
currency will thus be demanded all along, and a rise in prices would
in most cases not demand a retirement of money from circulation,
but a temporary raising of the interest flood-gate which governs the
volume of the daily issue

That, as Tooke and Newmarch have proved by many facts,
an increase in the money circulation does not necessarily bring
about a depreciation, is also illustrated by the case of Brazil, given
in the report of the Committee on Indian Currency, of 1893 (par
92) "The case of Brazil is perhaps the most remarkable of all, as
showing that a paper currency without a metallic basis if the credit
of the country is good, can be maintained at a high and fairly steady
exchange, although it is absolutely inconvertible, and has been
increased by the act of the Government out of all proportion to
the growth of population and of its foreign trade The case, it
need hardly be said, is not quoted as a precedent which is desirable
to follow The Brazilian standard is the milreis, the par gold of
which is 27d A certain number were coined, but have long since
left the country, and the currency is, and has since 1864 been, inconvertible paper The inconvertible paper was more than doubled
between 1865 and 1888, but the exchange was about the same at
the two periods, and very little below par or 27d " Besides, an increase in the money issue may not mean an increase of the money
circulation The money may be kept in the vaults of the Treasury
or State Bank, at the disposal of its depositors who opened a check
account with it The checks thus drawn may be the main circulating medium as they are in our time

The method proposed by Fonda to effect a regulation of the
money issue· the raising of the interest rate, or even a suspension
of loans, may meet with a certain prejudice, because we meet with
the application of this method under absolutely opposite conditions,
where it has an aggravating effect At present the rate of interest
is raised and credit is limited to a minimum in times of financial
crises which force the banks to such steps These steps in their
turn intensify the crises, no matter how much they may be demanded
in the interest of the banks The mere proposal of raising the interest rate must therefore call up unpleasant associations A closer
observation, however, shows us that the new conditions produce
totally different effects To-day we find the interest rate raised to
an abnormal height at the beginning of a crisis in consequence of
the scarcity of money Under the reign of the new currency the
reverse happens for the scarcity of money finding its expression
in a general fall of prices government forces more money into the
market, by reducing the interest rate so as to stimulate a demand
for the new money issues At the very time which sees our banks
lock up their money and raise their interest rate or refuse loans

altogether, a flood of new money submerges the market at reduced interest rates, to spur on enterprises, so as to enliven the demand for labor and its products The raising of the interest rate, on the other hand, comes when money is plentiful Thus at the very time when now the rate is lowest, stimulating speculation and forcing up prices, a rise of the rate acts like the drawing of a bridle to regain control over a runaway horse The supply of money is reduced and the prices of goods return to their normal height.

One objection will have to be met before we pass over to the effects of the new currency on the process of circulation in the next chapter the influence of the trusts on prices apparently partly independent of the money circulation, which has been exhibited in this country during the past six years Though the relation of the money stock to the turnover of merchandise has been an ominous one, prices have been artificially forced up by the great combinations, and even in the height of the financial crisis we are passing through, while I am adding these lines in the first days of January, 1908, no noticeable reductions have so far been made, except in copper, in which an unprecedented overproduction had taken place Pretty well everywhere else the combines have been able to meet any lessening of the demand caused by the money stringency by a limitation of the output, without a reduction in prices The main cause for this phenomenon must be looked for in the fact that it is not the quantity of legal tender money, but that of the currency which has an effect on prices, as has been shown before The money quantity comes into play only indirectly, through its influence on credit and consequently on the currency Now the financial power of the great combines has enabled them to force up the credit building to an unheard-of height, as the bank statistics of 1907 have shown us; and even now, during the financial crisis, this power has not entirely lost its hold Independent of this however, it is evident that where a number of combining business giants have obtained such a power over the production of a country that they can hold back competition at lower prices where financial causes tend to force on such competition, we can not expect to see economic laws produce their usual effects The monstrous growths are not doing their nefarious work in this field alone The continuance of their despotic power might not merely render the best currency system inoperative, but might have far more deleterious consequences, through their interposition against the natural effects of supply and demand, by curtailing the supply and preventing its adaption to the demand, through an adjustment of prices Chapters VII and VIII will show how such obstructive tactics can be dealt with, without special legislation.

CHAPTER IV.

CIRCULATION.

The currency is the economic body's life blood.

THE preceding chapter describes a money that can be created free from two defects of metallic currency It costs little to produce by dispensing with the immense cost of the precious metals. Its quantity can be regulated and thus kept from those changes in value to which all commodities, and especially scarce commodities like the precious metals, are unavoidably subject

We have seen how money preserves an unvarying standard of value, but we have not obtained any information how it could be made more easily accessible to the money users than coins. This will be the object of the present chapter.

We have to consider two kinds of money circulation One is that from the consumer to the producer, and from him as a consumer, to another producer, and so forth. We include here the intermediate stages of the middleman and of purchases not meant for direct consumption, but temporarily to help production, such as the purchase of tools and raw materials, freightage, etc.

Another kind of circulation is the payment of money for land, mortgages, bonds, or similar investments I shall try to illustrate the great difference between the two kinds of circulation by the transactions that take place between Plutus, one of our multi-millionaires and two other parties The one is Giles, a producer who obtains cash from Plutus for some kind of merchandise, the second is another producer, Jones, who receives money from Plutus for a piece of land.

In the case of Giles, circulation is not impeded; what has been paid out by him as a producer comes back to him, for though sales may occasionally entail a loss, as a rule the producer who sells goods to a consumer makes wages or even a profit This is well understood, so well that it has been assumed to apply to the other kind of transaction likewise. Our economists could find no difference—as far as the process of circulation is concerned—between the transaction in which the capitalist buys directly or indirectly from the producer any product of labor, and the one in which he merely pays or lends to the producer the money for something which is not a product of labor; in our illustration land. And yet the difference between the two transactions is ominous.

We assume that in the possession of Jones the land had been an instrument of credit His bank took a mortgage upon it, which has to be paid off when the land is sold; and thus the money obtained from Plutus merely takes the place of the money formerly obtained from the bank by Jones. No new money has been paid into his business funds, and not one single penny has been added to his purchasing power

"But," will be replied by our economists, "the credit given to Jones by the bank and repaid by him will now be given to some-one else, who will use it to purchase goods with, and we are prac-tically right in saying that, as far as the process of circulation is concerned it can make no difference whether this purchase has been made by the land-buying Plutus or by some other person to whom his money was passed over."

This would be true if the bank had to refuse further loans on good real estate security until the debt of Jones was repaid, but such is not the case—would only be the case if the bank merely lent out real money. We have seen that this is not the system of banks all the world over.

The loans and discounts of the banks and trust companies of the United States, including the savings banks, exceed ten billion dollars, while the total gold stock of the country hardly reaches one sixth of this amount. What they do is merely to lend the money, but mostly the money promises brought in by one set of people, to another set. They act as bookkeepers and credit insurance agents for the business people of the country, who indirectly thus lend each other their money, or rather their hope of getting money in case it is wanted, for comparatively little money passes or even exists in the country.

The whole arrangements remind me very much of a story I once read. The Mississippi had overflowed its banks. Hundreds of fine logs were rapidly drifting past a crowd of negroes who had gathered on the shore. They looked shiftlessly at the timber, when a white man, a stranger in those parts, addressed them.

"Boys," he said, "I will give every one of you as salvage one-half of the logs which he lands!"

With a will the men went into the water, and soon quite a number of valuable logs were piled on the shore. They took half of them for their labor, and the stranger took possession of his share and sold it to a neighboring sawmill.

"Fools, those negroes!" the reader will say. "Nothing pre-vented them from securing the timber for themselves, without giv-ing a share to a stranger, who had not moved a finger, and who had not the least claim on the timber."

Certainly; but, my dear friend, are you not acting in the same manner whenever you pay a bank for the right of an overdraft? The bank, in this case, only allows you to make use of your neigh-bor's labor or its products, whom you finally repay indirectly by the products of your own labor. The bank only does the service of a clearing-house for you. It provides the tokens required for this mutual exchange, and for this service, the work of bookkeeping and for the guarantee undertaken by them, the banks have en-riched themselves by billions. The mere fact of having as good as no money does not in the least deter our banks from giving credits from allowing debtors to draw checks, because they know that the checks will come in as deposits on the other side, and generally real money will neither be demanded, nor could it be paid if demanded in the generality of cases

The results, therefore, of the transactions between Plutus and Jones will be that a rich man, who does not overdraw his account at the bank, bought land, on the strength of which a poor man had drawn a certain amount of checks, which he now repays with the check obtained for his land from the rich purchaser. Thus the currency originally given to the capitalist by his rent or interest debtors does not return into circulation, as the transaction has not enabled the land seller to increase his right of check drawing. Jones merely repaid his debt to the bank, and there the matter ends

The debtors of a rich man pay him their interest or their rent The money, or the right of demanding money, has been paid to them by other workers, who expect to find employment through the continued circulation of this money, but they are disappointed The money has left the market, and it is kept out of the market, or, rather, a right of check drawing exercised before is now suspended Nothing has happened but a change in the basis of a given worker's check operations The check of Plutus simply took the place of the mortgage as the security upon which Jones' checks were drawn If land, bonds, or other securities of this kind, on which the banks allow overdrafts, were unlimited in amount, this would not matter, for someone else would obtain a credit on such security from the banks, and the checks drawn on this new account would take the place of the repaid overdraft in circulation. But the quantity of such securities is limited; and, while in normal times credit is not refused to those who can supply them, from year to year more of these securities come into possession of a class of people too rich to require credit, and who do not use them as a basis of credit money, of currency circulation, as the parties who sold them had done "It isn't money that is scarce, it's collateral '

In this way the accumulations of the rich disturb the equilibrium between supply and demand, in this way the means of circulation obtained by them does not return into circulation

The subject is too important and too new to meet full understanding at once, and yet without clear comprehension at this point, a vital part of the problem must remain an unsolved riddle. I therefore beg my readers not to skip, but, on the contrary, to thoroughly study, again and again, this momentous relation between wealth distribution and the supply of the circulating medium To give all possible help on my part, I shall now sum up the subject by condensing its principal features into as few sentences as possible.

M is the stock of the universally recognized legal tender money of the world, practically represented by 5 billion dollars of gold

coins and bullion Part of the stock circulates, part of it is
hoarded by parties who do not issue any credit money for it, and
the balance lies dormant in the vaults and safes of the banks, the
government treasuries and the business world to serve as the basis
of a thirty-fold credit currency circulation C (money promises or
representatives) To simplify, we shall leave the circulating real
money out of account as too insignificant when compared with the
total of the circulation, and also the hoards used or not used as a
basis of credit money, for this latter kind of money has practically
disappeared from the world for a time and we shall consider 30 C
as representing the whole circulation

Thirty C is not enough to supply a means of exchange sufficient
to enable the expansion of trade T, to keep step with that of
productive power P, so as to preserve its level with buying or
purchasing power B Unless $B = P$, commercial depressions and
want of employment are unavoidable Through improved machinery and other causes P doubles to 2 P, but B can only advance to
2 B if T can advance to 2 T This is only feasible if 30 C can advance to 60 C * (The increase of M itself through mining—after
abrasion, use in the arts and hoards not serving as the base of C
are deducted—is too insignificant' when compared with the
enormous increase of P and T to need consideration) Such an advance is dangerous, even where the best of securities are offered
as long as M alone is legal tender, for it signifies that 60 instead of
30 promises of money are to rest on one single M as their basis,
but let us suppose our capitalists risk this danger in normal times
where what they consider good security is supplied These securities (collaterals) are principally only of two kinds 1 land or
monopolies connected with it, and 2, the bonds of governments or
public bodies The latter may safely be left out of consideration
where such a large amount of new securities is required as the increase of 30 C to 60 C implies, though every year sees an average
issue all over the world of over $500,000,000 new government bonds
We must also take into account that a very large part of these
bonds are in, or gradually come into the possession of rich people
who do not use them as collaterals for credits

Nor are new collaterals needed; for—though the land surface
does not increase, land values—L—grow with P But as shown
in the case of Jones and Plutus, L is continually passing from the
possession of those who use it as a security for the issue of C into
that of men who require no credit In the chapter on interest, the
principal cause will be shown, which tends to accelerate this trans-

---

* Of course, this is not mathematically correct for a great deal depends
on the rapidity of the circulation The same amount of currency can supply
a much more extensive trade where telegraphs and railroads exist than
where more primitive modes of communication obtain But assuming an
existing intensity of the circulating process as remaining unchanged for the
time, my formula can safely be adopted

fer, and so increases the rapidity with which the gulf widens between the demand for larger quantities of C and the possibility of supplying the security, the collaterals, without which C is not forthcoming. The form which C takes is immaterial, whether it be that of overdrafts or bill discounting As C lags behind the demand, B, T, and P have to suffer, and the crisis is inevitable.

It is here where the land question sends its offshoots into the circulation problem and where land nationalization produces its most important effects The influence on the distribution of wealth, due to the monopolization of natural opportunities by a minority, can hardly be exaggerated, but this monopolization until now has directly interfered with employment only in exceptional cases as far as this country is concerned. As a rule, the land owner is willing to let the land at leases corresponding with the tenant's paying capacity Practically, private land ownership interferes with circulation only by transferring the principal credit basis, the best collaterals, from the possession of the masses, who used them for the extension of the credit circulation, into that of the few, who do not require any credit Thus credit is prevented from keeping pace with the increase of the turnover, at all events, of keeping pace as far as the narrow money basis finally permits

When the foregoing causes of the growing discrepancy between productive and purchasing power are well understood, the occurrence of crises will cease to excite surprise, the difficulty will be to understand how we can ever have good times as long as the described fundamental cause is at work. Even this, however, can easily be explained We must not forget that the real nature of the evil is almost absolutely unknown. A few students of economic science may have an inkling of the truth, but the masses, including our captains of industry and commerce, have come to look at commercial and financial crises somewhat in the light of meteorological phenomena, certain to occur at more or less regular intervals, forgotten as soon as they are over—just as a fine sunshine will make us turn out light-heartedly in thinner garments, unmindful of the fact that only yesterday we were caught in a shower. In the same way, the least sign of returning prosperity finds us all eager to make up for the depression we have just endured, and this very hopefulness must naturally have the effect of stimulating business It matters little what may have produced the first signs of reviving trade. It may be a war, with its destruction of labor's products, and its requirements of life and property annihilating armament, its withdrawal from the labor market of thousands of strong men, whose consumption temporarily increases, and whose absence from competition enables those who remain to obtain full and paying employment, and thus also to augment their consumption. Or there may have been expensive changes in armaments such as followed that onslaught of the *Merrimac* on the wooden ships of the Union fleet which introduced an era of armored ships;

or just as the Prussian victories in the sixties forced all nations to exchange the obsolete muzzle loader for modern guns. Or some great progress in the technic field, such as the last three decades experienced in electrotechnics, may have called forth a large demand for labor and products of labor. Or a San Francisco earthquake and fire may make room for new production, a Panama canal and new railroad constructions set labor in motion. No better proof of the general ignorance in this field can be supplied than the fact that the very phenomena here recognized as having a prophylactic effect are often proclaimed the causes of the crisis, we hear of "a frantic speculation which started new enterprises beyond our means; of the growing war and marine budget; of destructions through war, earthquakes and fires putting forth increased demands on our national capital"

Of which means, of which capital do such men speak? What was required for the production they mention? Certainly not labor and land; for where both are obtainable all other means of production are accessible. Machines, tools and means of transportation are also products of labor and land. Now, independent of the fact that even during the prosperity period thousands of workers looked in vain for paying employment, is not the very essence of the crisis found in the difficulty in which millions find themselves of securing a chance for the application of their productive power? And the land? Do not landowners look in vain for labor provided with the means of production—which in their turn are the outcome of labor and land—to make use of their land above and below the earth's surface? Their prices may be driven up by speculation but not beyond purchasing or renting power.

On the other hand, if as they pretend we had not enough capital at our disposal to replace all that wars and nature destroyed, or produce the new instruments of peace and war, how did we actually do this work? We did it without anybody having to suffer for it, on the contrary, enabling millions to live better, who otherwise might have swelled the army of the unemployed. If all of them had been fully employed all the time, with the best machines, much more wealth could have been created, and nothing hinders us now from continuing in wealth production on a greater scale than ever, nothing, but the absence of *sufficient means of circulation*, and here is where we find the capital deficit of which we hear so much. Can that be called capital which can be supplied in any quantity and practically without cost?—However the temporary revival came about, its effects are over-estimated and its transitoriness is ignored. At once hope rises on all sides, and this effect reacts upon the cause. The retailer gives larger orders than the increased demand warrants, the merchant lays in a large stock to meet the requirements of the trade, and the factories working at full pressure increase their facilities by adding new buildings and more machinery. The so-induced demand for more workers, temporarily raises wages, consumption is correspondingly increased, the demand becomes greater and thus is seemingly justified the assumption that at last the good times have come

But the same forces have been at work all the time; have been, in fact, intensified by the revival The increased demand for goods has further stimulated the inventive spirit, enterprising manufacturers have introduced improved machinery, which enables them to produce more with the same number of hands For a time the banks have been a little easier in discounting and allowing overdrafts, and capitalists, who otherwise would have invested only in the best securities, are infected by the general hopefulness, and invest money in business They become silent partners, buy stock or bonds in newly founded industrial companies, or lend money at interest to the trade Only the small fry, however, are caught in that way, the multi-millionaires are too old hands at the business not to know that, though temporary profits might thus be obtained, in the long run nothing is gained—that, in fact, the final losses overbalance temporary profits

It is stated that £404,000,000 of the capital invested in companies in Great Britain alone from 1892 to 1899 have been liquidated, and the Inspector-General in Companies Liquidation says "It appears that the total number of abortive or liquidating companies during 1899 was in the proportion of new companies registered 60%, as against 56% during the previous year ' That such losses generally do not affect the very rich as much as the poor is shown by the further remark "About 37% of the capital belongs to the more or less solvent class, while the remaining three-fourths in number, or 63% of capital, represent the insolvent class " Among the 37% we shall no doubt find very little money of the multi-millionaires, for this kind of men have learnt by experience that he who is satisfied with the 3% or 4% obtainable on good securities, is better off in the end than the speculator who hopes for 100% It may once in a while pay to buy a single lottery ticket, but if all tickets, or a very large quantity of them, are habitually bought, loss is certain.

If we go through the lists of dividend-paying stock companies we shall find that their average rate of profit does not exceed what could have been realized on good rent and interest investments If we include the no dividend-paying companies, this rate of interest has not even been equalled. Werner Siemens, the departed chief of the Berlin firm of Siemens & Halske—one of the most successful manufacturers in the world—once said that when they built their works, they discussed the policy of buying a whole block of land, but finally desisted, and limited themselves to the purchase of the actual site. The result proved that if the firm had carried out the first intention, it would have made more money through the increase in value of the land than it ever made in business

And this was an exceptionally successful firm For one house of this kind we find a thousand who never live over the first years of their existence We have only to consult the lists of Dun and Bradstreet to obtain an idea how numerous the commercial failures and how immense the losses are

A prominent attorney of Los Angeles, California, told me in August, 1907, that of 3,000 stock companies he incorporated in ten years approximately 40% had bursted after one year, 65% after two years, 75% after 3 years, 85% after four years; and after 5 years only 8% were left and paid dividends

The experience of large capitalists has shown that great fortunes can only be preserved and increased by investments in monopolies, and whether such monopolies consist in the possession of farms, building-sites, mines, quarries, forests, oil-wells and pipe lines, telegraph lines, canals, or railroads, they are all summed up under the heading of land-ownership or land control if we leave patents out of sight as of only short duration The millionaires therefore let the little ones buy the stock of the ordinary manufacturing concerns, while they themselves are content with owning the land on which are produced the food, cotton, hemp, flax, wool, oil, coal, iron, copper, tin, and other raw materials needed by the factories, as well as the transportation facilities, certain that in time all must come to their mill, just as the oil refineries had to submit to the oil and transportation monopoly All they do beyond this to help the new companies is to give them credits on the strength of their land and monopolies; certain that sooner or later the whole property will fall into their hands without further outlay The gradual passing of lands out of the possession of the masses who have used them as a basis of credit-money, into the hands of men who do not need any credit, is bound to continue all the time, and finally to produce its effect on the currency The relative restriction of credit and of currency circulation through these permanent causes continues, while the inflation, through the transient causes, can only be of temporary nature; for the exceptional demand due to a war, etc, ceases sooner or later, and the increased taxation which the war entails further reduces the purchasing power of the masses, while the influx of the dismissed soldiers, now competing in the wage market, depresses wages and thus further reduces the demand of consumers Add to this the increased output from all the new factories built during the revival, and it will easily be seen that the shopkeepers find themselves loaded with more stock than they can expect to sell for some time in consequence of decreased demand, and that they will be even forced to ask prolongations of bills from the merchants, who, being met by the double trouble of diminished orders and slower payments get into difficulties which in turn reach the manufacturer and farmer Credits in the bank are reduced, and the interest rate paid by the traders rises just when both the demand for goods diminishes, and when the money for sales comes in more slowly *

Workers are dismissed, others put at half time, which again decreases consumption, and thus further strengthens the effects of the depression

The depression soon degenerates into a crisis, and when a few large failures have frightened the banks into greater caution, and thus into precipitating fresh failures, the crisis becomes a panic, and the panic intensifies until the strongest business men do not know whether they will be able to weather the storm

The course of events here described is not uniformly the same. Crises do not always develop into panics and panics sometimes precipitate a crisis, or rather the transformation of a chronic crisis into an acute state. An example of the latter phase can be found in the American panics of 1893 and 1907. The sudden crash of the credit edifice, which far exceeded its usual height, suddenly withdrew the means of exchange from business, and brought about the acute depression which otherwise might have been delayed. This accounts for the distinction often made between industrial or commercial crises and financial ones; a distinction without any essential difference, somewhat like the difference between the fall of an exhausted man through lack of sustaining power, and the hastening of such fall through the intervention of an obstacle in the road. Without this obstacle the man might have dragged along a few steps further, without his exhaustion the obstacle would only have affected him temporarily. Practically, any business crisis is a financial crisis and vice versa. Business can only continue if enough money or money-promises are offered in the market for goods, when this is not the case it is absolutely immaterial whether the crisis is assigned to an oversupply of goods, or an undersupply of money. It is, as stated elsewhere, a quarrel whether John is taller than Charles, or Charles is shorter than John

Business now offers the phenomenon of a river which has been stopped in its course by some obstacle It rises until the moment arrives when the stored waters burst their bonds with terrific effect Thus the temporary arrests of the chronic crisis stream, called revivals of business, have no other effect than to substitute the crash for the gradual descent To use another metaphor, these business revivals are only the advancing waves of a receding tide The careless observer, seeing one particular wave come inshore farther than its immediate predecessors, may conclude that the tide is rising, when, in reality, it is rapidly running out So those who look

* "On the first intimation of a scarcity (of money) the rate rises and they who must have money to pay the current expenses of large establishments or to meet their outstanding obligations are at the mercy of the lender The captains of industry, and, through them, their laborers, are no longer the masters but the servants of capital"—Robert Ellis Thompson, "Political Economy" (p 152)

superficially on business revivals are too apt to ignore the fact that the tide is still running out in spite of the few advancing waves which impress us.

We have now arrived at the point where the full effects of a scientific paper currency can be understood So far, we could only see how such a currency could put a stop to the sudden collapses we are so used to, by means of its elasticity and its price-maintaining effect, but we could not discern how it could prevent the chronic crisis· the slowly but surely widening gulf between productive and purchasing power We have realized that credit, our real means of exchange, the basis of circulation, and consequently the condition without which production becomes impossible, is founded on a limited amount of securities, and that these are gradually passing into the possession of the creditor class from that of the debtor class the producers Thus the production, and consequently the purchasing power of the latter, is more and more crippled. Therefore, unless the new currency can be made accessible—not only to the owners of land values and bonds, but to the producers at large—we can never expect it to give any relief in our chronic disease of under-production, alias over-production I say advisedly a relief, not a remedy, for only currency cranks expect a thorough social reform from a mere currency reform The diagnosis of the disease given in the opening chapter has shown us that production is impossible without a corresponding consumption which we do not get where the part of the product obtained by the producing masses is too small, where their wages are too low Currency reform can help only in so far as it increases this part, as it raises wages, i. e, their purchasing power, an effect which can never be reached to the full extent needed, without a concurrent reform of our land laws.

The greatest accessibility of the proposed currency to the producers is reached by bringing into the foreground a new class of securities, which, under present conditions, plays a relatively unimportant part in finance Merchandise, the product of labor What at present causes its partial exclusion from the rank of credit collaterals, and restricts the security value of certain classes of merchandise, which are accepted as collaterals, is the risk of a decrease in their value Part of this risk, caused through their perishability, can, to a certain extent, be eliminated by insurance and safe storage This risk is comparatively small with most products which do not partake of the nature of food-stuffs and goods which are subject to fashion The risk due to price variations, however, is comparatively great, as the daily market quotations prove, and especially the results of auction sales It is well known that the latter, except for certain raw materials of very extended use, often bring only a fraction of cost price· and as auctions must always serve as the simplest means for a creditor to realize on his security, it is not astonishing if, in present circumstances, capitalists are very chary of giving credits on merchandise. This would entirely change in the case of a money based on the prices of merchandise, especially when the prices realized at auctions are taken into account proportionately to their share in the general turnover   The more the reform makes advances on merchandise the financial rule, instead of the exception, the more will this share grow in importance.   The very result of the reform on prices realized under these conditions will tend to give to the auction system the pre-eminence in the methods of whole-sale distribution which it now has only for that of a few staples. Manufacturers and farmers, producers of all kinds, will resort to this simple method of disposing of their produce at wholesale, in pref-erence to any other, as soon as a certain reliance can be placed on the prices obtained   And, on the other hand, this reliance will be strengthened in the same measure in which auctions predominate, for as auctions predominate, their prices will gradually become the almost exclusive gauge for the price tables of the Government's money-issuing department, and the effect of the money issue, in its turn, will steady the auction sale prices.

The new basis of credit thus created in most departments of production is of such an elastic nature that its monopolization be-comes an impossibility   Its limits are co-equal to those of produc-tion, which in our time are practically formed only by the demands of consumption provided with purchasing power.   The want of customers limits our present production, which does not begin to approach the extent of our latent productive power   If the goods could be sold, our production, even without new inventions, would soon double, treble, quadruple its present total; and new labor-saving inventions will be forthcoming as soon as the demand for the product justifies their use.   It seems certain that within a very short period a ten-fold increase of production could be reached, principally because the waste of power inherent in the present sys-tem, especially in the department of distribution, would disappear with the demand for more goods; of which more in Chapter VIII The certainty of obtaining a market at regular prices will to such a degree eliminate the risks of business that practically the product will finally not even be demanded as a basis of security.   The pro-ductive power—*i. e*, personal security—will largely take the place of the lien or pawn, as it already does with the German Raiffeisen banks, whose losses, even under our existing bad system, are abso-lutely insignificant   As I already indicated in the preceding chapter, these co-operative banks will then probably take the place of the present capitalistic institutions   They would be appropriate me-diums between the money-issuing state and the money-needing masses.   Aided by the Postal Savings Banks, and by the Mutual Banks (see Chapter VII), they would disseminate the fertilizing credit-element far and wide; changing arid deserts into luxurious paradises

The recognition of the problem's real nature has been **greatly** retarded by the false theories of the economists of the Adam Smith, Malthus, and Stuart Mill type In Chapter II of Book IV of his "Wealth of Nations," Adam Smith summarizes in the following sentences what he has explained more elaborately in Chapter II of Book II.

"The general industry of the society can never exceed what the capital of the society can employ As the number of workmen that can be kept in employment by any particular person must bear a certain proportion to his capital, so the number of those that can be continually employed by all the members of a great society, must bear a certain proportion to the whole capital of that society, and can never exceed that proportion No regulation of commerce can increase the quantity of industry in any society beyond what its capital can maintain It can only divert a part of it into a direction into which it might otherwise not have gone, and it is by no means certain that this artificial direction is likely to be more advantageous to the society than that into which it would have gone of its own accord"

This *wage fund* theory is also the foundation of John Stuart Mill's "Principles of Political Economy", it is likewise at the bottom of Ricardo's fallacies, and of hundreds who followed these beacon lights into a disastrous shipwreck.

I use these last words with full deliberation, as an expression of my firm opinion that these teachings have helped more than any other cause to retard our advance, by obscuring the real problem, and thus preventing its earlier solution This is easily proved

What capital does Smith mean? Food and raw materials? We have seen that they are in abundance, once the land is freed from monopoly's fetters Money? Not so long as we can make paper and build printing presses Tools and machines? It certainly cannot be proved that the employment of workers ever depended on the amount of tools possessed by the society of which they formed a part. There is not a single case in the history of nations of men being permanently unemployed merely because they could not procure tools of production, though there certainly are plenty of cases where there was too much work through the imperfection of such tools If the old Egyptians had had our modern machinery a fraction only of the hundreds of thousands employed in constructing their gigantic stone monuments, which so eloquently speak of the waste of human labor, would have been employed on this work; or more work of the same kind would have been produced. It is not the lack of perfect tools but the very efficiency of our modern machinery, which is directly responsible for the want of employment our workers complain of, whatever the indirect cause proves to be; as we have seen in the introductory chapter

But it may be replied that wherever more perfect tools are generally used, inferior tools practically become worthless, because competition by means of their use has become impossible, and that, in this sense, Smith and his followers were in the right My answer is that

1 Men provided with inferior tools have mutually supplied each other, and are supplying each other with the necessaries of life, without being in the least interfered with by others who use better implements Even in some of our most civilized European countries communities are met with, especially in mountain districts not yet opened by railroads, where the people live comparatively well, and where scarcity of employment is as good as unknown. though their tools and processes of production belong to a period lying at least a century behind us It is only when our modern implements intrude into their mountain solitudes that the justly named "scourge" of modern times begins to make its appearance. During one of my tramps in the Bavarian mountain districts, I entered into conversation with a peasant. We talked of the railroad which was going to be built through the section. "Formerly the peasant drove the gentleman, now the gentleman drives the peasant," was his criticism, which, in a few words, contains a deep meaning. He wanted to tell me that before the railway comes the peasant drives the travellers, and thus makes money, enabling him to purchase the things he wants Now the capitalists of the city carry the peasant on their railway, and, instead of making money through the use of his carriage and horses, the peasant himself has to buy a railroad ticket if he wants to travel, as he had to sell his conveyances for want of customers An income has gone; his expenses have increased Now, if these people are fully employed and make a good living as long as they are only using their primitive tools, and if, as soon as modern improvements arrive, the same troubles and difficulties as to employment arise ·which obtain in more civilized parts, this can certainly not be ascribed to the want of capital; rather to an intrusion of too much capital.

2. In fact, a want of tool capital never needed to exist by itself as long as our world has been inhabited by man. When the pierced bone was used as a needle, a curved stick as a plow, and a sling as an implement of the chase, as many pierced bones, crooked sticks and slings were produced, as the workers wanted And in our time, when the sewing-machine has taken the place of the bone needle, the steam plow that of the stick, and the Mauser or Martini rifle, the Bergmann pistol, the Krupp gun and Maxim quick-firer that of the sling—sewing-machine makers, instead of finding difficulty in supplying any amount of machines required, are only too anxious to obtain more orders; and were a machine needed for every man, woman, and child in the world, it could be forthcoming in a comparatively short time. Nor have I ever heard that steam plows and other implements could not be supplied in any quantity needed; unless there was a sudden unexpected pressure, soon to be relieved by increased facilities for production. The same holds good in regard to arms and any other thing produced by human hands.

There is hardly a single article against which the cry of "Over-production" has not been repeatedly raised

This complaint certainly does not show a scarcity of tool capital, but that its supply exceeds the demand and the demand fails because the workers do not receive wages corresponding to the increased efficiency of the machines   Our means of production, defective as they are to a certain extent—principally because we cannot let our technic progress have full play for fear of the consequences—supply at least ten times as much per day's work of one man as the more primitive tools of Smith's time, but it is clear that with these facilities there can only be work for all, if consumption also increases ten-fold   This it can only do if either the wages of the workers have their purchasing power ten-fold increased or the comparatively few people to whom the bulk of the purchasing power belongs, consume the surplus in their turn   But wages have by no means increased to anything like the proportion mentioned, and the number of people who obtain the lion's share of the product is too insignificant to enable them to consume the surplus, while the resulting under-consumption limits their demand for new means of production, which otherwise might prove a profitable investment   In consequence, they buy land and other safe tribute-claims, with the effect on circulation described in the dealings of Plutus and Jones   There can only be one result a reduction in the number of hands employed in production.   If the waste in distribution, through the unnecessarily large number of middlemen, the waste through militarism and destructive wars, the waste through devil Alcohol, through circumlocution offices, through flunkeyism, through strikes and other restrictions in production brought about by the labor unions, failed to tap off part of our superfluous blood, the social body would long ago have been subjected to a stroke of apoplexy

Want of employment in our time is not the product of too little, but of too much, capital, of a capital too abundant for our existing distribution of wealth and this settles the wage-fund bugbear of Adam Smith   It is not more wealth or wealth-creating power we want just now, but a more equal distribution of wealth

The new money, by taking out of the way one obstacle in this direction, will increase consumption accordingly   The increasing consumption must necessarily give a freer rein to our productive power, and call forth from latency into actual existence immense quantities of wealth   This wealth, in its turn by serving as a security for a money credit supplies its producers with the means of changing wealth into purchasing power—into money   There can be no danger of producing too much wealth under such conditions where demand keeps pace with supply, and where accordingly prices do not fall, as they now do, through a non-consumption of part of the newly created wealth—consumption in the sense of use for, to keep the economic machinery moving, it matters not whether the product of labor is consumed in the form of bread and meat, or of railroad locomotives, canals, and school-houses Such an under-consumption now results from the use made by our rich of their incomes, which restricts the market and presses down prices It is different under the new system, for when prices fall, new money appears in the market This is eagerly demanded by those who have paid their own money to their rich creditors The debtor class will be able to obtain this new money on reasonable terms, because the products of their labor will supply sufficient security, through the removal of the danger now presented by a fall in prices, and thus the withdrawal of money or credit, by the creditor class, will cease to do any harm Our next chapter will show the effect which the changed conditions will have on the interest rate, how they will reduce the interest tribute paid by the producers to the capitalists; and thus prove a potent factor in bringing about a better distribution of wealth

Thus the new money is bound to immensely increase production, for which a ready inland market is found through an equally increasing consumption This makes us independent of foreign markets, so that we can calmly face that great bugbear in the way of paper money, the international market

What is international trade even now when compared with domestic trade? It will play a ridiculously insignificant part when the full effects of scientific paper currency are produced in the home trade, effects which, as we have seen, must consist in an immense increase of production and consumption There is no country in the world whose citizens would not be far better customers for its products than any foreign or colonial market, if their purchasing power were kept at the level of their productive power, and yet, instead of tenderly nursing this purchasing power by just laws, we use up our strength in the attempt to conquer foreign markets, be it even by means of costly wars If any power, engaged in the unjust work of forcing nations—who want to be left alone—to fling open their doors to outsiders, would employ the means thus wasted and the human activity thus thrown away to organize production and distribution in its own domains, the additional turnover thereby obtained would far exceed any sales ever expected in the best foreign market One single dollar a working day more purchasing power given to 30 million American bread-winners would mean an additional home consumption of 9 billion dollars a year, or almost six times the total amount of American exports

I cannot refrain from quoting Miss Mara De Bernardi, the talented daughter of G B De Bernardi, the founder of the American Labor Exchanges, on the folly of looking for foreign markets while the demands of our home consumers are unsatisfied

"Tramping the highways and byways of the nations, shelterless, cold, shivering to-day under the blasts of a premature winter, doomed to bleak and comfortless nights beside the grudging fire of some discarded railroad tie, or, at best, to the shelter of some farmer's friendly surplus of hay, from Maine to California, and from Washington to the land of southern flowers, wanders the countless market for America's wood and coal, and lumber and brick and stone—the homeless, houseless waif of over-production. A humbled petitioner at the kitchen doors of the generous housewives of the land, with manhood crushed and dying beneath the awful Juggernaut of beggary, stands the numberless market for America's wheat and corn and boundless stores of food—the hunger-haunted victims of over-production. In their wretched rags, their cold, pinched faces, blue and strained, the tattered children of the land shiveringly proffer their claims to Dixie's cotton yield—the ill-clad victims of the nation's surplus stores. And they weary the pavements of our streets with their endless, aimless passing to and fro, and harass the very peace of the nation with their ceaseless importunities for the making and taking of the surplus of the world. And sometimes, when the struggle for human existence grows too great, some reckless, heartsick victim of too much unused clothes and food and shelter in the world, drifts off to meet the everlasting bounty and abundance of the hereafter, down some icy river, or on some outgoing ocean tide—a market lost to the over-production of the world by the crime of that world's own folly and neglect, a market which neither the sacrifice of human liberty nor the shedding of human blood was required to conserve, but which only the kindness and simple justice of a common humanity would have held inalienable; a market which could proffer not idle, useless, cruel gold, but honest toil for honest toil; a market which relieves alike the victim of over-production and the victim of over-work. A market for our surplus in China? It is praying for recognition, and dying of neglect, at our nation's very doors."

We have seen why this market, which prays for recognition at our very doors, is closed, and if a scientific paper currency opens this door, it matters little what effect this currency might have on our international trade. However, I want to show that even in this field, it is bound to exercise a favorable influence.

The larger the turnover, the smaller the percentage of business expense which has to be added to cost, and consequently the cheaper the goods can be produced. A factory which only works half time runs up nearly the same interest and rent bill as one that works day and night with its full force. The office expenses are nearly the same, and running machinery does not deteriorate much more, sometimes not as much, as when it lies idle. This part of cost of production is spread upon a turnover perhaps four times as large in the one case as in the other, and consequently amounts to only one-quarter as much under full running time as where only a quarter of the possible work is done. If, without exportation, only one-half of the plant can be kept employed, or the whole plant only half the time, it is evident that production for the home market would cost a great deal more than where, through exportation, the factory can be kept running at its full capacity. This is the reason why manufacturers often export at prices which would involve a loss, if they were obtained for the whole production of the mill. They calculate that the additional turnover thus obtained helps to bear general expenses, or, in other words, expenses, which have to be met anyhow by the domestic turnover, may be left out of account in the export department, which thus gives a small profit. Often this extra profit enables the exporter to pay out of his own pocket the foreign import duties to enable him to compete with the foreign manufacturer. The pretense that import duties are often paid by the foreigner is consequently not so unfounded as free-traders make out. I remember from my own personal experience as a manufacturer that I reduced my prices for a foreign country to the amount of a duty newly imposed by the foreign government, so that my customers could sell my machines at the old prices. The facts here given also account for the cheap prices at which some of our trusts sell abroad, and it is a fallacy to believe that they could always manage to sell at home at the same low prices. If the exports still leave a small profit, because general expenses are borne by the home sales, loss all round might be the result, if home sales were also made at a price only justified where general expenses can be left out of account, but impossible where they come in.

The results of currency reform would bring on a domestic turnover far in excess of the former total sales, home and international trade taken together. The saving in cost thus reached would not only amply pay for the higher wages—especially when we take into consideration the greater efficiency of the better-fed workers, but would also permit lower export prices. Exports thus could be made in sufficient quantity to pay for all the imports, in which case it is obvious that the currency system would not interfere in any but a beneficial way with the international trade of a passive country. If gold is sent or received from abroad, it will be as merchandise. In fact it is only sent or received now in this character.

But for all that, we have to investigate the possible contingency of an unfavorable trade balance, to find out what the paper currency will do in such a case. It need not trouble us that the free-trade school does not admit the possibility of such a contingency, on the ground that, as the French economist, Jean Baptiste Say, expresses it "Commodities are always paid for with commodities." It is one of those teachings which are on a level with Smith's wage-fund theory. The simple fact that England in the course of years accumulated a credit with other nations of not less than 2,000 million pounds sterling ($10,000,000,000) proves that England's exports have not always been paid for by imports, but that large amounts have been left on credit in one shape or another; bonds, mortgages, bills of exchange, etc. or investments of other kinds, such as land purchases, factories, shares and stocks of all kinds. The fact that Australasia, for instance, owes England nearly 500 million pounds

shows that English imports have not always been paid for by
Australasian exports, but partly have remained due at compound
interest   This is just what will happen to the paper currency country in the case of an unfavorable balance   If it has not a credit
balance abroad, like England, it will run into debt, as all of our
paper currency countries have done in the past, for such a currency
never was adopted except as a consequence of debt   A great deal
of the prejudice against paper money is due to this fact, people not
considering that the currency did not cause the debt, but, on the
contrary, the debt created the currency, which, in spite of the im-
perfect raw method of its issue, usually proved a benefit to the
country which adopted it.

We need not feel astonished that the theory of the economists
again is in flat contradiction to practice, as has been shown in respect
of the wage-fund theory   These gentlemen try to explain discord-
ant facts by false theories, without recognizing the disturbing element responsible for the contradiction   Closer study would teach
them the solution of the problem, but as a rule such study can only
be made by men acquainted with practical life, not by those whose
horizon is limited by desk and library

In the wage-fund difficulty they might discover that the only
fund really concerned is the land and money fund.   This would
sooner or later lead them toward the recognition of our land and
currency errors   They would find that unnatural land monopoly
and the artificial limitation of the money privilege to coins made of
one or two precious metals, are responsible for the equally unnatural fettering of productive power

In the case of their "commodities-bought-with-commodities"
theory, closer observation would show that the reason why this
theory does not conform to facts is due to the advent of another
factor, which falsifies the account   This factor is *Interest*   In the
next chapter we shall recognize the abnormity of this economic factor, and how it is entirely the outgrowth of the same pernicious
economic monsters private land ownership and money monopoly

Our return to nature at once operates an absolute change in
both cases   The last vestige of any limitation of productive power
will disappear with land and money reform   The wage-fund bogey
then will merely survive as a historical reminiscence in the chronicle
of human follies, and commodities will be really paid for with commodities, for there will be no other method of payment   Land and
interest values will be no more obtainable in the market, and money
of the new kind will be valueless internationally, unless converted
into commodities   Without interest it matters little to an individual
or a nation how soon or how late creditors will pay themselves
through a counter purchase of goods   In fact, the later the better;
for meanwhile the capital will be used free of charge

Under the rule of interest the case entirely changes   Interest
and its child, compound-interest, finally swell the original bill to

such unpleasant proportions that the debtor will too late recognize that buying in the cheapest market, according to the great free-trade principle, often spells buying in the very dearest market. One dollar due at 5% compound interest in one hundred years foots up to $140. Was it really cheaper to economize that dollar, at which the goods were bought and borrowed cheaper in the foreign market, than to make them at home without running up a balance against us, especially if in the interval our own workers were without employment through the foreigners not buying an equivalent from us? This brings the trade problem into a new light, which free-traders ought to make use of before they come to positive conclusions. Admitted that their pet policy is the only one which holds water, if examined from the pointview of the fundamental principle, the right of every man to satisfy his wants with the least effort. Admitted that from this point of view protection is an anomaly, is not interest, too, an anomaly, a negative element? A negative multiplied with a negative produces a positive, and a positive multiplied with a negative produces a negative. If we apply this rule, learned in our school-days, to the point in question, we must come to the conclusion that the negative Interest may be changed into a positive by the negative Protection, while the positive Freetrade, under the influence of the negative Interest, may produce a negative result. Under the iron rule of Interest a debt is always a danger, and to avoid it, measures may be found prudent, which, under freedom, are absolutely harmful. Satisfying wants with the greatest effort, without running into debt, may be found preferable to their satisfaction with the least effort, if it implies indebtedness.

To make this clearer let us substitute the case of individuals for that of nations. After all, what is the trade of nations but the trade of a number of individuals living in different countries. John, a tailor, needs some chairs. If he were fully occupied at his trade he would act very unwisely in making these chairs himself. He is not skilled in such work, and it would demand ten times as much of his time as Bill, an experienced cabinetmaker, requires to make far better chairs. John would do much better to make a coat, and buy chairs out of the proceeds, certain that the same labor time thus spent will buy more chairs than if he spent it on chair construction.

How would it be, however, if through a too limited demand for coats, John were only half employed? Would he not prove a better householder if he spent his idle time on chair-making, than if he were to buy those commodities on credit or with his savings, sitting in his shop, with his hands in his pockets. Now let us spin out the story a little farther and let us assume that Bill, too, is only half employed, but sadly needs a coat. Would not Bill, too, do better to make this coat by his own labor in his idle time, no matter how long this will take, than to run into debt for it, or pay out money saved for a rainy day? No doubt the most practical way for both would be to use their unemployed time to work for each other

John would make Bill's coat better and in a fraction of the time in
which Bill could make it, and the same thing would happen in regard
to Bill's taking John's place as a chair-maker.   Certainly both parties would fare much better by such an exchange, and no doubt
they would do this, if feasible   But the two do not know each othe
and barter between them is out of the question, as it practically is i1
the greater part of ordinary business affairs   John finds that h.s
cheapest way of getting chairs is to buy them at the next furniture
dealer's, and Bill buys his coat in a department store   Both these
middlemen—for some reason or other—have no use for the labor
of the two artisans   Let us say they can buy imported goods
cheaper   Both artisans borrow money from a usurer to buy the
things they want, or they run up a bill at the store   Would it not
be far more advantageous for John and Bill if in some way—for instance, by means of a prohibitive duty—they were prevented from
buying the cheap imported goods?   No matter what the addition to
the price might be, they would be better off if the goods were made
locally, and if they thus obtained employment   What would it matter if Bill had to pay $10 for a coat which could have been imported
for $5, and if John gave as much as $10 for the same chairs which
could have been laid down in the country for $5, when the real
result was simply that John made a coat in exchange against Bill's
chairs, and Bill made chairs in payment of John's coat   (For simplicity's sake, I leave out of account the surplus work done by both
parties to pay the middleman's profits)   In this case, the amount at
which both commodities figured in the mutual accounts would
prove absolutely indifferent.   Anything was better than to have
two willing workers sit idle in their shops that they might give employment to foreign workers.   Under such conditions, even an
absurd waste of power such as Adam Smith describes in the second
chapter of Book IV, may prove the lesser of two evils

"By means of glasses, hot-beds, and hot-walls, very good grapes
can be raised in Scotland, and very good wine can be made of them
at about thirty times the expense for which at least equally good
wine can be brought from foreign countries.   Would it be a reasonable law to prohibit the importation of all foreign wines merely to
encourage the making of claret and Burgundy in Scotland?"

My answer is   If the foreign wine-producing countries will
not accept British goods in payment for wine, while Scotch workers,
in consequence of this refusal to accept the products of their labor
in payment, cannot find any work to do, it would decidedly be better
policy to set them digging coal, making and laying steam-pipes,
building and heating hot-houses, therein to raise grapes, than to
reduce these willing workers to a pauper's state, fed by the produce
of other workers   The cheapest foreign wine for which we have
to run into debt, through compound interest, will finally be the
dearest we ever bought and workers, who otherwise would have to
be fed in idleness, can be looked at as working for nothing   Those

who always speak of the consumer who ought to buy in the cheapest market forget that at least 95% of the population are first producers before they can be consumers and that, therefore, the producer's interest must be nearest to their hearts. Unfortunately, those whose position gives them the power of directing the nation's policy, arise mostly from the non-producing minority.

This principle of reciprocity in trade, the great Scotch professor treated with contempt. In Part II, third chapter, Book IV, Adam Smith says "The sneaking arts of underling tradesmen are thus erected into political maxims for the conduct of a great empire, for it is the most underling tradesmen only who make it a rule to employ chiefly their own customers A great trader purchases his goods always where they are cheapest and best, without regard to any little interest of this kind"

It is exactly this policy of the great traders which justifies the interference of the state. Let us not forget that we only use a metaphor when we speak of America England, or Germany, as exporting and importing In reality, individual American, English and German traders export and import, and in doing so they merely consult their own personal interest, not that of the nation as a whole. An importer does not care which nation proves the best customer of his own country, when he gives his orders He merely compares price-lists and qualities, and then orders his goods In fact he can hardly act differently, or competition would swamp him

His country's passive trade balances in consequence of its effect upon the currency, may be followed by its indebtedness to foreign capital, perhaps by national insolvency; but what does he care about such trifles, trifles to him when looked at from the standpoint of his profits and losses? Why should he have regard to any little interest of this kind?" as Adam Smith expresses it

Not to be misunderstood, I must add a short explanation. Favorable, active, positive, or unfavorable, passive, negative balances of trade do not necessarily correspond with similar financial balances A balance of trade may be active and the financial balance passive, as is the case in the United States, and several other countries at the present time, and the trade balance may be passive and the financial balance very active England has long shown the most prominent example of such a country Its imports exceed its exports considerably, but most of the time the deficit does not reach the amount due from other nations on freight, interest, rent and profit account, while her colonies, in spite of their recent favorable balance sheets, have been running deeper and deeper into debt, because the interest debt due to England exceeded the balances of trade in their favor If their balances of trade were passive or if their exports just balanced their imports they would increase their indebtedness still more while England would become richer still if her balances were active.

It is the same case with this country, which had passive balances from the foundation of the Republic to 1873, figuring up to a total of $1,193,212,113 This debt, with compound interest, has had to be paid by the favorable balances accruing since 1873 These balances by this time figure up to six times the total of the former passive balances, but when we take into consideration the freights paid to foreign keels, the expenses of our tourists in the foreign countries, the dowries of our absentee daughters, the savings sent abroad (in 1907, $83,890,925 in postal orders alone), our losses on bonds and stocks sold abroad below par, and, more than all these items, compound interest, it is not at all astonishing that our debts abroad far outweigh our credits, especially if we include in the debts, the land mortgages, and bonds held abroad

Freetraders, like Louis Post of the "Public," look at our favorable trade balances, at our excess of exports over imports, as a loss of wealth This reminds me of a German humorous saying "Man verpuddelt eine Menge Geld mit dem Schuldenbezahlen" (a lot of money is frittered away in the payment of debts) Now there is only one way open for an honest man and an honest country, who do not like debts, and that is not to incur them, by refraining from buying more goods than they have money or goods to pay with. But freetraders of the Post school deny the very possibility of such a thing, for they believe in Say's old nonsense that "commodities are always paid for with commodities" They do not say when this payment is to occur, and forget that if the bill it not settled at once it is bound to run up, sometimes so high that there is no possibility of paying the mere interest in commodities, let alone the capital And this is just what happened to the United States during many years If it were not for the present favorable trade balances, the debt would rapidly increase, until bankruptcy some day settled the account; a policy which Mr Post would hardly prefer to payment by the favorable balances which he so dislikes

But does this excess of exports over imports really take wealth out of the country? Or, to put the question more correctly, would this wealth have been produced if it had not been designed for export?

Those who have followed me so far that they fully understand the predicament of our Twentieth century world, of its production painfully halting behind productive power, through an insufficient consumption, will easily see that increase of consumption must result in new production, which otherwise would not materialize. Now, this is practically the effect of exportation, which is consumption by foreigners Instead of taking the place of home consumption it practically creates additional home consumption, through the new chances of employment, which otherwise would not be obtainable—We owe such extravagances to the law of the pendulum, which finds its application in intellectual as well as in physical oscillations Our getting away from an error on one side often swings us into the error on the other side To stop in the middle seems to be almost beyond human nature. This fact has been observed in the wage-fund theory, where those who recognized the fallacy of Smith's doctrine went to the other extreme of absolutely denying the truth which hides behind the error the limitation of production through our wretched land and currency systems A specially interesting proof of this is offered by Henry George He saw that with free land, labor can produce all the capital required to make full use of the productive power of the country, without being limited by any wage-fund On the other hand, he did not recognize the significance of the means of exchange in regard to the turn-over, and consequently to production His argument that wages are only paid after their exchange value has been produced by the worker, and, therefore, that no wage-fund is required to enable us to produce, proves this clearly Of what use is the stock of merchandise to the manufacturer on pay-day if he cannot obtain customers for it at once, or banks who will loan him money on it? As long as all payments, those of wages included, are due in certain quantities of a scarce metal, so long shall we have a wage-fund, in spite of all the theoreticians in the world

It will be different when the exchange banks, described in Chapter VII, will change the product into market money, as soon as it is finished—and, in consequence of the credit system connected with exchange banking, even while it is as yet unfinished Then we shall certainly see disappear for ever the last trace of the wage-fund theory

Another case of pendulum swinging beyond the centre of truth, is supplied by Smith's relation to Mercantilism, an economic school which, though born in the previous century, still held sway in the great economist's time If the Mercantilists were at fault in overestimating the influence of the precious metals, Adam Smith and his followers, our modern freetraders, in the vindication of equal rights for all products of labor, without any distinction, swung too far to the other side with their mental pendulums, by forgetting the exceptional position given by law to the precious metals. To really defeat mercantilism, a thorough currency reform had to be the first step As it is, our whole commercial system, national and international, remains steeped in mercantilism The balance we are struggling for in both fields is not the wealth (products of labor) balance, but the financial balance We have not progressed so very far, after all, since the time of Colbert, the Mercantilists' great chief Smith justly denied that wealth consists only in money or in gold and silver, or at all events that the precious metals represent the most precious part of wealth He saw clearly that we might dispense with gold and silver more easily than with iron or copper, that we might even live without the two precious metals; while we cannot exist without food, clothing and shelter But here his perception of the real nature of the problem ended In Book IV Chapter I, he says "Though goods do not always draw money as

readily as money draws goods, in the long run they draw it more
necessarily than even it draws them. Goods can serve many other
purposes besides purchasing money, but money can serve no other
purpose besides purchasing goods. Money therefore necessarily
runs after goods, but goods do not always or necessarily run after
money. The man who buys does not always mean to sell again,
whereas he who sells always means to buy again. The one may
frequently have done the whole, but the other can never have
done more than one-half of his business. It is not for its own sake
that men desire money but for the sake of what they can purchase
with it."

Even a learned scholar cannot be absolutely blind to the facts
of every-day life, and I hardly believe that Smith could have made
such statements if he had lived a hundred years later. In the
twentieth century it is easy, even for a university professor, to point
out the absolute incompatibility of such theories with the facts of
real life. An immense increase of productive power has been the
signature of the hundred and thirty years that have passed since
Adam Smith wrote these sentences in his mother's house at Kirk-
caldy, in the quiet study of the scholar, carefully shut off from any
intercourse with the outside world. Our folly in making a scarce
yellow metal our exclusive legal tender money has since then
brought about a wild chase of goods after money, while the kind of
investments favored by our rich money owners clearly shows that
money can do other work besides buying goods. To comprehend
this, even if Smith had lived in our time, would, however, have presented some difficulty to him. The author of the "Theory of Moral
Sentiments" would indeed have found it hard to understand the
motives which can actuate our Rothschilds, Rockefellers, Astors,
etc., in their accumulations of millions. They can never expect to
use the money for the purchase of goods, for the greatest imagin-
able extravagance cannot conceive of such an expenditure. They
consume only a fraction of their income, and use most of the balance to add to their wealth; not in the form of tangible products of
labor, which would be equivalent to consumption as far as the
goods-purchasing use of the money goes but of tribute claims in
the shape of land titles, mortgages, bonds, etc.—mere cords to which
the world's money is attached, to be pulled in at the will of the cord-
holders. But whatever the motives may be, the fact remains that
immense amounts of money or money claims are thus used for
'other purposes besides purchasing goods' amounts exceeding
by far the whole money stock of the world. And the well-known
consequences of this fact are that everywhere goods of all kinds
go a-begging in vain for money, while money haughtily refuses to
buy goods, instead of "running after them," as Smith teaches.

I have no wish to depreciate the merits of the great Scotch
thinker, but he undertook here an impossible task for it is as impossible to do justice to economic subjects without practical busi-

ness experience as to bake wheaten bread without any wheat This is the reason also why Protection and Free Trade," by Henry George though written in his best style, is the poorest of his books Though more than Smith, he had never been, to any extent worth mentioning in mercantile business, and experiences, which to a business man have become flesh and blood, are to men of this kind undigested raw materials or *terra incognita* Most interesting in this respect is Chapter XIII of George's book, "Confusions Arising from the Use of Money," which ought to be styled confusions arising from ignoring the part money plays in business

Because a man who barters with another strikes the better bargain the more value he obtains in return for what he gives, George concludes that the more the value of her imports preponderates over that of her exports the richer a nation must be His reasoning, like that of all free traders is based on the 'commodities pay for commodities" fallacy, which assumes cases of barter where, in reality, purchase and sale, *i e*, money transactions, are carried on Under the money system a nation's imports, like an individual's purchases, represent not income but expenditure, unless they are obtained as a gift, while exports are sales, and represent income instead of expenditure if they are not given away gratis In this way George is kept from realizing the great difference involved in the use of money. His error is most apparent in the following parable found in the same book

"Robinson Crusoe, we will suppose, is still living alone on his island Let us suppose an American protectionist is the first to break his solitude with the long-yearned-for music of human speech. Crusoe's delight we can well imagine But now that he has been there so long he does not care to leave, the less since his visitor tells him that the island, having now been discovered, will often be visited by passing ships Let us suppose that after having heard Crusoe's story, seen his island, enjoyed such hospitality as he could offer, told him in return of the wonderful changes in the great world, and left him books and papers, our protectionist prepares to depart, but before going seeks to offer some kindly warning of the danger Crusoe will be exposed to from the 'deluge of cheap goods' that passing ships will seek to exchange for fruit and goats. Imagine him to tell Crusoe just what protectionists tell larger communities and to warn him that, unless he takes measures to make it difficult to bring these goods ashore, his industry will be entirely ruined 'In fact,' we may imagine the protectionist to say, 'so cheaply can all the things you require be produced abroad that unless you make it hard to land them I do not see how you will be able to employ your own industry at all '

" 'Will they give me all these things?' Robinson Crusoe would naturally exclaim 'Do you mean that I shall get all these things for nothing, and have no work at all to do? That will suit me completely I shall rest and read and go fishing for the fun of it.

I am not anxious to work if without work I can get the things I want.'

" 'No, I don't quite mean that,' the protectionist would be forced to explain 'They will not give you such things for nothing. They will, of course, want something in return. But they will bring you so much, and will take away so little, that your imports will vastly exceed your exports, and it will soon be difficult for you to find employment for your labor '

" 'But I don't want to find employment for my labor,' Crusoe would naturally reply 'I did not spend months in digging out my canoe, weeks in tanning and sewing these goat-skins, because I wanted employment for my labor, but because I wanted the things. If I can get what I want with less labor, so much the better, and the more I get the less I give in the trade you tell me I am to carry on—or, as you phrase it, the more my imports exceed my exports— the easier I can live and the richer I will be I am not afraid of being overwhelmed with goods The more they bring the better it will suit me '

"And so the two might part, for it is certain that no matter how long our protectionist talked, the notion that his industry would be ruined by getting things with less labor than before would never frighten Crusoe "

Of course, if it was a question of barter, if the importers took from Robinson goods which abounded on his island, and which could be supplied by him with much less labor than that entailed by the goods which the others gave him in exchange, his astonishment at the protectionist theories put before him would have been justified. Such a trade would have meant full reciprocity; and only extreme protectionists can object to free trade under such conditions Nor would it have made the least difference what time elapsed before the importers took Robinson's produce in payment In fact, the longer they tarried the better for Robinson, who could let his wealth breed additional wealth in the meantime. But let us suppose that it was not a barter transaction, but one of purchase and sale for money, and that the strangers' bill was higher than the value of the produce which they accepted from Robinson in exchange, so that Robinson had to run into a money debt, and that 5% interest was demanded for this debt, Robinson giving as security a mortgage on his island And let us further suppose that year after year elapsed, and no favorable balance of trade enabled Robinson to pay his money debt, his further bills against the importers not exceeding the amount of the new bills of goods they sold him, and gold not being obtainable on the island The debt remained, the interest on it accumulating all the time with the frightful velocity of compound interest; until one day a sheriff comes along who, as Robinson cannot pay his debt, in legal tender money, sells his island over his head As the proceeds are not sufficient to pay for the money debt, Robinson not being able to make a bid, because he possessed no legal tender money, all the other belongings of the poor man were also sold, and he is set adrift in the world, penniless, unless the new owners of his island consent to retain him as a laborer or as their tenant, who has to work hard from morning till night to pay his rent and to eke out a meager living No more imports are offered now, but most of Robinson's produce is taken away for rent Was it really Robinson's best policy, under such conditions, to buy the cheap goods offered to him? Was it not better to produce them by his own labor, though applied under much more unfavorable conditions, and to refuse the importers' goods at any cost so long as he could not pay for them with his own produce, but had to run into debt payable in money at compound interest? Anything was better than to become the interest-serf and finally the rent-slave of the strangers Fair trade, but not unconditional free trade, was the only not right-down suicidal policy open to Robinson, and as his supposititious case corresponds with the realities of individual and national trade, the illustration proves the very reverse of what was intended Fair trade is a certainty where metal money and its product, the interest-poison, does not come into the way Where it does, which is everywhere the case in our present world, however, counterpoison Protection, and even Prohibition of importation, may be found a good remedy.

Let me bring the state of things on Robinson's island still a little nearer to the reality of every-day life. Let us suppose that Robinson had made a specialty of the raising of foodstuffs and the production of raw materials; while an artisan, Jones, who had immigrated, produced furniture, cloth, and other manufactures required by himself and Robinson. The two exchanged with each other, each fixing money prices for his goods which remunerated him well for his labor, as they enabled him to obtain all he needed of the other's produce Now an importer lands, and offers all goods manufactured by Jones at one-half the price he charges Robinson at once ceases to give his orders to Jones and transfers them to the importer; for why should he pay more for his goods than he can get them for in the market? Jones, being out of work through the loss of Robinson's custom, emigrates After a little time the importer wants his bill paid. Robinson says that he has no money, and that his former customer, Jones, always accepted produce in payment, he could only settle his bill with produce. The importer agrees, but freights are high, and competition in this kind of produce in the distant markets is very sharp, which forces him to offer one-quarter of the price only which Jones had paid. Robinson cannot help himself, as he needs the goods of the importer, Jones having left; so that he either has to go without goods which have become a necessity to him, or has to make them in a much more primitive way with much more labor.

He thus finds that he pays twice as many bales of wool, or bushels of wheat, as he had to supply to Jones for the same manu-

factures He has some bad seasons, and he runs into a money debt
with the importer, who takes a mortgage on the island, which increases through compound interest until finally the island is sold,
and Robinson becomes the rack-rented tenant, or (at last) the laborer
of the new owner   After his death, in some poorhouse, the island
is turned into a deer park by the rich proprietor   The protectionist
thus proved to be in the right because he looked at the case from
the point of view of every day's business   Unfortunately for Henry
George, the business done by savages and Robinsons is not typical
of the regular business of civilized life, as George·supposes   In
reality, the business to be expected in the case of Robinson was
raw barter   In such a case the arguments of Robinson, or rather
of George, his representative, were correct   The more he obtained
in barter, and the less he gave in exchange, the better off he was
bound to be   But to look at such a trade as representing the ordinary business of civilization was a great blunder; for there those
are best off who spend least and receive most money, who consequently pay out less for their purchases (imports) than they obtain
for their sales (exports)

  This is proved by Portugal's economic history during the last
two centuries, as told by Friedrich List, the great German economist, in "Das Nationale System der Politischen Oekonomie" I
translate from the fifth chapter of the first book   List's quotations
from English sources are thus twice translated, so that the text may
slightly differ from the original, which is not at my disposal

  "When Count Erceira became Minister of Portugal, in 1681,
he conceived the plan of erecting woolen factories to work up the
country's own raw material and to supply the mother country, as
well as her colonies, with her own manufactures   For this purpose,
artisans were imported from England, and in consequence of the
support given them, woolen factories began to flourish so quickly
that, after three years (1684), the import of foreign woolens could
be prohibited   From this time forth Portugal supplied herself and
her colonies with her own manufactures, made from the local raw
material and, according to the testimonial of English writers
prospered thereby exceedingly " (*British Merchant* Vol III, p 69)

  The success of this measure is the more remarkable because
the country had shortly before this lost a great quantity of capital
through the expulsion of the Jews and in general suffered from
bad government and a feudal aristocracy which oppressed the liberty
of the people and agriculture (Ibid 76)

  In the year 1703, however, after the death of Count Erceira,
the celebrated English Minister, Methuen, succeeded in convincing
the Portuguese Government that Portugal would gain very much
if England permitted the import of Portuguese wines at a duty
amounting to one-third less than that of other nations, for which
Portugal was to permit the importation of English woolens at the
duty of 23% which existed previous to 1684   Immediately

after the ratification of this treaty Portugal was inundated with
English manufactures, and the consequence of this inundation was
the sudden and complete ruin of the Portuguese factories, a success similar to that of the later Eden treaty with France, and that
of the cessation of the Continental system in Germany

According to Anderson's testimony History of Commerce,
Englishmen were at that time so experienced in the art of declaring their goods under value, that practically they only paid one-
half of their duties fixed by the tariff 'After the prohibition was
levied" (says the *British Merchant*) "we carried away so much of
their silver that they kept very little for their necessary occasions.
Then we went for their gold" (Vol III, p 267)

This business they continued until recent times, they exported
the precious metals which the Portuguese received from their colonies and carried a great pile of it to East India and China, where
they exchanged them against merchandise which they sold on the
European Continent for raw materials The yearly importation of
Portugal from England exceeded the export to the amount of one
million pounds sterling. This favorable balance of trade forced
down the rate of exchange to the disadvantage of Portugal, 15%.
"We gain a more considerable balance of trade from Portugal
than from any other country" (says the editor of the *British Merchant* in his dedicatory memorial to Sir Paul Methuen, son of the
celebrated Minister) "We have increased our importation of money
from there to one and a half million pounds sterling, while formerly
it only amounted to 300,000 pounds" (Vol III, pp 15, 20, 33, 38,
110, 253, 254)

The consequence of this drain of Portugal's precious metals
and money was the institution of an inconvertible paper money
which, whatever services it rendered to internal trade, could not pay
the yearly debt resulting from the annual deficit of the trade bal-
ance-sheet, and other means of payment had to be found Then
began the usual cycle of mortgages on Portuguese land handed
over to British capitalists, of Portuguese Government bonds emi-
grating to England, of the dominion of British capital in Portugal—
capital imported in the shape of woolen goods for which no wine
was taken in payment, and accumulating in the usual way through
compound interest, until one of the richest countries became one
of the poorest, until national bankruptcy, more or less veiled, had
to alleviate the intolerable burden

Adam Smith, in his hatred of a reciprocity policy, "the sneaking arts of the underling tradesmen," could see no disadvantage to
Portugal nor gain to England resulting from these conditons, and it
is highly interesting to ascertain by what kind of logic such contra-
dictory facts were made to coincide with the preconceived results
of deductive reasoning He thinks that there can be no advantage
in thus obtaining gold and silver from Portugal, for "the more gold
we import from one country, the less we must necessarily import

from all others The effectual demand for gold, like that of any other commodity, is in every country limited to a certain quantity If nine-tenths of this quantity are imported from one country, there remains a tenth only to be imported from all others The more gold, besides, that is annually imported from some particular countries, over and above what is requisite for plate and for coin, the more must necessarily be exported to some others, and the more that most insignificant object of modern policy, the balance of trade, appears to be in our favor with some particular countries, the more it must necessarily appear to be against us with many others " (Book IV, Chap VI)

So many words, so many errors. Certainly Smith could not know 130 years ago that, while Portugal became bankrupt, England, in the year 1907 would become the world's creditor and capitalist to the amount of something like 10 billion dollars, merely through lending out her gold and silver, after having received it, or without at all receiving it, by letting the debts accrue which become due to her in consequence of her active balance sheets, which were not balanced by passive ones. He could not know this, nor did he know how affairs stood in his own time. He had the courage to write a book on political economy, without ever having been in active business life, without knowing more of it than a student can learn at his desk Henry Thomas Buckle, in his "History of Civilization in England" (Vol. I, p. 249), says· "The 'Wealth of Nations' is entirely deductive, since in it Smith generalizes the laws of wealth not from the phenomena of wealth, nor from statistical statements, but from the phenomena of selfishness, thus making a deductive application of one set of mental principles to the whole set of economic facts. The illustrations with which his great book abounds are no part of the real argument, they are subsequent to the conception " However, even a deductive philosopher ought to have known that money can be lent out at usury internationally as well as nationally, and that there is such a thing as land purchased abroad with gold, which land yields rent to its owner, whether that owner lives in England or in Portugal, also that there are really cases of generally favorable and of generally unfavorable balances

The worst trick in his speculations on international trade was, however, played on him by the wonderful discovery he made that "the general industry of a society can never exceed what the capital of the society can employ," which we had already a chance of admiring Upon this false premise, his whole ideas of trade policy have been built up, and it is no wonder that the conclusions thus drawn from a false major are absolute nonsense If it were true that a society could not increase its industry beyond fixed limits, it would be quite correct to conclude that the introduction of any new industry must correspondingly hamper one already existing and that therefore the industries for which the country is best adapted are preferable to those of a more exotic nature No use consequently, to protect any industry, for what cannot maintain itself without such artificial methods had better make room for what is more congenial to the soil As I have shown, however, the assumed fact does not exist, there is practically no limit to the extension of a society's industry. On the contrary, the more industries a nation possesses, the more industries it will have room for If spinning flourishes, weaving succeeds, and if both have reached a certain development, the manufacture of spinning and weaving machinery will pay, which in its turn gives more work to foundries, these to more iron and coal mines, etc

Unfortunately, authority plays a very pernicious part in public opinion Carlyle's "thirty millions, mostly fools," are too much in the habit of following some men with great names, like sheep running behind their bell-wether, or we should be farther advanced The first work urgently required before a sound building can be erected, is to clear out of the way the old ruins No headway can be made, unless the work done by certain men of renown is valued at its real worth, unless we fully recognize in which way these theory-mongers have managed to stultify themselves and the trusting public, which though it does not understand their reasoning, estimates their depth by their abstruseness It is taken in so much easier through the mutual support these philosophers give one another, through the flocking together of these birds of a feather.

Here, for instance, we have some wonderful theories on our present topic, hatched, in support of Smith's nonsense, by David Ricardo, a man who, though a speculator at the Exchange, had never any practical experience of mercantile business, which another theorist and deductive reasoner, John Stuart Mill, and still others of the same guild, are so delighted with, that they pass on the nonsense as if it were based on observations of real facts, and not merely on pure baseless inventions concocted at the scholar's desk. Adam Smith's deductively-found theories about international trade, culminating in Jean Baptiste Say's proclamation that *commodities are paid for with commodities,"* so delighted the imaginative Ricardo that he set to work to substantiate this assumption, even in the extreme instance of one country producing everything—without exception—cheaper than another country, as, for example, may occur in the near future with Japan If that country, with its low wages, continues to progress in industrial development as it has done during the last four decades, there may soon be hardly any article which cannot be produced more cheaply there than anywhere else in the world

The obtaining of a favorable balance of trade must therefore meet the most serious consideration of statesmen and. anyhow, they must look out that their country has favorable financial balances, which are as important nationally as they are in the case of individuals I repeat this for the purpose of cutting off shallow free-trader jokes like that of merchandise intended for importation, but burned at sea. "Its destruction," they argue, "diminishes imports, and thus procures a better balance of trade; *ergo*, according to the protectionists, it is better for a country if cargoes of this kind are lost than if they arrive in safety."

Certainly in such a case the actual imports are lessened, but the financial balance remains the same as if the ship had arrived, for the goods have to be paid for if they run at the risk of the importing country, and if they do not, other goods will take their place. So far as the trade and financial balance is concerned, the lost goods are as if they never had left their home port.

An explanation may be demanded why the international imports and exports do not balance, as they ought to, where the imports of one country are the exports of others. Instead of this, the imports preponderate considerably. The loose way in which exports are booked is mainly responsible for this. Imports are much more reliable, of which the custom houses take care. The booking of freight charges forms another item of inexactitude.

In modern financial balances the expenses of tourists have become of an importance they never had before. Some countries are almost entirely passive in this line, the United States, for instance. Others, such as Switzerland and Italy, are almost entirely on the active side. Very few foreigners travel in this country while the money which its people spend abroad runs into large figures. Switzerland, on the other side, has a yearly income of over thirty million dollars from this source. Italy and France show up hardly smaller active balances in this department.

Because I have tried to demolish certain errors which, unfortunately, are usually employed as weapons on the free trade side, I have been called a protectionist by some of its partisans. They do not reflect what a slap in the face they give their own party by such an imputation. It implies that the fallacies I attack are indispensable bulwarks of their school. I do not think they are. I believe that a man may stand up for free trade, if his country, according to his opinion, will profit more in the extension of its exports than it will lose by the increase of imports through such a policy, that its balance of trade will thus benefit by free trade. Another may be a protectionist on the opposite ground, or because he believes that you cannot convert other nations to free trade by onesidedly opening your own doors, like England, while the other doors are closed, but rather by closing yours, too, in the expectation that diminishing exports will preach them a more eloquent free trade, or reciprocity lesson, than the best free trader could supply. Disarming in the face of a forest of bristling bayonets has never been good policy, as the experience of history has proved often enough.

Each of two antagonists will have to prove his case by arguments based on such facts, for instance as a custom union between Britain and her colonies, or middle Europe and Argentine against the United States. The exclusion of his wheat and cotton from the world's market would soon make the American farmer a radical free trader. He never will, as long as the others endure American high protection without shooting back

This part of the question is so much of a side issue, compared with the great problems treated in these pages, that many reformers consider it positively harmful to bring in this apple of Eris so likely to divide allies in the main fight. As stated in another place, I here find one of the main arguments against the Single-Tax method of land restoration The Single-Tax must abolish customs, as there is to be no other tax but that on land values Thus its partisans are bound to stand up for free trade, antagonizing some of their best allies in the fight against land monopoly, who happen to be protectionists If I have had to attack balance of trade fallacies it was principally because the part played by money in international trade can not be understood without an explanation of the way in which international balances arise and are settled

For all that I do not stand up for protection; I merely defend it against attacks based on general economic principles. It is just as impossible to select certain principles of political economy from the rest without a disastrous failure as it is to take the best material and try to build with it on treacherous ground If we want to erect a dwelling on a quaggy bog, canvas and bark are better building materials than granite and oak, and to reject the flimsy stuff under such circumstances in favor of the more solid materials on the score of general principles of solidity, is just as preposterous as to decide for free trade under all circumstances merely because it agrees with fundamental economic principles. This would be correct policy only where all else is in line with first principles. With free land and money free trade fits in harmoniously, but with monopolized land and monopoly money, which form the quaking bog on which our economic building is erected, free trade may prove the heavy load under which the edifice will sink still more rapidly. Protection, just because it is opposed to true economic principles, may be the very thing wanted under such conditions We have no choice in the matter, either we stand up for true principles all round, or we have to go on the line of expediency, and if protection is found on this line we shall have to advise protection The decision will then have to depend on practical business conditions, usually ignored by the theoretician

Among these, the question of reciprocity stands in the foreground. The contempt with which it is treated by the Liberal party now in power in England, is due to the great reverence still paid to Smith's teachings. England is paying dearly for this blind deference to authority

The effects of the present commercial depression will make this clearer even than it is How sad to see the hopes of a land reform, to be brought by the Liberals, thrown back for another decade, through the certain victory of protectionist Toryism! The grower of hops, ruined by free American hops, the Sheffield manufacturer of steel goods thrown on the pavement by Solingen's overproduction dumped on the English market at any price, they and their workers are not the men who are accessible to hopes of the future based on possible land reforms The shirt is nearer to the body of the unemployed than the coat, the living, or rather starving present is more vivid than a distant future The question of the dear or cheap loaf takes the background of how to procure any loaf, cheap or dear, the same question which a witty Irishman so tersely expressed in these words. "In Old Ireland you can get a bushel of potatoes for six-pence, but the difficulty is to get the six-pence."

After we have thus settled the international bugbear, only one more international question remains to be answered Why do we find so many paper-currency countries who have made or are making all possible efforts to return to a gold currency—Russia, Austria, Italy and Argentine, for instance?

We might reply that a variable paper currency cannot compare with a scientific one as here delineated, which keeps up a more stable standard of value than gold, and by many the dangers connected with continual variations of the standard are considered greater than those inherent in gold This applies also to silver countries, like India and Mexico, whose governments try to adopt the gold standard

We have, however, to seek the main reasons for this state of affairs in the great influence exercised throughout the world by the creditor class, which benefits by the appreciation of money and in the prevailing ignorance in currency affairs Who are the men whose judgment usually prevails in such matters?

The statesman? I do not wish to estimate him as low as Adam Smith did when he spoke of him as "that insidious and crafty animal, vulgularly called a statesman or politician, whose councils are directed by the momentary fluctuations of affairs" (Book IV, Chapter II) But I must agree with Buckle when he expresses his opinion of the rulers of a country "Such men are at best only the creatures of the age, never its creators. Their measures are the result of social progress, not the cause of it." ("Hist Civ," Vol I, Chapter V)

Under party government the statesmen are supposed to represent the opinion of their party and in money questions the state of things which the historian Douglas found existing in the paper-money period of New England, and also in the French Revolution, still obtains all over the world "Parties," he said, "were no longer Whigs and Tories, but creditors and debtors"

The bankers and financiers? My personal experience of this class—of whom during seven years of banking experience I have known quite a number some of them being near relations—has taught me that these very bankers and financiers are of all men in the world least capable of pronouncing a correct judgment on the great currency problem   They cannot see the forest for the trees, besides being too deeply interested in the lumber business   If we are so entirely at sea in the currency business, if we have not yet been able to reach a safe harbor, it is because our ship is trying to steer its dangerous course between the Scylla of the scholar or the currency crank, who are all theory and no practice and the Charybdis of the financier who is all practice and no theory, who has no more the power to get out of his groove than Bismarck's dog mentioned in the last chapter.   The combination of theory and practice, of the study of monetary science with practical work in financial business is unfortunately rarely found, or we should be further advanced in the position to be adopted in regard to one of the most momentous factors in the great social problem *Circulation*

CHAPTER V.

CAPITAL, CAPITALISM AND INTEREST

The meaning of "Capitalism" can only be understood when we reverse the general definition of the relationship between Capital and Interest, when we see in Interest the father, in Capital the progeny

WHAT is capital?   Economists are at loggerheads when asked to define this important factor of their science, and their definitions mostly differ from what is popularly understood by the word So, for instance, may we hear every day Brown has invested his capital in land   If this means that Brown has bought and spread manure, made fences, dug a ditch for irrigation purposes or laid drains to desiccate the land, it agrees with the most general definition given by our economists, for Brown is using wealth (product of labor) for the production of wealth   But this is not at all what is usually understood when we speak of investments in land. If we say Brown has invested his capital in land, we generally mean that he has bought land which henceforth is his capital   The rental income from this land becomes now the interest of Brown's capital, and the sharp division which most economists make between land and capital, between rent and interest, is blurred together   Other economists by adopting a definition still more in accordance with the popular conception, escape this dilemma, but fall into another.   While defining as capital anything which produces an income, and thus ceasing to make a distinction between the products of man's labor and land— the substance and surface of our globe, the Divine Creator's gift to all men—they also include under the heading of capital, human talents and skill, such as a good voice, or the gift of acting, drawing, composing, the skill of the artisan, as well as the knowledge of the professor In this they keep in touch with the popular meaning, for we all know how often we have heard such expressions as ' Patti's voice is her principal capital," or "the most valuable capital possessed by Rubinstein was his wonderful art" Unfortunately here again we find two conceptions thrown together which to keep apart is even more important than the distinction between land and products of labor, *i e,* wealth no separation is made between capital and labor, between interest and wages I purposely do not say profit and wages as my business here is only with the interest component of profits Wages of organization and supervision, the other component, fall under wages, and what remains, besides rent, is risk premium, lottery gains, amply compensated by losses as we have seen in the previous chapter, or the tribute levied by monopoly, which a fundamental social reform will see disappear with its source I say this with a full knowledge of Marx's famous "Mehrwerth" (surplus value) theory, which finds the origin of profit in the power of the employer owning the means of production to exact unpaid working time A remarkable discovery consisting n the not only worthless but absolutely nonsensical substitution of a time profit to a product or money profit! At all events neither time nor product could ever have been exacted on free soil under free exchange   I hope I need not explain that any income received by a person from his work falls under the category of wages whether he works on his own account or for another individual who pays him a fixed or variable amount, whether it is physical or intellectual work, whether it is done by the carpenter's hands or the dancing master's feet, the throat of the singer the resisting powers of the professional faster's organism, or the thinker's brain.

As it seems impossible to give a generally recognized definition of Capital in the same way in which we can define what is meant by a horse a chair, or a house, we must formulate a definition which is useful and at the same time fairly compatible with popular meaning I consequently define *Capital as property which can procure an income without any work on the part of its owner*

This definition comes also nearest to the etymological derivation of the word from *kephalaion, caput,* the head, the principal, as distinguished from the expected interest or usury, the unessential In this sense Patti s larnyx is not capital, as it cannot be used to produce an income without her own work, nor is the skill of a worker of any kind his capital, whereas land is capital, as it produces an income without the work of its owner

I now proceed to give my reasons for considering this definition more useful than that mostly adopted, and often called the orthodox one

1 The orthodox definition cannot serve any practical purpose whatever for it regards as capital any kind of wealth used for reproductive purposes, and thus creates—not a category of definite objects—but one of temporary and changing uses. There is not a single kind of wealth which could not be simple wealth at one moment and capital the next The piano in my drawing-room, until

now used only for my pleasure, was simple wealth in the morning, but became capital the moment I gave my first paid music lesson on it in the afternoon   Bread bought for my table is wealth, but changes into capital with my change of mind which destines it to serve as provision in a fishing expedition   My horse was wealth as long as I used him merely to take my daily exercise on his back, but has been capital since I hired him out for money. On the other hand, even a machine may change into simple wealth from having been capital if it is presented to a museum   Of what practical use can it possibly be to create a special division of wealth with such flowing boundary lines?

2. The orthodox definition is not only useless, but positively dangerous, because, instead of bringing light into an important problem, it merely makes matters more confused

When an orator or writer has to reply to a socialist's attack upon capital as the oppressor of labor, he points to what orthodox economy calls capital, and speaks of our wonderful progress due to this capital, i.e, to our improved means of production and distribution; whereas his antagonist thinks of Government bonds, of land monopoly, of mining rights, of all kinds of tribute-claims selling at the stock exchange for certain amounts, and not at all falling under the orthodox definition of capital, though representing that capital which people principally have in view when they use the term   It is here that precision is of the utmost importance   It can by itself produce neither good nor harm whether we call a horse capital or mere wealth, the animal will not pull one ounce more weight, nor will a violin change its quality, whether it is wealth because we only use it for our amusement, or whether it changes into capital when we play on it for pay in an orchestra   But it is of great consequence to waive aside with a Podsnapian gesture the dangerous tribute-claims as not being capital, fixing our hostile gaze exclusively on the most harmless and even useful objects in the world—the means of production. We can better understand the fatal effect which such a classification must exercise upon an exact recognition of the social problem since we have realized in Chapters I and IV that the means of production would be far more abundant, and would be freely at the disposal of labor, were it not for that other kind of capital ignored by the panegyrist of the tool capital   We have recognized how this tribute capital is the greatest obstacle to the production of wealth by impeding exchange and consequently production through a reduction of the available money and the credit vehicles

My own definition makes no distinction between the chair on which I take a rest and the same chair when I sit on it to write something by which I gain my daily bread, but it excludes the means of production where they are at the free disposal of honest and solvent workers, and includes them where they are used as an instrument of exploitation   The substitution of the steam-plow for the crooked stick with which the savage tickles the soil, is certainly very beneficial; but paramount for the masses of workers is the question: Who owns the plow? We certainly can produce more with the steam-plow than with the stick, but the stick was owned by the savage, together with the soil cultivated by it, while the steam-plow and the land on which it works, belong to an exploiter. Some clear-headed men—Ruskin and Leo Tolstoy, for instance—have come to the conclusion that the advantage is not so unquestionably with the steam plow as many economists pretend, and that the question of ownership, of the free use of the means of production deserves as much consideration as that of their perfection.

3. My definition of capital alone legitimates its derivation: *Capitalism, ie*, the reign of capital as a means of exploitation. The increasing amount of machinery required for modern production, by itself cannot create and constitute capitalism, for even the socialistic state would not renounce technic progress. In fact, socialists expect from freedom a much more extensive use of machinery in the arts of production than has ever been reached under the system of exploitation.

We shall presently see that the productivity of machinery is not the cause of that main instrument of exploitation called *Interest*, that if it were not for the possibility of investing savings in land purchases and in a legal tender money made from certain scarce metals, capitalists would be glad to lend out their surplus free in the shape of machinery, or any other means of production to anybody supplying the work of preservation. That the owners of machinery can levy a tribute from labor, independent of their pay for the work of organization and supervision, is not a cause, but an effect of interest. The interest represented by tribute-claims based on monopoly of some sort is the father of the interest demanded and paid for the means of production produced by labor. If the root were destroyed, the tree would disappear. This root—the world's tribute-claims based on monopoly—once out of the way, through the withdrawal of the monopoly base, the workers would soon be the free owners of the means of production, and meanwhile would use all such means free of cost which would eliminate them from the capital category of my definition. Untrammeled productive power would create new means of production to an extent hardly realizable by a generation living under the influence of the overproduction bugbear. In other words, the destruction of capital, as here defined, would, to an incredible extent multiply capital in the orthodox economist's sense. Capital, correctly understood, is thus the arch enemy of wealth-creation, and not its friend. The socialist is right when he curses it as the worst enemy of labor. With the disappearance of monopoly, capital will vanish and wealth alone remain. This wealth, whether used for consumption or for productive purposes, will be deprived of all tribute-levying power.

Though half of the wealth now figuring in our tables of national wealth will thus be destroyed, we shall be richer than ever

before, because, when this branch of our so-called wealth which consists of tribute-claims, tabled according to their selling value, and
which practically is an obstacle of wealth-production is out of the
way, production will come up to productivity and our real national
wealth will increase immeasurably. The vanished value of the land
and mines, exclusive of improvements, the right of way of railroads,
river crossings, telegraphs, telephones, trams, gas pipes, lighting
and power wires, etc, will be more than replaced by the value of
new land improvements, houses, railroads, telegraphs, etc., whose
profuser creation this disappearance of monopoly will have rendered
possible.

We have seen how one of the roots of the tribute-levying power,
whose market value forms capital in its correct economic and popular
sense, how rent retires from the capital-breeding business through
land nationalization We have now to show how Interest, that other
prolific root of tribute-capital, also dies with the great reform, provided it is followed by the change in our currency laws proposed in
Chapter III.

The taking of usury has been condemned by the ethical and
often by the statutory laws of various nations, and only since a
comparatively recent period, that of Elizabeth, has the term *usury*
been confined to the taking of exorbitant increase, while the new
term "interest" has been substituted for what before was called
"moderate usury" So at least we are informed by R G. Sillar, the
indefatigable enemy of interest, who tells us that "when the first
usury law was passed, it was necessary to coin a word for legal
usury and we find the word 'interest' was first used in a public
document in 1623 in the Act of James I It was most likely used
privately before this, for Shylock says ∙ 'My bargains and my well-
won thrift, which he calls "interest," and he apparently says this
with a sneer "

All attacks upon interest were ineffective as long as the root of
the poisonous vegetation was not touched Finally the man of science
tried to justify what was universally practiced Only in this way
can we explain the defence of interest set up by political economists
threadbare sophistries of so flimsy a fabric that custom and prejudice
alone prevent every observer from seeing through them An un-
tutored savage would laugh at such teachings, or would think their
exponents possessed by evil spirits Try to make him understand,
when he borrows one of his neighbor's horses which the other does
not need, but only keeps in reserve for an emergency, that his feeding of the horse is not a full equivalent for the loan, provided the
use the animal is put to does not decrease its value Try to make
him see the possibility of a claim amounting to two horses after a
certain number of years, both as young and good as the original
horse was when he borrowed it, and that a time may arrive when,
though the borrowed horse long since went the way of all flesh, the
debt to his neighbor or his heirs shall have grown to the extent of

more horses than are possessed by the whole tribe A mere savage
will never succeed in seeing the possibility, not to say the justice, of
such a claim, it needs a civilized man to understand the effect of
compound interest, and an economist or jurist to defend the principle. And now let us see how these gentlemen go about it

Prominent among their theories is that which ascribes to capital
a certain *inherent productivity*, which is let with the capital, and is
refunded to the lender in the shape of interest The term "capital"
is here used in the orthodox sense of "means of production," but
excepting land, which produces rent, there is no means of production which will bring forth anything without being used by labor.
This, by itself, would not invalidate a claim made for capital of
part of the surplus which has been realized by its help; part of the
surplus, for unless labor gets at least some of it, labor would have no
advantage to use capital How much of this surplus will have to
go to the capitalist and how much to the worker, under free conditions, depends on supply and demand. A well-known example
used by Bastiat in defence of interest represents capital by a plane
and work by a carpenter If there were only an insufficient number
of planes in the world, not sufficient to supply the demand, Bastiat
would be correct in maintaining that as a carpenter can produce
more planed boards with the plane than he can with a more primitive
tool, he would find it to his advantage to borrow the plane, though
he had to give to the lender some of the surplus product due to the
use of this tool In Chapter IV., I have shown, however, that the
production of tools would always outrun the demand if no artificial
obstacles were in the way. In this case the supply of planes would
be more than plentiful, plane-owners would have a larger stock of
planes to lend or sell than there are cabinet-makers and carpenters
willing to use them Keeping these planes in stock would simply
mean the gradual loss of the capital; for mould, rust, fire, inundations, earthquakes, war, robbery of any kind, cost of storage and
cleaning, are all elements of depreciation; and at any time a new invention may make old patterns unsalable altogether, or salable only
at a reduced price Thus it might happen that the plane-owner would
do better in letting out the plane free of cost, provided the carpenter
agreed, under a sufficient guarantee for the fulfillment of the
agreement to replace the plane after a certain time by another worth
as much as the borrowed plane was at the time of lending Even
if, instead of paying interest, the worker demanded a certain percentage of the service rendered by him to the plane-owner, the latter
might find it to his advantage to strike the bargain This proves
simply that the interest claim is not due to the productivity of capital
but to supply and demand Unfortunately, there are artificial obstacles in the way which prevent the unlimited supply of capital, and
I shall presently show that interest takes an important place among
these obstacles We shall see that interest is partly responsible for the
unnatural conditions which to-day put a bridle on the productivity of

capital in the hands of labor , while the productivity of capital, when unfettered kills interest, which does not exactly indicate any parental relationship between the two powers. Stranger still than the attempt to trace such relationship are the errors of those economists who consider the element of time the father of interest In consequence of time's creative powers As far as the products of human labor are concerned, the work of time is of a destructive, not of a creative nature Unless new labor is continually applied, all products tend to lose in value Even where they are relatively indestructible— as gold or platinum for instance—they must be guarded if the owner wants to conserve them: and guarding is labor, while storage means rent besides Exceptions, such as the ripening of crops, the growth of trees, and the increase, through breeding, of domestic animals, are only apparent, and are caused by omitting the analysis of all the economic factors at work In the first place, the additional value is due to the labor employed Then we have the use of land, represented by rent in our calculations. If we also have to add interest, it is because interest is elsewhere obtainable for the capital thus invested, and consequently must be added to the price. If this capital were obtainable free of interest, the cost of timber of crops and cattle, of old wine and brandy (mentioned specially because their higher price, due to age, has been given as a proof of the interest-creating force of time), or any other product, would not exceed the cost of labor and rent In selling, profit may be added besides, but interest forms no part of it, unless interest has to be paid for the capital employed, in which case its addition to the price is *an effect*, and *not a cause*

There are also economists who make use of the element of time in another sense, in that of putting a higher value on the present than on the future possession of an object They are not so wise as the well-known boy who, when told that the early bird catches the worm, replied "So much the worse for the worm , why did it get up so soon?" He perceived both sides of the question, the bird's and the worm's side but those gentlemen cannot see that, though the present use of something may be more valuable to one party than its future possession, the very reverse may be the case for another For the hungry man a piece of meat to-day is worth more than one ready for him a week hence; but by the man with more meat on hand than he can eat within a fortnight, the taste of another's fresh meat will certainly be preferred to the *haut goût* of his own after a week has gone round Whether the service rendered to him by the other party, who supplies him with fresh meat a week hence in exchange for the meat borrowed to-day, will be as great, greater or less in value than the service rendered by him to the hungry man who might have starved if he could not have gotten the meat at once, is not to be gauged by the individual estimation of such value but by the assessment which the market makes on the basis of supply and demand The wanderer who lost his way and reaches a baker's shop in a starving condition may be willing to give all his wealth for the piece of bread he buys, rather than miss it, but for all that he will have to pay only one single penny, because the market does not consider the accidental personal feelings of certain parties, but the general conditions of · supply and demand   If our meat owner were the only party whom the hungry, meatless man could apply to, the case might be different; but if there are plenty of others who have more meat than they want, and to whom a service is rendered by giving them fresh meat a week hence for the meat of to-day, the mutual value of the services may not only be equal, but less meat may be demanded in return at a later period than has been given, for even half-a-pound of fresh meat is better than ten pounds of spoiled food

In fact, this case does not differ from that where the ready plane and one made after a certain period were in consideration The different degree of perishableness of both merchandise is of no importance; nor is that of their utility for production   A starving carpenter is as much hampered in production as one without a plane   If I thought it worth while to discuss it separately, it was because some most intelligent men have not been able to get out of this special dilemma—Professor Boehm-Bawerk, for instance

Also the source of Interest looked for in the traders' profit only leads to the element of time   Economically no difference can be found between the time spent by the merchant's bark between two ports or that spent by the grain of wheat between seeding and harvest

The habit of seeing interest paid in the transactions of daily life has so confused economists that they cannot lift their ideas from this rut and cannot gain a free outlook   This happened also to Henry George   He could not see how a tailor would not invariably sell a coat cheaper for cash rather than accept for it a note payable ten years later   The fact that, under present conditions, the cash received at once can be invested at interest, entirely hid from him the possibility that where such investment can not be made, and where any saver has to be content if he can invest his savings interest free, without being required to pay for the cost of preserving his capital, some good responsible customer agreeing to pay after a number of years, at a time when the money is needed, might be preferable to one who pays at once   Though I was not successful in making my friend see the case in this light, I had the satisfaction to hear him state publicly in the Manhattan Single Tax Club New York—where one of our discussions took place in April, 1893— that if I were right in asserting that interest would disappear with private rent, all he could say was —"So much the better" With these words he justified my attack made in "Rent, Interest and Wages" against his theory evolved in "Progress and Poverty" · that wages and interest rise and fall together, so that it is to the worker's benefit if interest is high.

The same force of habit is responsible for another claim often brought out and just as false the claim that *interest is the reward of abstemiousness* and that its disappearance would stop saving. We need not enter into the question once touched by the great socialist leader, Lasalle, we need not inquire whose abstemiousness is meant, that of the capitalist or of those whom he exploits; whether the interest paid in this world of ours is not produced by the abstention of the interest-payers Nor need we waste time in admiring the abstemiousness of our Rothschilds, Carnegies, Astors, Vanderbilts, and other interest-lords, but it might be worth our while to look a little into the second part of the wonderful thesis, the pretension that *capital production will stop if no more interest is obtainable*

It practically means that thinking and civilized man does not possess even the provident spirit of many animals, such as the bee, the ant, the squirrel, a number of birds, etc., who save for bad times and find the reward of their abstemiousness in its product, in the accumulated stock, on which they live at the time when production has to stop temporarily Could the bee reason, it would deem itself very happy in finding all the honey it has gathered undiminished at the time when it is required for apiarian consumption, the idea to stop saving, because no automatic increase of the store can be expected, would certainly never enter its insect head It needs the brains of a professional economist to breed such an idea Take, for instance, the following from the writings of Th Mithoff, professor at the University of Gottingen: "If he (the capitalist) did not cede the use of his capital to another, he would be able to use it himself for the purposes of production or consumption. In temporarily renouncing, therefore, the use of capital in favor of others, he makes a sacrifice for which an equivalent interest is due to him Doing away with interest would cause a great part of the capital now lent out for productive purposes to lie idle or to be used for consumptive purposes, and the growing difficulty of a paying use for capital must very soon reduce the future creation of capital But as the prosperity and the progressive development of economic life depend on the use of capital in production—doing away with the compensation for the use of capital in the shape of a part of the undertaker's income and of interest would result in a deep and permanent retrogression of the economic development "

So many sentences, so many errors

To begin with, capitalists only lend out their capital when they cannot put it to better use for the purposes of production in their own business There is a limit to such use The capacity of supervising industrial or commercial undertakings is limited even in the case of the creator of the capital, and generally much more so with his heirs. There cannot be the least doubt that if the descendants of Astor and Rothschild had to use their capital in business exclusively, and could not invest in land, bonds and similar securities, they would be ruined, as was the case with the descendants of our great merchants of centuries ago whose funds were left in business   If our multimillionaires had to invest their wealth in this fashion, the opinion we often hear announced—that the big fortunes disperse as quickly as they were gained—might be justified   The heirs of capable business men are often destitute of those qualities which made their progenitors great, and mismanagement as well as subdivision among the heirs, would soon dispose of the ancestral accumulations

Unfortunately, rent and interest on certain investments of a different nature have the double effect of not only securing a good income without any risk for the capital, but also of increasing the sum total of the capital much faster than the average number of heirs can diminish it, especially at the well-known low rate of family propagation of the rich   Facts have proved this.   Each of the present Astors, Rothschilds, Vanderbilts etc, is richer than was the founder of the family's fortunes—through the mere accumulative power of interest and rent

In my first book, "Auf friedlichem Wege," which appeared in 1884, long before trusts, Standard Oil and the railroad combines created multi-millionaires, I drew attention to the fearful danger which Interest was preparing for us in the quiet, almost unobserved accumulations it creates.   What is New York's unearned increment, enriching the Astors; what is railroad monopoly which built up the Vanderbilts, Harrimans, Morgans, what is the control of nature's resources, the root of the Rockefeller, Carnegie and Guggenheim fortunes, compared with the silent power of Interest, the creator of the Rothschilds?   In the book above mentioned I estimated their fortune at one thousand million dollars   Since then, through the mere force of interest compounding the thousand millions have more than doubled, have perhaps trebled   Standard Oil may be dissolved, railroads nationalized, the trusts broken up, but the quiet power which is behind the continuous growth of the Rothschilds and other excrescenses of the same nature, which increases their immense accumulations to unbelievable dimensions, with the impetus of a force of nature and the certainty of mathematics, will subsist   Interest will continue to do its destructive work until we sap its foundations.

The proverb, "three generations from shirtsleeves to shirtsleeves," has been deprived of its soothing power by well secured compound-interest

We have already seen how pernicious such accumulations have proved to our economic development, and how the very reverse of our professor's expectations as to the blessings we owe to interest has been verified by the facts of real life

But not only a productive use in their own business is impossible for our greatest capitalists, even self-consumption becomes almost infeasible.   Balls costing half a million dollars, weddings swallowing $400,000 in 15 minutes, of which $125 000 are paid for church decorations; what, in comparison is the cost of Lucullus' or Crassus' revels reported in the annals of Rome's worst times? And yet, what are such extravagances when compared with the incomes of the parties? They marvel at the bath of Vanderbilt costing a million dollars, but the gentleman might buy a million bath every month without consuming his income. I leave entirely aside the usual moral drawn from such prodigalities in a world in which millions of persons have not enough to fence them from hunger and cold, for the worst is that our millionaires are not extravagant enough. If they consumed their incomes, the world would be better off. It is just because they save a great part of their revenues that the workers cannot find employment. It is because they have not enough appetite that others have to go without a meal. If they could wear thousands of suits at a time, thousands of poor toilers would be able to buy some clothing. If every penny of their money were wasted in palace building, the poor would be able to procure slum dwellings. It is just to their saving and investing their savings at compound interest, in connection with our land and currency systems—that we owe most of our misery, as I have already shown. That this is being recognized more widely is evinced by the following remarks of John T. Gibson in the *Indianapolis News*.

"A few minutes' thought will convince anyone that the industrious man who lives up to his income, and saves nothing, is at least as large a factor in the accumulation of capital as the man who saves. Suppose for instance, that we would all start in to-morrow and narrow down our expenses to the last notch, 'cut off everything except oatmeal gruel, and make it thin at that,' with the idea of saving ourselves rich, how long would it be before we should find that, instead of being on the highroad to greater wealth and higher civilization, we should be on the back track to poverty and barbarism? There would be no demand for anything except oatmeal, and as no one could sell anything else that he happened to possess, he could not acquire the wherewith to buy oatmeal, and would have to produce it himself, or steal it, or starve. There would be no trade, no use for all our fine business blocks, nor for the railroads, nor steamboats, nor factories, nor any of the arts of civilization. The labor-saving principle of the division of labor could not be utilized except on the smallest scale in co-operative oatmeal production. Altogether we should be in a very bad way—a good deal worse off than the Indians were, for they had elbow-room and a game-preserve at their back."

If the rich spent their incomes, consumption of such immense amounts would give employment to millions who now are without work, and these millions could save, could gradually become owners of their own means of production, or could improve those now in their possession and thus bring about a great increase of the present general production. Instead of this, we have seen how the investments of the rich, restrict the access to natural opportunities, reduce

the circulation of credit money, restrict the credit building in which
our commerce is carried on, and thus prevent production from keeping abreast of productive power. We cannot produce unless we consume, and the masses are bereft of their full purchasing power
through the rent and interest tributes they have to pay to the rich,
either directly, or indirectly by means of the tax-gatherer or the
employer, while the rich, instead of consuming their share, invest
it in the purchase of more well secured tribute-claims, the only paying investment in the long run, as new production is a losing business where there is not a corresponding consumption

Thus it is not astonishing that the country which boasts of the
greatest number of millionaires, which estimates its national wealth
for 1907 at 110 billions, must also boast of harboring the greatest
misery in its cities I am not going to indulge in statistics without
an official census background For instance, those of Charles
Spahr in "The present distribution of Wealth in the United States"
(1900), in which the population is divided into four classes The
first consists of 125,000 families, one per cent of the population,
with an aggregate wealth of $32,880,000,000, or over one-half of
the total national wealth of 1890, so that the remaining 99 per cent.
of the population own less than these one per cent Fifty per cent
own nothing at all Seven-eighths of the population possess only
one-eighth of the national wealth Or R A Dague in the "Forward Movement Herald," of Los Angeles, according to whom the
producers' share in the national wealth, from 62½ per cent in 1850
has gradually gone down, from year to year, until in 1900 it reached
10 per cent, while the non-producers' share has risen from 37½
per cent to 90 per cent Or Senator La Folette's estimate that all
lines of industry of the country now are virtually controlled by 76
men

It is impossible to say how much truth there is in these statistics, for unfortunately though figures do not lie, liars write
figures This country does not possess the basis for any estimate of
the distribution of wealth, such as the income and inheritance taxes,
which produce valuable European statistics in this field Yet
these very European statistics prove to us that our American statisticians cannot be so very far from the truth, especially as with our
greater facility of locomotion we are marching towards the abyss
at a much livelier tempo than the rest of the world Highly respected English statisticians, for instance, such as Leone Levy and
Baxter, figure that the share of the English workers in 1867
amounted to 40 per cent of the national wealth, while estimates of
1886 gave them only 20 per cent, with a probable decrease since
then

Certainly any of the above statistics come nearer the truth than
the estimate of our Director of the Census, Mr S N D North, in
his letter to me of July 5, 1907, in which he says "The relative pro-

portion of wealth in the hands of a few cannot be, if any, greater than in 1850, or in the days of George Washington " We do not need statistical tables to recognize the enormity of the error contained in the above sentence, which will cause surprise wherever it is read. A look around us with open eyes proves sufficiently that one may be a Director of the Census and still have far less insight into the relations of the actual world than any poor laborer on the street.

I shall go on with my analysis of Professor Mithoff's lucubrations, asking the reader's pardon in thus seemingly wasting time but, unfortunately, Professor Mithoff is not the only one who believes that demon Interest is in reality a beneficent Ceres, out of whose cornucopia the incentive to all wealth-producing industry is poured over humanity The alternative given by the learned gentleman in the words *"to lie idle'* cannot pass either without a few words I wonder how the way in which this capital would lie idle *presented itself to his mind He can hardly have been so *naif* as to imagine that the rich would or even could put in a stock of gold or coins; for he probably knew that the whole gold stock of the world does not exceed five billion dollars, and that the savings of the rich in the United States alone outrun this amount more than ten-fold And even supposing that there were gold enough to be got for the purpose, the supply of the useless stuff would keep millions busy whose consumption and savings would fertilize industry in all other departments of production Even under this impossible supposition, the wealth accumulations of the rich would do more good than they are doing under the dominion of interest

If not in the vaults, how then are the savings to lie idle?

Does the learned gentleman suppose that the savings are received in the shape of products of some sort? Were this so, the rich owners of these products would have to pay for their storage, and for the work required to keep the goods from deterioration They would soon find that the best shape in which they could store their wealth would be in means of production of some sort, which the workers could utilize and thus make self-sustaining This certainly would not mean lying idle

Nor could investments in land be meant because they would bring a rental income, which means interest on the purchase capital, which cannot be called lying idle Besides the money paid for land as well as that spent for the other things, goes to somebody and thus circulates—does not remain idle

The greatest error of all we find displayed in our professor's statements is the pretension that the absence of interest would result in "a retrogression of the economic development" That the very contrary is the case is clearly perceived by Turgot, one of France's greatest financial authorities and economists, in his famous metaphor.

"The rate of interest* may be looked at as a kind of level below which all work, all culture, all industry, all trade ceases. It is like a sea spread over a vast country, the mountain tops rise over the waters, and form fertile and cultivated islands As the sea level sinks, the declivities of the mountains, then the plains and valleys, appear, covering themselves with produce of all kinds It is sufficient for the water to rise or fall one foot to inundate extensive shores, or to render them back to culture It is the superabundance of capital which enlivens enterprise, and the low rate of interest is at the same time the effect and the mark of the superabundance of capital."

The most superficial glance around us will show how Turgot's beautiful picture corresponds with reality. Thousands of useful enterprises everywhere, certain to benefit humanity at large, to increase its comforts, to cause a further advance of civilization, to raise the productivity of labor many fold—enterprises which would gradually pay back the outlay they caused, remain in the state of worthless projects, for the simple reason that a certain rate of interest cannot be got out of the capital invested. The Panama Canal would have been finished long ago, a tunnel would connect England and Ireland—perhaps also America and Asia—innumerable railways and canals would evolve from the state of visionary schemes into accomplished realities   Distant mountain-lakes and streams would quench the thirst of large cities now satisfied with impurer supplies, mountains over which the stage coach now winds its tedious way would be tunnelled, valleys would be spanned by viaducts and rivers—which now are crossed in primitive fashion—by bridges The whole face of the world would soon present an aspect differing in its progressiveness as much from the world we know as this is in advance of that remembered by our great-grandfathers What is in the way? Why have we to leave all this work undone? Can we not spare the labor? Can we not produce the machinery required, the raw materials needed? In a time whose chronic complaint is known under the names of over-production, want of employment and markets, commercial depression, such an answer can certainly not be accounted satisfactory   All know that no greater boon could be offered to millions than the opportunity of setting to work their productive power for the accomplishment of these and greater public works No danger either of not finding food, clothing shelter enough for the millions of workers needed to do the work. There is no department of production in which we could not multiply the output if there were a paying demand In fact, nothing stands in the way except one seemingly insuperable obstacle *Interest* The projectors may furnish ever so convincing a proof that the income from the improve-

---

* Of course, this means gross interest, the interest actually paid by the producer We shall yet see that a low net interest is often accompanied by a very high gross interest.

ment will sooner or later repay the cost, besides keeping up repairs, as long as they cannot also prove that a certain rate of interest can be depended on for the capital invested, they will preach to deaf ears.

With the disappearance of interest, these and thousands of other great works can be carried out within a comparatively short time. Innumerable inventions will come forth to diminish the amount of labor required, and they will no more be fought by trades unions, justly frightened over the prospect of a still greater scarcity of employment for their members The field of work will then grow with working facilities There is not a department of production and distribution where the disappearance of interest would not affect wonders What—even if he has the capital—makes the manufacturer build a shed lasting only a few years, where a stone cr concrete building would outlast generations, besides affording better conditions of health for the workers? *Interest.* The stone house would be cheaper in the end if it were not for the additional interest it costs, which figures up higher than the waste caused by the periodical repair or replacement of the shed It is interest which prevents the manufacturer or merchant from keeping more stock than is absolutely necessary, and thus precludes a more perfect division of work, as, for instance, in weaving, which demands continually expensive changes of patterns on the looms, where working for a certain length of time on the same pattern will cause a too great accumulation of stock, and thus a too great interest loss It is interest which may some day be mainly instrumental in vanquishing nations dependent on others for their food stuffs, because the fear of interest loss prevents them from storing enough cereals to last over more than a very short period. We have means to fight moisture, rats, mice and other vermin, and good conditions may preserve grain for many years, but we cannot protect it against the destructive effects of interest, which increases its cost with every passing day; so that, finally, it does not pay to keep stock, at any price, as long as we cannot destroy interest.

The disappearance of interest will take out of the way the greatest obstacle to money reform, a reform which in its turn is one of the most powerful weapons against the interest fiend Nothing restricts more the quantity of money which can be kept in circulation, or of free deposits in the banks, than the fear of losing interest— as we express ourselves when we either have to pay interest or miss a chance of obtaining it from others. From the poor wage-worker who carries at once to the savings bank every penny he does not absolutely require, that he may get interest, to the rich man who limits his ready money or bank account to his necessities, investing the balance as fast as he can to obtain interest—we witness a continuous restriction of the money stock held on hand The disappearance of interest would entirely change all this, would largely increase the money stock which could be kept in circulation or in the banks as a security for depositors

The beneficial effect produced by the disappearance of interest would be felt everywhere even in quarters where nobody would look for it at first sight   Who would think that it could be the most powerful means of introducing universal free trade, by making free trade what its defenders suppose it to be but what, as I have shown, it is not by any means fair trade?   It will not prevent the payment of imports with debt certificates, but it will withdraw the self-multiplying power from this debt, which now often makes the cheapest market the dearest in the end   Debt, as has been said in the previous chapter will then simply mean deferred payment by exportation   The delay, instead of causing loss, will only benefit the debtors who enjoy the free use of the capital in the interim

These will be the results of interest's exit from this world of ours, not those foretold by the blind bookworm of Gottingen University, and others of his ilk   The simplest calculation should have shown him the stupidity of his prognostics, should have taught him that, instead of stimulating, interest in reality tends to diminish saving and consequently production

If a man wants to retire on a yearly income of $500, he will save $10,000 if he can count on 5% interest, unless he buys a life annuity for even less money   The lower the rate of interest the more will he have to save, and if interest is unobtainable altogether he will have to save capital enough to last him for the balance of his life   He may have to go to an insurance company and pay in the sum corresponding to the average of years which statistics allow him, plus cost of administration   The calculation is much simplified by the absence of interest   If he wants to insure a certain capital to his family after his death, he will have to pay the yearly premium which corresponds to the sum, divided by the average number of years he is expected to live, according to statistics, plus a trifle for cost of administration   In either case he will have to save more than would be requisite in our days where the interest obtained by the company enables it to be content with smaller payments   If a life annuity to date from a certain age, or from invalidism, is desired, enough has to be paid in to correspond to the annuity multiplied by the number of years during which statistics promise him the enjoyment of the annuity plus cost of administration   Whether he pays the money in by yearly instalments while he is still working, or in one lump sum will then make no difference, as interest no more enters into the calculation   At any rate, he will have to save much more for such a purpose than he would in our interest-paying world.   Supposing he wants to retire at the age of fifty years, and to insure an annuity of $500 to his family, from then or his previous death up to the death of the last survivor. Let us say the number of years during which the annuity has to be paid is estimated as forty, the man will have to save something over $20,000, or at least double the amount he would need under present conditions And even then he will have saved only for the living generation if he wanted to commit the folly of saving also for unborn descendants, his accumulations would have to grow correspondingly, instead of needing only an insignificant increase under the interest *régime* Thus much more would be saved than in our time, and such savings would become what our present savings are wrongly supposed to be blessings, instead of the curses they really are through their restricting effect on consumption and consequently on production They would increase our means of production and communication, as well as all amenities of life They would help to raise the general income and welfare Until the saver consumes his economies they would take productive form, benefiting his fellow-men, and the world, as well as he, would be better off than if he had consumed at once what he produced More would have to be saved to live without work, but very much more could easily be saved in a world freed from the hampering effects of interest and the part played by its accumulations

We have seen how the creation of generations of do-nothings is by far the smallest evil resulting from such accumulations, but that the constantly increasing obstacles they oppose to the maintenance of production at the level of productive power are the very roots of the social problem of our time

So far, I have only shown what interest is not I have proved that it is neither the product of capital, the child of the element of time nor the just reward of abstinence I have made clear that, instead of stimulating production, it keeps it back For all that, I have not yet shown its real nature and parentage This we have now to elucidate.

Interest is a tribute due by one set of men to another That this is its nature, that it is a tribute and not a product, is made clear by the simple fact that all men could as little live on their interest income as all could live by burgling or by taking in each others' washing This striking illustration is due to Mr. L H Berens. Somebody has to pay interest, or others, could not live by it That interest is a tribute, and not a natural product of capital, time, or anything else, can also be demonstrated by simple arithmetical proofs

Proudhon says in "Qu'est-ce que c'est la Propriété" "If men, united in equality, gave to one of their number the exclusive right of property, and if this single proprietor placed with humanity a sum of 100 francs at compound interest, repayable to his successors of the twenty-fourth generation after the lapse of 600 years—this sum of 100 francs would, if invested at 5 per cent., amount to the sum of 107,854,010,777,600 francs, a sum 2,696 times as large as the capital of France, estimated at 4,000 millions (this was written 60 years ago), or 20 times as large as the value of the whole globe with all movable and unmovable wealth The Fourierists, those irreconcilable enemies of equality, the partisans of which they look at as sharks, promise to satisfy all demands of capital, of work, and of talent in quadrupling production. But even if they quadrupled production, if they increased it ten-fold, hundred-fold, property (he means land and capital with their rent and interest claims, and it is to this property to which he refers in his famous. "la propriété c'est le vol," or property is theft) by its power of accumulation and capitalization very soon would swallow products, capital, the earth and even the workers"

We know the old tale of the inventor of chess asking as his only reward that the Shah would give him a single grain of corn, which was to be put on the first square of the chess-board, and to be doubled on each successive square; which, to the surprise of the king, produced an amount larger than the treasures of his whole kingdom could buy. It is this kind of chess-game which capital is continually playing with labor. All exertions, all improvements in the methods and tools of labor, the strictest economy, the severest self-denial, are all powerless to compete with the rapidity of self-increase possessed by capital placed at compound interest, and they cannot keep up with its demands.

AN ALLEGORY

Ages had gone by since sinful man was driven from Paradise. The curse (not unmixed with blessings—like all punishment coming from such a source), which forced man to earn his bread by the sweat of his brow, had weighed upon the race with a heavy pressure. The crime had been severely punished; mercy began to prevail. A loving angel was sent down by the Great Master, charged with the task of lightening the burden. The angel's name was *Spirit of Invention.* He began his work by teaching man to make useful tools out of stone, wood, metal, and other formerly worthless raw materials. He taught him to tame animals to work for him, and finally he made him master of the elements, pressing them into his service. The mountain stream rushing down to the ocean was forced to turn wheels, and to grind the flour needed for bread, or to saw the logs with which houses were built, or furniture made. The wind, the merry son of the air, had to stoop to the same work, where water power was not available. The curse was lightened, but not taken off, man's wants had increased with the facility of satisfying them, and work was as hard as ever. But the hour had come when full mercy was to be granted to the children of Eve. Fire offered its service. The most powerful of the elements, though it had condescended hitherto to furnish some comforts to man, as often had proved his deadly enemy. It would have wrought him even more harm if a family feud it had with water had not enabled man to make use of the mutual hate of the two to fight one with the other. Now the time had come when the unrelenting antagonism between them was to be used as a means of taking off the ter-

rible weight of physical labor pressing upon mankind The deadly
foes were imprisoned together in bonds of iron and steel. A fearful
struggle began Water, maddened by the mighty embrace of its
enemy, foaming with rage till it turned into steam, tried all its
power to break loose from the iron bonds and to kill the fiery element The angel taught man how to use the terrible power so
engendered—to turn wheels, and to do all the heaviest work
Millions of iron giants were in this way pressed into his service,
working for him night and day Far down in the depths of the
earth they moved their powerful arms to free the mine from destructive waters, and to lift the treasures of the deep

Imprisoned in iron cars, they moved these with a speed exceeding that of the fleetest deer, drawing heavier weights than
could the strongest elephants, or hundreds of horses Pent up
in ships, they drove them forth through the waters faster, though
heavily loaded, than the best oarsman ever impelled his light craft
But this was not all

The angel *Spirit of Invention* again waved his magical wand
and millions of iron and steel goblins came forth skilled in all kinds
of work spinning, weaving knitting, sawing, grinding, printing,
sewing, shoemaking, etc, etc. They were practised in all trades,
and their delicate fingers went to work with lightning speed when
the iron steam giants were put behind to force them on

It seemed that at last the golden era had come of which men
had dreamed for ages past, without ever hoping to attain it. Without trouble, with almost no exertion, except that of supervision,
man had it in his power to produce boundless wealth for the satisfaction of wants which, in former times, even the richest did not
know or dream of. All the luxuries that art and refinement could
invent were at the disposal of the poorest, if free scope was given
to the wonderful giants and goblins, the number of which daily
increased in never ending varieties.

It *seemed*, I say, that the golden time had come, but it had
not come That envious spirit, that fallen angel, Satan, who once
before, in the shape of the serpent, had driven man from Paradise
by seducing him to sin, from the first moment had watched the
work of the beneficent angel with continually increasing disgust
and anger He knew very well that, if the plans of the Holy One
succeeded, Satan's empire would be over for ever. Once freed
from the cares and troubles of the struggle for existence and the
battle of life, man would turn to higher aims the powers God had
given him Art, science, and ethics would celebrate their greatest
triumphs, more and more would man break loose from the fetters
in which his higher spiritual being was held imprisoned by earthly
cares, and, getting into nearer contact with the eternal source from
which all spiritual life is emanating, would accomplish the great
purpose for which he was created.

The state of things looked desperate All was lost if some

stop could not be put to the work of God's angel, but what was Satan to do? As he looked over the dark army of vices, sins, and follies which had done him such splendid service in past time, to see whether any one of his great warriors could take up the fight with the angel, he perceived nothing but dejected faces   They all knew that they were powerless to battle with the heavenly messenger.   He despaired as he looked at that once valiant and victorious army, when, among the follies of man, he observed one little imp, who, instead of the despondent, mournful aspect all the others were wearing, looked at him in a self-conscious manner which attracted his attention

"What is the matter with you, Interest?" he asked the saucy imp   "You don't seem to be so dejected as your comrades are?"

"Why should I be dejected, master?" replied the spirit   "Am I not one of your favorite soldiers?   Haven't I always been victorious under your august guidance?   Why should I be less certain of victory now than I ever was before?"

"Alas!" answered Satan sadly, "you do not know the power of the enemy we are fighting now   You are no match for the *Spirit of Invention*"

'Well, there will be no harm in seeing about that," answered the imp   "Suppose you allow me to try a duel with the fellow?"

'You little imp!   Fight the powerful angel who is defeating all my army?" laughed Satan

"Yes, I alone, provided, of course, you allow my son, Compound Interest, to help me"

"Are you crazy?   You, with your weak little arms, want to throttle that immense army of powerful giants, and that more numerous one of wary goblins, who have filled the world by the command of the mighty angel whose brains conceived them?"

"I intend to do more than this, your majesty   I shall make them turn traitors to their duty   Instead of their being a source of blessing to mankind, I shall make them the producers of untold misery—worse than ever man suffered from thy hands   I shall make man curse them and the angel who sent them   He shall be made to consider them as the source of all his misery, and to use his best powers to fetter them and to keep them from their work by all kinds of repressive laws   He shall sigh for the good old times when machines did not yet take away the work from poor humanity!"

"You will do all this?" asked Satan, with an unbelieving smile

"Yes, and a good deal more, if you let me have my way," answered the imp, full of self-confidence

And Satan did let him have his way   The battle of giants began   Yes, it was a battle of giants, and yet only a game—a fight of titans, and yet only a noiseless sport in which the imp was the victor

Angel *Spirit of Invention* at first only laughed quite heartily when he saw the being who came to fight him

"Do you see those immense armies obeying my commands?" asked he "Well I have only to open the gates of my skull, and just as many more will come forward to fight you, poor little imp You had better return to the master who sent you, and tell him that his empire is ended for ever, even if he lets loose all the soldiers of hell he commands"

"There is no need for his doing that," calmly replied the imp. "I alone, together with my son, Compound Interest, whom you see peering from my pocket, can multiply our number to exceed any amount of iron and steel chaps from your empire. Look here, my friend, before we begin the fight, let us first muster our forces, and to end this business in a peaceful way, I will make you a proposal Look at this chess-board It seems just like any other chess-board, with sixty-four squares, but it has the peculiar quality of extending the dimensions of the squares, so as always to be large enough to accommodate all the soldiers we shall place upon them Now, listen well to what I propose I enter the first square with my son, and you match one of your warriors against us We enter the second square doubled in number, you send two more warriors—and so on every succeeding square We agree that we shall never more than double, and we further agree that when we arrive at the last square, and you have a single soldier left after occupying the same, we shall declare ourselves vanquished, and Satan with all his troops will leave this world for ever If I win, you and your army are to be at the commands of my master. Are you agreed?"

"Am I agreed!" laughed the angel, as he glanced over the untold millions of his soldiers "Why certainly, my friend. You had better send word to your master to pack his luggage as quick as he can"

"All right, we shall see!" said the imp, in calm, business-like tones And so the ominous game began.

In the beginning the angel laughed, for, though twenty squares were passed, no noticeable diminution of his forces was perceptible Demon Interest said nothing, but attended to business, quietly doubling his army on every succeeding square At the thirtieth square the angel ceased to laugh, and a few squares farther on he had to open the gateways of his fertile brains as wide as he could, urging on his new troops with all his might Only one field more, and he had to stop exhausted He saw he was lost.

"I despised you, little fellow." he sighed despairingly, "and I am punished for my vanity I see there is no use fighting against you. Demon Interest is more powerful than the *Spirit of Invention* I am your slave Command your servant!"

"I am only the servant of my great master," dryly replied the demon "Here I see him coming He will give you his orders."

And Satan gave his orders He commanded that the angel was to continue in his work with all his troops, which were to be increased with all possible exertion, so that humanity—which did not know the nature of the antagonist it had to fight against—would always keep in fresh hope of final success when the new troops were forthcoming But as fast as they appeared, Demon Interest was to send forth a larger army to capture the new forces, to enslave them, and—instead of their benefiting man—make them increase the slave-chains which weigh him down

It was a devilish thought, as could rise only in such a head Just what gave man new hope had to be the means of deepening his misery. What to every human eye appeared an unmixed blessing proved to be the incomprehensible source of greater need Satan had been victorious far beyond his expectations, for the consequences of the battle of life under such conditions—poverty, ignorance, crime, vice, and hopeless misery—appeared more in evidence from day to day, and there was no hope of reform, because the wise men of the world proved the impossibility of indubitable facts, reasoning that blessings could not produce misery.

I foresee the answer, that all this only shows *compound interest wrong,* that it does not prove anything against *interest proper,* but an objection of this kind can hardly be maintained after one moment's reflection What is compound interest? Is it anything else than the income from the investment of earnings of capital? In what way does the lending out of $100 paid to me as interest upon $2,000 differ from the lending of the original capital? If one is legitimate, the other is, if one is wrong, both must be wrong This objection would not hold for a minute, and therefore the mathematical proof is furnished that in the long run labor and nature can never produce enough wealth to pay interest at current rates

Jonathan Duncan, in "The Principles of Money Demonstrated, and Bullionist Fallacies Refuted," came to the same results 60 years ago from another point of view, when he contrasts the increase of claims through interest and the increase of money in which the claims are due:

"Neither is it just to charge metallic interest on the loan of metallic money, since the metal cannot sufficiently increase, and therefore the interest can never be paid in kind It must be commuted into labor, or the produce of labor, and infallibly leads to slavery '

Before I continue this quotation I have to intercalate that when Duncan wrote this he did not recognize the fact, yet visible only in its embryonic state, that in an increasing measure the claims are not "commuted into labor or the produce of labor," that money is insisted upon, though this money practically does not exist, a fact responsible for something worse than slavery the disdainful refusal of the slavery services, the denial of the daily bread for which they are offered.

"Suppose, for example, that England, at the present day, possessed the precious metals in coin to the amount of 28 millions, and having no paper money, were to require, as she does, increase on all loans of money at the rate of 5 per cent., every man who had borrowed £100 ought, at the end of the year, to be possessed of £105 in coin, or he cannot pay his debt with increase One hundred thousand such men, having borrowed 10 millions of pounds, ought, at the end of the first year, to be in possession of half a million more, and in twenty years, not reckoning compound interest, their debt, with interest, could not be paid with less than 20 millions of pounds sterling Now, where are these additional 10 millions to be found? Not in England, certainly—nor abroad, for all other nations take increase too, and their wants are in proportion to their capital. These men, therefore, go on for twenty years paying capital, by which time the whole of the money which they borrowed has been returned to their creditors, but the principal debt has not been paid, and now cannot be, they are insolvent to that amount "

It is related that Napoleon Bonaparte, when shown an interest table, said, after some reflection "The deadly facts herein revealed lead me to wonder that this monster Interest has not devoured the whole human race " It would have done so long ago if bankruptcy and revolution had not been counter-poisons

Counter-poisons, of which only the second one is available if no fundamental social reform kills demon Interest What enabled the world to stand the game so long? The destruction of the debt through the insolvency of the debtor no more suffices, since land values and government bonds have provided securities of such extension and reliability that the bankruptcy of the single debtor avails little, so long as others who need the land and who can be forced to pay rent and taxes take the bankrupt's place Only national bankruptcy, to the extent of a revolution that destroys vested rights, can help, and this help is approaching with rapid steps, with every year's further addition to the accumulated interest account, to the billions which are not consumed by their owners nor offered in the market for the creation of new means of production, but are spent in the purchase of new land values, bonds and similar tribute-claims, each of which increases the already unbearable load on the people's backs.

Nothing can save us from this inevitable goal, which approaches with the infallibility of mathematical progression with the next doubling of the capitalistic chess-board, nothing but a destruction of the source of Interest, which we now proceed to find. Even here we are not on untrodden paths. So long as almost four centuries ago the great reformer, Calvin, answered the arguments of Aristotle, who thought the taking of interest unjustifiable, because money put aside cannot produce money, by saying

"It is undoubted that money does not produce money; but

with money land is bought, which produces more than the returns for the labor applied to it, and which gives a surplus income to the proprietor, after all expenses for wages and other things have been met   With money a house can be bought bringing a rent income Objects with which things can be bought, producing incomes by themselves, can certainly be considered as bringing incomes themselves "

If I have $100 worth of goods of any description, with which I can purchase a piece of land, bringing $5 worth of rental income, I should certainly be foolish if I lent this $100 in money or goods of any kind to anybody unless he paid me at least $5 a year for the privilege of getting the use of my capital during that time.

Through making land an object of commerce, like boots and shoes, like watches and houses, we have given it a merchandise value, and rent has become the interest on the market price of land.   Rent by itself is no tribute in the sense of an extortion, but an addition to labor's product due to the ownership of land.   It becomes an extortion only where this ownership is usurped by individuals, not where it belongs to the community; where the yield goes into private pockets, instead of into the common purse.   One wrong leads to others   Through allowing monopolists to usurp the common inheritance, through making the property of humanity an object of commerce, a merchandise, the income which this merchandise produces has infected all other articles of commerce, all kinds of merchandise, for if the interest income from land values is not a tribute, but an inherent property of one merchandise, why should it not be that of all others for which land can be bought? Thus *rent*, through appearing in the shape of interest on land values, *became the mother and justificator of interest* on all other market values.

Not the only parent, though, for so long as we make one or two scarce products the sole legal tender, the monopolizers of these products can exact a tribute for their loan, and interest, with all its consequences, will continue to exist, in spite of common land ownership, as I have shown happening on Robinson's island in the first chapter   This also is not a new discovery, in fact, many of the enemies of interest have recognized that an *unelastic money is the father of interest*   The trouble only has been that reformers were usually satisfied with the finding of one parent, never supposing that there might be two of them, though such is the order of Nature.   However, the parents are near relations, and this consanguinity may be responsible for the monstrosity of their offspring The joint family name is *Monopoly*

We have yet to take into consideration the difference existing between gross interest and interest proper, *i e*, between the interest actually paid and that quota of it which remains after the risk-premium and wages of supervision are deducted, a very important difference

For the producer and trader it matters very little at what rate bankers can get money upon good collaterals, but very much what he himself has to pay for it without such securities   And, strange as it sounds, the lower the rate at which the bank lends money upon good securities, the higher the rate often is which the producer and trader without collaterals will be forced to disburse   It may happen that when the rate of interest paid at the stock exchange is almost at zero, the ordinary producer and trader cannot obtain money on any terms, while wages are lowest.   This paradox is easily solved

We must keep in mind that wholesale business is usually not done with real money, but by means of credit, and wherever prices are falling, through the sluggishness of the market, credit is reduced; or, as it is almost impossible to place cause and effect correctly in such a case, whenever credit becomes stiffer, prices fall. At all events, effect and cause react upon each other as they usually do   Where business investments tend to become riskier, capitalists prefer to retire their money from such investments, and temporarily place it where they can dispose of it at any time, even if they have to leave it interest free in their banks   Arthur Fonda says in "Honest Money" (p. 109) "The accumulation of money in banks in times of depression indicates, not too much money, but a general belief that its value is rising, or a fear that it will rise—testifying, if to anything, to too little money, in fact   Men do not hold a thing that brings no income, unless they expect to profit by its rise."

The investments preferred under such conditions are government bonds, loans upon the deposit of good papers, or discounts of first-class bills of exchange.   Smaller capitalists go to the savings banks and deposit the maximum permitted; often opening accounts in the name of wife, children, and other relations to get around the maximum clause.   The greater demand for this class of investments raises their price, or, which means the same thing in this case, depresses the interest rate   In this way the low interest rate of these investments and the increase of the larger savings bank deposits often is the sign of a stagnancy in business, of an increasing want of employment, and absence of confidence generally.   It is natural that under such conditions the risk premium rises, and that the low rate of interest at exchange is accompanied by a high 'rate of the interest demanded for capital required for productive purposes

These abnormal phenomena of interest, credit **and capital** are generally accompanied by the decrease or disappearance of many of the small deposits, a fact now hidden because generally deposit statistics are not classified, and thus its figures are made to prove the very reverse of their real meaning, to prove prosperity instead of poverty   The excellent New Zealand Registrar-General, Mr E J von Dadelszen, to whom I am indebted for his "Statistics of the Colony of New Zealand for the Year 1900," gives (p 309) the first classified savings bank statistics I ever met with   It is true they only give the accounts of the Postal Savings Bank, but this bank does seven-eighths of the New Zealand savings bank business Even here, however, there is room for further improvement The lowest class, not exceeding £20, ought to be further subdivided, and the average balances of each class should be given   Taking the medium figures of each class   £35 for the second "exceeding £20 and up to £50," £75 for the third of £50-100, etc , £600 for the highest, of amounts exceeding £500, and deducting the figures thus obtained from the total balance of £5,809,552, only £458 146 are left for the 142,368 depositors of the first class, or an average of £3 4s 5d   As there were in all 197,408 depositors, this would mean that 70% of the depositors only had an average balance of £3 4s 5d ($16) each, while 4 million pounds sterling—two-thirds of the whole —were deposited by 19,003 people, one-tenth of the depositors, i e., those with balances exceeding £100   But, of course, no exact calculations are possible as long as we are left without the actual average of each class

I add the following quotation from "The Public" of Nov 4, 1905   "Savings bank statistics as evidence of the prosperity of workingmen gets another blow through revelations in the settlement of the estate of Col Willard Glazier, the wealthy author and lecturer   Nearly all his fortune of $135 000 was found deposited in the savings banks of more than 50 cities scattered over 15 States In New York City alone he was a depositor in 18 savings banks These deposits show up in warm colors through the savings bank statistics, as an indication of that improving condition of the working poor of which statistics are so full and the working poor so ignorant "

We have seen how the proposed land and currency reforms, by striking at the risk premium, tend to lessen the gulf between net and gross interest and thus only render the fall of the interest rate of advantage to the producers, because only the fall of the gross interest rate indicates the degree in which capital is accessible to them, the terms at which they can obtain it and thus increase their share of the product. Losing sight of this important point produces the error into which many economists have fallen, when they see in the lower interest rate a relative decrease of the share which capital obtains of the product   The great whitewasher of capitalism, the French economist Leroy-Beaulieu a man of the Giffen and Atkinson type, goes so far even as to expect a growing equalization of wealth inequalities from the falling interest rate. "until a society is formed, in which the positions are more equal, activity more general and yet less overboiling, in which it is almost impossible to form large fortunes, difficult to acquire middle ones, and easy to attain prosperity " How wonderfully true facts have confirmed this prediction of over twenty years ago! The worthy gentleman never would have uttered such nonsense if he had studied more closely the works of his celebrated countryman and fellow-economist, Frederic Bastiat, who, in his fourth letter to Proudhon, says. "In the measure in which capital increases, interest falls, but so that the total income of the capitalist increases So when interest falls from 5 to 4, from 4 to 3, from 3 to 2, it means that capital has increased from 100 to 200. from 200 to 400, from 400 to 800, and that the capitalist gradually has an income of 5, 8 and 12 "

This is in accordance with the facts observed in everyday life, especially in the period passed since it was written over half a century ago The interest rate has fallen considerably, but the capital on which interest is paid has increased quite out of proportion much faster even than Bastiat imagined In spite of the lower interest rate, the relative share of capital, as a whole, has largely increased, that of labor has decreased

There was a time when the rate of interest exceeded 12%, in which the worker's share in the product of his labor was much greater than now when money can be obtained at 4% or less, for the few tools which he needed belonged to him or were easily obtainable, while now the costly machinery required is out of his reach What are his wages, brought down by competition on one side and monopoly on the other, aside of the millions paid out as dividends by the trusts? The total dividends of one single trust, the great American steel trust reached nearly one billion dollars up to the end of 1907, as much as the income of all American wage-workers during one month of the year. Compare the relative shares in the product of the independent cabinet-maker with his simple tools of the 18th century and the wage-worker in a furniture factory of the 20th, provided with the most perfect special machinery, or that of the spinner at the hand-wheel, and the hand of a spinning factory, with its thousands of spindles

The fall of the interest rate only proves that investment-seeking capital increases faster than profits available for interest distribution, and thus forces down the interest rate accepted by competing capitalists.

The well-known process, called watering, exemplified in Chapter II, showing how the interest rate is kept down where exceptionally large profits are made helps to illustrate Bastiat's proposition that the share of capital is in an inverse proportion to the interest rate

After what has been said in this chapter, it is hardly necessary to add that demon Interest will never be exorcised by legal enactments which forbid the taking of interest, so long as we leave his breeders intact our existing land and currency laws Signal failure has accompanied all experiments in this direction When the canonical laws prohibited the taking of interest, in the Middle Ages, money was locked up; and, as the inevitable result, where the money monopoly is given to scarce metals, trade languished In such a case it was a choice between the deep sea of stagnation in all intercourse produced by the blocking up of the circulating medium of exchange and the devil Interest whose enticements allured the money back from its hiding-places. The privilege of taking usury which was conceded to the Jews in those times was not meant as a favor to them, but was the result of an actual necessity.

No direct attack against the arch enemy has ever been of any use. Only by cutting off the roots private land ownership and the exclusive legal tender monopoly given to a money made out of the precious metals, can we kill the noxious weed. A well-known method by which the canonical laws were often circumvented illustrates this. The borrower made a bill of sale of some land to his creditor for the debt, by which the former owner became the tenant of the land whose rent represented the interest on the borrowed money. When the loan was repaid, the land reverted to the former proprietor.

Before closing this chapter I have to meet the objection that interest can only disappear completely when the foundations on which it rests are sapped in the whole world, for, as long as the reforms which insure its destruction are not carried everywhere, capital is supposed to emigrate to those countries where interest is still obtainable.

It is the threat of capital's emigration, which is so often dinned into our ears, whenever reforms that are unpalatable to our capitalists are proposed. Now let us see which capital can emigrate. That which comes under the definition of the orthodox economist? Buildings, machines, tools, stock? The buildings certainly cannot emigrate, nor can a great portion of the machines, because they would bring such a loss to their owners that no amount of interest thus obtained would compensate for it, which also holds good for the greatest part of the tools and for part of the stock, even if the other countries did not at once raise higher customs walls against such inundations of merchandise in these times of "overproduction." And what if the emigration of this kind of wealth really took place? How long would it be before the unfettered productive power of the country had produced better machines tools and stock of every kind and in any quantity? It is true the gold and silver, as well as large quantities of jewels, could leave but I need not explain how little damage would be caused by such an emigration, after the thorough treatment I have given the money question.

When we come to capital of my definition its main foundation, the land, certainly cannot leave us but the bonds mortgages and all other tribute-claims might emigrate.* The whole paper ballast of Wall Street might go abroad with or without its owners. What difference would it make? The tribute on which all this nominal wealth is founded gradually disappears with land nationalization

---

* When the corn laws were about to be abolished in England, the Peers threatened to leave the country and John Bright expressed the hope that they would leave the land behind them!

and money reform; as we have seen in the previous chapters, and meanwhile, with the people's unfettered productive power, it is immaterial where the tribute goes. Nothing remains finally but the real wealth which is behind all these bonds, stocks and other kinds of tribute-promising pergaments. Nothing can be claimed in the end but products of labor, and with our immense productivity such debts will be cleared off in no time. Future savings could only be exported in the form of merchandise, and with the tremendous productive power of the reform country, especially one like the United States, a glutting of foreign markets would follow, with the result that the losses on capital account would soon surpass any possible profit on interest account, in the books of exporting capitalists.

And how long could it be before the success of the reform work in one country would force the others to follow its example? At all events, the emigration-of-capital bugbear is not the creation of a logical brain. For what else is this emigration, under currency reform, but the very thing which the very same people have all along been putting before us as the highest aim of our commercial policy, the increase of exports, the conquest of foreign markets, the very goal for whose attainment the workers have been asked to reduce their wage claims? And suddenly the fear of these foreign markets, which might all at once become too eager for our products, is put forth to defend demon Interest!

No, the foreigner will not harm us in either direction, neither by refusing, nor by compelling our shipments. Just as the wonderful extension of the home market, through economic reform, would make us independent of foreign sales, so the colossal increase of productive power must enable us to export enough merchandise to other countries to pay our debts there in no time. Interest will die in the country in which no monopoly maintains it, no matter whether in other countries the vermin still subsists for a time or not *

CHAPTER VI.

DEMOCRACY

The best system of representation fails to insure government of the people by the people and for the people so long as the representative instead of servant may become the people's master

In the preceding chapters I have tried to ⋯ social reform can be reached evolutionarily, wi ical and social structure, and without recou⋯

* This question of the emigration of capita⋯ my "Rent, Interest and Wages," page 204-211 Reeves, London

THE ECONOMIC AND SOCIAL PROBLEM

tory on these lines, however, is not to be hoped for, without a thorough organization of the people. Otherwise they are powerless against the small but well disciplined army of plutocracy, securely entrenched within the fort of vested rights, as their monopolies are styled by them. If these men knew their real interests they would help in the work of peaceable evolution as the only possible defense against their real enemy the revolutionist, whose advance can only be staid by a destruction of the road over which he proceeds the general discontent.

The first step towards this organization demands certain political reforms, without which no true democracy can exist.

Democracy! I know that it is violently attacked by those whose comfortable seats on the back of the people are in danger of being lost through unruliness on the part of the poor beast of burden. This is only natural, though not reasonable, for any clear-headed observer must become aware that the penetration of education into the lowest strata of the population can only end in one result the demand for equal rights. Also, that not much time will elapse between the moment when this demand is made by the long-suffering and the occurrence of one of those terrible upheavals of the comfortable resting-places whereon the upper classes are so complacently philosophizing—of which history gives innumerable accounts. Now, all riders know very well that it is much pleasanter to get down from an unruly horse while it is standing still than to wait until it is disagreeably rearing and plunging.

Foolish as the stolid passivity of the governing classes may be, we can understand it. The riding business has been going on for so many thousand years, the habit of beholding the world from the backs of the oppressed masses has become so inveterate, that the idea of getting down is entirely superseded by schemes of better saddles, bridles and spurs. If such people declaim against universal suffrage and other conquests of democracy, we need not be surprised, but the case is different when some of the highest intelligences are found in the same camp when a Carlyle, with his "Niagara, and After," or a Huxley, are among the enemies of democratic rule.

I quote from an article contributed to the *Nineteenth Century*, April, 1890, in which I defend the theories of Henry George against an attack of Professor Huxley which had appeared in a previous number of the magazine.* Only the introduction refers to the

. . . and

other . . . . number of this review, Professor T. H. Huxley . . . . article "On the Natural Inequality of Men," in different . . . . . . it that Rousseau and the declaration of the rights wealth . . . . . founded grade Australia when Huxley's attack appeared, which . . . . for him. On his way back he wrote to me "I . . . . swer to Huxley. I may write some-threatened . . . . the country . . . . it did not discuss."
would leave . . . . the . . .

of man, in so far as they proclaim man to be born free and equal. As long as Professor Huxley confines himself to the special department of knowledge in which he is of a world-known celebrity, the domain of biology, he remains master of the field. His proofs that man is born neither free nor equal are irrefutable

It is true that a child is a helpless slave when it begins its career in this world, and it cannot be denied that even the children of the same family are by no means equal in their capacities and characters "Some are more powerful and honored than the rest, and make themselves easily obeyed"

So far all right, but the moment Mr Huxley begins to draw political conclusions from these facts, I am no more with him He brings nothing new when he launches his arrows against universal suffrage, pointed with the argument that only the capable ought to govern. Even the simile he employs is borrowed from Carlyle, where that great writer declares his opinion of the infeasibility of a ship getting round Cape Horn by calling the crew together and taking a majority vote as to the direction to take, instead of having the competent officers decide it by means of their instruments. If a real ship cannot be kept off the rocks by such means, how is the ship of State, with its much more complicated course, to be protected from the dangers besetting it from all sides, if numbers and not competency are to decide its direction?

Alas! it is an old, old question, as old as the world, this question of government given to strength and capacity, instead of being the outcome of majority votes Hero-worship v. popular rights— all the world's history is nothing but an infinite series of variations upon this theme

The proof of the pudding is in the eating, says an English proverb. If we apply this old and simple method to the working of the principles in question, we come to a result quite the reverse of the one anticipated by Mr Huxley. The tyranny and bad government of ages stands arrayed against the system of governing the masses by the classes, for this is what hero-worship comes to in the end Even heroes are poor human beings, full of human failings, among which vulnerability to the effects of flattery and adulation stands foremost. The foul emanation of these swamps will finally create a mist around the most pure and upright, through which the sun of truth will find it, harder and harder to penetrate The uneducated common-sense of the poor clown will see in a clearer light the real purport of the most momentous questions touching the public weal, than the despot in the midst of the haze by which he is surrounded

But this is not the worst by any means As long as the real hero lives, things may work tolerably well, but he is subject to another incurable failing, that of being mortal Who is to be his successor? We cannot get him elected by the popular vote, for that would be having the crew take a part in the guidance of the ship,

which is just the thing to be avoided   The hero himself, or the wise
ones appointed by him, will attend to it.   They did so since untold
ages.   What was the result?   Have they always picked out the
wisest?   Have they, has he, governed for the welfare of the people?
Emphatically, history answers "No" in the overwhelming majority
of cases   The frailty of our poor human nature brings it about that
irresponsible governors and legislators will first think of their own
interest before they give way to any other consideration   The final
result of aristocratic rule always has been, always must be, that the
governing minority will enslave the powerless majority, will make
them give up the land and the best of its fruits, will make them do
all the work for their superiors, who will finally believe themselves
of a higher blood, born with special privileges, entitled to the right
of spending their lives in laziness, and having the masses support
them by their labor   Labor becomes a taint, graceful loafing the
badge of gentility   Most of the governing done by them is to conserve, and, if possible, increase the privileges they enjoy   Commons
are enclosed without any regard to the rights of commoners, wars
are waged in the interest of the governing classes, whereas its
charges are borne by the people   No, no, Messrs. Carlyle and Huxley, that kind of governing the ship of State has not proved a success!   It may be that the crew will not always pick out the best
man to take the rudder, but certain it is that the monopoly of steer-
ing given to a privileged minority has mostly failed to bring out the
best pilot   And who would blame the poor slaves in the hold of a .
slave-dhow that they think it better for them if they can get the
mastery of the vessel, even though they know that they have not
got the captain's science and experience?   It is true that he would
be much more likely to bring the ship safely into port than they in
their ignorance, but what kind of port is it he brings them to?   The
slave-market, the place where they are to be sold like cattle to hard
and inhuman masters.   Do we blame them if they do not care to
arrive in such a port, and that they would rather run their chances
of getting into another place, be it even a desert island, or of meeting death in the waves of the ocean?
    There is only one clear course marked out for a man loving his
brethren and mindful of their real good   that is to give them the full
power over their own destinies, and to work with all his might that
they may get sufficient instruction to use this power   Nobody ever
learnt how to swim without going into the water, and if we want a
crew to know how to steer a ship we must give them a chance to
learn, not by jealously keeping them away from the rudder, but by
letting them steer, and standing by, showing them how to do it
Instruct the people, and cease to be afraid of their ignorance if you
succeed   Success is impossible, however, unless you look to something else first, and that is their being sufficiently fed, clothed, and
housed, for there is no way of getting knowledge into starved brains.
And this brings me to the main question, to which Mr Huxley gets

in the course of his article, that of land ownership for there is no possible chance of ever really improving the people's social position without first righting this fundamental question.

Though economic liberty is unattainable without political liberty, political liberty is a mockery without economic liberty This has been fully recognized by a Conference at Buffalo, State of New York, in July, 1899, attended by nearly 900 delegates The following is an extract from an address to the people drawn up mainly by Professor George D Herron, which was adopted by the Conference

"We would urgently emphasize our belief that the militarism which menaces us as a people is but the offspring and incident of the greater menace of plutocracy, which has established monopoly government in the place of government by the people.

"Monopoly rule is intrenched in every branch of national, state and municipal government. By economic force based upon special privileges in law and natural resources, upon indirect taxation and consequent limited competition, monopoly is centralizing the wealth of the nation in the hands of enormous trusts, which are becoming irresponsible economic despotisms which are using legislation, the judiciary and all the functions of government, as the mere instruments of private property, and which are reducing the entire people to economic serfdom or enforced wage-slavery.

"*Political liberty is a mockery without economic liberty* No man is in any sense free, either in practice, or religion, or science, so long as he is in enforced dependance upon some other man for the opportunity to earn his livelihood No individual or political rights are secure without security and equality of economic opportunity Equality before law and institutions must be based upon equality of opportunity and access to the resources which the common Father gave to all people in common If the State permits a few men to own the earth, then these few own the rights, liberties, and moral well-being of the people who must live upon the earth Even the further extension of the suffrage, so as to grant political citizenship to women, which extension we urge and advocate, will avail little or nothing without economic freedom to all

"We, therefore, make urgent appeal to the people to co-operate with us in the institution of such movements, and the support of such men as shall propose a social political programme"

The intimate relationship existing between political and economic liberty is my justification for devoting one chapter to politics in a book otherwise exclusively concerned with economic questions. I begin with the foundation The *Franchise, or Suffrage*

In the good old times armed robbers, styling themselves conquerors, attacked peaceable populations, forced them into submission, after taking away their land and whatever valuables they possessed and made laws which deprived the conquered of any participation in the government of the country, reducing them to slaves or serfs, without any rights but the right to work for their masters

No wonder that in a few generations a great change could be observed in the people The rough warriors gradually made use of the leisure afforded them through the work of their serfs to cultivate their minds, to acquire some of the knowledge their time possessed, while the poor downtrodden human cattle became mere savages, though their forefathers had perhaps been far more advanced in culture than the wild clans who overthrew them. When civilization advanced, when it became unfashionable to govern by right of the physically stronger—principally in consequence of a little invention made by a German monk who looked for gold and found gunpowder, which enabled a baby's finger to overthrow an armored knight—when declarations of independence and "droits de l'homme" were the order of the day the continued oppression of the poor, ignorant masses was justified on the ground of their poverty and ignorance Which practically meant that all those who had become poor and ignorant because their ancestors had been forcibly deprived of their rights were to continue without these rights because they were poor and ignorant And even in our days of universal suffrage we still hear the murmurs of the wealthy and educated against the injustice of giving an equal vote to a learned university professor and an ignorant boor, unable to read and write, knowing as little of the history and laws of the country which his vote is to govern as a savage in Central Africa, the injustice of giving no more than the same vote to the owner of untold wealth, whose estates cover an area larger than many a dukedom, with thousands obeying his mandates, than to the citizen of the slums, with a few rags as his only earthly possession, a man "without any stake in the country," as the other expresses it, quite forgetting who stole that stake!

Miserable hypocrites! where would you be if you had been brought up in the same surroundings? And these surroundings, these conditions, are they more likely to be changed where those who profit by the helplessness of the slave are the exclusive governors of the land, or where the masses are given the power? History is here to answer How long is it since men in the Southern States risked their popularity, if not a good deal more, by teaching the negro slave to read and write? And would there be half the pains taken to educate the masses possessing the vote if experience had not taught the danger of letting the ignorant govern?

I think I have said enough to dispense with discussing property or education tests We need not call to our aid Benjamin Franklin's sarcasm, when he asked whether the man who had voted under the hundred dollar franchise, because the mule he owned was worth as much, but who had lost his vote when the mule died, had really had the franchise; or whether, after all, it had not been the mule Nor need we look at the educational franchise in the light of our late experiences in the Southern States, referred to in the following extract from the New York *Worker* "We know that such qualifications are never honestly applied It is notorious that in those Southern States where the law requires that the voter shall be able to 'read and explain' the Constitution of the United States, the most ignorant man can register and vote if he is known to be a safe supporter of the dominant party, while the poor man who is suspected of intending to vote the opposition ticket is called upon to explain some constitutional point that the Supreme Court of the United States has never been able to agree upon, and so is convicted of ignorance, no matter how he expounds it. All this talk about the ignorant vote is nothing more or less than a screen to conceal the intentions of the dominant school of capitalist politicians and gradually to take the ballot away from the working class, lest the workers use their lawful power to abolish capitalist exploitation"

But it is not enough to allow every citizen a vote, it is also essential that this vote should be made effective. Every voter ought to be represented in the Government of the nation as fully as every other. I need not say that this is not the case in most countries— in our republic less than in monarchic Germany, for we have not even got the *second ballot* With us a relative majority still elects a candidate, though the absolute majority may be deadly opposed to him If the Republican candidate has 2,000 votes, the Democratic one 1,900, while the Socialist polls 1,500 the Republican is declared elected, though the 3,400 voters on the other side may be opposed to him. In Germany, in such a case, where none of the candidates has an absolute majority, a second ballot would be called between the two candidates who polled most heavily—in the above case, between the Republican and Democratic candidates As the Socialists might, in all likelihood, have more confidence in the Democrat than in the defender of capitalism, their votes would probably swell those given for the Democratic candidate to 3,400, so that he could beat the 2,000 Republican votes. Thus a totally different result might follow through a more rational system This does not mean that the latter might not sometimes work against new parties by enabling the old ones to unite against them in the second ballot As a rule, however, the old system stands in the way of new parties, because many of their adherents are afraid of voting for them for fear of thus ruining the party of their second choice, whose candidates their votes might have elected That such a simple reform has not yet been carried in this country is explained by the greater chances which the old method gives to the domination of party leaders Party machines hold the votes together, while free votes are likely to be lost by dispersion. Thus a well-united minority vote ensures a continuance of power, though the great majority of the country may be irreconcilably opposed to it In a similar manner a few individuals, or one man, may obtain the lead in the party caucus where the nominations of the candidates are made, thus conferring the dominion of a party upon one man Under such circumstances, we can hardly expect such a "boss" to be eager for a more democratic ballot system

For all that, the second ballot is only a clumsy attempt towards justice, towards the attainment of a fair proportional representation. There are far better systems, but, anyhow, none could be worse than the one we are used to. Its unproportionality is best evidenced by an exaggerated though possible case.

Let us suppose the case of constituencies of 6,000 voters each, of whom in each electoral division 3,001 vote for the 'A party and 2,999 vote for the B party. In this case, the parliament will consist merely of members of the A party, while the B party is not represented at all, though half of the voters have endorsed it. Under the proportional vote this result would be impossible; each party would elect one-half of the members. There are different systems of the proportional vote. The free list plan is used in Belgium and Switzerland. The official ballot has the nominees of each party arranged in separate lists each under its party heading, and each party gets the proportion of members to which it is entitled. The system has the advantage of simplicity and least disturbance of present methods. Its great disadvantage is that it leaves the selection of candidates to the caucus, and consequently to the party chiefs, unless primary elections take place, which necessitate double work for the voters.

The Japanese system, which has multiple districts in which each elector obtains one vote only, reduces this difficulty, making it easier, in spite of party domination, for a number of electors to give their nomination and vote to the same candidate, who is elected upon receiving his quota of votes; but this system has the great disadvantage of non-proportionality through a waste of votes, as under the plumping system, discussed further on. All the votes given to a candidate after his quota has been reached are wasted, for they cannot be counted for another candidate to whom the surplus votes otherwise would be given in preference. Gove and Hare do away with this defect. They arrange for preference votes. Under the Gove system the candidate, before the election, publishes a list of his fellow candidates to whom his surplus votes are to go, in the order of his choice. This has the advantage over the previously mentioned systems that the work is lessened and automatic machines can be used; but it still leaves the elector dependent on the selection of others, it limits his own choice of candidates.

The Hare system is the only one which leaves him fully free in this direction without requiring primaries. This system does away with the single constituencies. Every voter in a collective district, let us say a whole State, can only vote for one candidate, running for a special office, but all the votes given for a candidate in the whole district count for him, so that a number of minority votes in each section, which under the present system would have been lost, and for this reason in most cases would not even have been polled, are collected and may help to elect provided the total of the candidate's vote in the whole State reaches the figure which elects. This figure corresponds to the quotient resulting from the division of the total number of votes polled by the number of candidates to be elected. For instance, if the total number of votes cast in a State is 200,000, who elect ten members of Congress, 20,000 votes will elect one member.

Hare takes care that the surplus given to a candidate is not lost, but is counted for another candidate. On his ballot the voter marks each candidate with a number, according to the preference he has for him. His vote counts in the first line for the candidate to whom he gives the number "1". If the number "1" on a list is elected, all the additional ballots on which the same name is now found marked "1" are counted for the number '2," and if "2" is elected, for number "3," etc. The ballots which are given for a candidate who has not reached the minimum figure required to elect him are now taken up, beginning with the file which has the smallest number of ballots. These are now distributed to the number "2" on each, or, in case 2 is already elected, to number '3, etc. This goes on until the number of files left corresponds to the number of candidates yet to be elected, when the candidates to whom the remaining files belong are declared elected.

The subject is of such importance that I should like to make it clear to everybody and as there may be some among my readers who are fond of legal phraseology and who would like to see how the reform proposal reads when embodied in the project of a law, I repeat my explanation in this form.

Project of a Law on Proportional Voting —All elections of members of the Legislature in the State of . shall be conducted in accordance with the system known as the Hare system hereinunder described.

In this text the expression "full quota" shall mean the amount of the quotient resulting from the division of the total number of votes polled by the number of candidates to be elected (leaving any fraction out of account).

After the nominations of candidates for election have been closed, each voter shall number in the order of his preference on the voting paper, commencing with the number "1," the names of as many candidates as there are to be elected (or if he so desires, the names of more or fewer candidates).

The vote of each voter shall be used for one candidate only, according to the order of the voter's preference.

The result of the voting shall be ascertained as follows —Each voting paper shall at first be filed under the name numbered "1" thereon, and when all the voting papers are so filed, the votes on each file shall be counted, and if any candidate shall have received more votes than the full quota, the votes last filed in his favor shall be taken from the file, until the votes remaining thereon are reduced to the full quota

Every candidate who shall have received the full quota shall be deemed to be duly elected and his file shall be closed, and no further votes added thereto

Any voting papers taken from the files of any candidates who shall have received more votes than the full quota shall be distributed over the remaining files, or over new files if necessary, as votes for the candidates whose names are numbered "2" on the voting papers so distributed, or according to the name of the candidate numbered next highest not already elected, in case the candidate whose name is numbered "2" on any such voting paper shall have been already elected

After such distribution the votes for each of the candidates shall again be counted, and where any candidate shall have received more than the full quota, his votes shall be reduced to the full quota as hereinbefore provided, and the surplus votes distributed over the other files, or over new files if necessary, according to the names numbered "3" on the surplus voting papers, or according to the name of the candidate numbered next highest not already elected, in case the candidate whose name is numbered "3" on any such voting paper shall have been already elected, and so on, whenever any file shall have a surplus of votes over the full quota

After all surpluses of votes (if any) have been redistributed as aforesaid, the contents of the file containing the smallest number of voting papers shall be distributed over the remaining files, as votes for the candidates whose names are numbered with the next highest number on such voting papers not already elected. This process shall be repeated with the voting papers on the file for the time being containing the smallest number of voting papers, and so on, according to the numerical order of the remaining names not already elected on each voting paper taken from such small files, until the voting papers are, as far as possible, redistributed over the files containing fewer votes than the full quota

Any surplus of votes arising from the redistribution of the votes from the files containing the smallest number of votes, for the time being, shall be dealt with as hereinbefore provided

After the voting papers have been redistributed as above, as far as possible, the candidate or candidates (to the number necessary to fill the number to be elected), who have received the greatest number of votes shall be declared duly elected, whether or not they shall have received the full quota of votes

In the event of the necessity to decide between two or more candidates who have received an equal number of votes, the Chairman or Presiding Officer shall decide the election by his vote.

An article from a periodical may serve to show how the system works in practical operation

"On March 19, 1901, Tasmania held an election for representatives in the Federal Parliament, using the proportional representation system The island elected six senators and five representatives For the senators 18,403 ballots were cast, besides 419 invalid at the start from improper marking, and 1,112 became inoperative in the course of the count, because, when those ballots were reached, all the candidates on them had either been elected or 'eliminated' in the course of the count, leaving 17,291 voters who aided in the election of the candidates to represent. Thus nearly 92 per cent. of the voters were represented, while in ordinary elections sometimes a little over half the voters, and sometimes a deal less, are represented, and very inadequately at that, being compelled to vote for the nominees of the machine."

Similarly as to the House, 18,039 voted, of which 1,014 were "exhausted" in the count, besides 533 mismarked, leaving 17,025 electors represented, instead of half of them being practically disfranchised

All were elected who received the highest vote on first choice, so that the transfers from second, third, and subsequent marks of preference made no difference in the result ; but the voters knew that, as a rule, they ran no risk of "throwing away their votes" in voting for the men they deemed most competent for first choice, because, if not utilized for these, they would be for less popular candidates marked "2," "3," "4," or "5."

No difficulties or complications whatever were experienced in the count, although the ballots were brought from all parts of the island to be counted in Hobart, located in the south-central portion

One important effect of this proportional voting system will be that *it democratizes the caucus*, and thus deprives the politician of his most effective weapon. President Garfield said men in his State had gone to the polls for thirty years, with no more chance of seeing a candidate of their own way of thinking in Congress, than if they had lived under the Czar of Russia

The Hare system not only elects according to the preference of the voters, but also nominates as the people desire Anybody can propose nominees for the party, and if he finds a certain support, can have his man on the list. It does not matter if by that means many more candidates are on the list than there are places to fill, because not a single vote will be wasted Each elector adds numbers of preference to the names on his list, and according to these numbers will his votes be counted If he has given his number "1" to a man who has not the shadow of a chance, his vote will count for the man to whom he gave number "2" on his list, and so forth, until it is counted for someone on this list who receives enough support from other votes to obtain the necessary quota In this way every voter has a chance of nominating his own candidates, and of testing the popularity of these candidates, without any special primary election If he succeeds in obtaining a sufficient number of votes for his nominee, he will carry him through ; if he does not, his vote is not lost for all that, as it finally counts for somebody of his or another party whom he likes next best to the nominees preferred by him   The business of the caucus thus will have been given over to the whole people, as it ought to be

The most important effect of the system is that it would gradually break up parties altogether or, at least, parties in the present sense of the word   In a general sense, there always will be parties, for two men who agree to vote only for men advocating a certain policy, already form a party   What I mean by party here is the erection of a few big pens, mostly two only, into which the electors are forced, according to their preference, if they do not want to waste their votes   Whether certain principles, or only the names of certain leaders are affixed to the pens' doors, is immaterial The proportional vote would leave it to the electors to decide how many different pens they want to erect, and in which special pen they feel most comfortable

The proportional voting system has been objected to on the ground that it would bring a number of *faddists* into Congress

So it would, no doubt, but where is the harm?   Faddists are men with one idea, of whom Prince Bismark once said that he did not dislike them, for they had one idea more than most men

The progressive laws of to-day which are applauded by vast majorities were the fads of yesterday   And why should not every citizen have the right to send somebody to the House who represents his favorite idea, even if it is a fad?   Is it less correct to vote on such ground than to vote for private interests?   Who is the better citizen of the two—the one who forgets the interests of his pocket and votes for the men fighting for a great social reform, or he who has no other ideal than his personal advantage or local patriotism, who gives his vote to the man who pays him or who is likely to procure the greatest amount of Government patronage for his section of the country?

It may be inconvenient for the chief of a party to keep the reins of government, if the loaves and fishes of which he is the distributor lose their charm for electors and elected, but only where he lacks a noble enthusiasm, which makes him forget everything else but the desire to obtain the greatest good for the greatest number. A party chief of this nature will rejoice in the nobler task set before him and the possibility of accomplishing it   Instead of employing his political arithmetic in the direction of figuring where his official patronage will tell most on the support he can obtain, he will investigate which progressive law is likely to command most votes, and he will work in this direction   Is it not worthy of his best efforts to fight for that reform of the electoral system which promises the possibility of such a change in electoral tactics?

It has also been urged against the proportional vote—that it *favors the rich*, who can get up an agitation in the large district which would be substituted for the present small constituency, to the exclusion of the poorer man who can only canvass his own locality, not being able to work the larger district   The very opposite is true   For the best men in the country, who have nothing to recommend them but their devotion to the people's interests, without financial means to back their candidature, it will be easier to obtain a seat under the new system than under the present one A valid proof of this is supplied by the electoral statistics of Germany   The poor men's party the Social Democratic party, polled 3,250,000 votes at the last election (1907), representing almost one-third of the total vote cast, but obtained only one-ninth of the representatives elected   If Germany had the proportional vote there would be 117 Socialists in Parliament, instead of 43, out of 397 members.   The Clericals, with only 1,850 000 votes, would only have 69 representatives instead of 105   And to think that men, calling themselves liberals, rejoiced at the outcome of a miserable election system because it injured an antagonist!

If it were merely a question of money, social democracy would be nowhere, and plutocracy would govern without hindrance; but fortunately money is not the only power   After all, the appeal to the higher motives in man is a far greater force in the direction of human affairs if it can be made under the conditions that render it effective.   These conditions are supplied by the proportional vote and its system of large constituencies

Here is a man whose life is devoted to a great principle. He fights for it day and night, his powerful voice is heard all over the land, and his adherents are counted by the hundreds of thousands This is the very man whom you will never see in one of our present parliaments elected on the single constituency system   The men who can grasp his ideas are not very thickly scattered over the country   Though combined, they would be able to elect their leader, if the total of their votes were counted, they would not have the shadow of a chance in any single constituency   Talk of wealth profiting, of poverty losing, by the proportional vote! This man and his adherents are too poor, perhaps, to contest a single constituency against the plutocrat who dominates in that section, they have so little influence in each separate constituency that even if they could collect money enough to pay for election expenses, they would be at the bottom of the poll   The master-mind would succumb to a stupid local politician, whereas under the P V, without any expensive canvass, all his friends in the country would put his name foremost on their list and thus elect him

Henry George would not have had the smallest prospect of being elected if he had been running for Congress, in at least ninety-nine constituencies out of a hundred; but under the proportional vote, he would have had "1" on all the ballots of his partisans in the country, and of many thousands besides, who, though not in everything of his opinion, were at least convinced that they voted for an honest, incorruptible man with wide views and an urgent desire for the public welfare. I am confident that in such a case no other Con gressman would have polled so many votes as the first preference of the voters

Instead of making the whole country one single constituency, as Hare proposes, it has been suggested as a compromise to throw together only a certain number of constituencies, half a dozen, for instance. I believe that the change thus proposed is for the worse, and that the original and unadulterated Hare System is in every way preferable. The larger the constituency, the greater are the chances for minorities of being represented, the more constit- uencies, the less hope there is for struggling progressive thought to find a representation in the council of the nation. Take the case of New Zealand, for instance, with its 74 constituencies, and let us suppose that 148,000 were the total of votes cast at an election, which makes 2,000 votes the number electing a member Now, let us suppose there were 80 Socialists in each constituency Under the present system they would not even dream of putting up candi- dates, as the 80 partisans in each district would not have the slightest hope of success But even if the country were divided into 6 voting districts of 12 members each, they could not elect a single member, as their vote would nowhere exceed 1,000 If, on the other hand, the whole country formed one single constituency, they would send 3 members to the house With constituencies of 6 members, even 250 votes in each local district might not give them a single mem- ber, while on the centralized plan they would obtain as many as 9 representatives, and by joining with other progressives, might largely infuse legislation with Socialistic principles

I think the incentive to thus improve an excellent plan back- ward was the fear that the work of counting the ballots might be a little too complicated I am not so sure of this but there need not be much more work for each voter than in the other case He would simply pick the list he specially favors from the rest, and would vote for it by affixing the numbers according to his prefer- ence Of course, there would be more names on the general list than there would be on each district list, but it will never be neces- sary to number all names. It suffices to mark those specially pre- ferred, while the others will be taken in the sequence in which they are printed, if they should be needed. The case where men of other parties and lists will be added to, others struck out from a special list by the voter, will be exceptional, and even then the additional work is almost nil

Anyhow, the advantages of the larger constituency are so great that minor considerations must be relegated into the background. The larger the constituency, the more effective will be the vote of the whole people The smaller the constituency, the more of the evils inherent in the present system are preserved

The more effective we make the vote, the better do we obtain a true expression of the people's will. The new system will make elections tell a different tale from that of to-day; not money will profit, but intellect and character Principles, not men, will be elected, which means a back seat to that class of men called politicians, who treat politics as a business—a lot of nobodies who all over the world bring parliamentarism into contempt Only a party leader who himself belongs to this stamp will feel an instinctive horror of the new system. A leader capable of great thoughts, preferring to be the first among equals to being the master of servants, will welcome the proportional system

The bitterness of party strife will lose its venom, and the participation of the people in elections will be more general Many who now abstain altogether from voting, because the proposed candidates constitute to them a mere choice between evils, will interest themselves in the political contest when they have a chance to vote for men of their own choice

Opinions and principles may not be the only rallying points of the future voters It is very likely that different trades will send their own delegates—practical men, who know better what the people want than the lawyers who constitute such an undue proportion of our existing parliaments. (In the U. S. Senate 74 out of 92 members are lawyers.) Unfortunately, for good talkers are seldom great doers Doubtless a certain danger might still exist in this case that the interest of the community could be neglected for that of the trade, but, aside from the fact that the totality of trade interests forms the totality of community interests, even this would be preferable to a narrow local interest representation Quite a different tone would govern the discussion of such parliaments, as every one can see who studies the business-like and concise addresses and discussions at co-operative congresses, that of Great Britain, for instance. A co-operative congress does more business in one day than many a parliament does in a week

By-elections, when a member resigns his seat or dies, are unnecessary under the proportional vote on the Hare system, as the unelected candidate on the same list who obtained the next largest number of votes would simply take the vacated place

The proportional vote must not be confounded with the *scrutin de liste*, which also collects a number of single member constituencies into a large one of many members, a very objectionable method of doing away with the defect of the small constituency the subordination of the common to the local interest. It is a device of party politicians, because nothing strengthens more the autocratic power of the caucus of nominating candidates Cases happen under this system that a candidate is strongly opposed— even by the majority of his own party—in his own local district where he is known, but is elected by an overwhelming majority, because the other districts that vote the straight party ticket, not knowing the man, gave him their votes. In fact, it could occur that each single candidate on the list is rejected by the people among whom he lives, and yet the whole list pass with a large majority, because each district of the constituency, not knowing the candidates from the other districts, gives them an undivided vote, as the party leaders have nominated them The defects of this system have been used with the ignorant to throw disfavor on the proportional vote, with which it has nothing in common but the throwing together of electoral districts, whereas the fact that under the P V. each elector votes for only one candidate enables him to select whomsoever he prefers and to leave out altogether those he does not know or like, thus preserving the advantages of the many-member electorate, without its drawbacks

Plumping, or the multiple vote, is an improvement on the *scrutin de liste*, through the faculty given to the voter to concentrate his votes on one or more candidates whom he prefers It is the most primitive of proportional systems, for it wastes all those plumped votes which a candidate does not need If Jones needs only 2,000 votes, while 5,000 are concentrated on him, through plumping, 3,000 votes are absolutely lost, while under the Hare system they are used for the man second on the list, and so forth, so that all the votes are in any case given for some party friend

The *secrecy of the ballot* ought to be combined with the greatest convenience of the voter I understand that in Queensland the vote can now be given by postal card I do not know how they secure the secrecy, but can see no difficulty in this direction Each voter might be supplied with a parcel of cards of different colors, each color for a different election or referendum vote The cards would be numbered, and if no record is allowed to be kept where each number was sent, a control of the vote by the officials would not be possible The influencing of the voter cannot be avoided by the most ingenious systems of secrecy, but social reform would put an end to economic dependence, and at the same time would greatly raise the financial value of the vote for each shareholder in the State. No briber could afford to pay as much as the vote would transfer to him from the common pocket, for this would leave him no profit, and no voter could, on the average, afford to take less, or his loss on one side would exceed his profit on the other You can afford to bribe one shareholder of a limited company to vote for something which is against his interest, by paying him more than he loses, but you cannot bribe all for their loss as shareholders would either exceed their gain by the bribe, or your profit would not reach the outlay A well-known saying is "You can fool some people all the time, and all the people some time, but you cannot fool all the people all the time "

The greatest danger of the present system is the indifference of the voters many of whom do not go to the polls; just as small shareholders in stock companies mostly do not attend at the general meetings or do not even send proxies unless somebody specially asks for them. Their other interests outweigh too much the one influenced by their vote to make the sacrifice of time worth their while. Social reform will change this

The administration of the people's land under land nationalization, the management of the currency, organization of distribution, perhaps also of certain branches of production, are public measures so deeply touching the self-interest of the voter that he will be as eager to be represented as the large shareholder is certain to look after his own interests in a stock company —Even with the best systems of voting, and the most general participation of the people at the elections, it is not possible to be absolutely certain that the views of the voters are really faithfully represented. Leaving even the question of honesty apart, it is not to be supposed that one man will exactly hold the same views on every point as another, and generally the elector must be satisfied if his representative is at one with him on some important points, though he may diverge in others An *imperative mandate* might obviate this inconvenience. Each representative represents as many votes as he received, and has always to deliver the votes of his mandators where he has not been given full liberty to vote as he pleases The principal objection against this system—which caused its abandonment after it was tried in the beginning of the French Revolution, when the representative arrived with his *cahier*, which directed his votes—no more exists The general ignorance then was so great that no hope of reform could be entertained except by sending the most intelligent men to mutually enlighten each other Binding the delegate beforehand meant simply renouncing every hope of arriving at any useful solution. This has entirely changed in our times Our public school system, the public meeting, the press, and the accessibility of literature, have disseminated general enlightenment, and the representative is sent less to form his own opinions than to give vent to those already held by his electors The cases where speeches in Parliament influence the votes have become more and more the exception The party meeting often decides beforehand how each member is to vote, and the speeches are usually made for the constituency, or for the people at large, which could be reached by other means A reader of certain parliamentary debates is often struck by the strange fact that some bills are passed by a large majority after almost every speaker has opposed them The majority, certain of the result and not wishing to waste time, keeps silent, and lets the opposition do all the talking Many members sit in the refreshment-rooms or chat in the lobbies, and only come in when a division takes place

The single change which an imperative mandate would bring into the system, would be the substitution of the elector's mandate for that of the party meeting It is therefore mere nonsense to consider such a mandate as derogatory to the dignity of the member who feels no such scruple when he votes as the party dictates There is still plenty of work to be done which requires the exercise of his personal intelligence and initiative, such as the wording of laws (the principles only of which have been decided for him), the perusal of the public accounts, the investigation of abuses, the control of the executive, etc   A lot of useless talk could be done away with, if each elector's imperative mandate were registered at the beginning of every session, and debates avoided where a decision has already been arrived at by the majority of the electors, or as soon as a majority is reached through additional votes sent to the chairman during the debate   Such votes may come from electors who have reserved their mandates or from the representatives as far as they possess free mandates, i e , full power to vote as they please   In such a case the debate would at once be closed   There are plenty of other possibilities to get rid of suppressed speeches, without spending the people's time and money thereby!

However, there might be some inconveniences connected with such a system, and in any event another remedy against the despotism of the representative has been obtaining great popularity the direct vote in its modern form, *the Referendum and the Initiative*

This system was first adopted in Switzerland, where it takes the place of the old Germanic and also old Greek and Roman custom—as yet existing, as the *Landsgemeinde*, in some Swiss cantons, and in the New England town meetings—of having the people decide by their direct vote, in public meetings, what laws they want and what expenditures they authorize   The old system would not be applicable to the administration of a modern state, and the referendum—the referring of decisions to the approval or negation of the people's vote—has taken the place of the old *folkmote*   The Swiss have two kinds of referendum, the *optional* (facultative) and the *obligatory*, or compulsory   The one is taken whenever a certain number of voters demand it, the other has to be taken before certain laws become valid, or before expenditure, beyond certain limits, is allowed   The right of the Initiative enables a certain number of voters to propose a law   It would be useless to deny that the referendum has not always given the best of results, if the results are judged by the most intelligent section of the community   A river cannot mount higher than its source, and a people will not dictate better laws than their understanding permits   The intellectual aristocracy, who think themselves fitted to educate the masses, believe they can best do so by passing progressive laws, even if these laws go beyond the people's wishes for the time   They feel sure that the masses will soon be educated up to the laws   It is the system of benevolent despotism, of which some think that it produced good results in its time   The safest plan, however, and the only possible one under a real democracy is to wait until the people are ripe for progress, instead of presuming to force on them the progressive measures in the expectation that these will accelerate the ripening process

The rising sun first illuminates the highest peaks, whose brilliancy announces the coming day The complete victory over the sway of darkness, however, is only gained when the whole body of the mountains and finally of the lower country is lighted. So the world's great men merely indicate the lines of future advance, but this advance is only accomplished when the intellectual progress has become the property of the masses from the monopoly of the few The Swiss progressives have long since learnt this, and they humbly bow to the will of the people, even where the best laws are rejected by the referendum vote So, for instance, when the law for workers' insurance against disease and accident—the result of ten years' hard work—was passed by the two houses of the legislature but when it was submitted to the popular verdict, May 20, 1900, the Swiss people refused it, with 341,254 against 146,954 votes The further education of the masses since then had the result of bringing out another law, which is under discussion while I add this, in June, 1908, and which has the best prospects of adoption by the people

· This proves how little the representative sometimes represents the people's ideas also, in the middle of the nineties, a military law was adopted by a vote of 111 to 9 by the Nationalrath, and by 30 to 12 by the Standerath, and was rejected by the referendum with 269,751 against 195,278

The Referendum is a reform urgently demanded, and one which no really democratic country ought to be without. One State of the Union after another is adopting it as the surest remedy against boss rule and graft * The Initiative, though not quite as important, is also desirable, to enable the people to overcome the inertia of their legislators, sometimes caused by impure motives, and their subsequent failure to pass certain laws which are demanded by popular opinion The *Recall*, the right to dismiss at any time a representative, when a majority vote against him at a poll taken upon the demand of a certain number of his constituents, proves that he no longer enjoys the confidence of his electors is another commendable democratic measure. The main result of this right would be to strengthen the impulse to resign, engendered by decency, whenever a representative becomes doubtful as to his position with his electors Any sensitive man would in such a case submit to the test of a new election of his own initiative, rather than continue in a dubious position The Recall would also be a wholesome strengthener of an elected candidate's faithfulness to election promises It would not be applicable, however, under the proportional vote on the Hare system, and at all events is not of great importance where the representative is kept in order by the referendum bridle.

* "Equity," edited and published by C F Taylor, 1520 Chestnut Street, Philadelphia Pa keeps its readers posted in regard to the progress made by the referendum and the proportional vote The Prop Rep Society, 28 Martin's Lane London, only attends to the prop vote

For constitutional changes, a majority vote of the people—
of all entitled to vote, not only of those actually voting—ought to
be demanded, and among such constitutional laws that which re-
stores the land to the people ought to be placed. In fact, from an
ethical point of view, the people have no jurisdiction here; they
have no authority to give away the heirloom of unborn generations,
they have no right to re-create private land monopoly after it once
has been terminated Every new child born into the world could
claim the privilege to nullify any enactment that deprived him of
his full share in God's gift. Any other obstacle to changes in the
constitution but the requisition of such a majority of the whole
people might turn justified conservatism into a clog to legitimate
progress We must not forget that a majority of all entitled to
vote means considerably more than a mere majority of those actually voting

To introduce such a radical change into the constitution of the
United States will not be found an easy matter in consequence of
the power given to the smaller States to resist constitutional changes
demanded by the majority of the nation, but the final victory of the
latter cannot remain doubtful. Archives full of once valid but long
since worthless State documents, and many a bloody page of history, show us which way as a rule victory finally went in the battle
of which is to govern the people or the parchment? The change
must come or the United States will cease to be a democracy.

The question of constitutional changes brings up that other
one of the constitutionality of laws Who is to decide whether a
certain law keeps within the bounds of the constitution? The
United States allow such power to the courts, who thus override
the law-giving power of the people, delegated to the State legislatures and to Congress We know that the courts make a liberal
use of this power I need only recall the Income Tax Law, passed
by Congress and the President, but annulled by the Supreme Court
of the United States, or rather, as has been a common thing lately,
by one judge, who gave the fifth vote against four on the other side
Or that recent decision of the same Court and single vote, affirm-
ing the unconstitutionality of a law of the State of New York
which, in the interest of health, limited the working hours of New
York bakers It is highly instructive to note the grounds on which
sometimes laws are declared unconstitutional The New York law
was supposed to infringe the freedom of contract guaranteed by
the Constitution of the United States—freedom of contract, where
one of the contracting parties has to starve, if he does not accept
work regardless of terms! Or a late decision of a San Diego court,
which declared this city's Referendum law unconstitutional, because
it was on the lines of a pure democracy, while "the law-making
power of a city must remain in a representative legislative body."
As if it were not the business of the people to choose the means by
which they will give expression to the views of the majority! It is

no wonder that the power thus exercised by the courts, a power which subordinates the legislature to the judicial department, grows in disfavor The people, as the source of the constitution, are the final judge as to the constitutionality of laws, and to the people the last appeal must lie in each case where a court declares a law unconstitutional. If they decide by a majority vote, such as will authorize changes in the constitution, that the law stands, then the judgment of the court ought to be annulled The simplification of such changes, as here proposed, will make such appeals less cumbersome than they would be with the present apparatus, at least as far as the national constitution is concerned The pastime of declaring laws unconstitutional might be less frequently indulged in if the third failure of any judge in such an attempt would involve his incapacity of further serving on the bench

One of the most important questions which will come up when future changes in the constitution are made by the people will be the composition of our present second chamber, the Senate of the United States Second chambers, often wrongly called first chambers, are, anyhow, in very bad repute with democrats My old friend, J Morrison Davidson, than whom no better and sincerer democrat ever drew breath, makes out their bill of indictment in his "Politics for the People" (London, Reeves), especially that of the mother of second chambers the British House of Lords, an anachronism, and a dangerous one at that Mr. Davidson has drawn up an ominous list of its sins against the people, in proof that it has opposed any kind of progress, and usually has only yielded out of fear But its very origin must condemn it, for its authority is based on the foulest wrong ever committed against the people of England the robbery of their land Its only title is that of usurpation based upon usurpation The lords first stole the people's land, and then founded their hereditary privilege of governing the country upon the possession of the soil As the same author points out, the American Senate was nothing but a servile copy of a bad precedent, with its own goodish quota of sins in addition, especially in the matter of slavery "Suffice it to say that, but for the existence of the American Second Chamber, the Republic would have been spared all the horrors of the Civil War, with its holocaust of 900,000 lives and its loss of £1,400,000,000 of treasure," is the summing up of the history of the Secession War by our friend "Wherever two chambers exist, one must be master, and, unfortunately for the Western republic, the master is the plutocratic upper chamber. Hence Lord Salisbury's admiration for the American Senate, in which the little State of Delaware is put on a footing of equality with that of New York, with more than thirty times its population."

It seems to me, however, my worthy friend goes too far when he concludes, from cases where the so-called upper chambers did not represent the people's will, through an unjust composition, that second chambers by themselves are a bad institution, and that, if the second chamber represents the people as much as the other chamber, it simply supplies a needless repetition of the same vote. Two bodies, though of the same origin, may have different ideas on some points. We have seen, in discussing the referendum, that the representative does not always correctly represent the people's wishes, and two representatives elected by the same vote often differ. The history of the French Convention, on the other hand, proves that the pendulum has its good uses. It is true that to a certain extent the referendum can undertake its regulation, but a second chamber might in many cases save the trouble of recurring to the referendum.

Certainly it would be far better if a second chamber could be obtained which in a high degree represents popular opinion, without being a mere duplication of the other body, but how attain this end? A different division of the electoral districts would not be feasible under the proportional vote. Wealth should be as little a determining factor in the franchise for one chamber as for the other, especially in a country where common land ownership makes the whole people proprietors. Nor are appointments by the Government to be recommended, for the legislature ought to control the Government, and an administrator ought not to be allowed to select his own auditor.

I think a good idea would be to limit the franchise of the second chamber to all citizens above a certain age, say forty. Not the passive franchise, as in Sparta's Gerontes (Council of the Aged), but the active franchise. Only the citizens beyond a certain ripe age have the right to vote for the second chamber, but I see no objection to their choosing younger men if they wish to. Wherever younger men are elected by their elders, we may suppose that they possess a greater ripeness of judgment than the average men of their age.

Most of us who have lived a certain number of years are astonished to see, when we look back on our state of mind as it was in our youth, in what different aspects men and things appeared to us, how much we owe to a ripened experience. There is a great difference in the judgment of the average man above forty and the average man below forty. They have a joke against a certain country in Germany—Wurtemberg—that the people there only become reasonable at forty. A cooler reflection on the consequences of certain measures, the outcome of temperament and experience, gives the riper men a decided superiority as critics, and thus they are eminently fitted for the work in question.

The referendum is not the only institution for which little Switzerland, the purest democracy in the world, might afford America an object lesson. Its Executive is also far superior to ours. There the Parliament appoints a committee which carries on the executive work of the Government, each of the members undertaking a special branch of the administration, and which elects one of their number as their president for the year The two chambers meet together and elect the seven members of the Federal Council for three years The President is only the chairman of a board, without any other privilege The system works to perfection, and yet there is an agitation towards a change in the constitution, which would place the election of the Council in the hands of the people—changing the indirect election into a direct one, which constitutes a real progress only under a good proportional voting system Without it, the direct system is certainly more democratic in theory, but in practice, as we have seen, in our country, a miserable nomination system clogs it with the defects of the indirect system, and without preserving the advantages of the latter. Practically, the nominating caucus of one of the two main parties elects, and, as a rule, this caucus is not elected by the people as a whole, but by political clubs, usually domineered by a few politicians The attempts made by some of our States to substitute the regular vote of the whole people for that of unauthorized self-elected political clubs are certainly in the right direction, and, if the people voting at the primary elections selected their delegates on the Hare system, nothing further could be desired This would combine the advantages of the indirect with those of the direct system, where one or a few officials are elected by a large constituency It would be the system which ought to govern our Presidential elections The nominations would not be left to irresponsible conventions, without any mandate from the people, but to the product of the primary election, the Electoral College, to whom the present constitution entrusts the election But this college, far from being a meeting of dummies, ordered to elect the President whom the majority party has nominated, into which custom has transformed it, would then be a congress of independent delegates, entrusted with the task of nominating and presenting to the people's choice two sets of candidates Of course the members of the College ought to be elected on the proportional system, so that all parties are fairly represented among the delegates from each State Those members of the College who have no chance of bringing through their own candidates would then use their influence to insure the nomination of their second choice candidates, i e., those candidates selected by another party who are most acceptable to them or, at all events, the lesser evil, if they cannot pass their own Under the present system they are not only absolutely disfranchised, but their very attempt at carrying through an independent third party candidate may insure the victory of the party most obnoxious to them

The reform here proposed would not only free the birth of new parties from such risks it would do more than that It would bring to their ranks many thousands of voters whom the danger of insuring the victory of their worst enemies to-day keeps from voting for the men of their first choice Nominations by an independent college, issuing from the direct proportional vote, would thus facilitate in this country the peaceable success of new parties which hardly anything short of a real revolution could bring to the top under existing circumstances   At the same time the new system would protect the old parties from sudden discomfiture by a revolutionary minority, though relative majority, by enabling them to defeat the common enemy at the last moment, through their joint vote.   All this could be accomplished without any more work and expense than are entailed by the present system, because we should do away with the whole claptrap of the existing convention business, the jugglery by which the bosses and their tools manage to endow with the appearance of life the corpses of old rotten party organizations Those to whom this appears a harsh judgment had better remember the election of 1904, and the part which plutocratic influence played in the Democratic nomination   Does anybody really believe that an official convention (the new Electoral College here proposed), chosen by the proportional vote, would ever have made such a nomination?   Or, in other words, that the Democratic party, as a whole would have really enlisted under such a standard?   The answer was given by the thousands of Democrats who either abstained, or else voted for the opposite party, rather than vote for the candidate of bosses, bought by or acting for plutocracy

The members of the cabinet could be nominated by the same Electoral College and elected at the same general election, or they could be appointed in the present way.

This chapter would become too long if it treated all the reforms our Constitution requires to make it an instrument for the expression of a free nation's will, instead of a curb upon democracy   As an instance, I only mention the absolutely undemocratic system which delays the entrance into office of the newly elected President and congressmen for four months, so that in the interim often men legislate and govern who have lost the people's confidence   The last four months of President Buchanan s administration supply the best proof of the fatal consequences   If Lincoln and the newly elected members of congress could have taken their seats immediately after their election, the Southern States would not have been given the time for that preparation for the Civil War which Buchanan's inactivity afforded them.

CHAPTER VII

CO-OPERATION.

Between the isolated peaks of Individualism and the storm-tossed sea level of Socialism the fertile fields of Co-operation are espied

SO far we have been engaged in studying the reforms which can only be attained through the law-making machinery of the State, we have also discussed the improvement of this machinery Even the greatest optimist will agree with us that the hope of making an early progress on these lines, in any way commensurate with the pressing need, against the fearful power of plutocracy, is very slight. Whoever is in a position to know the intimate convictions of the masses realizes that the prevision of a bloody revolution is spreading fast. A very bad sign, indeed, for when the people begin to despair of any improvement by peaceable methods, the beginning of the end is near, unfortunately an end which would be only the prelude to further battles. A co-operation for the destruction of the old house might perhaps be obtainable, but a fearful fight would rage over the plans of a new building, meanwhile rain and storms would chill the shelterless. The danger is so imminent that it would be imprudent to rely on one single method. The work in the political field does not exclude action in another direction, where we can beat the adversary with his own weapons. Meeting combination with co-operation, we must oppose to the Trusts co-operative production and distribution, to the money monopoly, the organization of credit, to the capitalist's banks, the workers' Mutual Banks.

The history of co-operative production has not been a very brilliant one. In fact, it is only since co-operative distribution has made such wonderful progress in Great Britain that we see a little advance in this department. This is easily explained, for the difficulty producers find all over the civilized world, in our epoch of a so-called overproduction, is not the organization of production, but the sale of the product. Where even experienced business men fail by the thousand, what can be expected from workingmen, who, however proficient they may be in their special work of production, have no experience of trade and its ramifications? Their means, as a rule, are too limited to command business talent of a high order. Their experience is too small to effectively control the commercial manager and to avoid the fate of that gentleman who, having supplied the capital and his partner the experience for the concern, after a year found his partner had got the capital and he the experience.

It wanted the previous success of co-operative distribution to

supply the missing links sufficient capital and custom to allow production full scope Since 2,332,754 men and women, representing
ten million consumers, have united in Great Britain to establish co-
operative distribution with a joint capital of 160 million dollars,
yearly sales amounting to 500 millions have been made, with a
profit of 55 millions   (Report, 1906) A market has also been
opened for the products of co-operative labor. The result is that
though we are only in the beginning of this branch of co-operation,
40 million dollars' worth of goods sold in the co-operative stores
are manufactured by co-operatives This does not include what is
bought from co-operative productive societies, whose total trade
amounts to about 25 million dollars

   Yet close observers of the co-operative movement have lost
much of the enthusiasm which they once felt for it   More and more
we have seen distributive co-operation restricted to the sole purpose of reducing the cost of goods, with a complete blindness to
the fact that any general success of this work might finally merely
result in a fall of wages, hastened by the appearance in the labor
market of the former traders thrown out of work   Cost of merchandise has been greatly reduced by even more powerful agencies
than co-operative distribution, and the result has been anything but
beneficial to the masses of the population   The attacks against co-
operative stores, therefore, are justified so long as their efforts remain one-sided, so long as they are mainly directed towards the
cheapening of articles of consumption   It would be quite different
if the profits obtained were used to force on economic reforms in
the direction of creating employment, and consequently raising
wages   If the fifty-five million dollars yearly profits made by British
co-operators, instead of being distributed as dividends, were used
to purchase land for the co-operators, as many as fifty thousand
workers, or a population of a quarter of a million, might be settled
every year, relieving the labor market in a double way: (1) by
changing laborers into farmers; and (2) by increasing the demand
for co-operative products in exchange for farm produce   Co-operation could then make use of a powerful weapon for the increase of
its circle, so as to make it embrace the bulk of the nation within a
measurable time. This weapon is *Exchange-Banking.* Let us first
understand the general features of the system.

   Exchange-banking, or scientific barter, tries to combine the
advantages of the monetary system with those of barter, or rather it
tries to secure the benefits of money as a means of universal barter,
without the obstacles which it puts in the way of exchange   In its
most primitive form, that adopted in Robert Owen's labor exchanges, as far back as the thirties of last century, and in De Bernardi's American labor exchanges, founded about thirty years ago,
but disappearing after a decade or two, stores are organized in which
goods are deposited, or at whose disposal labor is offered, the payment not being made in money, but in orders payable in the goods

and labor offered by the store. As salable labor is also a merchandise, I shall in this chapter include it in the term "goods" for simplicity's sake Each depositor pays himself with the goods of another depositor, the orders through which this is accomplished becoming the money of the circle

A great improvement on this plan was that of the great Frenchman, Pierre Joseph Proudhon His "Banque du peuple," which, unfortunately, remained in the embryo state, was to issue the orders to all who held goods at the disposal of the bank, and who thus could pay themselves in turn by the goods of other members The store was extended so as to include all the stores of the members, in fact, all their productive and trading power It was Proudhon's ambition to so extend the circle that it would gradually embrace the whole of France This is best evidenced in the Memorial which he addressed in the year 1855 to the Prince Napoleon in regard to the use to be made of the Palais d'Industrie. (Appendix to "Théorie de la propriété ") He wanted to establish there a permanent exhibition of all producers of the country where orders could be accepted (and I suppose, for certain not very voluminous goods, as far as stock went, also executed on the spot), the payment to be made in exchange paper issued by the organization, a paper which, through being payable in all the products of the country, was bound to have the full purchasing power of legal tender money It is a great pity that this "Société de l'Exposition Perpétuelle," his best work, is so little known Nothing else the great genius has produced shows him so little of a crank and so much of a practical man of business In a masterly way he sketches the immense influence which such an institution would have on production and circulation, on interest and rent, on the waste caused by superfluous middlemen, and on the general distribution of wealth Nothing is impracticable in the grand project, not even the enthusiasm of the author who never for one moment flattered himself with the vain hope that the dreamer on France's throne would really accept his proposal If the moment when the founder of the Bonaparte dynasty dismissed Fulton with a jest, addressed to his surroundings as to the impracticable projectmaker, decided the emperor's fate by depriving him of the only chance he had of conquering England, we may say that the neglect of Proudhon's grand idea deprived the second Emperor for ever of the possibility to make France the first industrial and commercial power in the world, and to establish her national wealth on the most solid basis

Proudhon's agitation had at least one practical result the establishment of *Bonnard's Exchange Bank* at Marseilles in 1849 (Proudhon had published his "Banque d'Echange" in 1848). In 1853 the business moved to Paris, where according to Professor Karl Knies, in *Credit*, the turn over from 1854-55 amounted to 45 million francs. It still existed in 1897 under the name of "Comptoir Central de Crédit." J Naud & Co (Naud was Bonnard's son-in-law) It not only existed but prospered. Its yearly publications showed a very large list of firms who accepted the bank's exchange paper. This consisted of engagements backed by promissory notes, signed by the members, who had accepted a credit from the bank to supply within a fixed term a certain amount of their goods or to pay in cash their notes deposited as collaterals. The credit was, of course, only given in the shape of a loan to the members, consisting in the engagement of some other member, whose goods the borrower needs. A commission of from 3% to 5% was taken by the company, which was not co-operative, but a stock company working for dividends. Its success proves to co-operators how important is the mine of wealth they have left untouched.

The co-operators of Great Britain could at once make a success of the scheme. A co-operative currency could be issued by the Wholesale Societies of Manchester and Glasgow, differing from ordinary currency in not consisting of a special commodity like gold or a promise to deliver gold on demand but an engagement to directly supply the things for obtaining which the present currency is finally used. Or, let us rather say, ought to be used, because exactly the fact that in many cases it is not so used, but is employed as an instrument for the exaction of usury, is responsible for most of the evils we are suffering. The notes issued by the Exchange-Bank department of the Wholesales would not promise to deliver gold to bearer, as otherwise the law against the issue of bank-notes would be infringed, but to supply goods to bearer at cash prices. Such notes can be issued in England up to forty shillings without paying stamp duty. They would be made redeemable in any one of the different co-operative stores of the kingdom. The stores would accept them readily, as they could pay for their purchases from the Wholesales with them. Those stores which are not yet members of the Wholesales would here find a strong inducement to come in, because the acceptance of the notes would mean additional business brought to their doors. In a population of ten million, the members of the co-operative societies and their families, this currency, to a certain extent, would be as good as the present money, and they would be ready to accept as much of it in payment as they could pass on. They would consequently be ready to buy these notes from their employers for the cash received for wages, the only way in which, for the time being, the Truck Acts, made for an entirely different purpose, permit the transaction. The employers, being able to pass on the paper to their employees, and also to buy with it from the stores any goods they required for their own use, would accept the paper from the Wholesales for at least part of the goods supplied. Manufacturers do anything in their power to obtain custom, and the Wholesales are large buyers and good payers, to whom everybody tries to sell.

It will be readily seen how an entirely new class of members, or customers, would thus be recruited for the co-operative societies

Not only the manufacturers and farmers who accepted the notes for their goods would come in, but also those of their employees who are not already members; also many of the purveyors of these manufacturers, farmers. and employees, who are just as anxious to obtain orders, etc   All these would buy their supplies in the co-operative stores, if obtainable, while the stores would gradually extend their lines until anything could be obtained from them at regular prices.   The traders of the circle could even afford to pay a little more for the goods they buy with the new currency, because every such purchase means a corresponding sale of their own wares What store would not rather pay 5 per cent more for a merchandise, if the purveyor agrees to take in payment goods on which 15 per cent net profit is made?   In the same way, all who sell to the Wholesales for Exchange notes could afford to give better terms to those who accept the paper from them, their own purveyors and wage workers   The latter would obtain the additional advantage of a greater security of their positions.   Their acceptance of the notes would ensure to the employer a corresponding custom, and consequently enable him to keep them in preference when other employees are dismissed because cash business is slack

In this way, the co-operative circle would rapidly increase, until it would gradually monopolize the greater part of the home trade, until most producers and most consumers of the kingdom would form part of it.   The amounts of the new currency thus kept floating would then exceed that of all the present banks of the country.

The interest saved by the co-operative societies through the use of their own money and the profits made through the additional sales brought about by the new currency need not be paid out in dividends.   The new members thus brought in do not come to get dividends, but because their acceptance of the paper procures them employment or custom.   The extra profits thus made could be used for the development of co-operation, for its redemption from dividend-grabbing, and finally to the establishment of a *Co-operative Commonwealth*, in which anybody willing to work would find paying employment of the sort best adapted to his capabilities   Then co-operation would be looked at in a different light by the private trader, who now must be its enemy as long as it only deprives him of a living, without at the same time offering him the chance of a better one, with which the new system would supply him

My own efforts for an experiment in this direction were made in vain   In the years 1896-7 I lectured in a number of British co-operative societies, wrote in their organ, the Co-operative News, and spread a booklet, "The Real History of Money Island," in which I gave the imaginary history of an England as it would evolve through the adoption of my plans   I showed how the Trades-unions concluded to push the acceptance of the new currency among their members, to whom the co-operative societies supplied it for the purpose of starting co-operative production, a weapon found far more practical than the exploding strike revolver, which as often hurts the marksman as it hits the target. Gradually in this way the workers produced for themselves all they consumed, and in using part of the profits for the purchase of land made cheap through their refusal to work and live on the land of private owners wherever they could get land of their own co-operatively, they gradually rendered themselves independent of land owners as they had freed themselves of the capitalists. The two congresses which yearly met to fix prices and to debate questions of common import. the congress of the producers and that of the consumers, consisting of the same parties in their two capacities, gradually became the parliament of the country, general well being and happiness were attained, with universal peace and general disarmament, following the adoption of the system in other countries, and all other blessings which any decent Utopia is in duty bound to paint in glowing colors. The great social revolution was thus peaceably carried through.

The Real History proved that I did not make any particular impression on conservative co-operators, and I left England for her youngest colony, New Zealand, there to try the work independently.

If the co-operatives had taken up the plan the element of risk would have been reduced to a minimum, the risk that members become insolvent and fail to honor the society's orders. How inconsiderable this risk would be, even where the exchange-bank is organized by the ordinary trade, can only be realized when we fully take in the basis of Proudhon's plan the substitution of merchandise credit for money credit.

We all know the great difference between the two credits. There is hardly anybody so poor that he is entirely deprived of merchandise credit, or is not giving it to somebody else. In fact, the poor, as a body, grant commercial credits besides which those given by some of the largest commercial concerns dwindle to a mere trifle. The wage workers deliver their merchandise, i e, their labor, on credit and get paid only after a certain time has elapsed. If only 150 million wage workers all over the world have to wait for pay day on the average not more than half a week, all the year round, and if we average weekly wages at only three dollars, the sum thus continually credited by the workers to their employers amounts to 225 million dollars. In reality this credit is partly given, not by the wage workers, but by their own creditors, the boarding-house keepers, retail dealers. house owners, etc. There is hardly a worker so poor but he finds one of these parties giving him credit for the necessaries of life until pay day comes round. And going up higher in the circle we find numerous dealers and manufacturers, who could not raise a dollar at their bank, owing thousands for goods of some kind supplied to them on credit. and who could easily obtain many thousands more from the only too-zealous salesmen. who call on them and move Heaven and earth to obtain orders.

Now let us consider that, after all, what we now call merchandise credit is in reality a money credit, for, as a rule, goods are made payable not in goods, but in legal tender money, a money which, as we have seen in Chapters III and IV. is practically unobtainable in at least nineteen cases out of twenty when it is wanted That under such conditions this indirect money credit is so easily obtainable can only be accounted for by the very intensity of the struggle for the scarce means of exchange, without which existence is imperilled It is the life belt which alone can keep the swimmers above water, and for the majority, the sale of goods or services is the only way of obtaining this belt

To effect such sales every nerve is strained, great risks are taken; and where cash sales are impossible credit is offered Nevertheless, the risk is too great not to interfere seriously with the general exchange of goods and services Proudhon and his successors recognized that this strangling of exchange was due to the intrusion of money, an intrusion which forces all trade through the narrow gate of money and credit. Hence they proposed to substitute the merchandise promise for the money promise, the merchandise paper for the money paper

In our present system of currency we discern an ever-growing disproportion between base and superstruture; in the suggested system we have a never changing relation between the two, and thus an end of the danger due to their disproportion. The Exchange Bank, by giving to merchandise money wings and making the merchandise note take the place of the money note, creates a new money credit which at the same time is a real merchandise credit Of course, it is money credit only in a limited sense, for real money is accepted by everybody, while the merchandise money is accepted only in a certain circle. The more this circle extends, the more its money will, to every end and purpose, resemble real money The form of the exchange note may be various; in New Zealand I mostly adopted that of the bank-note, with the following text· "The holder of this note is entitled, on or within a reasonable time after presentation, to goods or services to the value of. . .from those members of the New Zealand Commercial Exchange Company, Ltd, who are liable to supply goods or services." If new issues were made, the words "or within a reasonable time" could be left out In the case of purchases made with ordinary money, goods cannot always be at once forthcoming when the money is tendered If we order a suit of a cloth which has first to come from a distance, all the treasures in the world could not produce it at once I had put in the provision only in order to guard against any confusion with the terms valid for our ordinary bank-notes and checks The goods promised in these—gold coins—have to be handed over the counter at once, though it is just as impossible to carry this out, if demanded by all creditors, as it is for the tailor to supply at once a suit ordered to measure

Experience has since made me prefer the check form, as recommended by John Armsden in "Value," preserving only the small bank-notes for change. My reasons are

1. The company ought not to rely on the interest demanded from the debtors as a revenue to pay current expenses Our fight must be against interest, and we ought to make the interest charge as low as possible, after a sufficient reserve fund has been obtained The revenue necessary to pay expenses ought to be mainly derived from a commission on the turnover, as in Owen's labor exchanges, though a much lower percentage than his—8⅓%, a penny for each shilling—could be demanded Now, it is impossible to control the turnover of members where the goods are sold, not in the store of the company, but in the member's place of business, if the payment is made by means of notes to bearer. Only when the payment is made with checks, not transferable, which the member who receives them has to bank directly, can the turnover be controlled Of course, the bank must insist on having the name to whose order the check is made out filled in in the same handwriting as the rest of the check, to avoid the leaving open of such name, so as to change it into a paper on bearer for the purpose of saving commissions. Evasions are punished by exclusion.

2. Only in this way can the bank prevent outsiders from reaping without charge the benefits enjoyed by members, and only thus can exclusion, the most powerful weapon to keep members up to their engagements, be made effective

In the commencement of a new undertaking like this, confidence is everything, and checks are more likely to inspire it when drawn by somebody known to the receiver, though the guarantee they give is not greater than that given by the notes to bearer The two forms of exchange paper only certify that bearer is entitled to receive goods from those members liable to supply these goods because the owner of the paper or the party from whom he obtained it has supplied such goods to others, or is at any time ready to do so The text of the check might read "Exchange Bank· Deliver to Mr. X $ in merchandise, to the debit of Y" The bank certifies checks on demand, if in order The company has no capital beyond its reserve fund to make good any failure of members In case of losses exceeding the income from commissions, interest and the reserve fund, higher commissions would have to be charged to make good. However, it is supposed that—as has proved the case in practical work, even with the discouraging circumstances under which this work was done—though outsiders may force a member into liquidation for cash debts, the Exchange Bank itself will rarely have to resort to such extremities. For every hundred men who have to suspend payment because a certain yellow metal is not obtainable, not one would refuse to supply goods (or labor) for his debt. The very fact that there is not enough demand for these goods is responsible for the activity of our courts of bankruptcy The risk of loss through insolvency of the members decreases still more with the extension of the circle, because the exclusion from the membership, the ultimate consequence of any non-fulfilment of engagements, might spell total ruin for the member Each would use his utmost efforts to make good sooner or later We must not forget the great difference between the Exchange Bank and the ordinary money-bank The latter merely supplies money to its customers wherewith to buy goods or make payments of any kind, it does not insure that the money thus paid out will come back to its spender to purchase goods from him The Exchange Bank alone has a right to say (what was mere nonsense on the part of Adam Smith) that "Money necessarily runs after goods, but goods do not always run after money" (See chapter IV) Exchange money is not a merchandise by itself, as ordinary money is, but only an order for merchandise, which sooner or later will be presented by somebody to the party who issued it Or, to be quite exact, for the order which he puts into circulation some other order will be presented to him, so that buying also means selling Any acceptance of an exchange-note (or check) means the compulsion to spend the same amount in the circle, for the notes are cashed only in this way. Each note becomes an active propagandist for the system, better than any advertisement could be To present the whole system and its effects clearly to the mind of the reader, it may be useful to reprint an explanation I gave in my "Pioneer of Social Reform," the organ of the N Z Exchange Bank, or "The New Zealand Commercial Exchange Co." I have made a few slight improvements

"The Commercial Exchange Company is a society whose members are men of different trades coming together to do business with each other   They are grocers, butchers, bakers, tailors, shoemakers, farmers, and so forth, who need each other's products, but barter, the simplest way of getting them, is out of question   Barter may do between two parties of whom each needs what the other wants to get rid of, but not between a hundred, of whom number one wants what number two can spare, number two what three wishes to dispose of, and of whom finally only number one hundred has any use for what number one offers in exchange   Under such circumstances, a medium of exchange—money—is necessary to pass from one to the other until it returns to the party who began

We all know how our butchers, grocers, tailors, shoemakers, etc, obtain this medium of exchange at present if they are not fortunate enough to own it through having received it in payment before they needed it   They go to a bank or a loan office and borrow certain pieces of a yellow metal, called sovereigns, or, in reality, they obtain the privilege of drawing little paper scrips, named checks, with which they pay each other, until finally, after a check has passed from number one to number two, from two to three, etc, and number one hundred has paid a check to number one, the latter recoups the original bank   For the right of drawing these paper scrips the parties pay an interest tribute to the bank, and are only

too happy if they are allowed to do so, for the banks are very particular, and do not allow everybody the privilege of a credit, but
only to those who can supply sufficient security that they will repay
the loan at any time at which the banks demand it   If the banks do
not obtain such security they will not give the loan, they will not
allow the parties to draw the little papers unless they have paid in
a corresponding number of the yellow coins called sovereigns, or
their substitutes principally checks certified by other banks.

This is the way in which things have been going on for some
time now, and have been getting more unpleasant the more prosperous the people became   This sounds strange, but it is a fact,
nevertheless, for the greater prosperity of the people resulted in a
more extended trade, and this trade extended much faster than the
stock of yellow pieces or—what amounts to the same thing—of
gold bullion which the Mint coins free of cost for anybody.   This
had the natural result that it became more and more difficult to induce the banks to allow the drawing of the paper scrips called
checks, for the danger grew that such scrip-drawing without a previous deposit of the yellow metal might result in general bankruptcy
of the banks and their debtors, for paper scrips are only accepted as
long as the people believe that sovereigns can be obtained for them
The very moment there is any doubt about this, nobody wants the
papers, but everybody will insist on receiving gold, often even refusing other kinds of scrips called bank-notes, which in some countries differ from the checks only in being drawn on the banks by
their presidents, and payable to anybody who presents them at the
banks, without their subjecting him to the trouble of signing or
proving his identity   Here, in New Zealand, the stock of gold in
the bank vaults amounts to only one-fifth of the deposits, that is, of
the amount of sovereigns due to parties who have brought sovereigns, or an order for sovereigns to the banks, and this does not
include the debt to the holders of bank-notes who also have paid in
gold for them, nor does it include the debt of the savings banks.
Including these the relation is only one-eighth   A very favorable
proportion, for in April, 1907, in the United States, it was only one-
twenty-sixth

Now, the very moment these depositors become afraid that
they may not be able to obtain the gold due to them, they will at
once call for it, and as the banks are well aware of the danger thus
threatening them (this threat has often turned into a reality) they
become more particular about giving credit, the more the excess of
scrip circulation over the gold stock increases   We have such a
period just now, for trade has increased very much all round, while
the gold stock has relatively diminished   Consequently, the demand for the paper scrips had to increase also, because without
them no trade is possible, as sovereigns are too inaccessible to
keep up our trade for a single day   The greater the demand, the
greater the danger that the small gold stock might be depleted, and

the more particular the banks are about giving credit, even at a high rate of interest. In this way it comes about that of all those people who want to trade with each other, a great many cannot obtain the right from their bank to draw the checks they need to pay each other, and many cannot even get a loan from the loan offices. If they do, they have to pay interest up to 60 per cent

Now, these people, or a certain number of them belonging to different trades, meet in their club, called the Commercial Exchange Company, and say to each other "Are we not great fools? Why do we go to the banks and usurers to obtain the right to draw paper scrips upon them, to pass them from one of us to the other, and finally to the banks again? Why not agree to draw those paper scrips upon ourselves, and to hand them back to ourselves? It may be done in a very simple way We first appoint a number of trustees whom we name the Board of Directors These print scrips somewhat like the banks' scrips, called checks and bank-notes, only with the difference that these scrips are not payable in gold sovereigns, but in the goods (and services) which the members require from each other In reality, the present scrips of the banks are nothing else for most of us, for we take them, not because we want gold for them—in fact, we take them though we know that if it came to the pinch we could not obtain the gold—but because we know that those whose goods we require take them in payment Now, if this certitude is all we need, what remains to be done is that we agree to accept our own scrips, and then we can borrow these scrips, or the right to draw them, from our trustees, and repay the trustees when we have received other scrips from members of the club All we have to do to feel certain that we can safely accept the scrips from each other is to instruct our trustees to make sure that no member obtains the scrips on credit, unless we can absolutely rely upon his supplying goods at cash prices for scrips when some one of us calls on him for such goods. Of course, we shall give him a reasonable time for this delivery, because such time is given even where we come with sovereigns in our pocket With millions of cash money in our possession, we cannot claim a pair of boots made to measure, at a moment's notice, but must give the necessary time to make them

Here we have the whole secret of the Commercial Exchange Company Its members supply to each other a means of circulation with all the qualities of that at present in use, merely omitting the roundabout way of occasionally claiming gold pieces, which in most cases are only wanted to pay for the goods which our papers promise directly Thus we not only avoid the interest-tribute due to the owners of the gold pieces, but the danger inherent to promises of things which to a large extent do not exist The task devolving on our trustees, of making sure of our members' solvency, is easy, when compared with that undertaken by bank managers. The most cautious of these cannot always avoid disaster, for nobody can be sure of always being able to deliver things, the stock of which is too limited to go round. Our trustees are under no such difficulty, for the productive power of our members will always exceed the demands upon it. The general complaint of "Over-production" shows that our trouble is not want of productive power, but the difficulty of selling the products. This difficulty will be much lessened when selling is no more exchange against a scarce commodity coined into certain round pieces of which not nearly enough can be obtained to satisfy the demand, but exchange against the products of others. With the lessening of this difficulty, the principal cause of failure in business will be out of the way. Honesty, capacity, and freedom from dangerous outside debts, will be the only criterions required by the trustees—by the Board of the Commercial Exchange Company—and the danger of loss by failures will be reduced to a minimum, for which a slight risk premium paid by the borrowing members will provide.

We hope that this explanation will make clear to every one desirous of information what the Commercial Exchange Company really is. It is a club of producers and traders founded to furnish each other with a means of exchange, a set of counters and a mutual credit, jointly secured, for the purpose of enabling them to trade with each other. There is nothing to prevent our club from gradually embracing all members of the community, and it is in the interest of every member to help to extend the circle so as to have it finally embrace all trades, so that anything wanted by the members can be supplied in mutual exchange. Then it will be the affair of the members to decide whether they wish to continue the club in its present form, or whether they prefer to merge it into that other club called the State of New Zealand, making of the old club a department of the larger club under the name of 'The State Bank of New Zealand'"

Another extract from the same paper may serve to illustrate how the system works in practice. It is entitled, A Co-operative Bacon Factory on Exchange-Bank Principles.

"More subscriptions are just now solicited for the Co-operative Bacon Factory at Woodville, more capital is required to purchase the full amount of hogs which the institution can cure. Naturally, it pays better to keep the establishment going at full speed, and so it seems a matter of course that more money is needed for the purpose. At first sight, every business man must approve of the proceedings; and yet, when we investigate them carefully, we shall see how unnatural the whole thing really is, and how little the shareholders of this Co-operative Society are possessed of the co-operative spirit, the spirit of mutuality. If they really appealed to this spirit they would find at once how unnecessary it is for them to solicit new subscriptions for the purpose. Would there be any idea of raising more money if the farmers who supply the pigs took bacon in payment? Certainly not. In this case, the whole transaction would be reduced to a simple booking operation. It would provoke laughter if the Bacon Factory tried to raise cash to pay the farmers for the pigs, and then demanded the farmer's money for the bacon.

"Does the case change when one more member is added to the circle, when the storekeeper takes the bacon from the farmer, and the farmer takes his groceries from the store? It would be just as ridiculous for any of the parties to borrow money for the transaction, for there might simply be two separate barters, the one between the farmer and the factory of pig for bacon, and the other between the farmer and the store of bacon for groceries. Or if the process is simplified by the storekeeper's taking the bacon direct from the factory, the farmer might pay for his groceries by means of an order on the factory for the amount due to him for the pigs, and the storekeeper pays his bill at the factory with the farmer's order. This way of doing business, however, becomes a little less easy when another member is added to the circle. Let us suppose, for instance, that a wholesale grocer X, at Wellington, is the buyer of the bacon. In this case, X might give to the factory an order on the storekeeper Y, who buys his groceries from X. Y pays the order by one on the farmer, his customer, and the factory passes on the order to the farmer to pay for his pigs. Still no money is needed, but there may come in more links in the chain of trade between the parties; so that finally the buying by orders of this kind becomes absolutely impracticable. To provide for this difficulty the Co-operative Society called the New Zealand Commercial Exchange Co, Ltd, has been founded. It is nothing but a clearing-house between its members, under their supervision, exercised by a board of their own selection—a selection made on the most democratic system the Hare proportional vote. Let us see now how the parties would deal with each other under this system. To begin with, the factory would become a member of our company, and would borrow our exchange-notes to buy pigs with, or draw checks on us on credit. It would find no difficulty in placing the notes or checks among the farmers for pigs, provided it can satisfy the farmers that the country stores will accept the paper. This is easily accomplished if one single store in a section is won over; for, in that case, the others are bound to follow suit if they do not wish to lose the custom of the farmers. The stores only want the certainty that they can pass on the paper in their turn, and this certainty will be given them by the wholesale grocer who is ready to accept the paper for groceries; because he purchases the bacon from the factory and can pay it with the paper, which the bacon factory can either pay back to us, or, by passing it on again to the farmers for pigs, begin the same circulation over again.

"Every one of the four parties here concerned has benefited by the operation. The factory has obtained cheap money, and a customer who will do all in his power to sell the co-operative bacon, because the more he sells the more groceries can he sell to the country stores, who otherwise might give their custom to others   The storekeepers likewise are sure of obtaining a custom which, in many cases, would have gone elsewhere.   The farmers do well, because they have a certain sale for their pigs at remunerative prices, for there will be no cutting in the circle as in cash business   The reason for this is a very simple one.   Cash can only be obtained in the world's market, and this market suffers from an excess of a demand of cash over the supply, with cutting of prices as a natural result   When this money is eliminated, and when goods are bought with goods, as in our exchange circle, business improves

"Every purchaser with our paper necessarily obtains a customer who pays with the paper.   He is certain of making a profit on a sale, and therefore can afford to pay well for what he buys   There is no need of cutting in such a case, 'Live and let live' is the motto of all members of the circle "

To show how wage workers could benefit by their membership in the Exchange-Bank I reprint the following dialogue from "How to do Business without Money," published by the New Zealand Commercial Exchange Co in 1899

"Question   Your Exchange may, perhaps, increase the income of the employers, but how can it benefit the wageworker?   I can understand why he favored De Bernardi's American Labor Exchange, an institution in which, if he found no employment, he could directly sell something he produced, and make himself paid by the produce of other workers, but in which way is your system to help him?

Answer   Certainly the advantages of the American plan are more obvious to the worker, though I cannot understand how it can benefit the great mass of workers, who do not see their way to produce on their own account any goods for sale, but have nothing else before them than to work on wages for an employer, if they find one.   You also must see that De Bernardi's combination of storekeeping with exchange banking has fastened a heavy clog on the system which makes it almost unfit for a wider application   Our method is free from this incubus, and by interfering as little as possible with the existing business systems, by adapting itself to the present machinery, it opens the path to an easy and speedy victory.   What could a New Zealand wage worker bring into the Labor Exchange if we adopted the American system?   A few shoemakers might bring shoes, but they would not find any leather in the shop, because tanning needs too much capital to be undertaken by workers who have nothing but their hands   We are past the primitive methods of production, in which such a system might have directly benefited any worker   To do any real good we must adapt ourselves to the complicated systems of the twentieth century, or we are doomed to that failure which finally overtook the American Labor Exchanges

And now I am going to show you how a wageworker can get

the benefit of his membership in the exchange bank on our system Let me suppose you to be a shoe manufacturer, totally unacquainted with our institution, and me, a wage worker, out of employment, but a member I come to you and want work, and the following conversation ensues —*You.* "Have no work, sent off already several applicants to-day" *I.* "Yes, because they wanted money from you; I do not." "No money? You do not mean to say you work for nothing?" "Certainly not, but I take shoes in payment." "What can you do with them? You cannot open a shoe shop, besides, the Truck Law does not allow me to pay you anything else but money." "I know I mean that I at once repay you your money, and buy an engagement from you that you will furnish your goods at regular prices for the amount I paid you to anybody who comes with my authorization." "I would be perfectly willing to do that, and to give you permanent employment on such terms, even if you want to keep some of the money, because the only reason I could not employ you before was that I had little money, but plenty of boots and shoes Yet I cannot see how you can manage to sell your order for boots and shoes"

And now I explain to you the organization of our Exchange, which enables me to pay for all I want with such an order for shoes This order you give me in the form of notes or checks of the Exchange, of which you become a member, accepting a credit on the force of your stock and the new goods produced by my work

But this is not the only advantage given by the Exchange to the workers if they join in sufficient numbers The reserve fund, which will grow from year to year, could supply them with the capital they may need to set up as independent producers. Their co-operative organization may supply the necessary security, and the progress brought about by the Exchange system would put out of their way the present most serious obstacle to their success, the difficulty of disposing of their produce In a market in which even the skilful and experienced business men often succumb in struggling for the scanty gold stock, the co-operating workers have a poor chance Their commercial management is rarely as efficient as that of the capitalist. After the new currency has rendered it easier for a producer to sell his goods, co-operative production will thrive"

To show how the business done through the exchange bank creates an absolutely new production, that it does not take away one man's bread when it procures employment to another, as is often the case with the circulation based upon our monetary system, I might add that thousands of townworkers have to refuse fruit and vegetables to their children, whose health badly needs it In consequence of this, farmers and gardeners, who need shoes and other products of labor, cannot buy them, because they cannot obtain money. Owing to this fact their fruits have to rot on the tree, their vegetables run to seed, because there is no custom for them The exchange bank puts both parties into communication and obtains

employment for them, which otherwise would be unobtainable By
this it does not deprive anybody of his bread, but procures bread for
all, by transforming latent productive power into a real one

I desire to call attention to another advantage which the bank
gives to its members it supplies an effective weapon against the
Trusts, as it deprives them of their boycotting and discriminating
power, visited upon those who buy from competitors, for it protects
the competitor's continuance in business because the circle will give
him its custom   I repeat that buying from a member in the circle
means selling goods to others, and thus even a higher price is practically cheaper to the amount of the profit made on the goods sold
in exchange Of course, the trusts might also join the society, but
as unfair dealing entails exclusion, their continued membership
would only be rendered possible by a renunciation of their tricks
Where the trust has no competitors in the circle the members can
start such, with the help of their custom, for this custom is more
important than the capital required, which is always obtainable
where a sure profit can be shown

The circle needs no protective tariff to insure full work to its
members, for even if a foreign competitor sells cheaper, the
society's producers will not lack custom Its reciprocal system insures it Importation by the circle will only be possible if, directly
or indirectly, it is paid for by exportation, for only in this case is the
circle's paper of any use to the importers who accept it in payment
for foreign goods The circle's system insures *Reciprocity* far better
than any tariff tinkering I refer to Chapter IV, in which I have
shown the fallacy of the free-traders' contention that goods are always paid for with goods, and that therefore imports insure a corresponding amount of exports Our present money is an international commodity which may or may not come back to buy goods
in the country from which it was obtained for goods Our exchange-paper, on the other hand, *must* come back, if it did not, the
goods purchased with it abroad would have simply been given away
for nothing

I cannot leave the subject without referring to certain difficulties in the way of an Exchange-Bank. or "Mutual Bank," as it
is also appropriately called In the first place we have the danger
of domination by wealth, the fate thus far of all great corporations
in this country, a danger easily avoided by attaching the vote to
membership and not to share capital, each member needing at least
one share of the company, but no share by itself entitled to a vote.
In this way outsiders who buy shares cannot vote and members
cannot increase their voting power by purchasing more shares than
one By limiting the dividend to the usual percentage obtainable
on capital there will be no great demand for shares on purely mer-
cenary grounds The bulk of the profits would be used for
strengthening the organization Another danger. that of controlling general meetings by means of proxies, can be easily over-

come. A confirmation of all decisions made by the general meeting through a referendum of members voting directly by postal cards specially issued by the bank may be made compulsory at least in all important matters. The referendum, democracy's protection against the representative, is also available to protect the stockholder against the proxy holder. If, besides, the directors are elected on Hare's proportional system, as described in Chapter VI, all the necessary safeguards against domination by capital will be supplied. This does not mean that plutocratic wrecking is thereby excluded. In fact, this is the point where the new institution will encounter its greatest difficulties and dangers, as my practical experience in New Zealand showed. In that country I found that the greater the extent of a business, the more dependent it is on bank credits, and, though the exchange-bank could gradually free its members from money-bank credits, it cannot do so in the initial stage; so that the fear of suddenly being called upon to settle with their banks kept the best firms from joining, who otherwise might have become members. This naturally had a discouraging effect on others, and thus brought an element of weakness into the work.

In the United States, where plutocratic influence is stronger than anywhere else in the world, institutions of the kind here proposed will meet with greater difficulties. The case of the People's United States Bank in St. Louis shows how these influences can set in motion the power of the State to get rid of inconvenient competition. Nobody would have imagined that the United States Post Office, an institution whose object is to serve communication without any regard of persons, could one day be used by plutocratic interests to ruin a bank which stood in their way. A simple decision of the postal authorities sufficed, and against such a decision there is no appeal to the courts. The Crumpacker bill, which was passed with but one dissentient vote in the House of Representatives, would have terminated this absolutism; but it did not pass the Senate, being kept back until the close of the session. The president of the bank was also the publisher of two monthly journals, with a combined circulation of two and a half million copies. To increase his affliction, this enormous business was suddenly stopped by Geo. B. Cortelyou, the Postmaster-General, by refusing their customary right to the mails at the lawful rate and subjecting them to an arbitrary and ruinous postage. The bank was an enterprise in which more than three million dollars cash capital were invested, against which, in spite of all efforts, no illegal methods could be proved, and which was so thoroughly solvent that, in spite of the shameful persecution to which the Post Office subjected it and the enormous costs its defense involved, all its creditors were fully satisfied, and even the shareholders had their money almost fully paid back (87%). This enterprise was declared fraudulent and its officers were excluded from the mails, so that even its president was isolated from all postal connection, not permitted to receive letters from his own

mother This is a sort of punishment not even inflicted on a condemned murderer. And this happened, not in Russia, but in the
United States, and in the 20th century!

Well, the People's United States Bank was an innocent baby
compared with an exchange bank, so far as the interests of our
existing banking world were touched by it for its only offense was
the saving of check-cashing and money remitting expenses, whereas
the exchange banks would put an end to a considerable part of the
turnover made by our present money banks

While this book is being prepared for publication a long expected event occurred, which on the one hand must bring an acces-
sion of strength to exchange banking, while on the other hand it will
diminish the antagonistic influence of money banks The financial
crisis, foreseen in these pages, came over us suddenly, with elementary force, and with it a host of explanations, out of which I
select one, because it will specially amuse those who have so far
followed me Its author is Frank Arthur Vanderlip, who enjoys
in this country some reputation as a financier. According to him,
the crisis is explained by the enormous loss of capital the world
sustained during this decade by the Boer and Russo-Japanese wars,
preceded by the American war with Spain, and followed by the San
Francisco earthquake and fire. This shows that even the "chiefs"
of our financial world have no true conception of the real nature of
this crisis

What sort of capital was destroyed in the catastrophes mentioned? Evidently only the products of agriculture and industry
But what is the main signature of the crisis? Clearly, in the first
place, the want of paying employment in the domains of production Consequently, according to Mr Vanderlip, the exceptionally
great demand for the products of labor that followed the destructive
events mentioned is the cause—not that, as every person with some
common sense would guess, there must be an extraordinary demand for labor of all kind—but that demand for labor and its products has decreased Isn't that wonderful? I hope I need not mention that it is absolutely indifferent which products of labor have
been destroyed, for there is not a single one—beginning with articles of consumption, including war materials, and ending with the
tools of production—for which producers would not be most happy
to obtain more orders Then what kind of capital can be meant by
Mr Vanderlip? Money? Now, I cannot conceive in which way the
events mentioned could have destroyed money Much money has
changed hands, and in this change of hands the United States, who
to a large extent had to supply the destroyed goods, especially food
materials, for which they received money or its equivalent, have
certainly not been the losers Besides, it is well known that during
the decade in question the world saw such an unprecedented increase in the production of the yellow metal that many attributed to
it the rise of prices and talked about another change of our standard

of value In which way, then, can the events referred to have caused the crisis?

As a matter of fact, the very contrary is true; these events, instead of causing the crisis, actually postponed it Without them, it would have arrived long ago, because the turnover of the world in merchandise of all kinds has more and more run ahead of the money stock, so that credit had to supply the means of exchange in ever growing measure The cash extracted from hoards by the new war loans and San Francisco insurances increased the money circulation and expanded credit, which brought about and kept up a great business revival If we study the history of crises we find that they often break out two years after the termination of a costly war, not as consequence of the war, but because the increase of circulation due to the war, which for a time had postponed a crisis, became exhausted after two years. On this ground I predicted the present crisis for August, 1907, two years after the peace of Portsmouth, and was only two months wrong.

There was no need for such far-fetched explanations of what brought on this crisis as Mr Vanderlip's It required a continual presence in the midst of Wall Street's skyscrapers to lose the free outlook over the financial world to the extent exhibited by this bank manager. Otherwise the gentleman would not have needed artificial explanations to realize that where the banks owe thirteen thousand million dollars, with only one thousand million behind the debt, of which not quite one-half consisted of legal tender coins, a mere breath of distrust must bring about a downfall of credit. It was not alone the increase of the turnover which can be made responsible for such abnormal conditions Speculation in watered stocks and bonds had its goodish share in the enormous excess of deposits over the cash stock The owners of these water papers borrowed on them from the banks, and though only a part of the quoted value was taken into account, still the sum by far exceeded the value which remained after the crisis press had begun to squeeze out some of their watery components The amounts thus borrowed formed a considerable part of the deposits, for which real money had never been paid in. They actually only formed water foam that had condensated into gold debt Unfortunately, no matter what formed the origin of this part of the banks' debts, they had the same claim upon the attenuated gold stock which the real depositors were entitled to And, still more unfortunately for the latter, these foam-born deposits belonged to experienced financiers, who, knowing the watery origin of their own credits at the banks, for which no real money had ever been paid in, fully understood the danger thus threatening all depositors Thus they were among the first who called for their money, or rather that of the real depositors, who, as a rule, were less initiated into the state of things and consequently came too late The latter had to be content with clearing house and cashier's certificates, those illegal forms of paper money which were the product of the crisis.*

It can easily be seen that all this materially changes the prospects of exchange banks The reputation of their enemies, the money banks, has not only sunk in consequence of the lending manipulations just described—in which not merely the New York banks participated, but directly and indirectly many of the other banks of the country, who lent their legal reserves at a high interest rate to Wall Street's water-born paper, but the banks have deprived themselves of their best weapon. This weapon, the appeal to the old superstition that only paper backed by cash has a right of circulation, has perhaps never been used with less right than by those who made 13,000 million gold debts upon a backing of 500 million cash and 500 million of bank notes, guaranteed by the government, the basis of the check circulation of this country. But, as if this were not enough, the banks have added another weapon to the arsenal of their rivals by the issue of those money-substitutes, unknown to the law, just mentioned, the clearing house or cashier's certificates, of which millions circulated. The partisans of exchange banking have a perfect right to say that their paper is based on a far surer foundation than the scrip just mentioned Exchange paper is based on real goods held ready for it, while the bank's certificates practically have no gold behind them. This must finally lead to the failure of the promising party All business based on them leads through the narrow gold door, while the promises of the exchange bank are built on the productive power of able men, whose solvency is no longer exposed to disastrous shipwreck on a hidden gold rock At all events, though the chances are greatly improved, a severe battle can hardly be avoided, and a strong reserve fund will be found of great importance to the new institutions

The commission on sales and the interest on loans ought to be fairly high, in the beginning, to collect a good reserve fund; but as this fund is mostly supplied in goods held at the disposal of the bank, it will have to be turned into cash with the help of disinterested friends, who only deal with the circle to help the work and purchase exchange-paper for cash, or open an exchange-bank account by paying in cash, which then is redeemable in exchange-checks only. Officials with cash salaries,

---

* These certificates were not promises to pay money but engagements to accept them as money, as the following copy of one shows.
"Los Angeles Clearing House Certificate
No ——— Los Angeles, California, November 5, 1907
ONE DOLLAR
Securities having been deposited with the Clearing House Committee of the Los Angeles Clearing House Association. this certificate will be accepted for the sum named by any of the Banks composing said Association or any Bank clearing through a member thereof.
J A GRAVES, President
V H HOLLIDAY, Vice-President and Secretary"

independent men living on their incomes, may choose this way of establishing better conditions. The larger the cash fund, the more able the bank will be to help those members whose adherence may subject them to attacks from the money power   Attacks most effective in the commencement, through the necessity of paying rents, taxes and freights in cash, until the circle has extended so far that its paper is taken everywhere.   Discrimination in favor of landlords and railroads who accept the paper; use of the reserve fund to buy land and a controlling interest in railroads or to build new lines and then to boycott the refractory roads, until this is no longer needed, and last, not least, political education of the members and full use of their vote to obtain government ownership of land and public utilities, and the use of exchange-paper by the government to pay officials and other expenses so as to render possible its acceptance for taxes, must do the rest.   When the corporation is once so rich that it can procure all the land and railroads the members require, so that it can force down the value of the remaining land and roads and finally control all, thus forming an organized co-operative commonwealth, a state within a state, its political power will have become so great that the ballot can do the rest, can materially accelerate the final victory.

To further the great work, an institution may be recommendable which I found very useful in New Zealand the issue of a periodical, in connection with the Mutual Banks, as their central organ.   This organ will not only give the lists of new members—until the membership becomes so extensive that it may be less troublesome to publish the names of those who do not accept the people's paper—besides other notices of the institutions, but it may also become, what the name of its New Zealand precursor implied, a *"Pioneer of social reform"*   Its main task would be to unite the members on the great reform work yet to be performed by them in their quality of citizens, independent of parties, especially Mutual Banking.   To insure to the paper a larger circle of readers than any other paper possesses, and thus to make it also a powerful protector against annoyances by the financiers, the arrangement I made in New Zealand might be copied. The paper might be given in the place of a dividend on the one bank share which every member must own   If $5 shares are made, a dividend of 5% (with the advertisements) would pay the expenses of a weekly   This would save the work and the cost both of paying out the small dividends and of collecting the subscription fees.   The second-class privilege, forfeited by free delivery, would thus be secured.

One detail merits a short reference. the question of territorial extension of the bank's organization.   Are we to have a United States bank with local branches, or State banks federating?   I think the latter plan better adapted to our institutions, without wishing to see obstacles put in the way of members joining the organization of some other State, instead of the one where they live, if they prefer it. However, in the beginning, a concentration of power in one single organization might be preferable   As they strengthen, branches might gradually become independent and remain in contact with other similar banks through a central clearing house, with control over its members   Much must be left to local initiative, and no projector can foresee all contingencies of practical work in the future. In all this I merely intend to give the results of my own ideas and experience, which, though they may obviate the necessity of similar experience for others, cannot pretend to surmount new difficulties which may present themselves

Proudhon's writings, Owen's work described in George Jacob Holyoake's "History of Co-operation," the experience of Bonnard and his successors, the writings of John Aimsden, of William B. Greene, A Whittick, Arthur Kitson, Hugo Bilgram, Alfred B. Westrup, etc , may supply additional help. Faithful pioneers, all of them, for the great work, whose victory they prepared. Perhaps at last the great moment has arrived which sees the fruit of so much labor, seventy-five years after Owen and sixty after Proudhon spread the first seeds   The Crisis of 1907 is a splendid propagandist   I have tried to condense its lesson in a paper which appeared in "Out West" in January, 1908, under the title, "The Crisis in Jackassville." I here quote the little story with which the article begins

"Jackassville was in great trouble   This is how it came about. An epidemic had broken out in the town, and the doctors were at a loss as to its origin, until one of them, wiser than the rest, attributed it to contamination brought about by the circulating coins   Upon this the City Council at once decided that all the coins in the place had to be thoroughly washed with soap and water and then allowed to dry in the open air on the common for 24 hours. Faithfully the programme was carried out   Unfortunately, there passed that way a tramp, who was not at all afraid of infection, and took the risk of carrying off all the money he found spread out on the common, even stealing a good sack from the miller for the purpose   The next morning there was howling and gnashing of teeth, and a messenger was sent at once to the seat of government with the request for immediate help, for the city was absolutely destitute of money, and starvation would soon ensue   The Governor at once repaired to the place and took in the whole situation   The town was well provided with wheat, cattle, vegetables, fruits, wool, cotton, fuel, timber, and, in fact, all raw materials necessary to feed, clothe and house the people.   There was plenty of skilled and unskilled labor of all kinds ready and anxious to do all the work needed to change the raw materials into bread, meat and other food, into clothes, boots, houses, furniture, and so on, as had been their wont. All this was in the best order, and so the Governor told them, but I am afraid it cost him votes at the impending election, for the general opinion was expressed in the indignant words of the Mayor, who replied 'We know all that.   But don't you see, Governor, that we have been robbed of the last cent, and that nobody has any money left to buy the good things he needs? We thought we had made the case clear enough when we notified you of the general poverty into which we had fallen through the shameful act of that tramp' The Governor saw that it was no use insisting on the fact that people do not live upon money, but upon the products of labor which they require for their sustenance, and that of these there was more than plenty in the town So he decided to teach them the lesson they needed in some other way Telling the assembled City Council that they were right, and that he had thought of that before he left the capital, he pulled a roll of large bank notes from his pocket and handed them to the Mayor as a temporary loan from the Government. The money was received with many thanks, but the great difficulty at once presented itself that there was no small bills and no 'change'; that the bills were altogether too large to be used in the ordinary business intercourse of the place. 'I'll tell you what we will do,' said the wily official. 'You deposit these notes with me and I will act as your trustee, who keeps the money as a security for the cheques you are drawing to pay each other with. The Mayor, who knows you and your transactions, will, of course, certify only the cheques which are all right—which means those which you draw for goods actually received for services rendered, for which you are at any time ready to deliver goods or services in turn Those who can be relied upon to do so are solvent, and their cheques will be certified' And then the Governor went away, and business prospered in Jackassville as it had never prospered before. The cheques were every day cleared by the Mayor—which means that he kept a large ledger, in which credit was entered to each man for whatever cheques he brought in, while the cheques which he had drawn were deducted from his credit. As the citizens did not draw any more cheques than they received, the accounts always balanced If this was not done the same day, it was mostly done within a week. If there were a longer delay the Mayor did not mind it if he knew the parties were solvent. Nobody ever called upon the Governor for any of the money he loaned the Mayor, and which the Governor held in trust As a consequence, at a public meeting held one day it was proposed to authorize the Governor to pay back the money to the Government, as they did not need it, and might as well save the interest they had to pay for it. This was done, and business flourished as well as before in Jackassville A strange story, isn't it? So much like another just now told of a certain people, called the American nation."

I then applied the story to the prevailing crisis, by showing how the country is rich in everything that human beings require, and that only in consequence of our folly of making a scarce metal our only legal tender we find ourselves without adequate means of exchange That now the hour of delivery may have sounded, for our money banks are the very parties to show us the instrument of reform. Their scrips, though without any legal authorization and security, did the service demanded of them.. in spite of their being only accessible to a minority, to the few who had money due them by the banks or who could supply sufficient collaterals The moment may come which sees our business world—perhaps under the initiative of its Chambers of Commerce—create a means of exchange, which cannot be locked up and monopolized, which is accessible to every one without any further security than the proof of his productive power and his readiness to supply it, the best security in the world. Meanwhile the law givers at Washington debated which of the two miserable palliative measures was to become law the emergency currency of Aldrich or the asset currency of Fowler, not being able or willing to rise to a real reform action, such as the creation of a postal savings bank, with a check circulation which gradually might do the work of a central bank While a valuable opportunity was thus lost, the manufacturers of the country, the owners of railroads, the merchants and the farmers of the country, with such of the bankers as are capable to tear themselves away from a selfish onesided personal interest policy, might unite for the issue of a new Declaration of Independence, the independence from the gold fetish, by creating a currency based on the surest foundation, upon the labor of a great nation freed from gold fetters, by setting in motion that gigantic force, which even now, under the load of the mightiest burdens, calls forth the astonishment of the world—*Credit.* Then the workers, kept in forced idleness, will set in motion the resting and rusting giants of iron and steel Panting freight trains will cross the country with reawakened activity; the stores will fill with a renewed crowd of customers, the nation's life will throb with hopeful forces, so soon as the great banner of liberty is raised, the banner on which the proclamation is made in gigantic letters *Product for Product, Work for Work!* In hoc signo vinces! Under this sign, that of free exchange, thou shalt conquer, poor hard working humanity, freed from the golden fetter which cuts so deeply into thy flesh; but not otherwise, for without free exchange labor cannot possibly develop to its full capacity It is true gold is not the only fetter Land-monopoly and others will for a time still oppress us, but we shall easily throw them off after the heaviest one of all has been annihilated What then will become of the nation's official money? Its legal tender need not trouble us much, so long as the unlegalized tender is universally accepted It may still find its use as change, or it may serve as a hoarding material It may for a time serve to steady prices, still made in legal tender money, though hardly ever paid in it, except in small dealings, to finally give place to a scientific currency on the lines drawn in Chapter III It matters little, for, important as a steady money-standard may be, it is only a secondary quality of a good money; its first and fundamental endowment is its *accessibility.* Even a money with a variable purchasing power, which is easily obtainable by any one who wants to work in exchange for it, is far better than a money with the most stable standard, which the usurer may lock up

I am unwilling to close this chapter on co-operation without alluding to three forms of co-operation which are not without some importance. The one is that presented by the experiment now made in England under the name of "Garden Cities," of settlements near large cities where manufacturers can have their works in the good air of the country, in proximity to the farmer, and where the workers and people of leisure can have all the advantages of the country and the town combined * The land owned co-operatively, bought at agricultural prices, is supposed to be raised to city value through the access of population The increasing income through the rents, which rise with the growing demand and with public improvements, after a moderate interest is paid to the stockholders, is spent for these very improvements, which thus swell the source they spring from. Fairhope, in Alabama, is organized on this principle, mixed with the idiosyncrasy of paying tenants' State and County taxes out of the town's rental income, because they want to call it a Single-Tax colony

The other co-operative scheme is concerned with *Co-operative Houses and Associated Homes* When we want to produce cotton goods, the steam engine takes the place of thousands of wheel turners, but when we wish to produce roast beef, thousands of cooks have still to perform a work which dozens could do far better under a system of centralization

I need not enter into the complaints about servants, nor is it necessary to say anything about the other worries of housekeeping, which so absorb the average woman that she has little time left to educate her children, and still less to improve her own mind The estrangement from the husband, who looks outside for the intellectual intercourse he cannot find at his own fireside, and the whole tragedy which ensues in "home, sweet home," has too often been treated to need discussion here And yet no reform could be simpler Even if associated homes should meet with too much opposition, a beginning ought to be made with associated cooking, washing, and house-cleaning

The next step would be to build a number of homes without kitchens around a central kitchen, to which a laundry, kindergarten, swimming bath, social hall, etc. might be added, as means permit. Servants could be kept in the central building who work by the hour for the single houses on business principles They would be as independent as factory girls, which, combined with better pay, might induce thousands to devote their time to this kind of domestic work in preference

All this and much more could be done, and the system would afford a good deal more enjoyment to the members, and at less cost than the present wasteful practice but it will be the last reform we shall get We shall perhaps have the socialist commonwealth before

* Letchworth near London, is the first, which, two years after its birth, has already 6,000 inhabitants.

we have a general adoption of the Associated Home system, before our millions of galley slaves, called housewives—with or without the scourge of underslaves—will be relieved from their wearisome drudgery

I have reserved for final consideration one class of co-operative schemes which deserves a history of its own, much more extended than the numerous records given us by Nordhoff, Semmler, Noyes and others   It is the socialistic or communistic settlement, especially well represented in the United States where a number, mostly on a religious basis, already exist. It would take more space than the plan of this book affords, to give details.   These settlements are on the garden-city plan, in so far that they hold their land in common, while some of them also embody the co-operative household   They go beyond these limits by carrying on co-operative production and distribution in common   They try to show on a small scale that socialism, or even communism, can be made successful on a large scale by whole commonwealths. Most of them wish to be looked at as object lessons. It would not be fair to socialism and communism if we accepted them as such, because conditions on a small scale are altogether too unfavorable to admit of sound judgment on the feasibility of the scheme when tried by a whole nation   Labor has become so diversified that it needs more workers than the most successful of these schemes ever possessed, to produce, under the best conditions, many of our necessaries. Of course none of the settlements ever produced more than a few specialties, and had to sell some of these to provide other kinds of goods not made in the circle   This alone has made it impossible to show the enormous saving of labor and waste attainable by mutual production and exchange   However, even without the advantage of such economy there ought to be no reason why a number of people working on free land might not succeed in producing in common most necessaries   To a certain extent this has been accomplished where religious enthusiasm formed the cement which kept the colonists together and subordinated them to a capable management   In all other cases failure had been the final result; mostly in consequence of the personal element   My participation in one of the well known American attempts of this class· the Topolobampo Colony, Sinaloa, Mexico, in the early nineties, decided me to refrain from any future work in this direction   It is too late for object lessons when all hands are needed on deck to bring the ship of state through the perilous tides which are surrounding it on all sides   However, I recommend to those enthusiasts, whom the failures do not frighten off, the constitution which, worked out by me for Topolobampo at the time of its crisis, was unanimously adopted in its main features, but never had a chance of being tested   It provided for common land ownership and common trading for exchange notes, the money of the colony, but for united production only in cases where private enterprise proved extortionate   In fact it meant to show on a small scale the feasibility of the reforms which this book proposes. Perhaps it was fortunate that the scheme was never tested, for its failure under such conditions might have been used against reforms, which, after all, do not aspire to success unless carried out on a national scale.

CHAPTER VIII.

SOCIALISM AND TRUSTS

"Our present social inequality materializes the upper class, vulgarizes the middle class and brutalizes the lower class"—*Matthew Arnold.*

THIS work, so far, has pursued strictly individualistic lines. Its individualism, however, has been a logical one, very different from that pseudo-individualism and liberalism which permits a minority to monopolize the ownership of the globe and then preaches against any interference with the liberty of the individual Land restoration has, therefore, been the first demand on our path to free individualism, land restoration with all it includes state ownership of farm and town lands, of mines, forests, quarries, oil wells and roads. However, something more was needed to permit the free development of the individual under the new conditions brought about by the advance from barbarism, a universally accepted and accessible means of exchange, elastic enough to adapt itself to the demands of trade To leave its production free was impossible, for the very nature of a serviceable money is its general acceptance. If every one could manufacture money this universal acceptance could never be secured Universal free exchange and consequently free production are impossible without a general agreement as to the means of exchange We have seen how unfortunate the choice of coins made out of precious metals has proved We have seen how a new monopoly was thus thrown into the hands of those who could corner the precious metals and the possibility of providing a far better means of exchange, a money which could not be monopolized by individuals We further saw that with untrammeled opportunities and circulation unlimited, freedom in production and distribution would no longer be harmful. No use for usury laws when interest, the child of land and money monopoly disappears with its parents No need of protective tariffs where the absence of interest makes international exchange a barter of commodities for commodities No need of labor-laws, limiting hours of work, fixing a minimum wage, organizing arbitration, insuring against sickness, accidents, old age, or unemployment, where production keeps up with productive power, so that wealth, including the means to pay for insurance, is at the disposal of all who are able and willing to work The unfettered forces of supply and demand can then be relied upon to produce that self-adjustment between the economic factors now erroneously supposed to exist by those who believe that solid buildings can be erected without a solid foundation

It has been disputed whether political economy is a science. The doubt is perfectly justified, when we observe the discrepancy between its theories and their practical results   But no science can give any correct results when we depart from fundamental principles, which in the case of political economy are two   (1) The land, the very foundation of our existence, must belong to the people at large, and (2) the circulating medium must be easily obtainable by all who have products of any value or efficient labor to sell   Only by building on these immutable principles can results correspond to theory, and only then will political economy become a science. Without such a foundation it is merely an exponent of expedients, whose beneficial effect is proportioned to their departure from first principles

No greater improvements in manufacturing and distribution were ever made than by the combinations called *Trusts*   Under free conditions they would be a real blessing, but as it is, they fully deserve the curses launched against them   In the existing world, whatever economises power is a misfortune, whatever wastes and destroys is a blessing   Thus W. S. Gilbert, in his letter to the London Times, says "he could never fully understand the prejudice against burglars   A burglar gives work to innumerable telegraph, police and railroad officials, and possibly also to surgeons, coroners and tombstone-makers.   As soon as he is in custody, the service of a whole army of lawyers, judges, petty and grand jurors, reporters, prison administrators and turnkeys are put in requirement.   Certainly the burglar effects more good than harm "

This can be proved by a very simple test by which we judge whether, under existing unnatural conditions, any measure will produce good or bad results   We simply investigate whether its principle is correct or not   If it is correct, then the measure won't do, but if the measure is based on a vicious principle, it is ten to one that the best thing is to vote for it   It will be easy enough to prove this strange paradox

Is it good that millions of men are kept unproductively under arms from day to day, from year to year, that Europe's peace establishment alone now exceeds four million men?   Certainly not!   Such a state of things is entirely opposed, not only to economic laws, but also to those great principles preached from the Mount, which form the basis of that Christianity professed, though not practiced, by a great part of our civilized world   The conclusion is that this armed peace, this forcing of millions into a busy idleness, is an excellent thing from an economic point of view, as long as we do not make fundamental economic changes   We talk of over-production now, but what should we have to say if these millions of our strongest, healthiest and most energetic men, instead of merely consuming, were set to work to produce more wealth, imploring a market? This explains why there are far more unemployed in England and, in spite of her wonderful resources, even in the United States than in the military countries of Europe. On the other hand, when is business brisker than in war times? Business was prosperous during and immediately after the Crimean, the American Secession War. the Franco-German War, and is not the revival, which terminated in 1907; mostly due to the Boer and Russo-Japanese wars? This is natural, for war is the greatest consumer; war creates that wonderful arcanum for which we all sigh and often fight: a market for our surplus production. Things have come to such a pass that business men all over the world look at wars, if only they do not involve their own country, as blessings, which a poor, overstocked merchant ought to be very thankful for. I know they do not say so publicly, and their press organs are duly praising the blessings of peace with a grateful upturning of their eyes, but I know what is said behind the scenes, for during nearly half a century I have been an initiated member of Mercury's Stock Company, called the commercial community. If this had not been so, if I belonged to that learned clique which the world over have monopolized economic and social science, I should speak differently. I should possibly praise the beneficial effects of peace, I should curse the destructive tendencies of war; I should declaim against the waste of militarism; I should expect universal prosperity from general disarmament, I should do all this, and I should be as great a liar as they are under the existing state of things. Moral peace societies, stop your nefarious work! Nefarious, as long as you do not help us to lay those foundations of the peace temple, without which the higher you build the more surely will your baseless structure fall, and bury you under its ruins. the foundations I have been trying to specify in this book.

It is a truism that *alcoholism* is even a more terrible scourge than war. For one victim of the battlefield, more than a hundred are killed by the bottle. But supposing prohibition or any other method were successful in exorcising the fiend, what would be the result under existing conditions? A terrible increase of over-production and unemployment. as long as every worker produces four particles of wealth, and is only permitted to consume one, while those who are entitled to the lion share are over-satiated and cannot consume all the wealth falling to their share. Consequence. more unemployed and more drink. For one man saved from drink in such circumstances and now producing with all his power, instead of destroying wealth, two may lose their job and turn to drink in their despair. Proofs are not wanting that misery produces drunkenness far more frequently than drunkenness produces misery. "In Rent, Interest, and Wages" I gave an interesting example from the North of Ireland, where a drunken population became sober 'through obtaining a continuous paying employment   I here add an article from the *Binghamton Independent* in the same direction

"A table has been prepared by Professor Warner, of Stanford University, based on fifteen separate investigations of actual cases of poverty, numbering in all over 100,000 cases in America, England and Germany   These investigations were conducted by the charity organization societies of Baltimore, Buffalo and New York City, the associated charities of Boston and Cincinnati, by Charles Booth in East London, and for Germany we have the statements of Mr Bohmert as to seventy-seven German cities   They include virtually all the facts that have been collected by trained investigators, unbiassed by any theory   From these figures it appears that about 20 per cent of the worst cases of poverty are due to misconduct, and about 75 per cent to misfortune   Drink causes only 11 per cent , while lack of work or poorly paid work causes nearly 30 per cent

All evidence worth considering goes to prove that poverty and crime are both results of forced idleness or low-paid labor. As a rule, men who are steadily employed at some productive work, and who get in return for their labor what they consider to be a fair share of the product of their efforts, are temperate and moral   If all men could feel sure of steady work at fair pay there would be practically no need for policemen or temperance societies. If the preachers would study theology less and political economy more, and then go into their pulpits and preach practical Christianity for every-day use, they would be doing a far greater work than they are when they talk about patient submission here, in order that reward may be had hereafter.

Poverty and crime are results of laws which men have made, and we will have both so long as these laws are in operation. It is not the fault of God, or Nature, or whatever you may term the creative cause, that many men are poor, shiftless and intemperate   The fault lies with the people, and with them rests the remedy and the responsibility   When the people are wise enough to remove the cause, the evil will disappear   It is about time for men to stop repeating that antiquated statement that intemperance is the prime cause of poverty, and take up the study of how to remedy the real cause—enforced idleness "

Moral· Temperance promoters had better help in taking away the worst cause of drunkenness, which is not, as they think, the supply of alcohol, but the social conditions which drive men and women into the bar-room.

In any case, most of our temperance promoters are too radical; instead of working for mere temperance, they fight for total prohibition, and thus make enemies of many who detest the abuse of alcoholic drinks, but shrink from infringing the freedom of the individual   If they took example by those countries which are working on the Gothenburg or related systems—aiming at decrease of drunkenness—they would be much farther advanced Fifty years ago the annual consumption of alcohol in Scandinavia was 30 litres (nearly 7 gallons) per individual It has now been reduced to 2 litres, and in Norway *delirium tremens* has become an almost unknown disease

An anti-treating law—fining the publican who serves liquor to any person who does not pay for his own drink—might do away with one of the most prolific causes of drunkenness, and one of the most idiotic limitations of personal liberty in this country the unwritten law which compels every member of a party of friends who meet at a bar to order drinks and pay for the whole group, so that each individual pays in turn, and each drinks far more than he would have imbibed otherwise—with inevitable consequences

Thrift, if generally practised, would under present conditions prove one of the worst calamities that could befall us, as has been already shown in Chapter V. Does it not mean an increased productivity accompanied by a restriction of consumption and consequently of production? As long as we complain of overproduction or underconsumption the waste of the well-to-do is beneficial, their economy of evil effect Let us all live the simple life, let us restrict private and public expenses to the lowest limit and see how we can keep alive the millions of additional unemployed that under the present system would result!

Moral· More waste, more useless officials at good salaries, more million dollar baths, more $50,000 balls, more $400,000 weddings, more yachts, more palaces, etc but for Heaven's sake, no more thrifty, industrious workers! This adjuration is required to-day even more urgently than it was twenty years ago in England, where I penned the following lines; because compound interest has continued its nefarious work all this time·

"The praise of industry sounds from every pulpit and platform, is dinned into our ears by millions of leaden soldiers from the type-foundry regiment, leaving the impress of their footsteps on millions of tons of paper which go forth as dailies, periodicals, or books How strange that we find a growing fear of industrious workers, and that we do our best to send them out of the country, or to prevent their getting in. Emigration societies are founded, laws against the immigration of foreign workers are enacted or demanded. The rich drone is welcomed everywhere, and glowing advertisements set forth in rose colors the advantages of different towns in order to attract him; whereas workers are warned off in every possible way It is a natural result of the unnatural state of things we live under, for consumers are wanted, and producers shunned in a world in which the purchasing power of the masses lags more and more behind their producing capacity."

The whole aspect of the case would be changed by a reform which kept the purchasing capacity of the masses parallel to their productive power Anything which increases the one must then result in an equal increase of the other, so that production will no more be fettered by the elements which are meant to promote it Peace, temperance, and thrift, the stoppage of waste of all kinds, will not only cease to deprive the workers of a chance to make a living, but will enable them to earn more, with less labor. Labor-saving inventions will prove the real benefit to the working masses which they are now wrongly supposed to be They will increase wealth production while lessening toil and working time. They will enrich the worker, and enable him to become his own employer, working with his own tools, or dictating his terms These terms will be quite different where two employers compete for one worker than where two workers compete for one employer No more strikes or lock-outs in such a case' There ought then to be no more antagonism between the two camps who now waste their best energies in fighting each other Instead of being at loggerheads about factory acts, about working time, and minimum wage, both ought to unite in fighting their common foes private land monopoly, an inelastic currency, and the dire offspring of those twain—interest

The conflict is no more between employer and employed, or between wealth and poverty, but between monopoly and freedom Monopoly rides on the back of mankind as the Old Man of the Sea sat on Sinbad the Sailor gripping firm hold with its two knees Land and Money and the suffering mass need no further concession than that the monster shall get off its back. The quarrel lies not between the competitive system and co-operation, as Socialists think—whatever reforms may yet be found desirable in that domain —for both systems can be practised under slavery. It is simply a fight between liberty and slavery It is the power of preventing free competition by monopolizing land and money which causes the struggle, the devil-take-the-hindmost fight we are daily witnessing

A theatre is burning, in headlong flight old and young, weak and strong, men and women try to gain the outlet—a single small door blocked by a frantic mass of fighting humanity Hundreds of corpses are found the next day, and people are discussing the cause of the disaster Some pretend that if, instead of this mad competition for the only outlet, there had been peaceful voluntary co-operation, or if the authorities had maintained order and forced the people to walk out in a regular procession, all would have been well Perhaps so, or perhaps only half the spectators would have perished, because, even in the calmest and most methodical manner, all might not have been able to pass through so small an opening in such a limited time But a sufficient supply of doors would have allowed all to escape, no matter whether order reigned or not. Open the doors widely for really free competition, and people will cease to cry for State intervention'

Liberty is the perennial source from which alone a higher civilization can flow ; slavery proves to be a curse for the master as well as for the slave Yes, also for the master, if it were for no other

reason than that given by John William Draper in the "Intellectual
Development of Europe" "The high caste is steadily diminishing
in numbers, the low caste is steadily increasing In impervious
pride the patrician fills his private jail with debtors, he usurps the
conquered lands *Insurrection is the inevitable consequence—foreign
war the only relief* " What was true of old Rome is true of our
times The tendency of concentrating wealth in a few hands is even
more marked now than it was in the days of which Draper writes
and the danger is quite as great.

Those who are on top forget how insignificant their number
really is. They meet in their drawing-rooms, their clubs, in their
boxes at the theatre, their ball-rooms, and public drives; and seeing
each other so often, they obtain the impression of large numbers, as
we do in the case of those histrionic armies composed of the same
few men who march out at one side of the stage to come in again
on the other, occasionally changing their helmets and arms if there
is no time to don another uniform Thus our upper classes do not
perceive how thin is the shell which they form on the social globe
We hardly realize the flimsy nature of the envelope which protects
us from the volcanic underlying masses We quietly go about our
business and pleasure, until an earthquake or an eruption disturbs
us in our careless dream-life, reminding us of the terrible powers
beneath So our plutocracy lives from day to day, investing and
speculating, accumulating and wasting, without thinking of the turbulent masses on whose shoulders their palaces are built, until a
social earthquake, an insurrection, sometimes growing into a revolution, shakes them out of their indifference And all the while, the
very forces which should prove the greatest blessing to all, our
progress in science and the arts, serve to increase the tension Our
Divine Master has not given us a very long time for that peaceful
evolution of humanity which may yet prevent the most frightful revolution this world has ever witnessed We may guess the power
of the reaction by that of the forces at work towards a culmination
of the evil You who have the capacity and the means to hasten
the day of reform, hurry up in your own interest while you may!
You cannot secure your own future, and certainly you cannot provide for your children, in any other manner Those fortunes which
you may leave to your heirs will crumble to dust, for they are nothing but mere titles to slave services, they become waste paper on
the day that sees the slaves break their chains But you can leave
behind you something immensely more valuable and indestructible,
a free world, in which every talent has scope, in which easy and
pleasant work, less exhausting than those so-called pleasures, which
now absorb your time, will provide your children with all they need;
a world which the gratitude of millions would transform into a
paradise for you and yours.

But I leave to others the task to appeal to your higher motives.
Experience has shown me the futility of such appeals, where the

mind is so immersed in selfishness that the eyes cannot see beyond the artificial wall of prejudice. Be selfish, if you cannot help it, only, in your selfishness, be at least as practical as you are when you give orders to your stockbrokers. Weigh in your mind which enterprise offers the best chances of investment: the stock company—in which you are as yet a main shareholder who is busily engaged with the sawing of the branches on which you are sitting, endowed with an immense capital to do the work as speedily as possible, with golden saws tipped with diamond compound interest teeth, or that other company, whose share register has as yet few subscribers, but whose object—among others indifferent to you— could be also to supply you with a safer support than the branch on which you so strangely rely.

Oh, Carnegie! oh, Rockefeller! great monopolists and promoters of education, think of it for one single moment! What you are now doing can only help in the branch sawing business, for every one of those thousand poor scholars whom you provide with the means of education will, at the end of his studies find himself in a world where knowledge and ability become every year more incapable of making headway against stupid mediocrity that is the inheritor of monopolies, the slave-driver swinging his whip over the skilled and the unskilled worker, over the scholar and his intellects as well as over the common laborer with his brawny arm. Then will they curse the larger vision you have helped them to achieve; for they will see beyond the mists which as yet veil the truths of life from the ignorant many, and they will discern that your benefactions to themselves were fruits of that very system—that Upas tree —which has poisoned the whole anguished world.

Oh, Carnegie! oh, Rockefeller! a fraction of the sums that your philanthropy is misdirecting would launch a reform propaganda which—controlled by your genius of organization—could transform this planet! Peacefully would the marvelous change be effected, and long before it can be reasonably anticipated by other means. Men like you, and still more especially, men like Tom L. Johnson, the creature of monopoly, who exerts his power and his wealth to combat monopoly—could become important factors in the march of progress, could advance incalculably that peaceful and brotherly development longed for in the heart of the human race! Not through strengthening that longing by direct appeals, which so many good men at this time are making in press and pulpit, for it is not a mere ethical question. Let rebating stop, let the trusts disband, let franchises be kept by the community or leased at their full market value, let corruption disappear and people treat each other like brothers; but let rent accumulate in private pockets, let interest go on compounding, and things will get worse to-day than they were yesterday, to-morrow than they are to-day. Unless we change economic foundations, we work in vain, we waste our breath and ink in preaching and writing. We resemble that poor woman who was given a lift by a kind driver, to whom she replied upon his question why she did not put down the load she carried on her back "I do not want to presume too much on your kindness It is hard enough on the poor horses to carry me along without imposing on them my load too "

Rent and interest press with the same unbearable weight on the wheels of industry, wearily dragged along by the laboring masses, whether the passenger takes some of the load on his shoulders or puts it down on his seat

While I am writing these pages the tide of "muck raking" is running high, and in the violence of personal aspersion few remember that man is the product of heredity and environment, and that to look for improvement in a reformation of individuals is like trying to cure the small-pox by cutting off the pustules The wealth of the Rockefellers and Carnegies is neither the outcome of their personal capacities, great as they are, nor of illegalities, but of laws which permitted their monopolization of raw-materials in the womb of mother earth, and of roads aided by laws that restrict our means of exchange and others that kill foreign competition through high tariffs It has been well said that dirt is wealth in the wrong place The ability of men like Rockefeller, exercised in the right place, can produce untold good It has become a fashion to rail against the *Trusts* and even to make laws against them * It is the merit of socialists to point out that the principle which underlies trust formations is sound, and that these organizations will benefit the people the moment their fruits are not monopolized by the few, but belong to all These fruits are savings of waste in the processes of production and distribution, due to competition

Competition! I come back to this strange actor on the economic stage, adored as a saint by one party and cursed as a devil by the other To the one, competition is the source of all progress; to the other, it is responsible for the social chaos Here we learn that "competition is the life of trade," there, we find all our miseries referred to as "the competitive struggle." Which is right? As usual, there is truth on both sides. In the political economy built on the false foundations of private land ownership and our existing legal-tender money, competition results in the domination of the land and money monopolist, of the trust; while in an economy built on free land and a really elastic currency, competition becomes beneficial, and even the Trusts, deprived of their legal monopolies, would change into useful wheels of the economic mechanism

* I use the term Trusts because it is generally employed, though the most powerful industrial combinations are not independent producers doing business through a central office, a Trust, but simple business corporations, stock companies (in England they are called Limited Liability companies) which differ from others chiefly in their dimensions Instead of one factory, they own a hundred but their legal status is not changed thereby, no anti-trust law would hit their organization

Socialists always remind me of Lamb's Chinaman, who burnt his house to roast a pig, because he did not know that a few sticks might be made to produce the same effect. So socialists cannot see how the people's welfare can be advanced, how the roast pig of general prosperity can be obtained, without a total destruction of the individualistic structure which our civilization has evolved out of the barbarian's communism. They propose to abolish our present system of ownership, production and distribution, without considering whether, after all, a change in our system of land ownership, combined with rational currency reform, might not be sufficient to produce the same beneficent results. This investigation would teach them that they need not demand the nationalization of the means of production even, for if labor owns the land it can soon bring forth all the other means of production, so that common land ownership by itself is absolutely sufficient to accomplish the desired results, provided, of course, that circulation is not impeded by giving an exclusive money monopoly to one or two scarce commodities

Let us suppose the whole United States soil owned by the workers of the country, freely exchanging their products, while the capitalists possess all the houses, machines and capital of any kind, what would be the result in a few years? On the one hand, the enormous development of productive power would have enabled labor within that time to produce better houses, machines, capital of all kind and more of all than now exists in the country, while the capitalists would not know what to do with their decaying houses, rusting machines and ruined stock, unless the workers kindly took them off their hands

I do not want to be misunderstood when I attack the "competitive system" shibboleth. Though I had to prove this slogan a misleading catchword, when the real clue to the great problem is looked for, I do not thereby wish to indicate that I am standing up as a defender of the kind of competition we are used to, the better name of which is *Waste*

(At all events it is a far better slogan than that of "the capitalistic system of production" (Kapitalistische Productionsweise) used by the German speaking socialists, for, as I shall show further on, it is not so much the system of production as that of distribution which ought to be arraigned.) With or without socialism, the whole trend of progress is against it. Parallel with the advance from hand work to that of steel levers and wheels, from the primitive tool to the complicated machine, went the progress in the methods of production and distribution, and this progress was altogether on the line of lessening competition through a more extended co-operation. The factory took the place of the little shop, as the railroad train took that of the coach and cart, and the Trust unites the factories and railroads. At each step division of labor became more perfect and the cost price of the product less. Trusts, department stores, and co-operative stores are advance steps in the processes of production and distribution; and the fight against them is of the same kind as that against machinery, a fight quite as justified under existing conditions, on the already illustrated principle that in a world which is upside down through our departure from fundamental principles, what is good in principle is bad in practice, and vice versa The socialist Wilshire's motto "Let the nation own the trusts!" is certainly more rational than the cry "Down with the trusts!" There is a third way, however, more on the line of organic evolution and in the same direction, in which we found the remedy against want of employment and overproduction Freedom Freedom from land and money monopoly once accomplished, any device by which more wealth can be produced and distributed with less effort will be welcome. With monopolized land and money and the consequent growing chasm between productive power and production, every such progress must be harmful Either we go back to first principles or we are condemned to march in the line of expediency

The economic field is not the only one where we have to follow this course. Love is the great life principle which should govern our actions, but if barbaric hordes attack our homes, burning and killing as they advance, expediency must take the place of this great principle, and automatic rifles will be temporarily preferred to bibles. It would certainly have been far better to prevent the invasion by observing the laws of justice and love, but if we do not destroy the evil at the root we have to cut down the branches If we do not reform fundamental economic evils, we have to protect ourselves as well as we can against their effects, no matter how dangerous the remedy by itself.

Even Communism, the remedy of despair for thousands who can see no other way out of the calamity, is preferable to a continuance of present conditions, without fundamental reform. This is in agreement with the well-known words of John Stuart Mill. "If, therefore, the choice were to be made between communism with all its chances, and the present state of society with all its sufferings and injustices; if the institution of private property necessarily carried with it, as a consequence. that the produce of labor should be apportioned as we now see it, almost in an inverse ratio to the labor —the largest portions to those who have never worked at all, the next largest to those whose work is almost nominal, and so, in a descending scale, the remuneration dwindling as the work grows harder and more disagreeable, until the most fatiguing and exhausting bodily labor cannot count with certainty on being able to earn even the necessaries of life, if this or communism were the alternative, all the difficulties, great or small of communism would be but as dust in the balance " * * * "The restraints of Communism would be freedom in comparison with the present condition of the majority of the human race The generality of laborers in this and most other countries have as little choice of occupation or freedom of locomotion, are practically as dependent on fixed rules and on the

will of others, as they could be under any system short of actual
slavery."

The extraordinary division of labor introduced into all branches
of production has made most of our workers mere wheels in a gigantic machine, a fact not at all affected by the system of enrolling
the managers of the machine Certainly no one can truly believe
that the transfer of this management to men elected by the workers
would result in less liberty than our existing method of government
by absolute self-elected masters, whose decision allows no appeal,
who at any time can deprive the worker of employment, can even,
where blacklists exist, altogether cut him off from any chance of
earning his bread by the work he has been brought up to How
little, after all, coalitions of workers can accomplish where they are
faced by a union of employers, experience has repeatedly shown—
as, for instance, in the great English engineers' strike or that of the
Chicago teamsters Where trusts dominate over a whole department of production, the chances of labor unions are certainly still
further minimized, as proved by the failure of the American steel-
workers' strike In considering this question, the upper classes are
only too inclined to forget that for the masses there is no really free
competition even now As a general thing, the difficulty of finding
another situation makes our employees more dependent than they
ever could be under a socialist *régime*, which would at least allow
their votes to elect the manager But, through the trusts, even the
employers are one by one losing their independence Not to follow
the mandates of the Rogerses, Morgans, etc , spells ruin The independent employer becomes the official of the trust, and is forced
to obey orders just as strictly as the public employee in the socialist
state Even when not absorbed by the trust, he is dependent on
the ever more exacting and less certain customer, and his position
has become so precarious and unpleasant that the main endeavor
of many in this country is to find a good situation in the public
service—which, however, does not prevent the same parties from
declaiming against the absence of liberty in the socialist state It
would be difficult for them to prove why the employee of a state
which provides work for everybody has less liberty than the State
official of our day, whose situation is longed for by a number of
competitors anxiously anticipating the moment when his trembling
hands shall lose their hold The consequent subserviency to superiors is only natural So we see that even the despotic communism
put before us in such books as "Pictures of the Future," by Eugene
Richter, cannot be so very repellent to the masses, because it can
hardly restrict any liberty of practical value possessed by them in
our time, while it would at least ensure them a permanent competency That this actually would be the case, and that the bogey
of famines and general misery put forth by Richter exists only in
the fancy of such blind leaders of the Manchester school, needs no
proof after calculations which show that one single hour given daily

by all who are capable of work—under a systematic organization, without any waste—would provide all with the necessaries of life An hour's work ought to be got out of every man and woman, without any compulsion other than that of sheer tedium. Many of our well-to-do people devote part of their time to pleasures which demand greater exertions and risks than most employments of paid workers Mountaineering, hunting, deer stalking, rowing, yachting, cricket and football, coaching, autoing, ballooning, etc, prove that work of some kind is imperiously demanded by our nature. Whether a certain action figures as work or as a pastime often depends on its being done under compulsion or voluntarily

But abler pens than mine have often enough shown up in their real light objections of this kind, which, however justified they might be when looked at by the citizen of an ideal state such as never existed, are certainly worthless as regards the actual world in which we live Here the one stereotyped answer can be given to all such detractors of socialism and its possible results. "And to-day? Are things not much worse?"

When the disheartening picture of general sameness is unrolled before us—of barracks for homes, uniforms for garments, messes, and even State-regulated amusements, ridiculous fancies though they are—let us ask the poor proletarian whether he would not prefer even this mode of living to the one he is used to. Barracks are better than slums, uniforms are preferable to rags a well garnished mess is decidedly pleasanter than a private table around which the children vainly cry for bread, and even entertainments organized by the State are preferable to those offered by the saloon

The following incident, which happened in Apulia, is related by Mr. Edward C Strutt in the *Monthly Review,* under the title, "Famine, and Its Causes in Italy"

"Three young women from Allisto were brought before the Prætor of Ugento, charged with stealing olives on an estate belonging to the municipality The pinched and starving features of the defendants, the eldest of whom was barely twenty-five, their ragged clothes, and their half-hopeful, half-despairing expression, excited the sympathy and pity of the kind-hearted magistrate, who, though unable to acquit them, sentenced them to the minimum penalty— viz, three days Then a tragic scene took place Bursting into tears, the prisoners flung themselves at the magistrate's feet, imploring him to give them the shelter of the prison for at least three months. With the touching ingenuousness of children, they told how the theft had been a preconcerted affair in order to escape the terrors which the winter (a particularly bitter one this year) held in store for them, and how they had even consulted a lawyer, who had planned the whole scheme, assuring them that, according to the Penal Code they would be sentenced to three months at the very least. And now the poor girls saw their dream of prison paradise, with its bed and blankets. and daily soup and bread, and meat twice a week—a princely fare—vanishing like a mirage before them, just as they thought themselves on the point of entering the blessed portals!"

People who regard the jail as an Eden from which they are debarred will not be inspired by that horror for Richter's barracks and messes, with which well-fed, well-dressed and well-housed gentlemen regard such accommodations

Though the limitations of the second-class may appear unpleasant to cabin passengers, to the man from the steerage they will seem paradise. And Atkinson, Giffen, Richter and other glorifiers of individualism with all its blessings seem not to remember that the immense majority of passengers in the ship of state travel in the steerage, and not in the saloon Do not let us forget also that this immense majority own the ship, and that they will not be for ever deterred from taking possession by the contention that it is impossible to give them all first-class cabins. They will reply, not without justice, that they do not claim cabins like the present first-class compartments: but that an equal partitioning of the ship into a number of well-furnished rooms, with one good table for all, would certainly improve their position, however it might affect that of the present first-class passengers. Nor can they be frightened by the prospect of their subordination under the orders of the ship's officers, for though these officers may not drink champagne with them as they now do with the saloon passengers, they certainly will be politer towards men who are the recognized owners of the ship than they are towards poor steerage folk

What effect is produced upon the poor proletarian when you tell him that communism would stifle the inducement to exertion, because profit is no more obtainable, and that without this incentive progress will be arrested? He will answer like the servant immortalized by the German humorist, Fritz Reuter. The man called his master to account because of the insufficient and poor food he was getting, and the master defended himself by asking the Court whether beef and plums is not an excellent dish The man replied. "Certainly, beef and plums is an excellent dish, but, gentlemen, I never get it" Let us admit, for argument's sake, that our wonderful progress in the arts of production and distribution has been brought about by the desire to gain What has this progress done for the masses of our population? Statisticians of weight, such as Thorold Rogers, Beissel, Janssen and others prove that their wellbeing is less than it was in the fourteenth century. They show that the average wage worker of our time cannot purchase as many necessaries of life as he could five hundred years ago, when production was yet in its infancy. It is true there are more recent periods that would give a relatively favorable aspect to our time, and optimistic statisticians of the Giffen and Atkinson type generally take such periods as standards of comparison They quite ignore those statistics just referred to, which present the somewhat hard nut

to crack   In those more remote times when the productivity of
labor was not one-tenth as great as now, why was the purchasing
power of wages higher, and why were the workers comparatively
well off?   They pick out the worst times labor ever went through,
and from the top of this dunghill they flap their wings, and crow
lustily   "Workers, see how much better off you are, stop com-
plaining, and things will improve still more!"

In his "Problems of Poverty," John A Hobson gives them
this answer   "The period between 1770 and 1840 was the most
miserable epoch in the history of the English working classes
Much of the gain must be rightly regarded rather as a recovery
from sickness than a growth in normal health   If the decade 1730-
40, for example, were to be taken instead, the progress of wage
earners, especially in Southern England would be by no means as
obvious   The Southern agricultural laborers, and the whole body
of the skilled workers, were probably in most respects as well off
a century and a half ago as they are to-day   .   Although a
'sovereign' will buy more for a rich man than fifty years ago, it will
buy less for a poor man   The prices of most of the comforts and
luxuries of life have fallen considerably, but the prices of most of
the necessaries of life have risen   The man with an income of £500
a year finds he can buy more with that sum than he could half a
century ago, for almost all manufactures and imported articles have
fallen in price   But a family living on 20s. a week spends a small
fraction of their income on such goods   The prices which most
concern them are the prices of shelter. of bread. fish, meat, groceries, vegetables, dairy produce, etc.   Bread, sugar, tea, cloth is
cheaper (see 'Life and Labor,' by Booth, to see how little of the
latter the very poor spend)   Rent is 150 per cent higher, vegetables, milk, eggs, butter, cheese, coals, meat, oil, etc, are dearer,
20 per cent. is to be knocked off money value of wages to find real
rise."

What can it benefit the worker if he can buy cheaper carpets,
objects of art, and other luxuries which are mostly only attainable
by the wealthy?   They are "beef and plums" to him.   Of infinitely
greater value to him than all these luxuries is the certainty of always finding employment, and this existed in a much higher degree in those distant days than in our over-production-shrieking
times   This question of permanent employment is very often lost
sight of when wages of different periods are compared   The weekly
wage may have risen. and yet the yearly income may have decreased   30 weeks at $30 wages yield a smaller income than 52
weeks at only $20

At the present writing (January, 1908). there are said to be
four millions, of unemployed in the United States   It has also been
asserted that similar conditions recently existed in Australasia
The following is from the "New Zealand Herald" of 1900
"There are 5,000 applicants for billets (situations) in the New Zea-

land Railway Department Here is the state of things in Victoria. For 387 vacancies in the Railway Department there are—how many applications, can you imagine? No fewer than 12,000 The rush to Bendigo was scarcely a circumstance to it. Wages from £1 to £3 a week—possibly £3 10s at the most Just fancy! It has taken an army of clerks to open the letters and note the particulars of each applicant The greater part of the applicants are country lads—a reflection on our vaunted productive industries In 1897, for almost a similar number of vacancies, the applicants were less than 2,500 What accounts for the immense increase it is impossible to divine Both wheat-growing and dairying are brighter now than then Yet the fact remains that 12,000 of the youth of the colony are eager to get a billet in one of the poorest branches of the Civil Service Surely there cannot be any more possible candidates." Which, by the bye, strangely illustrates the anti-socialists' bogey of the general slavery to be expected from state management!

Said a West Australian paper "A man in want of work called, among other places at an iron foundry on the bank of the Swan, and asked for a job, but was told there was no vacancy A day or two afterwards he saw the body of a man being dragged out of the river, and was told it was one of the hands of So-and-So's foundry Off he rushed to the manager, and again asked for a job, and was told there was no vacancy 'But,' said he, 'one of your men is drowned I have just seen his body taken out of the river' 'You are too late,' replied the manager 'A man who saw him fall has got the job'" That this story is brought out in a country so thinly peopled that its natural resources could support a population at least thirty times as large as it possesses, makes it as fit to illustrate the employment problem as books filled with statistics. For those, however, who prefer the latter, I cannot recommend more instructive reading than the volumes of "Life and Labor of the People" by Charles Booth, and "Poverty" by Robert Hunter

Then there is the working time, in regard to which we certainly are not ahead of the past Eduard Sacher, in "Die Gesellschaftskunde als Naturwissenschaft" tells us (p 277) that in the eleventh century the working time in mines was only 4 hours Thorold Roger believes that in the fifteenth century the average working day in England was 8 hours only.

I am sure that the most optimistic statistician will not pretend that incomes and purchasing power of the masses have kept pace with the productivity of labor, which—after taking into account the labor spent on the building of the necessary machinery—has increased at least ten-fold within a few centuries Therefore, if instead of earning less, workers (including intellectual workers, who, relatively are most underpaid) had to-day twice the purchasing power of those distant periods—and the most optimistic statisticians dare not go beyond this—they would only obtain one-fifth of what they would receive if productive power were taken as a measure. I say "productive power," potential production, not actual production I maintain that without working longer hours or any harder, they could have at least a five-fold income, if all waste of power, through forced idleness of millions, deficient organization of production and transportation, militarism, flunkeydom, etc, were stopped, if everybody were employed on the best method available, with the best of machines obtainable. If, however, the waste through superfluous middlemen, were also stopped, and if the part taken by rent, interest and profit were restituted, we might easily come to a fifteen-fold increase of wages

In the face of such glorious possibilities it is really nauseating to meet again and again with the presentation of the low average figures which the total income of a nation gives when divided per head of population, to prove that communism (even if it did not, as it would, according to such individualists, largely reduce this average income) would simply spell poverty for all Again and again we hear the "chestnut" about the communist, who, in 1848, wanted Rothschild to divide, with the result that the wealthy German banker handed him a florin as his share of such a division, telling him to send all the others, meaning to prove that an equal division would impoverish the rich, without doing much good to the poor Though an equal division in the United States, according to the census of 1900, would give to each family a fortune of $6,000, which would seem wealth to a large majority of the people, we have nothing to do with such calculations In the first place Socialism is not Communism, and does not at all exclude payment according to work done, in fact finds its weightiest attack against the existing system in the proof that the latter's method of dividing the national income is a gross and palpable contradiction of the principle of payment according to work done And then, the socialist's main argument is that the overthrow of the unnatural obstacles, which the existing system puts in the way of production, would do far more to bring production up to productive power than the absent stimulant of free competition could make it lag behind

But we have not done yet with our friend Competition We have a little nut to crack with those who drag him in at every opportunity, who fill our ears with him as if he were the life of society, as he is supposed to be that of trade These gentlemen arbitrarily limit his empire to the domain of the dollar, a paltry domain after all though its master be called almighty Is there not a far higher kind of competition in this world of ours, which we shall never lose even in the communistic State? A competition whose stakes are of a different nature altogether? In his "Merrie England," Robert Blatchford points to the lives of men like Galileo. Bruno. Newton. and indeed the bulk of the explorers, scientists, philosophers and martyrs who were not forced onward by the incentive of gain but by the love of truth, of science of art, or of fame. And He who laid down His life on Calvary to accomplish the best work ever done for humanity—did He work for pay, for wages, or dividends?

In a communistic commonwealth everyone would have to give a day or a couple of days a week to productive labor. Were we relieved of solicitude as to bread the motives just mentioned would stimulate us to undertake the higher tasks of philanthropy. The most celebrated Talmudists gained their food by handicraft; their wisdom was not sold for money. Spinoza made a living by grinding optical glasses, and refused to consider the Elector of the Palatinate's offer to pay him for his intellectual work with a professorial chair at Heidelberg, preferring to offer the fruits of his studies free to the world. Does the soldier offer his life for pay? Is it for the love of gain that he rushes on the enemy's entrenchments with almost certain death in view? Do we see a Milton write his "Paradise Lost" for pounds, shillings and pence? Is a Florence Nightingale sacrificing her health in the field hospitals for wages? Did Luther translate the Bible on piece-work or salary?

Carlyle never wrote nobler words than these, in "Past and Present": "My brother, the brave man has to give his life away. Give it, I advise thee—thou dost not expect to sell thy Life in an adequate manner! What price, for example, would content thee? The just price of thy Life to thee—why, God's entire Creation to thyself, the whole Universe of Space, the whole Eternity of Time, and what they hold, that is the price which would content thee, that, and if thou wilt be candid, nothing short of that! It is all; and for it thou wouldst have all! Thou art an unreasonable mortal —or rather thou art a poor infinite mortal, who, in thy narrow clay-prison here, *seemest* so unreasonable! Thou wilt never sell thy Life, or any part of thy Life, in a satisfactory manner Give it like a royal heart, let the price be Nothing; thou *hast* then in a certain sense got All for it! The heroic man—and is not every man, God be thanked, a potential hero?—has to do so, in all times and circumstances In the most heroic age, as in the most unheroic, he will have to say, as Burns said proudly and humbly of his little Scotch Songs, little dewdrops of Celestial Melody in an age when so much was unmelodious 'By Heaven, they shall either be invaluable or of no value—I do not need your guineas for them!' It is an element which, should and must, enter deeply into all settlements of wages here below. They never will be 'satisfactory' otherwise, they cannot, O Mammon Gospel, they never can!. Money for my little piece of work 'to the extent that will allow me to keep working', yes, this—unless you mean that I shall go my ways before the work is all taken out of me, but as to 'wages'!—!—"

In spite of competition's whip being absent there will be fewer loafers and tramps than in our time. In Dr. Rossi's report of a Brazilian anarchist colony's doings he specially mentions that the members worked too hard, because each felt himself under the

watchful eyes of his co-workers   Such fears of loafing often are expressed by people who never did an honest day's work in their life
The daughter of an English Squire advanced, in answer to one of my addresses, that the old "Mark" was broken up by the lazy fellows who would not work   I simply drew her attention to the amount of labor done by England's landlords   I might have told her the story of the American who had asked an Englishman, whose objection against America was that it had no gentlemen, what he meant by "gentlemen"   "Aw, aw, men who do nothing, you know!" "Oh," said the Yankee, "we have got them, too, only we call them tramps!"

We are also told that in the communistic commonwealth some will have to perform unpleasant work, that all cannot enjoy certain delicacies, or live in favored locations   We might ask whether—in our world—everyone is exempt from unpleasant work, and whether all kinds of enjoyments are accessible to any who desire them.   But socialism is not communism, and though communism could hardly make things worse in this respect than they are, socialism would decidedly improve them.   Those who do the unpleasant work would get better pay and work shorter hours, while pleasanter employment would be less remunerated   While to-day some bank managers receive over fifty times as much pay as the man who cleans our sewers, it might happen in the socialist State that the latter finds himself the better paid man, who could afford to purchase the costliest enjoyments and to live in the most expensive localities.   But, no doubt most of the dirty and unhealthy work would be done by machines, or under better protection against danger, and far less human labor would be employed for such purposes than in our time   The argument that work which presupposes a high education has to be paid better, to cover the outlay thus incurred, loses its force where education and maintenance of the student are paid for by the State   I should not have touched this simple matter if it were not for the fact that it is just this subject which disturbs the mind of more would-be socialists than any others of far more weight.   For this reason, Robert Blatchford devoted some of his most amusing lines to it in "Merrie England".

"Under Socialism. Who will do the disagreeable Work?   Who will do the Scavenging?

"This question is an old friend of mine, and I have come to entertain for it a tender affection.   I have seldom heard an argument or read an adverse letter or speech against the claims of justice in social matters, but our friend the scavenger played a prominent part therein.   Truly, the scavenger is a most important person, yet one would not imagine him to be the keystone of European society—at least, his appearance and his wages would not justify such an assumption.   But I begin to believe that the fear of the scavenger is really the source and fountain-head, the life, and blood, and breath of all conservatism   Good old scavenger!   His ash-pan is the bulwark of capitalism, and his besom the standard around which rally the pride, and the culture, and the opulence of society. And he never knew it, he does not know it now If he did, he would strike for another penny a day. We have heard a good deal more or less clumsy ridicule at the expense of the socialists We have heard learned and practical men laugh them to scorn; we have seen their claims, and their desires, and their theories held up to derision But can any man imagine a sight more contemptible or more preposterous than that of a civilized and wealthy nation coming to a halt in its march of progress for fear of disturbing the minds of the scavengers?

"Shades of Cromwell, of Langton, of Washington, and of Hampden! Imagine the noble lord at the head of the British Government awing a truculent and radical Parliament into silence by thundering out the terrible menace 'Touch the dustman, and you destroy the Empire!' Yet when the noble lord talks about 'tampering with the law of political economy,' and 'opening the floodgates of anarchy,' it is really the scavenger that is in his mind, although the noble lord may not think so himself—noble lords not being always very clear in their reasonings For just as Mrs Partington sought to drive back the ocean with a mop, so does the Conservative hope to drive back the sea of progress with the scavenger's broom."

After all, everything depends on the degree of social recognition bestowed on occupation, and if scavengers are as much thought of under socialism as other tradesmen, there is no reason why many should not prefer scavengering to certain other occupations which are much sought after at present The knacker's work is still more unpleasant than the scavenger's and yet not more unpleasant than that of the anatomist, with the only difference that the latter's business requires a lot of brain exertion, which the knacker's does not Now, on the same school benches we find boys who would rather do this unsavory work without racking their brains in addition, sitting side by side of others who delight in intellectual exercise The ones will rather be knackers, the others anatomists. For pay, the hangman and the officer kill, in the State's employ, the one in perfect safety, the other at the risk of his life But are there not plenty of Falstaffs who prefer to kill without any personal danger to themselves? When everyone has become penetrated with the idea that any kind of honest work is honorable, there will perhaps be as many applicants for work now considered the most despised as for that presently regarded as the most conducive to social esteem

Another objection often heard is that *nobody would save under socialism* In Richter's book there is actually a description of a revolt caused by the confiscation of savings, as if the vast majority of workers in our time could save anything worth mentioning, and as if saving were to be precluded in the social commonwealth! Under communism the saving would be done by the community, not by the individuals; and under socialism, while the community would be the principal saver, individual saving would not be precluded Every one gets credit for his work, upon which he may draw at leisure, spending his income when and how he pleases, and we can safely assume that even individual savings in the socialist commonwealth will be much larger than under the existing system, because earnings will be much higher and more general Certainly there is one great difference between the savings of the two periods The savings of the socialist commonwealth do not breed, they do not yield any interest; they do not enable the saver to extort tributes from other workers. They represent stores put aside during times of abundance for the days of want, on the principle we observe in the animal kingdom. To be sure, man has made a great progress in the art of saving. Instead of hoarding perishable goods, of which part will prove to have been destroyed or stolen when the saver wants to consume his stock, he lets his savings take the shape of means of production, whose use more than covers the cost of storage and preservation, so that when the time of consumption arrives the saver can obtain the full amount due to him out of the day's production This process, which we can observe in our present world, would find its counterpart in the social commonwealth, but without the interest now paid to the saver I have already treated this subject amply in Chapter V

If there are antagonists of socialism to whom the impossibility of saving causes heartburn, there are others who find in saving their principal argument against communism, the only kind of socialism they ever heard of Who has not met with that idiotic argument which forms the stock-in-trade of the ordinary Philistine "And if you divide everything to-day, you will soon have again rich and poor men Some would be thrifty and would save, while others would spend all, so that soon the old conditions would return." What are you to say to people who do not even know that communism does not mean division, but throwing together?

Under socialism, personal saving will certainly yield advantages to the thrifty, and there will probably exist more rich men than in our time; but there will be no oppression of the less favored brethren, because one man will no longer depend on another for the means of living In fact, there can be no poor where society is so wealthy that it can secure a certain minimum to all This minimum might include as much as a house, with garden, plain furniture, clothing and food Our productive power is so enormous that a deduction from individual earnings for such a purpose would hardly be felt

The mere conception that we should have to take from the rich to provide for the poor proves how little such enemies of socialism know of the facts in point We have neither to meddle with our existing wealth nor with our new wealth at present produced

from day to day, but with the potential wealth, the wealth which
could be created under improved conditions, when once the obstacles to free production are removed. Instead of confiscating
wealth, society would only destroy obstacles to the production of
wealth   There is a great difference between wealth, the concrete
product of labor, and wealth, the capitalization of tribute-claims.
We have seen in previous chapters how the latter dangerous class
of wealth arises and how the reforms therein treated will destroy
the factors out of which this kind of wealth is created   Wealth, the
concrete product of labor, can never be productive of any permanent danger, not so much because of its evanescent nature due to
time's destructive powers, but because its possession in no way
hinders others from producing the same kind of wealth   The wealth
which consists of tribute-claims, however, plays a most ominous
part in our economic and social relations, for it is imperishable as
long as the laws subsist which form its basis, and its possession not
only enables its owner to extort the product of others' labor, but
entails also the still more formidable right of absolutely preventing
the exercise of this labor   The workers need not grudge the existing wealth of the rich, whether it be justly or unjustly got, but they
have a right to claim that monopolies of all kinds be abolished
which enable the rich to exploit them, and, what is much worse, to
prevent them from producing wealth.   No wealth is to be taken
away from the rich, only obstacles to the general production of
wealth   It is not a question of dividing the existing stock of goods,
but one of opening the flood-gates of unlimited wealth and permit-
ting an inflow far exceeding the present totality

The enemies of socialism forget that, to a certain extent, we
are already living within the boundaries of the socialistic state, that
it is no more a question of whether we shall obtain socialism, but
how far socialism is going to be extended   Sydney Webb showed
in his pamphlet, "Socialism in England," which appeared in April,
1889, to what extent at that date one of the most individualistic
countries of the world had adventured into socialism

"Besides our international relations, and the army, navy, police,
and the courts of justice, the community now carries on for itself, in
some part or another of these islands, the post office, telegraphs,
carriage of small commodities, coinage surveys, the regulation of
the currency and note issue, the provision of weights and measures,
the making, sweeping, lighting, and repairing of the streets, roads,
and bridges, life insurance, the grant of annuities, ship-building,
stock-broking, banking, farming, and money-lending   It provides
for many thousands of us from birth to burial; midwifery, nursery,
education, board and lodging, vaccination, medical attendance, med-
icine, public worship, amusements and burial   It furnishes and
maintains its own museums, parks, botanic gardens, art-galleries,
libraries, concert halls, markets, fire-engines, lighthouses, pilots,
ferries, surf-boats, steam-tugs, life-boats, slaughter-houses, ceme-

teries, public baths, washhouses, pounds, harbors, piers, wharves, hospitals, dispensaries, gas works, water works, tramways, telegraph cables, allotments, cow meadows, artisans' dwellings, common lodging-houses, schools, churches, and reading-rooms. It carries on and publishes its own researches in geology, meteorology, statistics, zoology, geography, and even theology."

I may add to this enumeration that Glasgow provides hydraulic power, and from other countries the corporation of Vienna has a brick-yard, Tarnopol a municipal bakery which provides citizens with bread at cost prices, and Valparaiso has a municipal music school. From its municipal horse-races Paris draws $50,000 annually, and its municipal nurseries, segar factories, and greenhouses are profitable. Life insurance factory laws, poor laws, public health acts, workers' insurance against accidents and sickness, New Zealand's arbitration acts, old age pensions, grading of dairy and gold products, are all of them socialistic measures.

In Germany fire insurance is not only carried on, but to a certain extent it is even monopolized by the State, who makes it obligatory for buildings. Its railways, which are almost all owned by the State, yield an enormous revenue and are well managed; so are the State mines and the domains. In different countries the telegraph and the telephone are worked by the post-office, that gigantic monopoly which the world over is managed by the State. Then there are the national salt, tobacco, matches, and alcohol monopolies and other socialistic organizations.

The enemies of socialism, when they talk about the injustice done to the diligent and intelligent worker, whose surplus product is to be accaparated for all under socialism, forget two things. The first is that by far the greatest number of our intelligent and diligent workers are now deprived of the lion share of their product to the benefit of a minority, and secondly, that at any event a very small fraction of the product is due to the individual exertion of the worker.

How much is produced by the most skilful worker, manual or intellectual, after we deduct the parts which past generations have had in his work. From the time when first a savage discovered the use of fire to that when this fire first made the ore yield its metal? From the stone hammer with which the hot metal was shaped, to the mighty steam hammer which, though capable of gently breaking a nut's shell, could have smashed the powerful mammoth into atoms within a few minutes? From the firebrand that made darkness visible, to the sun-like arc light? From the clumsy sledge—made of branches—wearily dragged across the wilderness, to the express train flying with the speed of the hurricane? From the fish-bone needle to the sewing-machine? From the word of mouth heard with difficulty at the distance of a few hundred yards, to the wire-carried whisper that is understood a thousand miles away? From the pointed flint scratching signs on a slab of stone, to the type-writer and cylinder press?

Let us not forget that about twenty years is the longest monopoly given anywhere by law to the inventor of the most wonderful
improvement, and after this period anyone has the right to its free
use. Furthermore, that under land nationalization the work performed by Nature, all the advantages due to location and to the
efforts of the community will be common property The part of
the product due to the personal work of the man of one generation
is so small that under such conditions, it will not be worth while to
separate it at that future time when unfettered production has created additional progress, compared with which all that has been done
in the past may appear insignificant The mere expense of keeping
accounts will then be far greater than any possible benefit expected
from a discrimination between the different workers' rights in the
product

But technic progress is only a small part of the immense debt
of gratitude due by the individual worker to the past and present
work of others The product of his own personal work is merely
plucked by him from that wonderful tree which we call our *Civilization*, of whose roots the inventor's activity only forms one fraction.

From the battle of the first savage who killed a cavern bear
with a stone, to the valiant little body of Spartans defending Greek
independence against Persian despotism at Thermoplyæ; from there
to the common soldier unknown to fame who fell at Gettysburg, or
to the German peasant whose strong arm helped to repel French
aggression—millions of silent partners have contributed to the earnings of a Carnegie and Vanderbilt, and even to those of the hum-
blest laborer. From the first shepherd who, in the silence of the
night, ruminated over the nature of the distant shining orbs, to a
Copernicus, Gallileo and Newton; from the unknown bard or bards
to whom we owe the *Iliad* and *Odyssey*, to a Shakespeare and
Goethe from the philosopher forced to drink the hemlock cup and
from the glorious martyr of Calvary, down to the humble writer of
our own days starving in a garret, all have contributed their share to
the root fibres from which sap has been conducted to the tree Civilization. All these have helped to produce the dividends paid by
the great steel trust or by the farms, factories, railroads, ships, etc,
of the world

If I do not add "and the wages of their workers," it is because
it is more than questionable whether—taking it all round—much
has been added on this field by civilization Some wise men even
claim that the average savage, in the full enjoyment of the freely
accessible resources of nature, is better off than the civilized worker
of our time, with starvation wages and the permanently present
Damocles' sword dangling above his head of finding himself without employment For all that, there is also a lesson of modesty for
our socialists in the above passage, which might be brought home
to them when they eternally trot out their "man with the horny fist"
as the creator of all wealth I well remember the day when a hun-

dred such men with the horny fist swung the flail from morning till
night, until one man—with very soft hands, perhaps, but with brains
—brought forth the idea of a machine which automatically now
does the work of our hundred horny fisted ones, does it, too, without
murmuring or of pride in its achievement And the steam plow,
the reaper, the sowing machine? Or the brick making machine, the
saw-mill, the steam dredge and digger? And how about the horny
fists that made all these wonderful steel and iron giants? Why, it
once needed a hundred of them with chisel and file to plane one
single plate, forming a part of some machine, until some soft-handed
but hard-headed gentleman brought out the planing and the milling
machines, of which each single handed performs better work than
the hundred horny-fisted ones ever did in the same time I know
that all these machines are built and worked by the horny fisted, and
all honor to them; but with what right do they each of them, claim
the rights of the hundred whose place they took, or rather of the intellects who, inventing, constructing, organizing, often risking their
all in the attempt, mitigated the waste of human energy employed
for the gross needs of our bodies, through the application of those
wonderful God-given endowments which differentiate man from
the beast?

When we take all this and much more into consideration, we
shall cease to wonder at the strange simplicity of those single-minded
men who believe that a time will come when, saving all bookkeeping
drudgery, we shall no more discriminate between the individual
mite's and the community's share in the production of the immense
wealth-store flowing with such abundance that a few hours' daily toil
supplies more—for all—than the greediest could consume Communism may after all see its day arrive, and God's Kingdom, the
milennium, be given us on this side of the grave

We may not even have to wait for that problematical date usually given by the average bourgeois "It may do when once men
are angels, but," etc. Nobody ever gave a better answer than Henry
George in his "Standard." He presented as an object lesson the
observations he had made on the Pacific steamers. At that time, it
seems, their steerage passengers were not oversupplied with food,
so that at all meal times they fell upon the victuals like ravenous
wolves in a "the devil take the hindmost" struggle, while the saloon
passengers who sat at a well-supplied *table d'hôte*, behaved quite differently, eating and drinking as educated people are in the habit of
doing And yet it was not character or education which was responsible for this remarkable difference of behavior, but the inequality in the food supply George was confident that if the positions
were changed, if the saloon passengers had been transferred to the
steerage and the steerage passengers to the first cabin, we should
soon have seen the new steerage passengers fall upon the scarce
victuals like voracious animals, and the former steerage passengers,
now well provided, politely hand each other the dishes before they

served themselves, and in every way behave in as kindly a manner as their predecessors. If once everyone can with ease procure as much of the necessaries as well as of the luxuries of life as he desires, the disappearance of the mad struggle for the means of existence will result in a totally different picture of human character from the one we are used to.

My friend, John Richardson, of Lincoln, England, in his excellent book, "How it can be Done,"* recognizes fully the difficulty of introducing complete socialism to a generation brought up under the individualistic system, and proposes to begin by educating the growing generation for socialism. The system of schools he advocates is highly ingenious. Its main feature is that not only the mind is to be fed, but also the body; for it is impossible to develop starved brains His pupils are fed, clothed, and, if necessary, lodged at the school Great attention is to be devoted to physical exercises, so as to grow a healthy body as well as a healthy mind. The expenses incurred are obtained by taxation in the beginning, but the productive work carried out by the pupils is supposed gradually to make the schools self-supporting; for in the highest class, the continuation school, half the time is devoted to the different branches of knowledge, and the other half—four hours a day—is spent in the fields and workshops, where all trades are taught At the same time—unlike the system usually pursued in our present industrial schools and technical institutes—what is produced in the workshops, gardens, fields, laundries, dairies, kitchens, etc, is to serve for practical use, to feed and clothe the pupils, and to sell in the open market so as to pay for outlays This system is not only of great pecuniary advantage, but offers much more encouragement to the pupils than the ordinary methods which utilize their work for educational purposes, but otherwise mostly waste its results

The children begin in the elementary schools, where they spend four years. From these they come into the second-grade schools, and then they proceed to the continuation schools, where they stay between the ages of 15 and 18. Above these is the university, where the pupils are from 19 to 21 years old. Here, too, a certain amount of productive work, enough to pay for the tuition and maintenance of the pupils, has to be given, unless a corresponding fee is paid This would mean no loss of time for the studies, for only a certain amount of knowledge can be forced into the brain, and those who spend half of their time at work which exercises the body, while it relieves the mind, will finally get far ahead of those who cram from morning till night.

Before I leave this part of the subject it may not be amiss to point out that, just as there is no strict dividing line between individualism and socialism, there is also none between socialism and

* The seven best chapters have been published in a penny edition under the title, "The Education Problem and its Solution" (Twentieth Century Press, Ltd, London and Glasgow).

communism. Though rational socialists want to pay each worker according to the work done, many of them demand payment according to the time given to a certain class of work. This is the system of many trades unions; practically the communists' demand of "each according to his ability." Now, our productive power has grown to such dimensions that with the elimination of the waste due to the existing system, or rather want of system, one hour's daily labor supplied by each adult would provide all with the necessaries of life. An other hour would add all reasonable luxuries. Certainly two hours a day do not exhaust the ability of any healthy worker and thus we could easily provide what communists demand in the second part of their motto for "each according to his necessities," without thereby limiting the workers' liberty to freely produce and exchange during their spare time—i e., 22 hours out of 24—in excess of the quota supplied by the community whatever the satisfaction of their fancies might further demand.

The antagonism between communism and socialism, yea, even between communism and individualism, is, after all, not one of principle, but one of conditions. The inhabitants of a tropical island, which supplies man's needs without any labor on his part, might enjoy nature's bounties in common, each taking according to his wants. Any other system would not be individualistic, but monopolistic. However, their communism would not be disturbed by allowing the woman who fabricates a sunshade because she prefers it to the palm leaves used by others. The contrary would not be communism, but robbery. In her case, but under such conditions only, where all have plenty, and not under those for which they were written, where the large majority was in want, where often those who worked hardest obtained the smallest, the drones the largest share—the witty lines of Ebenezer Elliott, the Corn Law rhymer, might be justified.

"What is a Communist? One who has yearnings
For equal division of unequal earnings
Idler, or bungler, or both, he is willing
To fork out his penny, and pocket your shilling."

The fact that I am not an enemy of socialism should attach weight to my opinion, that whatever the future may bring forth, the practical programme of our day does not call for such a thorough revolution of the existing system as would be involved in the socialistic demand for the exclusive ownership and use of all means of production and distribution by the State. If I had no other reason to offer for this conviction, the mere fact ought to suffice that the great majority of our generation is opposed to such a revolution, a majority which includes the most intellectual portion of the community. Moreover, I have shown that great progress can be effected without giving up the competitive system. Where through-tickets are unobtainable we have to book from station to station.

Not that I should like to advocate competition in the whole
field. Even the extreme Manchester school draws the line at the
post-office, well knowing that the waste incurred by competing post
offices would be much greater than any possible saving through better organization   If ten competing post-offices brought us each one
letter from different parts of the world, a letter would cost far more
than if brought by one post-office, centrally managed   In that all
are agreed except a few extreme individualists, who, judging from
the fact that for a time, through a loophole in the law, private letter
deliveries in cities have underbid the post-offices in some parts of
Germany, argue that they could do so in the general delivery   It
is evident that, where the profits from the city delivery help to pay
the losses from deliveries at great distances or on difficult roads,
those who undertake the profitable business only can afford to manage that specialty on better terms than where they would have to
do the whole work indiscriminately.

From the mere transportation and delivery of letters, parcels,
etc , to the sale and delivery of merchandise is a long step, but even
this the state has already taken. For instance, the wholesale and
retail trade of tobacco is monopolized in France, Austria-Hungary,
Italy, Spain, Roumania and Japan   The great economy in the cost
of distribution effected by the post-office would of course be enormously multiplied if extended to merchandise, and there is no reason why this economy should not be so adopted   It is hard to see
where the waste, which would be caused through ten letter carriers
doing the effective work of one, is different from that incurred in
sending ten milkmen, bakers, butchers, and grocers through the
streets, each only serving a few houses and then passing into another street, there to seek a few customers, instead of having one
service for each street or quarter   Or why ten post-offices in one
little town would be more wasteful than are the ten or even twenty
groceries which now do a business that one could efficiently attend to

Competition in production and competition in distribution are
two entirely different things   Whereas in the one case individual
efforts result in improving the processes of production, with the
effect of reducing cost price or bettering quality, competition in distribution only wastes power, increases price and decreases quality.
Whether State production could do as efficient work as private enterprise may be open to discussion, but there can be no doubt that,
under a State monopoly of distribution the average State official
could do far more effective work than the best of merchants

To those who can fully appreciate the great qualifications required for a successful pursuance of the mercantile career, and who
at the same time have had some experience of official red tape, my
statement must appear rather paradoxical, and yet it is not difficult
to prove its correctness   The greatest part of our merchants' ability
is required for the purpose of fighting competition—a function en-

tirely done away with under State distribution, which would be mere routine work, as is the case with the post-office   Capable business men would certainly be required in the central office to assort and to place the orders, but outside of this, any ordinary functionary could do the work required   Where no cajoling of customers is needed, because nobody can attract them elsewhere, where the art of pressing on them things they do not want—inferior qualities at high prices— is of no use, the remaining work the showing of goods, taking orders, shipping and money-collecting operations certainly does·not require great genius   All this has been well proved in the tobacco-monopoly countries. Everything is successfully organized there in the way here indicated, and the public are well served   There are only as many selling places as are required, in France, for instance, one per 900 inhabitants· in Austria, one per 400.   A commission of 10-15% is paid, and persons who have served the State or members of their family are employed, thus saving pensions to the State   The prices are not unreasonable, but if the large profit mostly obtained by centralization and consequent absence of waste in distribution, instead of being made to yield immense amounts to the State—over a million a day in France—and a proportionate saving of taxes, found its expression in a reduction of prices, no country in the world could supply cigars as good and cheap as are sold under the tobacco monopoly. Even as it is, I have heard the system praised by smokers as giving them the advantage of finding at once anywhere in the whole country cigars of the same quality for the same price, whereas elsewhere it takes them weeks in a new place to find exactly what they want.

(This was written before the days of the tobacco trust, which improved things in this respect. but also supplies the proof that the State's monoply does not shut off free competition, but private monopoly   The final difference is found in the fact that millionaires pocket the profit which otherwise would accrue to the community —an argument made use of by socialists in regard to production and distribution in general)

Now, what can be done for one article can certainly be done for a hundred—in fact, for all kinds of goods—and it is evident that the saving must increase with the extent of the monopoly   If party shibboleths, through the power of habit, had not prevented discrimination, socialists would long ago have noticed that when they speak of the waste through our "anarchic system of production," they mostly illustrate their meaning by giving examples taken from distribution

In this department facts speak too distinctly to escape anyone's notice   A walk through one of the principal thoroughfares of a modern city will teach people who never read a single treaty on economics that an enormous waste is going on which needs looking into. We count 20 shops selling the same class of goods, where one could well do all the work, with a saving of 19 rents, 19 advertise-

ments, at least 10 salesmen, and so on as to heating, lighting, etc
But that is only what we see at first sight   Behind this row of shops
we can find quite an army of commercial travelers who supply the
goods which they offer to the public, spending millions for railroad
fares, hotel bills, etc.   Behind these we have another army of wholesale houses and agents, with their rents, advertisements, bookkeepers, correspondents, etc,; and only after we have got beyond
this last barrier do we reach the producer.   Even here we have not
done with the waste in distribution   Commercial travelers have to
be engaged to visit the wholesale houses, advertisements swallow a
considerable amount; correspondents, salesmen, rents of show-
rooms, exhibitions, etc, still further swell the amounts which have
to be added to the original price of goods to cover the expenses of
distribution   Various calculations have been made to find out the
addition to first cost paid by the consumer of the product, and they
vary from 30% to 100%   With certain articles 900% is added, i. e.,
the final price paid by the consumer amounts to ten times the
original cost   Let us take the middle course, and assume the addition to be 66⅔% on the average, which means 40% of the retail
selling price   I quote a few calculations from Professor Adler's
"Kampf wider den Zwischenhandel" ("Battle Against the Middleman")   "Taking 100 as the original cost price of the goods, the following figures show their prices at retail   Simple victuals, 120-150;
kerosene, 120; coffee, 150-200; ordinary cotton goods, 120-150;
woolen goods and more expensive cotton goods, 150-200, hardware
and fancy goods, 200-500; alcoholic liquors, 200-500, tobacco and
cigars, 150-500; glass goods, 200-300; paper, 150-300, books, 200-
300; pamphlets, 300-500, etc."

He thinks that the average addition to original cost made by
the middleman amounts to 50%.   Another author, Gustav Maier,
states that in Zurich, a city of 150,000 inhabitants, 1 million francs
a year are spent for advertisements in the newspapers. while those
of another kind may amount to as much again, so that of the 30,000
families each had to spend about 65 francs on this head alone   The
increase of middlemen in Germany from 1881 to 1891 has been almost 40%, while the increase of the population in that period has
only been 11 65%

I add a calculation given by W. G. Moody, before the United
States Senate Committee of 1885.   "A farmer sells his wheat to the
middleman at from 40 to 60 cents a bushel, and it goes into consumption at $1.50 a bushel.   We, the consumers, are paying here
$10, $11, $12 a barrel for flour, and as there are 4½ bushels of wheat
in a barrel, anybody can make the estimate of how much is paid in
the way of toll."

Now let us see how much could be saved of this percentage if,
with production left to private enterprise, distribution were monopolized by the State, just as France, Austria, Italy, Spain, Japan and
Roumania monopolize that of tobacco in its different preparations

That in these countries a part of production is also monopolized by the State need not disturb us, for the system of distribution would not be changed in the least if the production were entirely left to competition. No merchants, no commercial travelers, no advertisements (except perhaps those of manufacturers who draw attention to their goods to induce the public to demand them in the State's shops) raise the price, and only as many selling establishments as the convenience of the public requires, deal in tobacco and its manufactures in the above-named countries. There being no credit, a lot of bookkeeping and costs of collection are saved. The saving must be greater still where the distribution of all goods is monopolized by the State. Delivery, for instance, being centralized as in the post-office, one cart would serve a street where 20 now follow each other. The greatest saving however would be that in rents, not only through having fewer shops, but through paying less for the floor rent at each of the few remaining selling places required than the present shop has to pay. For two reasons

1   There would be no such competition for land to build stores on, as only one-twentieth of selling places are needed, and consequently the ground would not cost more than that used for private dwellings

2   Immense central magazines of many stories would be erected, with elevators, providing more floor space than the present average store for the same land surface. This land once bought by the State, no landlords could raise rents in proportion with the increase of profits, according to their present amiable and remunerative custom

3   Attending to customers would require much less of the staff's work, and consequently less space. Competition now forces salespeople to waste a great deal more of these with each customer than would be needed if no more subserviency, and just as much system, were shown as the public gets in the post office. I have been told that many ladies go "shopping" just for amusement, visiting one store after another to price goods, often without buying anywhere. A good part of the staff's time is taken up that way. The State's store might exhibit books and shelves containing samples and patterns systematically arranged, which every customer could personally examine until quite satisfied, when he or she would simply fill out an order, giving number, quantity and price. The goods would be sold only in certain minimum quantities or the price would be correspondingly increased to pay for the additional work. As wages would be much higher, the masses could afford to buy more at a time

Taking all this into consideration, I think 6% of the retail price would suffice for the work of distribution, instead of 40% Mr William Maxwell, president of the Scotch Wholesale Society, calculated that co-operative distribution only costs 7½%, instead of 33½% of private enterprise, without taking into account better qual ity. This would not include the saving through the prevention of adulteration I do not discuss the injury wrought upon the health of the people by this last mentioned abuse, so intimately connected with our present system of distributing merchandise I leave out of sight the innumerable graves dug by this murderous practice, especially in this country, even where ministering to the sick is the object of the trade. Ghent, in the below mentioned book, quotes from Dr. Lederle's statement in "The Health Department," published by the City Club, New York, in 1903, that out of 373 samples of phenacetin, purchased from druggists in Manhattan and Brooklyn, 315 were found to be adulterated or to be composed of substances other than phenacetin Only 58 were pure Wood (methyl) alcohol is used for ethil alcohol It is a rank poison, known to have caused Saint Vitus' dance, paralysis, and total blindness It is exceedingly harmful even when used externally An investigation showed that 35 5 per cent of all from whom samples of various drugs were bought for analysis were selling adulterations I limit myself to the mere financial aspect of the case W J Ghent, in "Mass and Class," pp 181-2, has the following estimate

"Finally, Mr A J Wedderburn, a special agent of the Department of Agriculture, who made a thorough investigation into the whole subject, reported in 1894 that 'these sophistications can be truthfully said to be as broad as the continent,' and that the extent of adulteration was not less than 15 per cent, approximating $1,123,000,000 yearly This total, tremendous as it is, relates only to food, and is exclusive of the adulteration in wine, whiskey, beer, tobacco and drugs, and the glaring fraud of patent medicines "

The most stringent laws have never been able to prevent adulteration It is a graft intimately connected with private trading, and can only be effectually eliminated through nationalization of distribution The Government's experts in each department would exclude from purchase adulterated goods of any kind Where the public demands an adulterated article, the real contents should be marked on each package, then the real value only would be paid and demanded

We have to take into account also the saving made by the producers, who would only have to send wagon-loads of their goods to the State's magazines, without a penny's cost for wholesale selling expenses, and without the trouble and charge of packing and forwarding smaller lots all over the country Another great saving to the producer would be specialization, rendered possible through central buying The buyers of the State would have before them the orders from all the selling places, they could easily assort them, and arrange with the manufacturers that each gets an order for certain numbers only, so that instead of hundreds having individually to manufacture a hundred numbers, each of them will only produce one number, and thus save a large amount of cost through a correspondingly increased sub-division of labor, allowing special machinery, greater skill applied to the work, an easier supervision, etc., a great advantage already made use of by the trusts, an advantage obtainable without the nationalization of production by the mere nationalization of distribution.

There is no other way of saving the independent artisan, who once played such an important part politically and socially There are few articles of which one single number could not be made as cheap in a small workshop, if it were made as a specialty, as in a large factory or group of factories. Better supervision, cheaper labor (not lower wages), and saving of expenses, which the large place cannot avoid, would more than make up for certain disadvantages, if it were not for one insuperable difficulty, and this is the impossibility of selling the specialized article in competition with the larger concern, which sells the whole line at not more expense than would be incurred by the specialist for the sale of his single number   In fact, in most cases, he would not obtain an order for this single number, even if he undersold the large concern who sells the whole line, for the customer would find it too much trouble to buy from a hundred parties what he can obtain from one. Such an underselling is still more difficult where the large concern resorts to the dangerous and perfidious artifices used by our trusts temporary price-cutting, followed by high prices after the ruin of the competitor has been accomplished. The boycott of dealers who favor competitors and the employment of blackmail, which enforces compliance through the threat of underselling and boycott, would be avoided. Here, too, the State's selling monopoly would save the small producer   Boycott and blackmail can be used to intimidate a smaller competing dealer, but would fail against the State   The dodge of temporary price cutting can be cut off by the State's continuation of orders to the small producers at the regular price, unless the trust guarantees the lower price for an extended period, which it cannot where it has no greater facilities than the small man, where neither a monopolization of natural resources nor that of specialization procures an advantage

Our next task is to investigate the relation the laborer's wages bears to his product of merchandise   Only in this way can be found the relation of the purchasing power of the masses to their produce. In my former writings I had given this relation as being between one-fifth and one-sixth, which was optimistic when compared, for instance, with the calculation of Bersford in his "Pocketbook of Statistics," who gives the relation of wages to retail prices as 13½ to 100, about one-eighth   Bersford fell into the same error to which I succumbed, and which the latest American census tables, those of 1905, for the first time permitted me to correct, all the previous ones having shown a deficiency in this respect   This census enables us to separate the manufactures which form the raw materials of other manufactures (in German "Halbfabrikate") from the total of manufactures, which by their inclusion in the old tables falsified the result. For instance, the tables gave the leather twice; first as the product of the tanner and then as part of the shoe-maker's and belt manufacturer's product, except where the shoe factory had its own tannery, in which case the leather was not given at all and correctly figured only in the value of the shoes The wages paid out for raw materials, on the other hand, were omitted because they figured in the census of agriculture and mining, or not at all, if the material was imported. Either the raw materials had to be deducted from the total of manufactured goods or the wages spent on them had to be added to the total of wages, and neither had been done. After making these rectifications, and after adding to the price the retailer's profit, I found the relation of wages to retail price to be one to four, which is bad enough, but not quite as bad as it at first appeared It means that the workers can buy only one-fourth of what they produce, when measured by the price they actually pay for goods the retail price.

If the 34% which centralized selling could save in the field of distribution were kept from being gobbled up by the capitalist and landlord, through land nationalization and currency reform, as they would be without these reforms, the saving of 34% in distribution could reduce prices 34 per cent or could increase wages 136 per cent If as much as 9 per cent of the saving were used for fiscal purposes—which would suffice for national public expenses and would permit to relieve the people of all other national taxes—then wages could be doubled The immense increase of consumption thus obtained would create such an additional demand for goods of all kinds that those displaced middlemen who are not required for the national work of distribution, and the unemployed workers would find remunerative productive work, while such a reform under present conditions, when every saving merely swells rent and interest, not wage account, would simply make matters worse, especially for the poor middlemen, most of whom are forced into bankruptcy by department and co-operative stores and their own frenzied competition, for—as I have already illustrated in opening this chapter—anything based on a correct principle must produce bad effects so long as we disregard such fundamental necessities as the people's free use of the earth and a means of exchange freely accessible to all who want to exchange their products

I have spoken here much of wages though I know our friends in the socialist camp do not like to hear of wages when we look into the future What they really mean, however, when they declaim against the *Wage System* is not so much the system itself, for it is by no means certain that where two parties join in production, the one to whom a certainty is insured in advance is always better off than the other, who takes what is left after his partner has been paid What the socialist really hates in the wage system is the system of low wages He can hardly be blamed, though, for his generalization, as the practical business men of the whole world do their best to prove the necessary identity of wages and low wages Of all disgusting things I am meeting with in my special field of study, nothing beats those exhortations addressed to the union man who tries to force up wages, in which two points are usually made: 1 "High wages mean dear products, and the purchasing power of the wages sinks in proportion to their rise." 2 "If you want too much you will not get anything at all, because we shall not be able to compete in the world's markets."

This is the nonsense usually dinned into our ears by employers of labor, by economists, by editors of all colors, who generally agree on this point at least.

If wages were the only component of selling price, the argument that the worker cannot profit by higher wages, as they must result in a correspondingly higher price of everything he buys, might be plausible But wages form only one-quarter of the retail price and consequently the increase of the selling price, due to a rise of wages, need only be one-quarter of the wage increase If W (wages) $= \frac{1}{4}$ P (price), a doubling of W needed by itself only raise P to $1\frac{1}{4}$ P, which means, that with a doubling of the money wage the workers would only pay one-quarter more for their goods, their actual purchasing power would have risen 60 per cent Now, when we consider that such an increase would entail a corresponding consumption and thus would make free room for new production, more than five-fold in excess of all our exports, not only need we not trouble about the foreign market bogey, but we can open before the employer's eyes such an immense field of increased business and profits to make him grasp the important truth that he is the party who profits most by higher wages paid all around If employers understood this, they would combine for the purpose of raising instead of reducing wages.

I attach very little importance to the question what forms production will take, after once the workers of all kinds obtain a fair share of the outcome. The probability is that all kinds of forms will subsist side by side There will be production organized and carried on by the State or municipality, there will be co-operative production and there will also be work under employers, mostly, no doubt, with a participation of the employees in the profits of the enterprise, a system which forms the bridge from simple employment on wages, to co-operative production, as the constitutional monarchy is that between absolutism and the republic

Let us suppose that all the difficulties under which present co-operating producers are suffering, are removed They have easy access to raw materials, money and credit, and through co-operative or State distribution the greatest obstacle in their way, the commercial work, the hunt for the customer, is eliminated. Under such conditions only those employers can keep workers from entering co-operative shops whose organizing ability is so great that, in spite of paying as much and even more wages than the independent workers are earning, they can still make higher wages of supervision and organization, of management for themselves than they would receive as paid managers from labor-copartnerships They are, so to speak, managers on piece work.

Where the landlord has gone, where the tribute-claiming capitalist has disappeared; where the employer is only a skilled worker, what becomes of the so-called *class war*, the most invidious and fatal battle cry that was ever invented; a battle cry which hardens the hearts of thousands who, with a feeling of complete solidarity with the lowest and poorest; and anxious to fight for their cause, are held back by the bitter prejudice manifested towards them.   This is unjust, because the living men are made responsible for conditions due to historical wrongs which created monopolies It is also impolitic, because history repeatedly shows that the men who led the proletarians in the battle against oppression belonged to the very class which benefited by the existing state of things. From Moses to the Gracchi, from Mirabeau to Marx and Lassalle, the most important fighters for the masses, their greatest leaders, have come from the classes. The fight ought to be against private land-ownership, not against land-owners, against interest, not against capitalists, against monopoly in any form, not against monopolists If a war against persons comes at all into play it would be directed against a small number of plutocrats, who, instead of recognizing in time the impossibility of keeping up antiquated institutions, risk their all on the maintenance of oppressive laws So much the worse for them, for the question whose will be the final victory cannot be doubtful It is their interest to bring about a peaceable compromise, which is possible only on the lines here sketched. To them and their coadjutors, to that small minority who as yet hold the reins, this book appeals in the first instance I am not conceited enough to hope that it will obtain many adherents from the extreme party on the opposite side, from the revolutionists They believe themselves to be right, and, to a certain extent, they are I think that the road here proposed is better adapted to the present conditions of the soil, but, in any case, the worst road is better than an impassable quagmire. It will be for those whose crushed corpses may perhaps have to make the treacherous soil of present conditions passable to bethink themselves that the time for the construction of a good road is not yet past Will they be in time, or will history once more record another set of fools who believe that their unaided arms can hold back the express train on which the human race is travelling towards its destined goal? God alone can tell!

The great change will come; that is certain, only the road as yet is hidden from our sight, the road which may lead us through peaceable evolution or through a bloody revolution The choice lies still in the hands of the masters, who control the safety valve Sitting on this valve, when the boiler is under a high tension, is not conducive to safety and sometimes proves an expensive operation,

as the Southern States once experienced   If the termination of
chattel slavery had been the result of peaceable compromise, instead
of a bloody wrangle, ample compensation for the liberation of the
slaves might have been paid and billions of treasure, besides untold
human lives, could have been saved   Extreme measures, such as
granting the political franchise to the existing negro generation,
with the inevitable reaction we are witnessing, might in such a case
have also been postponed

A task of infinitely greater magnitude than the settlement of
the negro problem would await the victorious socialists at the conclusion of a civil war brought about by our existing economic
anarchy   Forcing their ideals upon a nation, united in the attack
against existing abuses, but hopelessly divided in regard to the
necessary work of organization, would be found a Herculean task.
Attempts at any progress for which the majority is not ripe are
followed by reactions such as overtook England in the seventeenth,
and France in the nineteenth century. The road of peaceable evolution is far safer and better adapted to an undeveloped marching
capacity of the people

It will not be the same everywhere   In continental Europe,
where State ownership of railways, telegraph and express service,
municipal ownership of tramways, waterworks, gas and electric
lighting have more and more taken the place of private ownership,
they have already found out how little this special progress in State
socialism has helped on real social reform, and millions of voters
are pressing forward for more radical work. The United States
and England will yet learn the same lesson, unless the octopus
swallowing business is carried out on a far wider scale than that at
present held in view by radical democrats, who are considered hopelessly in advance, though they only demand what has been attained
in countries far behind theirs in political progress, in countries
where even the most conservative would not advocate a return to
an antiquated system which delivered the control of the arteries of
commerce into the hands of private monopoly.

Of course, every effort ought to be made for the nationalization
of our railways, telegraphs, parcel delivery, savings-banks, as well as
our fire- and life-insurance now in private hands, for the municipali-
zation of our tramways, waterworks, gas and electric lighting, but
only as a side issue, not as the main programme. Currency reform
ought to take a foremost place if we wish to carry through real
social reform work   The palliative measure under contemplation
while this is written, an emergency currency to be issued by the
National Banks, whatever other objections can be brought forward
against it, has the great defect of being only a drop in the bucket.
The amount it would add to the currency of the country is far too
insignificant, when compared with the normal increase in the volume
of our turnover and the corresponding demand for currency   Only
an elastic currency, whose supply expands with the demand, can

free us from our worst peril, the permanently impending financial crisis

The next step should be the nationalization of the land, and only then may we be ripe for the nationalization of distribution, in the sense of exchange   This great reform, too, may be reached in Europe before we begin to touch it in this country   On the European continent the tobacco and alcohol monopolies have already paved the way for the idea of State distribution so that it is no more a question of a new principle, but merely one of extension. In England the elimination of competitive trading might be reached through the extension of distributive co-operation, which has already made much progress

Though the work of distribution lends itself far better to nationalization than that of production, and ought to precede the latter for reasons already given the opposite course might prove easier in this country, for the reason that important branches of production have been almost monopolized by the trusts, while millions of little folks find their independent bread in the work of distribution. These clamor loudest against the trusts, though in their bulk they themselves are by far more voracious and dangerous leeches, drawing the people's life blood, than the most tyrannical trusts. That the masses do not recognize this, is most natural and has always been so   Long before there has been any record of human history man hunted the huge carnivori   Their destructiveness was as evident as is now that of the big trusts; and yet how insignificant was it compared with that of those microscopical beings, the bacteria, which only our advanced science, armed with powerful instruments, has begun to discover, and of whose existence the old lion hunters were absolutely unconscious   The trade parasites are far more dangerous to human welfare than the trust tigers, but it is easier to shoot lions and bears than to destroy bacteria or even to discover them

So it is a much more difficult task to organize national distribution in the place of the teeming powerful middlemen hive than to nationalize our principal industries; for anybody can see clearly that the substitution of the people as a whole for the present trust shareholders is a very simple matter, need not even change the trusts' system of administration, nor even the personnel; for the same managers, foremen, bookkeepers and correspondents could attend to the work   The only difference would be in the persons of the dividend-receivers. And so, though it is not the way the scientific reformer would choose, the American people perhaps will begin with the nationalization of production, or, anyhow, with that of the trusts The distribution of the trusts' products might then also be carried on by government officials, and the rest would be a mere question of extension, until we arrive at the realization of the socialistic ideals, the whole of production and distribution carried on by the consumers on their joint account

In this way the co-operative commonwealth the downfall of

the competitive system, may be reached by peaceable evolution There is little hope, however, of such a consummation, unless we first thoroughly reform our system of government in the direction indicated in the chapter on "Democracy." Without the referendum and the initiative, which destroy the representative's power for evil, we cannot kill corruption, which surrenders the legislative apparatus into the hands of the big corporations, allowing the wolves to constitute themselves the guardians of the sheep. The briber will disappear when the bribed "cannot deliver the goods." The proportional vote, besides the advantages elsewhere enumerated, will finally eliminate the greatest difficulty which we generally have in our mind's eye when we think of State management of industry and commerce under the present accidental majority system. The proportional vote enables each trade to send its own representatives to the capitol, and these representatives would show more fitness for the work of industrial and commercial management undertaken by the community than the advocates of the monopolists, who dominate in our existing parliaments. The co-operative commonwealth would be administered by men selected as leaders by the workers in their special branch of trade or by men holding like opinions scattered all over the country, not by the vote of men living accidentally in the same district of the most diverse interests and opinions

State management carried on by men so selected would be totally different from that which we could expect from the fruits of our present voting system And yet this simple, easily attainable change is not comparable with the much more momentous one we may hope for from a systematic education of the future voters and statesmen in schools in which the young are prepared for universal peaceable co-operation, for human solidarity with "one for all, and all for one" as the leading parole, instead of "make money, honestly, if you can, but make it anyhow, for the devil takes the hindmost. Only take care you keep out of the penitentiary!" the banner under which the present system marches, which teaches the struggle of all against all.

To socialism belongs the future; many of the world's best men and women agree in this, though they may differ in regard to the methods of attaining the lofty goal The step by step method here proposed may, after all, prove more practicable than the radicalism of Social Democracy, to whom Henry George said twenty years ago . "We both want to reach the Pacific (the people's good). You think we shall reach it only in Yokohama (Socialism), while I believe we shall already be there at San Francisco. (Land restoration) Well, all I have to say, is let us go by one of the Pacific railroad trains to San Francisco—which anyhow is on your way, too. If you are right, I shall go on with you; and if I am right, you save the trouble of going farther "

Unfortunately the blind conservatism of vested interests is the worst obstacle in the path of peaceable evolution, which perhaps will continue stemming the flood until it breaks through all obstacles in one mighty all overpowering deluge

And for all that the defenders of these vested interests are the very men whom we hear declaiming against the despotism the people would be subjected to under Socialism'

It is not the least amusing among the many vagaries of the strange transitory period through which we are passing that it is usually the despot, and those belonging to his coterie, who paint with vivid colors the despotism to be expected from the Socialist State   It is not the poor factory worker or agricultural laborer working as hard as a slave, and with the submission of one, who trots out this bugbear, but the employer, to whom present conditions have given powers resembling those of the slavedriver   Or the landlord and capitalist, who, without responsibility of ownership, own their miserable tenants and debtors as thoroughly as if they were mere chattels   Or those who in books and newspapers take up the cudgels for capital   After all, there will not be the least need for the Socialist State to extend her business* undertakings beyond distribution, transportation, communication, and, perhaps also, the production of the necessaries of life—leaving the production of luxuries to free competition   The painter of portraits and landscapes may be as severely left alone as the performer on the 'cello or the writer of a novel   But even in all other branches of production full liberty might be granted   Let them compete, if they can, after the land belongs to the State, after the means of exchange is accessible to everybody, and after distribution is nationalized   There will not be much to fear

Nobody forces us to take the railroad or to make use of the post office, the telegraph and telephone   We have the most unlimited privilege to walk and to send messengers, but the fact that anybody performs distant land journeys on foot or by any conveyance but the railroad has become more and more exceptional, while not one man in a hundred ever sends a messenger beyond the distance of a few miles where the post office, telegraph -or telephone performs the same service for a trifle   Under such conditions, there is no reason why seemingly irreconcilable parties might not work together after all   Even the most extreme communist does not like to sacrifice the liberty of the individual to work as and where he pleases, but he prefers dependence to the freedom of starving   A comfortable and certain living as a little wheel in a large machine seems to him preferable to uncertainty of employment as the price of independence—if we can call by this name the present state of things which forces him to become a part of a private machine   Hunger and cold, which now force him to undertake the most repulsive and

---

* Only the business, the economic task of Socialism, which is to supply it with the means for its important social reform work, is within the scope of this book   Abler pens have taken up this latter work and principally the State's relation to the family, especially to the child of the future

dangerous work, are more efficient means of coercion than the whole police force of the Socialist State   Is it astonishing that under such circumstances he does not share the aversion in which the well-to-do hold communism?   An aversion readily understood in the case of men to whom a comfortable position gives a certain amount of independence from which they are loth to part   For the very sake of this independence, however, the classes may be counselled to look at the question for once from the point of view of the masses, of the poor and down-trodden, who form the majority, and whose will must finally prevail

Who is to blame if this will should finally jeopardize the position of the others, may be their very existence?   Is it not their teachings that effectually inculcate the lesson how political power is gained by graft and oppression and used for graft and oppression?   Are these gentlemen, these owners of large corporations, the perpetrators of wholesale robberies, in a position to oppose important economic reforms or even downright Socialism because they call them "confiscation?"   Have the worst kind of step-paternalists a right to rail against the paternalism of the State?

They are the breeders of revolution and their present policy is impotent against its spread, for as a witty Frenchman once said   "You can do anything with bayonets, except sit on them"   That their antagonists are not despicable is shown by the latest platform of American Socialists, which for the first time has modified the preposterous proposal of nationalizing the whole of production in a manner which make it acceptable to earnest social reformers of all classes   It demands ·

"The collective ownership of all industries which are organized on a national scale and in which competition has virtually ceased to exist"   The preceding part of the programme which demands "the collective ownership of railroads, telegraphs telephones, steamships and all other means of transportation and communication, and all lands" only needs some slight limitations to make it come within the boundary lines of many adherents of the old parties.   As a whole I think it will be safe to predict that within a measurable time this programme, without essential modifications, will become the programme of all progressive Americans   Dr Johnson's axiom ·   "It is no use bolting a door with a boiled carrot" will more and more be recognized a practical policy.   Half measures are often worse even than standpattism

CHAPTER IX.

CONCLUSION

It is the fight for the truth, not for success, which is certain of final victory

I have done   What I give is the outcome of a quarter of a century's study, concurrent with half a century's practical work in the field of industry, trade and banking.   I do not flatter myself that the book will prove to be popular.   The public interested in sociological work is limited, and often wedded to some favored method of cutting off the hydra head of social misery.   Unfortunately, the beast has more than one head, as Hercules found out in the good old time when monsters yet abode upon the earth in their undisguised ugliness, so that heroes knew exactly where to strike.   They are much worse in our time, when hired pens so cleverly manage to hide them behind beautiful names, often impenetrable armors for the intellectual lances of the multitude.   *Capital, the friend of labor!*   Capital meaning the market value of the privilege to fleece labor.   *Interest, the reward of abstinence!*   The abstinence of those who have to pay it   *The instigator or saving!*   As if the bee needed interest to stimulate its honey-collecting work, and as if interest, by reducing the amount of savings, necessary to live without further work and by disabling the interest payers, etc, from saving, did not prevent more work than it stimulated.   *Free trade!*   Even if it means opening our own armor, while others double their protective shield   *Laissez faire!*   Even if the people starve   *Sacredness of property and full play to individual effort!*   Even though property means the soil of the country, and though life and work are impossible without land.   *Sound money!*   Even though soundness means a growing monopoly for the owners of a scarce commodity, which has been made the only legal tender for debts, the only standard of value, the only legally valid means of exchange   *Credit the soul of business!*   By exacting interest which kills trade   *Gradual equalization of wealth!*   Because the rate of interest goes down, in reality the sign of an unnatural overgrowth of tribute-claims competing for the limited quantity of safe tribute   *Free trade in land!*   To have the mortgage-lord take the place of the landlord, the plutocrat that of the aristocrat   *Over-population!*   With an over-production of all necessaries of life   *Over-production!*   With millions of needy people.   *Survival of the fittest!*   The fittest often being the useless sprig of a line of idle drones, who overcomes the honorable toiler

No wonder it is difficult to find the head of the hydra, the new head which has grown in place of the old one.   *Plutocracy* the ugly successor of *Despotism!*   Who will be the modern Hercules to cut off this head?   Will it be that great nation which has done so much already?   *Noblesse oblige*   Will its great Declaration of Independence from foreign oppression be followed by another much more important one, directed against the New World tyrant? Let us hope so, for nowhere has this despot attained such gigantic power, nowhere is his yoke more strongly felt.

This work would certainly court a greater popularity if it had followed one of the well known flags; for example, that of *Social Democracy* I have tried to do her justice, but I could not follow her lead, nor do I believe that the people as a whole are prepared to do so; for only the work of the day appeals to them, not that of the future. The flag of the *Single-Tax* is followed by some of my best friends. None of them can have a higher veneration for the great founder of their school than I. His great "Progress and Poverty" did more than anything else to speed me on the path of social reform work, but they are altogether too onesided in their aims and are wedded to special methods, which can never be successful. *Currency Reform*, necessary and urgent though it be, has been the banner under which false issues have been put forth, while the practical plan is almost completely ignored. On no other field have cranks and fadists held such orgies. Rarely have partisans been more deaf to other voices. *Tariff Reform*, a rag pulled to one side by protectionists—who in their narrow and usually selfish partisanship lose sight of all other aspects of the great social problem, but foreign competition—and to the other side by the nothing-but-freetraders—almost as blind Don Quixotes, riding their rosinantes to death and doing all in their power to make disobedient facts accommodate themselves to their theory

These classes are too deeply engrossed with their own specialties to heed the physician who contends that the disease of the social body cannot be cured with one remedy. They consist of estimable men who are far ahead of that ordinary run who go their way through the world without realizing that they, too, are called upon to work for the great change, which, though sure to come, could be reached much sooner if they all helped to the best of their abilities.

It is no easy matter to reach the masses; in fact in ordinary times it is impossible, but, fortunately, ours is not an ordinary time. We live in one of those rare periods of which the poet says "The time is ripe and rotten ripe for change," a period in which a great revolution is preparing, which is beginning a new chapter of human history We have seen several such periods since that great one which began on Calvary in far off Jerusalem One of them that which fourteen centuries later was marked by the introduction of letter printing, which made knowledge, once the monopoly of the few, the property of the people A little later, the discovery of a New World, destined to become the cradle of liberty, was followed by the great Reformation, that began the liberation of the human mind from ecclesiastical serfdom. Another century came which saw the sailing of the Mayflower with its wonderful potentialities, which witnessed the uprising of a nation and the fall of a faithless king,

followed by the peaceable revolution which confirmed the great principle of self-government for the Anglo-Saxon, the seed of 1776 and
1789.

The ground had thus gradually been prepared for progress of
a different nature in which Invention led the world to the conquest
of untold wealth and wonderful possibilities of wellbeing for all.   In
this miraculous mastery of nature's powers, these almost unbelievable transformations made by the Alladin's lamp of science and
technical progress, battle after battle was fought in such quick suc-
cession that the armies had not much time to pause and examine
their commanders.   When at last they did so, their observation revealed to the astonished warriors that, during their march of conquest, the leaders who had urged them on, had gradually usurped
such despotic power that a new kind of slavery had arisen, a slavery
all the more strange because so little to be expected as a consequence
of such wonderful achievements

The rage brought on by this discovery spreads quickly, but the
first storm takes the wrong direction.   It attacks persons and classes,
instead of looking for causes.   In this book I have investigated these
causes, after explaining the radical difference between the new
problem and the problem of the past   I have shown that it is a
question of clearing a free path for the immense productive power
we possess, and no longer one of the division of an insufficient stock
of wealth   We saw how land monopoly and inelastic money have
been the main obstacles which prevent production from reaching
the limits of productivity, and from thus creating wealth for all   It
was then easy to indicate how the land can be made accessible to
all users, without confiscation, or the imposition of new loads on
the workers' shoulders   It proved a little more difficult to explain
how an elastic money can be created, presenting an unchangeable
standard of value and easily accessible to producers and traders
Interest, the enslaving force through which billions of so-called
wealth—in reality only the market value of tribute-claims—became
the property of the few and the shackles of the many, needed no
special system of attack; for it sufficed to prove its dependence on
the two great monopolies; their downfall entailing its disappearance

After cutting the roots of those monsters known under the
name of Trusts by the two fundamental reforms, their final overthrow, or, at all events, their transformation into harmless and useful factors in the co-operative circle, was shown easy by the help of
another important reform, i e., the nationalization of distribution;
an economic factor of such potency that it would render unnecessary
the nationalization of production

But will such great transformations ever be reached by the
process of peaceable evolution through the ballot?   The political
reforms needed to make this possible were discussed; also another
path to the same goal, voluntary co-operation was surveyed   Mutual
banking, though not providing new money, at least supplies a credit

system, independent of money and land monopoly, and thus may help in the final battle against the main forts by mining their outworks. With its help, co-operation in distribution could obtain part of the power which the nationalization of distribution would completely secure, and thus might help to render the trusts innocuous

Not a single specific; but the plan of a complete campaign, making use of the most diverse forces. No such patent medicines as Single-Taxers, Freetraders or Bi-metallists prescribe, and therefore a plan likely to be proscribed by these gentlemen, who like the crank of an engine always come back to the same point in the revolutions of their mental mechanism, yet on that very ground a plan that ought to commend itself to all who are not yet married to an Ism; not only to the poor, downtrodden masses, but to the very men now looked at as their oppressors What tends to keep these men back from helping in the great fight and makes them limit their efforts to the domain of charity and education is that very appeal to a class fight which is the shibboleth of Marx and his followers.

We hear a good deal about classes, class consciousness, class fights, etc., but are these not rather loose verbalisms? While some simplify the task by merely distinguishing between the rich and the poor, others, believed to be more scientific, classify on the one side the owners of the means of production and distribution, and on the other those whose labor sets these agencies to work. Practically the fight is between employers and employed, and may be summed up in the endeavor of the employers to get as much work as they can obtain for as little money as the employed can be induced to accept, and the endeavor of the employed to give least work for as much money as they can extort Unions have been formed on both sides, and the war goes on with varying success At the outset the employers' unions are at an advantage, as not only prejudiced judges but also Hunger and Cold fight in their ranks, and not only weaken the resisting power of the united workers, but also recruit their worst enemy, the "scab" or non-unionist In the end, however, the result of the war seems beyond any doubt, for the working masses form the large majority of the nation, their will must finally become law if they put aside the poor weapon of striking and make good use of their political power. It is easy enough to see in which direction this power will be used, unless the fight is shifted to a new field At present the opinion begins to prevail among them that against the seeming tyranny of the employer the only remedy is his elimination, by making the workers their own employers who shall own their means of production in common. From such a narrow point of view Socialism necessarily is the only outcome. I have tried to show in the preceding chapter that for the toiling masses even this alternative is an immense progress from their present state but that another course offers which not only promises them greater advantages, but would be more acceptable to the reigning classes, who might be gained over if their antagonists met them half way This alternative has been presented in these pages. If it should not prove acceptable to the men who represent the cream of our workers the unionists, it is because they have been too long in the fight against persons to recognize the fact that it is not persons but certain institutions which hold the fort against which their attack ought to be directed. Unfortunately, many of the victims of these institutions do not fight against them, but try to use them as a ladder for their own personal elevation from the ranks of the downtrodden into those of the oppressors, who would be powerless without the cupidity that recruits the ever ready army under their command. It is this cupidity which makes the masses listen so readily to their worst enemies, the land owners, to whom are allied the men who make a living by selling or conveyancing land—those eloquent preachers against the wicked ones who want to despoil the poor worker of the little plot for which he has been saving up during so many years Or the money-lender, who rallies him to the defence of interest, pointing to the benefit accuring to the poor saver from his investments in the savings banks or life insurance companies Or the banker, vaunting the good old honest gold dollar, and warning the man of the people against worthless paper which is bound to ruin the industrial classes

It is the old story of the wolf who preaches to the sheep that the right of devouring other animals is one of the most sacred natural laws, equally beneficial to all creatures, and therefore not to be infringed by anyone without extreme danger ! "These agitators want to deprive you of the right you have to gorge yourselves on wolf flesh, just think of it !" Or the story of the slave-holder who tells his human chattels that slavery is a profitable institution to them "Has not Cæsar, a former slave, after buying his liberty, bought several slaves for himself? Why should not all of you have the same chance ?"

Let the worker calculate how much his share in the nationalized land would amount to, and how much on the average he can ever hope to own, under present conditions. I have shown in Chapter II. that the nationalized rent would yield enough to ensure him and his wife a higher pension for every single year after his retirement from work than, in ninety-nine cases out of a hundred, the whole value of the little plot of land which he can ever hope to possess free of debt, would figure up to I could equally prove to him that the amount of interest he pays during his life in the price of everything he buys or of every dollar he borrows, as well as in the loss caused by lower wages or unemployment, due to the interest paid by his employer, exceeds a hundred-fold the interest he obtains for his scanty economies from the savings bank or through the reduction on the premium he pays to the life insurance company But all this dwindles into the background when he takes a broader view, when he come to understand the part which the institutions thus praised to him play in the economic process. When he has once realized the truths which this book tries to inculcate that the social mystery of the past and the present century—the problem of want through superabundance, which has succeeded the familiar and explicable question of misery through insufficient productive power—that this seemingly incomprehensible problem is due to capitalism; and that capitalism must perish when its roots (rent, and interest) are destroyed, with the soil of private land ownership and hard legal tender money which they luxuriate in—when the worker has thus gained the solution of our present-day problem, he will behold the dawning of a new era Instead of clamoring for more labor laws, he will join his employer—after all, a worker, too—in the great fight against monopoly, the soul of capitalism, their common enemy.

Then and then only will victory crown their joint efforts, a victory without any vanquished, for the fertility of unfettered productive power is so wonderful that the compensation of the capitalists will be easily accomplished With the disappearance of private rent and interest as a continuous doubling force of their wealth, our rich will gradually consume it. It would simply mean that a certain number of people have deferred consumption, while others consent for a while to use the wealth thus saved in the shape of tools of production, to hand it back in the form of articles of consumption of all kinds at the time when the lenders want it. For the advantage reaped from the use of the tools, the borrowers would render the service of preserving their creditors' wealth intact. The longer the period during which wealth is thus freely lent, the better for the borrowers If the lender is so rich that, as in the case of the Rockefeller family, the mere consumption of the accumulated wealth, without interest, would give a yearly income of a million dollars during a thousand years, this would simply mean that generations after generations of workers need not at all think of reimbursement, that they may almost look at the capital as belonging to themselves Practically, the liquidation would probably terminate somewhat more expeditiously, for it is not to be supposed that, in a world in which the wealth-producing power of labor benefits principally the workers, and thus conquers for them the highest rungs of the social ladder, any body should want to continue living as a drone Where only the self-made man is honored, inherited wealth will finally be flung away as something derogatory.

An interesting precedent is supplied by history. Professor Roscher tells us in his "System der Volkswirthschaft" (Volume III, p 21), that in the year 1293 the citizens of Florence made a law, according to which "the Grandi (noblemen patricians), who had become members of a guild to enjoy the privilege of sitting in the Council, had to actually work in their trade if they did not want to risk the loss of their franchise. People could be ennobled as a punishment . After the expulsion of the Duke of Athens, the most popular noble houses obtained permission to relinquish their nobility In Pistoja all the disturbers of the public peace were entered into the register of nobility (1285) In Guelphic Parma all the Ghibellines were ennobled (as a punishment) in 1248."

This reads like satire, and certainly appears as strange as my prediction of the future; and yet it is historical fact, recorded by a careful German university scholar But results more wonderful would follow our land and currency reforms We have become so accustomed to the present state of things that it is hard for us to realize how difficult it would be to make anyone, unacquainted with our history, understand our present plight. It would be almost impossible to make him comprehend how, with such a wonderful productivity of labor, the workers could not soon free themselves from all their obligations—in fact, how they have not long since gained the ownership of all wealth Even if he understood how our ancestors committed the folly of selling their terrestrial birthright, or how they were deprived of it by fraud or force and thus recognized the fundamental basis of all our land titles, how explain to him that the workers, with their untold potential wealth, have not long since bought back the land? We should further have to tell him how it came about that we made a pretty yellow metal our fetish and our sole legal tender, that debts in this world are not payable in labor's products, but in coins made out of the scarce metal of which not enough exists to pay one-twentieth of the obligations contracted in its coins, and only then would he comprehend the rest. If possessed of any logic at all he could not fail to realize that, under such circumstances, the creditor class is bound to become richer, the debtor class is sure to grow poorer all the time The former play the bull game once worked with remarkable success at the New York Stock Exchange on the bears in Northern Pacific railroad stock. The bears had sold more of the stock than existed in the market, and, as a natural consequence, had to accept any terms the victorious bulls chose to inflict on them If, instead of claiming a comparatively moderate fine to free the others from their engagement to deliver something which was not obtainable, the victors had so forced up the prices of the stock that all the wealth of the world would not have sufficed to compensate them, there might have been no legal impediment, except that unwritten law according to which, as the German proverb says "Wo nichts ist hat der Kaiser sein Recht verloren" ("Where there is nothing, the Emperor has lost his rights") The bankruptcy of the debtors, after they had given up all their possessions, was the only practical limit, and the spoilers had reasons for stopping short of this extreme result of their power The world's creditor class is in exactly the same position towards the world's debtor class, the difference is only that the deficit between the money stock and the engagements to deliver it is by far greater than it was in the case of Northern Pacific stock. The debtors have promised to pay from twenty to thirty times more gold than the world possesses, and the creditors give them prolongations of the engagements against the payment of a fine, called interest, a fine which is payable in the same unobtainable gold so that in this twentieth century the interest dues of one single year by themselves alone by far exceed the whole gold stock in existence In spite of this fact, fines upon fines are added, interest and compound interest further increase the debt, until bankruptcy liquidates the account And even this is not all

By rendering the legal tender coins—the basis of our currency —less and less accessible to the producers and dealers (who imperatively require a means of exchange), the creditor class has succeeded in monopolizing, to a great extent, natural resources, on the score of their gold claims The rent tribute grew with the interest claims, and heavier and still heavier manacles were imposed on the purchasing power of the masses and consequently on production, so that this purchasing power and production had to halt more and more behind the growing productivity of labor, which enables less and less men to do the work formerly done by all Manifestly, then, growing numbers are thrown out of productive employment, or employed at wages lessened by the competition of the unemployed.

In this way progress necessarily produces poverty instead of bringing untold wealth to all, as it will when a small minority is no more able to use it as the cement of the strongholds in which their monopolies are entrenched the control of natural opportunities and the means of payment This final summing up intends again and again to impress on our workers the fact that a thorough reform may be introduced by simple laws which do away with certain well defined abuses without overthrowing our whole economic system

Observe, that I do not oppose full socialism as the great lodestar of the future, but as a practical proposal for adoption by our generation. Living men, women and children have to be fed, clothed and housed For living human beings practical methods have to be found at once. This is the purpose of the present book It appeals to those who, convinced of the impossibility of continuing in the old groove, look for simple and practical reforms; not for a revolution of the world they are familiar with, and these men and women form the majority of the nation.

Maybe full socialism, under present conditions, is the remedy of despair and ignorance, or rather despair through ignorance, for those who cling to it do so because the real source of the evil, as well as the way out, shown in these pages, lies too deep for the superficial observer. Agreed that it is far easier to declaim against "the competitive system," to draw castles in the air of a new co-operative world, at once ready for inauguration as soon as we have smashed the present one to pieces, than to diminish the waste of competition on practical working lines Be it so; but mark it well, ye favored sons of fortune, that despair is growing fast, and ignorance is fostered by your millions spent to keep out of university chairs, pulpits and popular newspapers any truthful man who possesses the courage

to show things in their real colors. Go on bleeding the monsters and
they will tear you sooner than you apprehend! Help, in the lines of
fundamental reform, and you will save yourselves by saving the
people!

As I do not wish to leave my readers with the impression that
the man who can issue such an appeal is an impractical idealist, I will
at once say that I am far from entertaining a hope of its success.
The appeal is inspired mainly by a feeling of duty. Practically, I
entirely agree with the words of Professor F W. Newman in his
letter to Alfred Russell Wallace "Our duty is to do what we can
in detail, but the longer I live the less hope I have of justice, without changes so great in the persons who hold power that it will be
called a revolution   I mean justice, not as to land-tenure only, but
as to many other things equally sacred, perhaps more vital   Until
popular indignation rises, I expect no result; and when it rises, it
may seem easier to make a clean sweep than carry a quarter
measure."

This is in accordance with the answer I once obtained from a
socialist after one of my addresses on land nationalization in Germany. He asked me whether I really believed that the proposal I
made, to nationalize the land, could be carried with the parties in
power in the country, and as I could not assert I did, he continued:
"Well, if we have to make a revolution by force, don't you think
that we had better take all at once?" It was the only question of all
put to me at my meetings to which I did not care to reply

However, I want to close my book in a more hopeful vein, and
I do so by quoting from "The Social Unrest" by John Graham
Brooks, a book which, though it misses a true conception of the
social problem, is nevertheless full of interesting information   In
Chapter X, after an enumeration of the symptoms that indicate a
conversion of German socialists from intransigent radicalism to parliamentary co-operation in practical reform work, he concludes:

"When party tactics are chiefly directed to agitation of this
kind, the Klassenkampf in its former sense if not quite dead, is no
longer alive   To have struck at its roots, this vicious growth of the
class fight, is the chief moral triumph in the changes here noted   As
these sectional hatreds are overcome, the ground is first reached on
which the longed-for social reorganization can begin   The conditions that shall make such reorganization possible can spring neither
from hate nor suspicion. They can come only from a completer
sense of a common and not divided social destiny " But even if this
passage into the serener seas of a peaceable political and social reform should not be possible without previously weathering the hurricane of civil war, this book will not have been written in vain
Flood tide is followed by ebb tide action by reaction, and, as history
has often proved, any political and social advance that outruns the
people's preparedness is sure to recede sooner or later to this fatal
boundary line of all solid progress   I do not think this line will in-

clude full socialism within the life of the present generation. If the revolutionary pendulum should swing to that line it is certain to swing back again, until further reaction is barred by the educational limit If this book helps towards the advance of the latter, if it contributes towards an improvement of prevailing conceptions regarding our land, our currency and our trade system, its author has not worked in vain.

FINIS.

Lightning Source UK Ltd.
Milton Keynes UK
UKOW04f1935140217

294418UK00010B/661/P

9 781245 973519